LONG
NIGHT'S
JOURNEY
INTO DAY

LONG
NIGHT'S
JOURNEY
INTO DAY

A REVISED RETROSPECTIVE
ON THE HOLOCAUST

Alice L. Eckardt and
A. Roy Eckardt

Wayne State University Press
Detroit, Michigan

Pergamon Press
Oxford • New York • Beijing • Frankfurt
São Paulo • Sydney • Tokyo • Toronto

1988

BT
93
.E25
1988

Library of Congress Cataloging-in-Publication Data

Eckardt, Alice.
    Long night's journey into day : a revised retrospective on the
Holocaust / Alice L. Eckardt and A. Roy Eckardt. — Rev. ed.
        p.   cm.
    Authors' names in reverse order in earlier ed.
    Bibliography: p.
    Includes index.
    ISBN 0-8143-2085-6 (alk. paper). ISBN 0-8143-2086-4 (pbk. : alk.
paper)
        1. Holocaust (Christian theology)   I. Eckardt, A. Roy (Arthur
Roy), 1918- . II. Title.
    BT93.E25 1988
    261.2'6—dc19   88-10668
                                                                        CIP

Published in North America by   Co-published in the United Kingdom
Wayne State University Press   and the world by
5959 Woodward Avenue   Pergamon Press
Detroit, Michigan 48202   Headington Hill Hall
                                       Oxford   OX3 0BW

British Library Cataloguing in Publication

Eckardt, Alice L.
    Long Night's Journey into Day:
    A revised retrospective on the Holocaust.
    —Rev.ed
    1. Jews. Genocide, 1939–1945
    Implications of Christian theology
    I. Title   II. Eckardt, A. Roy
    230
    ISBN 0-08-036571 X
    ISBN 0-08-036570 1 pbk

Grateful acknowledgement is made to the
John M. Dorsey Publishing Fund for
assistance in the publication of the original
edition of this volume.

The quotation from Elie Wiesel,
"Ominous Signs and Unspeakable
Thoughts," is © 1974 by the New York
Times Company. Reprinted by permission.
Quotations from *After Auschwitz* by
Richard L. Rubenstein, Copyright © 1966
by The Bobbs-Merrill Company, Inc.
Reprinted by permission of the publisher,
The Bobbs-Merrill Company, Inc.,
Indianapolis, Indiana.

FOR ALECK AND CHARLES,
TWO OF THE MANY
WHO HELPED ARREST THE
CANCER OF NAZISM

ELLEN!
WHERE ARE THE CHILDREN?

Ilse Aichinger,
Herod's Children

CONTENTS

FOREWORD BY
IRVING GREENBERG

In rereading *Long Night's Journey Into Day* for this foreword, one surprising word forces itself into consciousness: prophets. What constitutes a prophet? The ability to excoriate God's people for the sake of God, out of overflowing love and the desire that one's family be morally healed; the ability to challenge God for the sake of God's people and to demand better divine behavior out of passionate covenantal attachment; without fear or guile to shed a light of analysis so pure and decisive that the inexorable recognition comes: one is standing in the circle of illumination of the divine light itself, and there is no hiding. These qualities describe the achievement of Alice and Roy Eckardt in this book; prophet is as prophet does.

Of course, the fire of prophecy is so searing, so merciless in its integrity, so revealing in its compassion that we—as our predecessors—are far more likely to writhe in agony at our moral nakedness, to offer a hundred exculpations, to do everything to trivialize or, better, to evade reading the words! Thus, we cling to death, moral and spiritual, rather than release our idolatries, purge ourselves, and turn to life reborn. All too often, this response has been the fate of Alice and Roy Eckardt and of *Long Night's Journey*. This new edition offers us another chance to do better.

At the heart of this book's power is its unrelenting grasp of the truth that the Holocaust is an orienting event, "an event that twists our journey through space/time by 180 degrees" (p. 54). By the light this event sheds, the Eckardts take elements of Christian and Jewish theology, of the German people and various of its leaders, of scholars and individual theologies such as Jürgen Moltmann's and Wolfhart Pannenberg's—and yes, even of our understanding of God and covenant—and pass them under the rod and count and sift and fix their lifespan and write their destiny. The results are sometimes inspiring and sometimes devastating but always stimulating and thought provoking.

9

With all its intensity and weight, the book is written with wit, imagination, and even flair; sometimes all these elements are rolled into one. Witness the Eckardts' stunning articulation of the reality of the devil and unmasking of the diabolic strategies, their exposition of the unique uniqueness of the Holocaust, their proposal to redate the calendar B.F.S. (Before the Final Solution) and F.S. (in the year of the Final Solution).

Despite its capacity to upset our certainties and comfortable positions, this is a liberating and even ennobling book. It summons God to necessary penitence for having made Israel a suffering servant through divine election; simultaneously it calls humans to forgive and to open up "[to] the possibility of a trust in God in a dimension beyond but fulfilling history" (p. 90). The Eckardts are trying to evoke the best in our nature, giving us the courage to take responsibility—to use our freedom to self-correct. They guide us to restore the moral health of culture and religion, especially Christianity; we desperately need to heal the body of faith after the uncovering of the putrid, morally dead flesh that made the Holocaust possible.

Long Night's Journey is a model of integrity—for some, painful integrity—in both its capacity to pass judgment without evasion and its willingness to pay the price and understand Christianity in a new light in order to purge the incubus of hatred from the gospel of love. Many Christians bridle at its critique of the claim that the crucifixion be accepted as the determinative symbol of redemptive suffering. Speaking as a Jew, as an outsider, to my Christian brothers and sisters, I can only assure you that this is not a dismissal of Christianity but a call to modesty of theological claims and to deeper insight into the message of the cross. By the x-rays of the Holocaust, the Eckardts see more deeply; they see the event of Golgotha not as theological triumph but as a cry to humans to join in God's work of overcoming suffering and remove others from the cross.

The most difficult section for Christian readers is the Eckardts' reduction of the resurrection. (Let it be said, that this is no more difficult to integrate in a faithful Christian's *Weltanschauung* than it is for faithful Jews to confront the Eckardts' challenge to humanity and to admit that the covenant of demands on Jews is no longer morally valid and that only the Jews can restore it by reaccepting it voluntarily.) I plead with Christians: Listen carefully; certainly, do not dismiss the Eckardts as Christians. Christian faith should be exposed to their insight even if ultimately their position is not accepted. If faith be deepened by this encounter or if the insight be integrated into belief, then the Christian faith is enriched, as the Eckardts wish. If faith be wounded in the process, let it be recognized that, after the Holocaust, no faith is so whole as a broken faith. (Is this not the deeper message of Jesus' final words on the cross?) The bruises inflicted by the Eckardts are the faithful wounds of a friend/lover; they are closer to the Christian truth than the widely accepted imperialist claims of a triumphant Resurrection by which Christian superiority over Judaism—and all civilization—supposedly is "[unequivocally] confirmed by the God of Israel himself" (Pannenberg).

Ultimately, the lifelong mission of the Eckardts and this extraordinary book tower above all the arguments. They help tilt the balance of the world toward redemption. After all is said and done, *Long Night's Journey Into Day* summons all its readers—Christians and Jews and unbelievers alike—to believe in and work for that yet unrealized final and universal resurrection. This book and the Eckardts, by their lifework, bring us closer to that longed for day.

FOREWORD BY
FRANKLIN H. LITTELL

Roy Eckardt and I were active in the Epworth League and the National Council of Methodist Youth fifty years ago, and we have been friends, fellow seminarians and Methodist ministers, professors and professional colleagues since that time. How long ago it was—before World War II, before the Holocaust!

In the towers of theological training and in the bastions of ecclesiastical bureaucracy there are still many who show no signs of historical awareness. They continue to draw their supplies through a long tunnel, as has the traditional Christian apologetic for centuries, without regard to the weather outside. Ignoring the heat and cold, the fear and fortune, the starvation and mass death which are the lot of ordinary mortals, in intellectual conclave they have hunkered down and continued to debate timeless questions and profess timeless truths.

Roy Eckardt was formed in another school of thought. He has followed at this point the line of our great teacher Reinhold Niebuhr, to whom theology was a matter of confession with the life as well as with the lips, for whom the truth became clearer in the arena than it could ever be on the balcony. Since Roy Eckardt published his first great book on the Christian/Jewish encounter, *Christianity and the Children of Israel* (1948), he has relentlessly pursued the most difficult and the most painful of Christian theological burdens today: to rethink, rework, and reconstruct Christian preaching and teaching about the survival of the Jewish people.

In this work he has been accompanied and assisted by his wife, Alice, who, as their children grew up, entered more and more into the theological arena in her own right. In 1970 there appeared the first major expression of their literary partnership: *Encounter with Israel: A Challenge to Conscience*. The central theme is significant, for the restored state of Israel presents a major pledge of Jewish survival.

The Holocaust, in which 60 percent of European Jewry was slaughtered in the heart of "Christendom" (one out of every three Jews in the

12

world), seemed to many an extreme reading of Christian apologetic. Yet there was no getting around the fact that the churches had for centuries proclaimed that with the coming of Jesus Christ the Jewish historical mission was fulfilled and the Jews should disappear into the limbo of history. That they did not disappear was an offense to traditional Christian apologetic. That they survived the Nazi "final solution" was a miracle, especially considering the technological power mustered against them when powerless and abandoned by the so-called Christian nations.

There is no quid pro quo in the relationship of the Holocaust to a restored Israel. But one question brackets the two themes, a question that today puts Christianity to the question: *"How do you interpret the survival of the Jewish people?"*

Traditional Christian apologetic, having given the wrong answer for centuries, now ignores the question. The so-called Historical Revisionists, who simply deny that there ever was a Holocaust, are now generally viewed with contempt by decent people as well as amusement by trained historians. The theological denial is hardly so brash, but its effects are more pernicious to date. Yet there is a new breed coming, and there are seminars and dissertations in theological faculties and seminaries in the United States, Canada, the Netherlands, and West Germany that might be said to inaugurate a Christian reentry into history.

Roy and Alice Eckardt, having wrestled with the Angel of the Lord on this theme for decades, have earned the right to be called "blessed."

The present writing, already a classic, works through the problematic, challenges the traditional apologetic and its consequences, exposes the intellectual denials, and points the way that a reconstructed Christian preaching and teaching must go if Christian credibility is to be regained *post-Auschwitz*. Even where a colleague may differ with a given solution, no one can help but admire the precision with which the Eckardts identify the critical issues, the clarity with which they discuss the topics, and the vigor with which they challenge those with eyes to see and ears to hear.

PREFACE TO THE
REVISED EDITION

No event has made more clear the consequences of ideas than the German Nazi "Final Solution to the Jewish Problem." There could have been no "Jewish problem" to resolve had not almost two millennia of Christian teaching and preaching created it. There could have been no bureaucracy of highly trained civil servants and professionals willing to initiate and carry out mechanized and systematic mass murder without the development over several centuries of a technological and scientistic mindset that saw nothing wrong in using ruthless social engineering to create a national society from which all the human "problems" had been eliminated.

The ramifications of these ideas have neither been eliminated with the military defeat of the Third Reich, nor are they limited to that geographical locale. Dare we hope that they will be overcome, abolished? (Hope is not just optimism; genuine hope is chastened by sober realism.)

It appears that there are "key moments of history [when] possibilities for transformation emerge, which in turn create a new tradition. These moments are *kairoi*, times filled with the promise of the future and [perhaps even] expectation of new revelatory experience. At this juncture [people] can respond either by seeking to hold onto the past, out of anxiety about the new and untried future, or [they] can take the risk of the new."[1] Although the last decades of the twentieth century hardly appear to qualify as times filled with the promise of the future, or expectation of new revelatory experience, we suggest that we do, in fact, live in such a key moment. The *Shoah* (Holocaust) itself must be seen as a revelatory experience, "a negative epiphany" as Emil Fackenheim has described it,[2] and as such it has much to reveal to us. The memory of the Holocaust must be a life-shaping force that makes us significantly more sensitive to individual suffering, to the frailty and preciousness of human life, to the fragile fabric of society, and to the insidious ways by which religious, philosophical, and scientific ideas can lead us to justify life-destroying behavior. We have the freedom to transform our faith, our attitudes, and our teachings so that they will *not* carry the genocidal impulse or the impulse to subordinate any group or class of people. We can learn to be more humble in our confessions. We can learn to recognize the danger signals of old ideas and new absolutisms that claim the right to determine who has the right to live.

To undertake this kind of revolutionary about-face (*metanoia*) requires knowledge of what was wrong in the past, and a genuine experience of repentance (*teshuvah*). It also calls for courage to walk forward into the unknown and to try the untried. Our title makes clear that much of the book entails what Robert McAfee Brown has described as

> a nocturnal journey. Only fleetingly does day begin to dawn at the end. And that is as it should be. Any vision of dawn from such a night will turn out to be premature, a false dawn. Daylight here will not come automatically. . . . The psychic, even spiritual, daylight toward which [the Eckardt] book points can be had only by hard effort, painful confrontation, and the shedding of much intellectual and spiritual clothing we had thought would keep us warm in the night but actually was insulating us from the truth.[3]

The Third Reich waged a war against such traditional Jewish and Christian values as compassion, concern for the helpless and infirm, kindness, and ordinary humaneness; it built a state in which the forces of exclusiveness and hate and the idolatries of nation, race, and political creed garnered mass support. Tragically, many parts of the world have been overtaken by these very same sorts of forces, under banners other than Nazism. Most, or at least many, of these contemporary manifestations have different origins from that of the Nazis' antisemitism and racial doctrines, and for that reason they are outside the direct concerns of this study. That does not mean, however, that they may not have a similar etiology or that they should command less concern. Our endeavors are particularly committed to the eradication of all the strands of antisemitism—Christian, rationalist, political, and racial—and anti-Judaism that enabled the systematic murder of some six million Jewish children and adults to be carried out in the heart of Christian Europe.

The study and thinking that have emerged in this book in both its original and revised forms are the result of considerably more than a decade's consistent attention to the subject in response to teaching opportunities, the challenge and inspiration of friends and colleagues in both the Jewish and Christian communities, and the outpouring of

15

scholarly work and personal accounts regarding the Holocaust and the years immediately preceding (and following) the killing phase of Hitler's Final Solution. Above all, our engagement has been an intrinsic part of our long struggle to resolve the contradiction of Christianity's proclamation of divine love and salvation (and supposed liberation) and the church's persisting *adversus Judaeos* tradition. This is, in fact, the main concern of the volume. Consequently there is considerable attention to theological thinking, especially by some Christians. However, much attention is given to Jewish thinkers as well (theology is not a word widely used in Jewish circles) since some of the troubling faith questions are similar, and because it is time for Christians to listen to Jews.

The initial opportunity to devote full time to research, international discussions, and writing was made possible by a humanities fellowship from the Rockefeller Foundation. Our major research during much of that time was undertaken at the University of Tübingen,[4] the Center of Holocaust Research at Yad Vashem, Jerusalem, and the Division of Holocaust Studies of the Institute of Contemporary Jewry at The Hebrew University. Since then we have had the opportunity and pleasure of twice being visiting scholars at the Centre for Hebrew Studies, University of Oxford, where further work was undertaken and much of this revision prepared. Lehigh University has given us aid and support on all of these occasions, and we are pleased to be able to acknowledge it publicly. We have returned to Europe and Israel for additional research, and we have participated in a large number of national and international conferences on the Holocaust and on Christian-Jewish relations. We are members of a Christian study group that is seriously engaged in rethinking Christian theological positions that continue to have an impact on the Jewish people through attitudes implanted in clergy and church members. The study group came into being as a consequence of the awareness that hostility toward Jews, Judaism, and the State of Israel still persisted in Christian circles some twenty-five years after the liberation of the death camps. To say that condition continues today is hardly necessary. However, the influx of new blood into this group of scholars as well as into other concerned circles is one factor that sustains hope.

In several European countries and Israel we conducted a number of oral history sessions with scholars, literary figures, psychiatrists, religious officials, and lay persons. In addition, inquiries were directed to respondents in different lands, within and outside the churches. In both instances we made contact with persons most likely to have some reason for, in our view, taking the Holocaust, and the relevant "Church Struggle" (*Kirchenkampf*) into consideration: historians, biblical—especially New Testament—scholars and theologians, parish clergy, social scientists, interfaith workers, Christian missionaries, Jewish survivors of the Endlösung and Christian survivors of the German church struggle or other resistance. We have not attempted to make a statistical report of the many thoughtful responses, and we must ask our respondents' forgiveness if it appears that we have ignored their specific answers. Although we noted many throughout the book, we have taken into account in our own consideration of the central issues the other oral and written replies to our probing questions.

In addition to library and other research, a congeries of personal experiences forms much of this book's background. To mention a few of these: visits to the Anne Frank House in Amsterdam; pilgrimages to the sites of a number of concentration and death camps; a journey with a pastor from Reutlingen, West Germany, to an interfaith gathering in Strasbourg arranged by the secretary-general of the Jewish Consistory of the Lower Rhine; a visit behind the Berlin Wall with the family of a theologian resident in East Berlin; a journey with a Jewish friend (and his wife, also a Polish Jewish survivor) to a small Polish village to meet the Catholic family that had hidden him, his brother, and his mother at deadly risk and at the cost of continued ostracism by neighbors; encounters with distinguished literary personages and artists such as Hermann G. Adler, Yehuda Bacon, Abel J. Herzberg, Abba Kovner, and Manès Sperber; participation in a long and vibrant session with members of L'Amitié Judéo-Chrétienne, Paris; a visit to Kiev where the official Soviet guide pointed out with considerable enthusiasm a statue of Chmielnicki to our group of Holocaust survivors and scholars, unaware that this Ukrainian national hero was responsible for the largest slaughter of Jews prior to Hitler; a meeting with Danish resistance fighters who were stirred to anti-Nazi activities largely by the German authorities' decision to arrest and deport Denmark's Jewish population; the privilege of being able to express to Nina Lagergren our enormous gratitude for the daring rescue work undertaken by her half-brother Raoul Wallenberg; conversations with some of the Aktion Sühnezeichen/ Friedensdienste leaders and informal sessions with one of their groups of young people serving in Israel; a visit to two neighboring settlements in northern Israel—Kibbutz Lohamei Haghetaot, where survivors of the ghettos and death camps of Eastern Europe have looked to the future

17

while creating a museum to the past, and Nes Ammim, where Christians (mostly from The Netherlands and West Germany) have committed themselves to building a new relationship of solidarity with the Jewish people, especially in their new national home; an audacious presentation of our own findings and views to an Israeli audience that included many survivors of the *Shoah*, several of whom expressed supportive interest in our study along with an unshaken firmness in their Jewish faith; a marvelous evening with a group of German high school students during which time we plied them equally with refreshments and questions on their views regarding a play about prejudice that they were reading in one of their classes. Particular mention has to be made of the openness, trust, and friendship we have received from so many of those who went through the searing experience of the Holocaust. One of the continuing rewards of all our work has been finding year after year students at Lehigh University who persist in taking courses that can scarcely be considered pleasurable experiences because they want to know how and why and what needs to be done to prevent future destructions of this kind.

This book is much more than the effort of just two people, even though we bear, of course, the only accountability for its contents and point of view. To list all the persons who have aided our endeavor is impossible. We express gratitude to all. However, it would be ungracious not to identify the individuals whose names are listed in Personal Acknowledgments.

Without his knowing it at all, Elie Wiesel helped us to keep going.

The book honors Aleck C. Gaylor, Roy's friend of some sixty years, who was gravely wounded in Germany while serving with the United States Army during the invasion of Europe, and Charles H. Lyons, Alice's brother, who was fortunate not to be wounded during the same European campaign against the forces of the Third Reich and its allies. The dedication is also a reminder that the Nazi destruction of the Jews was finally stopped by people and bullets and bombs, not by such professorial strivings as this volume.

Finally, I am responsible for the specific work of revising and enlarging the original edition.

Alice L. Eckardt

18

PERSONAL
ACKNOWLEDGMENTS

The following are singled out either for the specific aid and counsel they gave us, or for contributing to the book's apperceptive mass, or both.

DENMARK

Anker Gjerding, Finn Henning Lauridsen

FRANCE

Claire Huchet-Bishop, Bernhard Blumenkranz, Roger Braun, Bernard Dupuy, Marie-Thérèse Hoch, Edmond Jacob, Bertrand Joseph, Léon Poliakov, Roland de Pury, Åke Skoog, Manès Sperber

GREAT BRITAIN

Hermann G. Adler, Caesar C. Aronsfeld, Lionel Blue, Albert H. Friedlander, Charlotte Klein, H. David Leuner, Jonathan Magonet, Dov Marmur, Gerald Noel, Dorothy and James Parkes, Peter Schneider, Ulrich E. Simon, W. W. Simpson, Ruth Weyl

ISRAEL

Adina Achron, Ora Alcalay, Yitzhak Arad, Yehuda Bacon, Shalmi Barmor, Avraham Zvie Bar-On, Yehuda Bauer, Eliezer Berkovits, Clara Gini, Israel Gutman, Cynthia Haft, Gertrude and Rudolf Kallner, Hilel Klein, Abba Kovner, Michael Krupp, Avital Levy, Bernard Resnikoff, Livia Rothkirchen, Chaim Schatzker, Pesach Schindler, Jacobus (Coos) Schoneveld, Verena V. Wahlen, Heinrich Zvi Winnik.

19

THE NETHERLANDS

Yehuda Aschkenasy, Jan Bastiaans, Hendrik Berkhof, Rudolf Boon, Samuel Gerssen, Abel J. Herzberg, Louis de Jong, David Lilienthal, Cornelis A. Rijk, Avraham Soetendorp, Willem Zuidema

NORTH AMERICA

Robert McAfee Brown, Joel Colton, Yaffa Eliach, Robert Everett, Rose and Emil Fackenheim, Eva Fleischner, Blu and Irving Greenberg, Raul Hilberg, David Hyatt, Josephine Z. Knopp, Nora Levin, Franklin H. and Marcia Sachs Littell, Donald W. McEvoy, John T. Pawlikowski, Donald L. Ritter, Alvin H. Rosenfeld, Michael Ryan, Roger Simon, Diana and Eli Zborowski

NORWAY

Leo Eitinger, Oskar Mendelsohn, Magne Saebø

WEST GERMANY

Ulrike Berger, Otto Betz, Armin Boyens, Volkmer Deile, Wolfgang Gerlach, Dietrich Goldschmidt, Franz von Hammerstein, Kristen Hausen, Martin Hengel, Ruth and Heinz Kremers, Hans Küng, Pinchas Lapide, N. Peter Levinson, Pnina Navè Levinson, Friedrich-Wilhelm Marquardt, Reinhold Mayer, Jürgen Moltmann, Frederick B. Norris, Peter von der Osten-Sacken, Dieterich Pfisterer, Elisabeth and Rudolf Pfisterer, Wolfgang Pöhlmann, Rolf Rendtorff, Eleonore Schmeissner, Dieter Schoeneich, Carola and Klaus Scholder, Gerhard Schultz, Linda and Dieter Splinter, Martin Stöhr, Hans Stroh, Volker von Törne, Rudolf Weckerling

1
RETURN TO
THE KINGDOM
OF NIGHT

[We] will never succeed in making the *churban*—the Jewish catastrophe of our time—understood to those who will live after
us. . . . "Even if all the firmament were made of parchment, all
the trees were pens, all the seas ink, and even if all the inhabitants of the earth were scribes, and they wrote day and night,
they would never succeed . . . "
                    Manès Sperber, . . . *than a Tear in the Sea*

Had the Jew Jesus of Nazareth lived in the "right" time and
"right" place, he would have been dispatched to a gas chamber. Many
of the Nazi executions of Jews were carried out by believing Christians.
When these two truths are put together, as, incredibly, they must be,
the rationale of this book begins to express itself. We seek here to deal,
in selected ways, with the contemporary impact and meaning of the
Holocaust. Our approach is moral, philosophical, and theological.[1]

Can the Holocaust event ever be explained? Perhaps it is not ex-
plainable. A few singular persons have brought that event to the fore.
Were it not for the work of individuals such as Elie Wiesel, the Holocaust would occupy a much lesser place in today's social conscience.
Psychohistorically speaking, the passing of a full generation since the
Nazi years has afforded a certain distancing that is important for scholars as a requisite to creative reflection and that has led a growing number of Christian and Jewish thinkers to grapple publicly with the subject. The concern of the Jewish community, generally considered, is
quite transparent in its origins: the Holocaust is the most horrendous
event in the long history of this people. Jewish thought and life have
been shaken to the foundations. On the Christian side, from which the
present writers speak, it is more and more acknowledged that what
Jules Isaac called the "teaching of contempt" for Jews and Judaism

21

helped make the Holocaust possible and perhaps even inevitable.[2] If only for this reason, the Holocaust is as much a Christian event as a Jewish one.

The vastness of the subject of the Holocaust and its aftermath, its many impalpable elements and its severely controversial aspects make for a measure of pluralism and tentativeness within any effort to grapple with it. The pluralistic and provisional character of our understanding of the event is linked as well to the differing kinds of questions analysts raise. Insofar as these parties involve themselves in problems of causation and social conditioning, they will consult sociohistorical and psychohistorical sources. Others, concerned with questions of meaning and value, will turn to literary creations and to philosophic and theological materials. Yet the lines are always crossing, for the latter sources are inevitably influenced by given social milieus, just as the former sources are conditioned by existential and moral experience. This means that to set one type of approach qualitatively above the other is not convincing.

DIE ENDLÖSUNG

Uri Zvi Greenberg's accounting in the prose poem "To the Mound of Corpses in the Snow" is an epitome of our subject. An SS officer demands that the narrator's father, an old man, remove his clothes. Never before had the holy man stood entirely naked even before his own eyes. When the officer saw that his victim still persisted in wearing underclothes, socks, and skull-cap, the brute struck him, and he fell. "He gave a groan that was like the finishing of a last prayer, after which there is no more prayer, only a clouded sky, a heap of corpses, and a live officer." The blood from the saintly father's face turned the snow red. . . .[3]

Let us consider how the concept "Holocaust" is to be understood.[4] We resort first to German phraseology for the sake of grappling, as though from inside Nazi demonry itself, with the eschatological and salvational nature of the *Judenvernichtung*, the total annihilation of Jews. The German Nazis determined upon *die Endlösung der Judenfrage* ("the Final Solution of the question of Jews"). This formulation was put forth officially on 20 January 1942 at a conference at Gross-Wannsee, although the actual decision was probably made earlier.[5] The Wannsee dictum was the logical consummation of, or it merely gave expression to, a resolve whose roots are traceable to 1919, when Adolf Hitler declared that his ultimate objective was "the removal of the Jews altogether." "Removal" became physical "extermination"—a term deliberately chosen for its association with verminous creatures—when such total elimination of Jews from existence was seen as the essential element in Hitler's apocalyptic struggle to create the new age of the master race.

According to the minutes of the Wannsee Conference, the eleven million Jews of all Europe were marked for death.[6] Yet it is misleading to comprehend the Holocaust solely within the *Aktion* of simple killing.

The Endlösung means that everything is permitted now, any and every method is to be utilized in the struggle—indeed, in the enjoying of the struggle[7]—to obliterate the single pestilence that is destroying the entire world: the Jew. The German Nazis taught that the Jew is the *Untermensch*, the contaminator from below. The Jew is anti-human, *Gegenrasse*. Accordingly, his name is to be taken away; he does not deserve a name. He is only a number tattooed into his flesh.

The Endlösung is the competitive "race of the dead" at Treblinka and elsewhere, a physiological competition that makes one man's survival absolutely dependent upon the next man's extinction. For the race of death decreed which prisoners would be murdered and which ones "spared."

At the heart of the Endlösung is the utilization of Jews as officially selected agents for reviling and torturing their fellow Jews. The Jew is turned into the accomplice of his executioners. Thus, the Endlösung is ultimate degradation: the attempted dehumanization of the Jew as well as the torture process that makes this possible. The Endlösung is meant to be total mental, physical, and spiritual breakdown. It is the ontic separation of children and parents, wives and husbands. Child, parent, wife, husband—all these are enforced witnesses to the suffering and annihilation of their loved ones.

The chronology of what the Dutch psychiatrist Jan Bastiaans calls "das perfide System" was: Declare the Jew to be the *Untermensch* or *Gegenrasse*; then do everything to make him this, thereby vindicating your major premise; and only then, kill him. In this respect, the Endlösung had nothing to do with the specific advent of death, for the ultimate shamefulness lay in staying alive. Objectively speaking, death was transfigured into a form of mercy. Death became salvation—although, of course, the manner of death incarnated the dehumanization and was the mirror image of the terror. It is often said that the nightmares of the captives were more frightening than their encounter with death.

Speaking of life in the Vilna ghetto, Abba Kovner, who helped lead the uprising there, attests that the most appalling thing was not death, but to be defiled to the depths of one's soul every hour of the day.[8] But perhaps the ultimate in attempted dehumanization was the German Nazi effort to obliterate the Jews and Jewishness from all human memory.

At the same time, we are not allowed to forget the complicity of those people and nations other than the persecutors themselves. There is much truth in Elie Wiesel's judgment that the victims suffered more "from the indifference of the onlookers than from the brutality of the executioner." Cynthia Haft writes that the futility of the agony is contained in the words "et ils savaient que vous ne pleureriez pas" (and they knew that you would not weep).[9]

Again, the Endlösung reached out even to those who gave the appearance of surviving it. Many could not endure the shock of "liberation." They died. For vast numbers of those who lived, the years after release were as dreadful as, or worse than, the horror of the camps. Most sadly, some no longer retained the strength that human beings are required to muster if they are to be happy.[10] Thus, to be freed was, in many cases, not to be freed. How could these people adapt to a life that they had lost? Many lacked the power to retrieve their former world, a fight that would demand enormous inner resources. Even those with some strength left found that the old world was gone. Their loved ones and friends, their homes and their countries: all had been destroyed.

But the starkness of the horror of the Endlösung is not fully appreciated until its official character is realized: the Final Solution was the official action of a great modern state.

Most of the Jews of Europe were simply trapped people; there was nothing they could do to elude a certain fate. This must be insisted on especially because of the all-too frequent assertion that they went "like sheep to the slaughter." This accusation is one of the more demonic methods by which responsibility for the murders is insidiously transferred from the killers to the victims. Some Jews, of course, were led to collaborate with the enemy, under a variety of those impulses that capture any human being who, facing persecution and annihilation, seeks desperately to escape. Yet collaborationism was relatively rare. To be sure, in the days and hours before death many victims had been brought to that terrible state which allowed no psychic possibility save "consent" to destruction. (The quotation marks signify the truth that these persons were in fact beyond compliance or noncompliance.)

We do not complete the correct usage of the term "Holocaust" until we include the fact of Jewish resistance to the German Nazi program.

The resistance was at once spiritual, moral, and physical. In Jerusalem the institution called Yad Vashem bears the official title, "Martyrs' and Heroes' Memorial Authority."[11] Who is a martyr? Who is a hero? Among the greatest of these were the mothers and fathers who sought to comfort their children in their final hours, before shared death, and older youth who chose to share their parents' deportation to death rather than abandoning them to escape to the forests or a clandestine existence in the "Aryan" world. Many were the Jews who went to their destruction in quiet dignity. It is said that in their final hours, numbers of the pious ones danced and sang in celebration of their God—a protestation of faith in defiance of agents of antifaith. Nor can we overlook the massive effort to serve life, to maintain normality, even in the ghettos and concentration and death camps. Schools and literary clubs were organized; plays, lectures, and concerts were arranged; child care, soup kitchens, and other charitable activities were fostered.

A number of Jews and Jewish communities engaged in physical and armed struggle against the foe. The Warsaw ghetto uprising is well known, the first armed revolt of any people within occupied Europe. There was a resistance movement even in Auschwitz.[12] There was an uprising at Treblinka, which, with outbreaks elsewhere, was inspired by the Warsaw revolt. The Treblinka revolt is even more unbelievable than that in Warsaw because a murder center was the scene, and, at least indirectly, the aim of destroying Treblinka was achieved.[13] In at least one known though exceptional case, an entire Jewish village rose as a single person against the Germans: Tuchin (Tuczyn) in the Ukraine, with a population of some three thousand. About two-thirds of them escaped to the forests, although many of these were later delivered up by Ukrainian peasants. The Germans offered safety to any Jews who would return, and some three hundred foolishly accepted the offer. They were promptly shot in the Jewish cemetery. A few of the escapees got through and joined the Russian partisans.[14]

These and the many other acts of resistance refute the misleading and immoral stereotype that the Jews of Europe simply went to their deaths with sheeplike compliance.[15] In this resistance the kingdom of night was confronted by the dawning kingdom of day.

Our understanding of the concept "Holocaust" itself poses momentous questions. For example, what is the relation of the Holocaust to different "holocausts," to other acts of mass human destruction? This Holocaust, whose weight we have taken upon ourselves—in what ways is it a singular event? Such questions will engage us throughout these pages.

There is the valley of the shadow of death. And there is the Endlösung, that much deeper valley of historical dehumanization, terror, agony, and final murder of the Jew only because he is a Jew. Yet there is also the historic resistance of the Jew to the war against him. A single light burns: the German Nazi campaign to dehumanize the Jewish people was a total failure. Jewry as a whole refused to fall to the level of the *Untermensch*. Only those who became the real *Untermenschen* did that: the enemies of the Jews.

DILEMMAS OF THE SCHOLAR

A student of the Holocaust and its aftermath may exhibit a form of detached, clinical objectivity.[16] In contrast, there is the approach of a participant, *un homme engagé*, an interpreter who insists that detachment is the adversary of human obligation. Along which path are we to make our journey? Or is it possible to travel both roads? It may be useful for us as authors to include an autobiographical note, not for personal reasons, but because it bears upon the methodological and moral dilemmas that pervade our subject.

In an intellectual-experiential way we came to the particular issue of the Holocaust, its meaning and its consequences. This occurred after we had attended for a number of years to the historical, ideational, and moral relationships between Christianity and Judaism, between Christians and Jews. Although we began a study in the latter general realm during the immediate post-Holocaust period (1945–1947), the effort was not primarily a response to the Nazi Endlösung; but it did deal with that reality and sought to grapple with antisemitism, especially Christian theological antisemitism.[17] The bare truth is that we did not come to the subject of the Holocaust, nor earlier to that of Christian-Jewish relations, through any traumatic personal encounters within or even outside the Europe of 1933–1945. Rather, it was the anti-Jewish problematic within Christian teaching and the history of Christianity that finally led us, probably inexorably, to concentrate upon the Holocaust.

The last thing we should ever imply is that personal participation in, or victimization by, the Endlösung makes the survivor incapable of comprehending and of placing the evil within a broad and deep frame of reference. On the contrary, such direct confrontation may be of crucial aid in achieving a theory of the event, in the highest and most practical sense of that term. Jacob Robinson points out that the judgments of some authors are weakened by the fact that they never experienced the Holocaust or any other mass disaster. Many writers did not even follow closely the development of the Endlösung.[18] By contrast, many who suffered in the Holocaust but who somehow managed or were enabled to survive it have attained, especially with the distancing years, a kind of creative objectivity in their very descriptions and assessments of Nazism.

Wherein, then, lies the relevance of our own accounting? There is the danger that the Holocaust will be appropriated only as a nightmare, a horrible episode that erupted within a brief span of years as part of a special ideological development or political tragedy or whim of an insane man, a nightmare from which we have long since awakened. There is the temptation to reduce the Final Solution to an aberration, a kind of cultural-moral mutation. In consequence, any comprehension of the event as the logical and even inevitable climax of a lengthy and indestructible ethos-tradition and Christian theological obsessiveness is readily lost. Against this eventuality, we must root ourselves in the fateful past—a possibility that has only of late gained a foothold within scholarly circles and within and beyond the churches. We seek for the grace that may derive from a certain historical perspective, from a kind of distancing that is at the same time nearness. Captivation by and concern for the centuries-long story of antisemitism, and particularly the antisemitism fatefully linked to one's own religious tradition, may serve to contribute to at least three consequences: it will aid us in avoiding a facile approach; it will help foster a concerned objectivity; and it may slightly offset the personal condition of having passed the Holocaust years at a protected distance.

Those who contend that one must have been a part of the horror in order to write of it face the difficulty that no written word can equal the experience itself. It is a Holocaust survivor, and not a mere onlooker, who has written: "Perhaps, what we tell about what happened and what really happened have nothing to do one with the other."[19] True, the nonparticipant's writing is at least twice removed from the reality. However, the participant's writing remains once removed. In

27

both cases there is a break with noumenal truth.[20] This is not to disagree that, in principle, a qualitative difference obtains between literature once removed and writings twice removed. To those who say, you must have been within the inferno in order to approach it and write of it, we can only respond, with Cynthia Haft, that "we too want this event, so unique, never to be forgotten, that we too feel obliged to join with them in their efforts to remind others and to bear witness, without in any way violating the sanctity of the subject matter."[21]

We trust that the struggle against false objectivity is carried forward through the elements of personal encounter upon which, in considerable measure, this volume is grounded. There is no way to separate one's acts as a human being from one's work without falling into a certain personality split. The two elements are bound together within the larger category of "calling" (*vocatio*). Objectivity without commitment contains temptations—most lamentably, those of neutrality and coldness. This condition must be fought. It is a fact that the very study of the Holocaust's aftermath becomes, inevitably, part of that aftermath, part of *Existenz*. There is objectivity for the sake of truth, and there is subjectivity for the sake of goodness. Truth and goodness are not separable. The objectivization of the Holocaust—that is, the removal of, or the refusal to make, evaluative judgments about the event—constitutes, in effect, a justification of the German Nazi program.[22] We either oppose Nazism or we support it; bystanders, by default, range themselves on the side of the supporters.

A further moral complexity manifests itself. Allusion has been made to the German Nazi device of setting camp inmates in competition for their very survival. We ourselves do not totally escape a related though nonlethal form of evil when we call attention to testimonies of and accounts about certain sufferers and not to those of other sufferers. Such representations are inevitably caught up in personal judgment: this piece is "better" than that piece; this reference is "more memorable" than that reference; or, at the least, this one is to be called to public attention and not the other one. In a fine study, *The Holocaust and the Literary Imagination*, Lawrence L. Langer regrets having had to omit from consideration such works of unusual distinction as Piotr Rawicz's *Blood from the Sky* and Charlotte Delbo's *None of Us Will Return*. Although the purpose of our book is not the critical assessment of literature of the Holocaust, we are obliged to offer a parallel apology. But does an apology resolve the moral problem? What we do is to honor the memory of some human beings and let the remembrance of others die.

28

Here is a special burden for writers, particularly those who, like the present analysts, are not survivors. There is the added fact that those who work in Holocaust studies profit, if only in reputation, from human torment.[23]

As long ago as 1969, novelist Cynthia Ozick declared that the Holocaust had become dangerously literary, dangerously legendary, dangerously trivialized to pity, and the pity to poetry.[24] Ozick was already telling us how embarrassing were the riches in the available literary, documentary, and oral historical materials representative of our general subject; and it is true that the human proclivity to mythologize the past is universal and sometimes dominating. But we do not believe that pity trivializes the Holocaust, unless or until it becomes the exclusive response. Whether pity is trivialized in poetry, we are not competent to judge. However, the real stumbling block to agreement with Ozick is that writers today are forced into the creation and transmission of literature, legend, pity, and poetry in the very acts of observing and guarding against the dangers in these and other pursuits.

This leads us to one other fundamental dilemma. The problem is tied to the bafflement many have confessed before the *Judenvernichtung*. They ask: how is the unspeakable to be spoken about? We ought to speak of it all right, but how can we ever do so? Again, how are we to engage in scholarly work upon a subject that staggers the mind and stabs the soul: the human effects of this crusading-political-technological annihilation of an infinity of children, women, and men? We place the children first in our listing, as a reminder that their destroyers robbed them of human completeness. Woe to those who despise the little ones! (Matt. 18:10). Very largely, this book is nothing more than a sequel to a children's story of a dread kind. In the Holocaust some one and one-half million Jewish children were destroyed. The youngest of children were chased, clubbed, and shot, as if vicious criminals, merely for attempting to smuggle food into the starving ghettos. The *Kinderaktions* (roundups of children for transport to the killing centers) were among the most brutal and thorough of the many SS-police seizures. Most children were immediately put to death upon reaching the camps. The older and stronger ones were put to work as laborers, usually for about six months. Then they were murdered.

The tradition of Jews remembering the suffering and deaths of their people in literary and liturgical laments is centuries old. Elias Canetti, a Bulgarian-born Jew writing in 1945, insisted that this tradition must now cease, precisely when there is the greatest reason for it. Why?

Because it will not decrease the hate non-Jews feel for Jews, but will only increase their awareness that Jews are totally vulnerable and need not be feared.[25] It may whet their appetite for a repeat performance. We are convinced, along with numbers of other Christians, that the Holocaust will become part of Christian consciousness and concern only when similar laments and occasions for their use are integrated into the churches' liturgies, professions, confessions, and calendar.[26]

It is sometimes contended that the basic lesson of the Holocaust is that there are no lessons. The Endlösung is too shattering for us to learn anything from it.[27] We do not dishonor such existential skepticism when we point out that the noumenal and ostensibly mysterious character of the event is one thing, but the consequences the event has had and is having within human life and thought are quite something else. The asserted bafflement of some parties itself exemplifies the second of these categories. We allude now to the phenomenal impact of the Holocaust, noting the aptness of the ambiguity in the concept "phenomenal": the word has come to mean "powerful" and "decisive," while also retaining its philosophical connotation of "empirical" and "observable." Yet in chapter 3 and beyond we dare to approach the noumenal dimension of the Holocaust.

The imponderability and *mysterium tremendum* of the Final Solution, together with the varying attestations to silence before its unspeakableness, have not prevented the appearance of an incredible amount of materials on the subject.[28] In this respect, a problem shared by all students of the Holocaust and its impact is not so much how to speak of the unspeakable, as how to grapple with such a number of publications, documents, and oral and written testimonies while at the same time they seek fresh interpretations and venture ideas of their own. Our challenge, all in all, is one of apprehension, another aptly ambiguous word. The ambiguity in "apprehension"—standing as the word does for both the claimed receiving of truth and a certain anxiety respecting the future, including in the present instance the anxiety of harming human beings through one's research and writing—invests that term with a certain fearful propriety.

One final word needs to be said before we concentrate on the ultimate nature of the Endlösung. Attention to the killing phase of Hitler's war against the Jews should not blind us to the inhumaneness and evil inherent in all the earlier measures the Nazi regime took against them (and, beginning early on, against those other Germans with the "wrong" political views and the "wrong" genetic inheritance).[29] Not only the inhumanity of those decrees and actions but also the denial of basic human rights, particularly under the cloak of legality, are to be deplored and rejected. We must recognize that many of those who later were appalled at the *methods* of the Final Solution were not appalled at the earlier measures *or the goals and ideology they were intended to fulfill.* Yet the denigration of any group by another strikes at the very foundation of the human community; it is an attack on the creation which God saw was good.

Many of the troubling questions with which we will be wrestling in the following chapters are equally pertinent to these less drastic actions of the German Third Reich,[30] although they may not be as apparent as when we face the ultimate in human arrogance and cruelty and their consequences for other human beings. Because such lesser attacks on human dignity and human rights may be more readily accepted by society, they represent the greater danger. Yet they were the first steps that led initially to Dachau and Sachsenhausen, and later to Auschwitz and Sobibor. Because the lesser evils were not opposed, the greater evil could be perpetrated. Accordingly our existential concern with antisemitism is not simply a peculiar obsession or an irrelevancy to the present. Similarly, the international movement to protect human rights and to protest against their violation is a significant reaction to the state sponsored and bureaucratically managed murder that has so proliferated in the twentieth century.

2
REMEMBERING

Let one never forget the day
for it has been.
Let one never forget the months
for they were.
Let one never forget the years
for they still are.
Let one never forget those six million
for they had been.

Leslie Konigsberg, "Remember"

We have introduced our subject and spoken of certain dilemmas
that face the analyst. In succeeding pages the challenge of moral obligation will occupy us because this is interrelated with a continuing
quest for understanding. This second chapter is concerned with a fundamental psychomoral problem.

We consider one facet of the Holocaust's aftermath today, the issue
of its remembrance as opposed to its amnestia. "Amnestia" means oblivion, intentional overlooking, the exact opposite of "remembrance."
We shall approach this matter through the enigma of responsibility and
guilt. Our primary experiential focus will be West Germany, although
the observations are also relevant to other peoples and nations even if
not as pointedly or poignantly.

THE TEMPTATION IN
REMEMBRANCE AND THE
DANGER IN AMNESTIA

Lawrence Langer contends that

the failure of the restrospective imagination to find meaning in history or in
the consolations of tragedy dramatizes the absurd position of man as Survivor: the act of recollection, instead of forging links with the past, only wid-

ens the exasperatingly impassable gulf between the dead and the living, creating a void which makes new beginnings for the future equally impossible until some way of reconciling the fate of those dead with the present can silence the influence they continue to exert on the living.[1]

The stress upon remembering is not without its problems, its temptations.

What does it mean to remember the Endlösung? Can remembrance somehow contribute to the reconciliation of which Langer speaks? What is the purpose of remembering? Elie Wiesel has spent much of his life expressing such remembrance. Yet he himself has asked, "Remember what? And what for? Does anyone know the answer to this?"[2] What are the virtues, the necessities in remembering? Would it not be better to forget? Again, there is the most vexing question: *How* is the Holocaust to be remembered?

Because of the very nature of the Final Solution, its remembrance tends to open up certain moral and psychological dangers. Death and destruction ever draw unto themselves human fascination. What horror tale can possibly compare to the Holocaust, replete with piercing screams, silent but endless sadistic "games" and macabre laughter, the lust of inducing pain and fear and cruelly ingenious medical experiments, blood flowing from the ground and walking skeletons all but drained of blood, rotting corpses and death without end, godlike impunity in determining how and when death would occur, and superhuman struggles to survive? The greater the horror, the greater the opportunity for macabre pleasures. That a pornography of the Holocaust should have long since developed may revolt us, but it can scarcely surprise us.[3] The suffering of Jews has so impregnated our conscious and unconscious selves that our very study of it, our very attention to it, may well foster a kind of tacit or unconscious consent, even a new, perhaps unrecognized reason for despising the victims.[4] Are we possessed of the inner resources and the will to keep the eye of our memory fixed where it belongs, upon the plight of the sufferers? Will not our gaze stray, ever so gradually, ever so imperceptibly, over to the persecutors, with hidden interest and secret sympathy, a sympathy so secret that we do not even confess it to ourselves? Those Nazis were men who rose above all inhibitions, broke all fetters, were prepared to tread down anything and everything that blocked their way. How grand it would be to be enabled to follow one's impulses, to be as presumptuous as the Nazi killers[5] and without ever having to make any decisions! The blessed rules of the Party rendered wholly unnecessary every burden of choice, every terror of responsibility. In a word, the superego is annihilated by the id. (The Führer taught that conscience is a Jewish invention.) May not the remembrance of the *Shoah*, especially in its obsessional aspects, kindle a clandestine drive to repeat 1933, 1938, 1944? In gazing down into the Abyss, may we not open the abyss within ourselves?

On occasion it is claimed that anti-Jewish attitudes and behavior among some German young people today comprise a means of getting back at Jews for making them feel guilty. Jürgen Moltmann of Tübingen once suggested to us that in the new antisemitism of younger people in Germany, self-hatred comes forth, gathering up "the hatred of the fathers." But from the alternative standpoint mentioned in the preceding paragraph, self-love and self-assertion ought probably be added to self-hatred. The desire to have a positive national identity, not an unusual desire, can provide strong motivation for turning on those who force one to confront the negative aspect, the dark face of the nation's history. The weight of a guilty past is openly denied or at least defied.

In April and May 1985, prior to President Ronald Reagan's trip to West Germany to commemorate the conclusion of World War II, most West Germans appeared to support their chancellor, Helmut Kohl, and President Reagan regarding the planned official visit to the cemetery at Bitburg where forty-nine members of the Waffen SS are buried. Only a few indicated a willingness to acknowledge that even an appearance of honoring the SS dead was unacceptable in view of the central role that the SS played in the mass murders. Despite public protests against the visit by a number of West Germans, spearheaded by Christian leaders, most Germans preferred to agree with Reagan and Kohl in exonerating the SS because they were simply following orders and fighting for their country. (See the discussion of the Austrian people's similar attitudes later in this chapter.)

President Reagan chose to ignore the fact that these SS troops are among those accused of murdering at least eighty-six American prisoners of war during the Battle of the Bulge. He also chose to ignore the declaration of the War Crimes Tribunal at Nuremberg that the SS was a criminal association, which played a major role in the Final Solution and other murders of innocent people. For the President, these dead Germans were *equally victims* of the evil caused by one man. Thus was World War II "falsified into a deplorable but . . . normal event." And West Germany and the United States were reconciled "at the expense, and at the exclusion, of the memory of the victims of the mass extermination."[6]

Johann-Baptist Metz is particularly distressed by the desire to put a "limit of liability" on Auschwitz, which he believes is "less the expression of a will to forgiveness from Christian motives (and indeed *we* have hardly anything to forgive!) than it is the attempt of our society [German] and of our Christianity (!) to decree for itself—at last—acquittal."[7]

One member of the American clergy reported to us that several Christian participants in a visit to the memorial of Yad Vashem manifested hostility in face of all the remembering. (Would this hostility have surfaced if guilt were not somehow being summoned up?) A Roman Catholic priest who served as an official Israeli guide told us that on one recent occasion some members of a group of German clergy declined to enter the Yad Vashem museum exhibit, protesting, "This has nothing to do with us." If, as we shall be arguing, the Endlösung constitutes the heritage of antisemitism in its final logic, may not the perpetuators of Holocaust memories be inadvertently keeping alive resentments and hatreds? May they not be acting, all unintentionally, in ways that sustain and aggravate *Judenfeindschaft* ("hatred of Jews")? This eventuality becomes a special menace whenever charges of guilt are brought without proper discrimination and care. At a 1975 conference in Hamburg on the Holocaust and the Church Struggle, Caesar C. Aronsfeld of London objected to a concentration upon guilt and repentance, contending that when people are forced to prostrate or humble themselves, they will eventually turn upon the party they identify as making this demand. Nathan Rotenstreich of the Hebrew University emphasizes that it is not easy to entertain or maintain feelings of guilt; they continually threaten one's pride and self-righteouness.[8]

In addition, the plaint is often made that concentration upon the remembrance of the Holocaust is a waste of energy and has harmful consequences. Such effort only serves to keep us from helping to resolve the really fateful problems that today plague mankind and, if they are not solved, will lead to man's extinction: the food shortage, overpopulation, pollution, wastefulness, annihilative weaponry—and, for that matter, genocides, not excepting potential genocidal acts against the Jewish people themselves. Every year, fifty million persons die of starvation, more than eight times the number of Jews destroyed by the German Nazis. A kindred attitude derives from a kind of baffled pragmatism. What, after all, can be "done" with the Holocaust? This outlook is exemplified in a statement by the German historian Golo Mann, son of Thomas Mann: "I think of Auschwitz once a week and have done so for thirty years. But you can't expect millions of Germans to don sackcloth and ashes and repent all the time. One likes to forget because what can you do with" such a memory?[9]

If there are psychomoral dangers in remembering the Holocaust, there are counterdangers in not remembering.

A former resistance fighter living in Israel, a man who advocates full discussion of the Holocaust, emphasized to us the unqualified right of individual survivors and their families to forget, if they so desire.[10] But in Israel, where the largest number of survivors live, this is not easy since observances of the Holocaust on Yom HaShoah, the national day of remembrance, are public events widely covered and carried by the mass media. Here is a moral complication: honoring the victims can inadvertently create problems for an individual victim-survivor. However, much depends upon who it is that is counseling forgetfulness and to whom the counsel is directed. There is all the moral difference in the world between a plea by a Jewish spokesman that his people turn away from the horrors of yesteryear, and the actual pronouncement by the West German chancellor (on the thirtieth anniversary of his people's surrender) that Germans have learned their lesson from the past. One may argue with the first party without necessarily charging him with an ideological taint or hypocrisy, but the issue of self-deception and the deception of others is unavoidably raised with respect to the second party. This latter response is also promoted by a moral reaction to the pervading public viewpoint within today's West Germany that the media ought no longer dwell upon the Nazi atrocities. The same critical response may be called for against all those whose counsel of forgetting is demonstrably accompanied by insensitivity or antisemitic attitudes. In a word, there is a licit forgetting, and there is a culpable one.

A certain professor in a West German university has sent the Holocaust off to oblivion. That is to say, she simply refused to discuss the event and its meaning. "Go talk to the murderers," she has said. "Do not ask us who are Jews. It is their problem, not ours." Such an effort to obliterate truth is perhaps understandable, although in this particular case the individual is not a direct survivor of the persecutions. She early succeeded in fleeing to Palestine and only much later returned to teach in West Berlin. Herein may lie part of her problem; very many authentic survivors are now fully able to speak of their experiences. This woman gave every evidence of being unable to face the facts of the

36

Holocaust. Yet as a historical scholar, if not as a human being, she has no real alternative but to assent to its actuality. She can hardly function as a teacher should she fail, time after time, to deal with students' queries on the subject. A possible outcome of her condition is some kind of split personality.

The foregoing case is extreme, but it comprises a relevant witness to the truth that while the remembrance of the Endlösung carries psychomoral dangers, a tacit or advocated forgetfulness bears equal or greater dangers. Personality wholeness and psychic health demand a reasonable harmony among the volitional, affective, and cognitive dimensions of the self. In a vital sense, this is also true at the collective level. In the words of Harvey Cox, "Psychiatrists remind us that the loss of a sense of time is a symptom of personal deterioration. . . . The same is true for a civilization. So long as it can absorb what has happened to it and move confidently toward what is yet to come its vitality persists." Alienation from the past induces decline and ultimately death.[11]

The Israeli psychiatrist Hilel Klein stressed to us what he called "the essential historical continuity of the generations." When parents have not discussed, or have been unable to discuss, their Holocuast experiences, their offspring have tended to develop psychiatric problems. For example, the children very often conclude that they have to be ashamed of their family history. Discontinuity between the generations compounds the development of fantasies and leads to mental illness. Klein insists that remembrance is essential to individual and social health. The truth must be known. It must be known by all.[12]

One rejoinder to the counselors of amnestia is that avoidance, suppression, and repression are aspirin tablets in the treating of cancer. The disease quickly reasserts itself, and when this occurs the forms are often as terrible as before. Nor does the passage of years necessarily help. Thus, in what has come to be called the post-concentration-camp syndrome, the longer the lapse of time, the more serious the survivors' symptoms and suffering. A final horror of the German Nazi system is its power to reach beyond the generations it ravaged, taking unto itself new victims. It is doing so at this very moment. Where, then, is the moral legitimacy in arguing that the Holocaust belongs to the past and ought to be forgotten?

Jürgen Moltmann has voiced concern that his people have suppressed and repressed their dark history. He says, "German guilt was never given expression, and so it could not be forgiven." In *Die Unfähigkeit zu Trauern* (The Inability to Mourn), Alexander and Mar-

37

garet Mitscherlich have argued, from a depth psychological perspective, that there has not been a sufficient and repentant working through and working out of the guilt of the Third Reich in postwar Germany. Dieter Hartmann reports that the lack of compassion for the Nazis' victims, so noticeable during the Third Reich, is still to be found in today's German society. This impaired capacity for compassion helps to keep Germans, and probably other responsible persons and societies, from accepting responsibility and then moving on to the logical next stage: repentance and change. The Israeli poet Abba Kovner attests that in accordance with "the way of our forefathers," penitence must take priority over mourning.[13] In the present context, the decisive question is one of penitence and confession rather than that of mourning. Although the phrasing of the Mitscherlichs' title is meant to refer to an inability to mourn that is *caused by* lack of repentance, when used out of context it may well suggest that certain deaths have occurred that appear incapable of inducing proper weeping and sorrow. (This may, of course, be an accurate, if unintended, description of the situation.) The alternative concept, "inability to repent," conveys a blockage in penitence respecting transgressions for which men are responsible.

In German writing and discourse of recent years a certain phrase appears again and again: *eine unbewältigte Vergangenheit*, "a past that remains unmastered." (The expression has even become somewhat banal.) Is the German past in fact unredeemed? Or is there legitimacy in speaking of its having been mastered (*die Bewältigung der Vergangenheit*)? Culpability for the Endlösung has sometimes been narrowed down to the reputed insanity of one man (but if Hitler were insane, he could hardly be blameworthy) or to his sane but all-destructive ambitions. Less restrictedly, the blame has been assigned to the relatively small Nazi elite. The moral-historical fault in both attributions lies in ignoring "the facts of participation by tens of thousands of Germans (and their satellites) in the physical destruction of millions of Jews. . . . Many of them could have avoided this awesome responsibility had they wished so." But the Nazis found that they could rely on "ready compliance and on ruthless adminstrative proficiency" from "legions of subservient" and even enthusiastic administrators of the genocidal program. Very few ever took advantage of opportunities for passive resistance.[14]

We have been using the phrases "German Nazis" and "German Nazi system." The wording is carefully chosen. To speak only of "Nazis" would be to misrepresent the truth of the wider and deeper German condition. But to speak only of "Germans" would mean lack of discrimination and fairmindedness. Furthermore, the designation "Germans" would not wholly avoid self-idolatry. As the noted Dutch Jewish writer Abel J. Herzberg insists, were we ever to claim that Nazi behavior was exclusively German, we should be pretending that we could never stoop to it ourselves. However, the phrase "German Nazis" is not felicitous from an objective, descriptive standpoint. It fails to convey non-German complicity in the destruction of European Jewry and in abiding antisemitism. When, for example, President Franklin D. Roosevelt was asked, five days after the Nazi pogrom of 9 November 1938, whether American immigration restrictions against Jews would be eased, he replied with a sharp and unqualified "no."[15]

The linguistic-moral challenge is how to avoid exculpating guilty parties while at the same time not being unfair. No single expression is sufficiently comprehensive to convey the breadth and depth of complicity in the Endlösung. To resort to such phrasing as "enemies of Jews" would be to fall into abstraction and to obscure responsibility, yet the phrasing "German Nazis" hardly overcomes our predicament. In this phrasing a problem is stated; it is not resolved. We are confronted by a special and overwhelming case of the human mystery of responsibility and guilt.

The English word "responsibility" is ambiguous, denoting both accountability and culpability. From the standpoint of moral philosophy, the entire human condition can be epitomized in and through this ambiguity. If man as man is responsible (*verantwortlich*, "accountable"), when is he also responsible (*strafbar*, "culpable")? Furthermore, the special enigma of collective guilt has always beset moral, philosophical, and theological reflection; it is most doubtful that the present analysis will dispose of the question of social guilt/guiltlessness, of moral responsibility/nonresponsibility. However, we may not forget Dostoevsky's insistence that to deprive man of responsibility for his acts is to lower him to a subhuman level and to rob him of his dignity.

SIX MORAL-HISTORICAL PROPOSITIONS

The responsibility of the German people (*Verantwortlichkeit* and *Strafbarkeit*) for the Holocaust years is a less controversial matter than the question of German guilt allegedly persisting into the post-Holocaust period. We venture upon several comments, in no way as a device for resolving the vexing and profound problem before us, but only as a possible means of living with its afflicting presence. None of us escapes the shattering questions: Where are you? (See Gen. 3:9.) What are you doing with that one space which you now fill? How are you expending your one life? What choices are you making? What decisions are you reaching and following out?

1. *Historical memory must take all available facts into account.*

Exemplification of this proposition is forthcoming from any and every quarter, and certainly as much from anti-German data as from more sympathetic data. Yet it is a moral fact that many Germans were victims, not victimizers.[16] Many of them fitted both these categories.

Just east of Tübingen lies the village of Pfrondorf, where we resided while conducting part of our research. Once a farmhouse stood on the very spot where we found living quarters. In World War II the dwelling was destroyed by an aerial bomb, reportedly with no warning. Were there children in the house? Did they die in the explosion? One could easily call upon much more dramatic and terrible events, such as the firebombing of Dresden. We allude to this particular instance only because the questions about the children kept repeating themselves to us, a fact doubtless occasioned by the personal circumstances. We never were able to secure any pertinent information.

In other instances we do have information, not only about German civilians as victims of massive bombing attacks by the American and British airforces or retaliatory treatment by Soviet soldiers but, even more significantly, also about Germans who risked and frequently gave their lives to either resist Nazism or aid its victims. The literature about this aspect of the Nazi era is frequently written by Jewish survivors or writers eager to demonstrate that there were two Germanies and to honor those who had "the courage to care" "when compassion was a crime." (The quotation marks indicate that these are titles of two of the books on the subject.)[17]

2. *A blighted historical memory is not restored to health so long as its original and fundamental inspirations remain within the body politic.*

Observers, as well as West Germans themselves, have expressed concern about some of the more open manifestations of Nazi sympathies and ideas within the country. In the late 1970s scores of our informants in the Federal Republic emphasized in particular a latent, and therefore all the more fearsome, anti-Jewishness that continues to exist there. Our own observations gave considerable substance to these worries. As we saw at the universities of Tübingen and Heidelberg, much of the young intellectual community was leftist and considered itself so free of the not-so-distant Nazi past and its ideology that it could be as hostile to Jews as it wished. These students, with some faculty companions, concentrated on denying the right of the State of Israel to exist and, fashionably, saw Palestinian Arabs as victims of genocide—at the hands of the people from whose memory these young Germans wanted to be free.

A sociological study gave further support to the judgment regarding antisemitism's continuing presence. A survey conducted at the Institute for Sociological Research of the University of Cologne in 1976 found that every second person in West Germany harbored some kind of adverse opinion of Jews. Of these, 15 to 20 percent manifested "distinct antisemitic prejudices of different kinds," while another 30 percent had "latent antisemitic prejudices." The most severe prejudices were found among farmers in the southern part of Germany, a small segment of the population, of whom 52 percent contended that the persecution of the Jewish people was deserved punishment for "their" crucifixion of Jesus.

The Cologne study has been criticized for, among other things, employing a type of leading question that tends to weight results on the side of an expression of derogatory attitudes.[18] With due allowance for the probability of exaggeration in the survey findings, it remains the case that those of today's antisemitic people living in Germany from 1933 to 1945 would have supported the Nazi anti-Jewish ideology and program, or at least they probably would not have opposed Nazism. This conclusion remains valid despite evidence that some admitted antisemites, even some members of the Nazi Party, did not approve of the final and murderous stage of Hitler's anti-Jewish campaign, and some small number of these individuals actually helped Jews escape their decreed fate.[19] And, presumably, any present or future assault upon Jewish existence would be welcomed or condoned by these people since they are aware of the consequences of such views held and acted on during the previous generation.

Some confirmation of this assumption was supplied by Eberhard Bethge in March 1986 when he reported to an American scholars conference on a number of antisemitic happenings that had occurred in West Germany in the ten months following President Reagan's controversial visit to the German military cemetery at Bitburg. Bethge was convinced, along with some other concerned West Germans, that the

41

American president's visit to Bitburg served to rehabilitate the SS and to remove the restraints on the public expressions of antisemitism that had prevailed in his country before that event.[20] In the frame of reference of the Holocaust's aftermath, what term other than "collective guilt" can accurately describe the objective moral condition of antisemites in Germany today?

Evidence of the abiding presence of the old antisemitism and anti-Judaism is to be found in a totally new milieu today—the Christian feminist movement in Germany. The deeply embedded stereotypes of the prejudices against Jews are "being spread about through new channels, from a completely different source."

Gisela Hommel observes that "what makes [the statements of German feminist theology] really dangerous is the fact that they follow very old patterns, already formed, strengthening and confirming them anew. Antisemitism is not only deeply rooted in the conscious mind, but even more deeply in people's unconscious emotions."[21]

3. *Although precise lines can never be drawn between authentic nonresponsibility and culpable responsibility, the truth is that historical memory is readily seduced by irresponsibility.*

Within humanness—that is, within "radical freedom" (as Reinhold Niebuhr defines humanness)—irresponsibility is an ever present temptation. Indeed, there could be no such thing as moral obligation without the immanent potentiality of its denial, a denial capable of marshaling great force.

More than once in different sections of Germany, we were told that Nazism was, of course, much worse and was accepted and practiced much more in regions of the country other than those represented by our informants. The script seemed to read: "Oh, yes, I remember all right. But it did not really happen here. It happened over there." In effect, this means: "We were only the victims; it was they who were the victimizers." These informants were being deceitful (to us or themselves, or both) at the point of both space and time. As we contend above, historical memory is subject to judgment by the facts; the principle applies equally here.

Jürgen Neven-du Mont's apologetic report upon Heidelberg in *After Hitler* helps sustain the fantasy and deception according to which Nazi behavior was always something that involved the other people: I and my parents and relatives would never take part in such harmful acts, and neither would anyone I know, including, for that matter, Party members. Even supporters of the regime did not, so one woman put it, "do bad things."[22] In a word, we are all good people. The truly fanatical Nazis and their supporters are invariably off somewhere else. But if that is so, then just where are they? It is as though Nazism has vanished into the clouds. Were one fully to accept this testimony, he would have to begin wondering how all the people could ever have been killed. The next step would be to ask himself, were they really killed? The final step would be the publication of a work denying that the Holocaust ever occurred as, in fact, increasingly is being done.[23]

Among the possible motivations for such testimony is the obvious one of seeking to escape any form of moral responsibility, of attempting to dissociate oneself from any kind of blame. For example, some Germans today claim to have had a place in the resistance movement that they did not in truth have.

On 8 May 1985 West Germany's President Richard von Weiszäcker challenged his compatriots' desire to deny or to forget. In a speech to the parliament he emphasized the unparalleled nature of the "genocide of the Jews," and the necessity of acknowledging that any German living in the Third Reich "could not fail to notice" the stigmatization of Jews, the destruction and plundering of their property, or their deportation. "All of us, whether guilty or not, whether young or old, must accept the past. We are all affected by its consequences and are liable for it. . . . [T]here can be no reconciliation [with Jews] without remembrance."

We have been speaking so far about the individual or personal process of remembering and recalling. But historical memory is also a society's shared memory by which those events not experienced directly are acquired as "inherited" memory. One of the most formidable shapers of this kind of collective memory and conscience is, of course, written history. If, in the first decades following the collapse of the Third Reich, little was written about the crimes the nation had committed, one of the present trends among German historians is to "normalize" the history and public consciousness of that period. One line is to argue that Hitler's annihilation measures were only reactions to the "Asian peril" that Stalin initiated with his social extermination policies against kulaks, his party purges, and his Gulag system. Thus, Auschwitz and the Endlösung are relativized and "de-singularized." Another line treats the National Socialist past as a normal or at least "quasi-normal" period of recent history that can, after all, be absorbed into an acceptable German nationalist perspective. Accordingly German soldiers are presented as not knowing "what was going on behind their backs [and as] not guilty of what was happening." They had to defend Germany and thereby also defend Hitler; they were caught in a "tragic conflict." Or, in another tactic, the concept of tragedy is focused on the cruelties experienced by Germans in the eastern provinces during and as a result of the war, including their eviction. But this is done without the necessary recognition of the disparity between this particular suffering, resulting from a war initiated by their own government, and the suffering of the millions ruthlessly murdered by the SS *Einsatzgruppen* and death camps, neither of which was required by the war. Still another historian's approach is to concentrate on the "everyday history" of the National Socialist period. This makes it possible to present a totally depoliticized picture of the National Socialist decades. Again, as with a previous example, one could easily conclude from this presentation that nothing bad really did happen.

The problem with all of these ways of presenting the history of the Third Reich is their ignoring of the victims. Just as "defending" Germany then made it possible to keep the death machinery operating, so, too, utilizing an argument today on behalf of the defenders repeats the abandonment of Germany's chosen victims. Just as German citizens could be persuaded then not to think about what might be happening to their absent Jewish neighbors or to the people of the conquered nations (even though "slave laborers" from those countries might be in their midst), so, too, today the attention of the German people can be directed away from them. Just as their concerns could be focused on their own undeserved suffering so they would make greater efforts to win the war, so, too, today the suffering of the German people at that time can be emphasized while the suffering Germans imposed on others can be forgotten.[24]

4. *One powerful force in the evasion of the moral demands of memory is the elevating to sovereignty of the self-contained individual.*

It is a historical-moral truism that before the dawn of individual conscience and individuality as we have come to think of these realities, the human being felt himself bound by and responsible for the behavior of his group. One dilemma within any modern moral philosophy concerns the measure in which the total emancipation of the person from collective fate may foster an inadvertent break with humanness. For is it not so that to be human is to belong to and to be responsible for the other? From this latter standpoint, atomistic individualism comprises an assault upon the integrity and dignity of the person.

44

Very few will argue that Germans born during or after the Nazi period bear "the sins of the fathers" in the sense that these younger ones are subject to guilt and punishment. But are we to conclude, morally speaking, that all the links between the generations can be or ought to be severed? A few German young people have told us that they do feel a special responsibility, on the very ground of their personal identity. They confront themselves with a special obligation to do what they can to see to it that a crime such as the Holocaust does not recur. Beate Klarsfeld is particularly known for her twenty-year self-imposed mission of tracking down war criminals and bringing them to justice. But until she went to France as a young adult, she had known very little about Nazi persecution of Jews. In France she found herself being looked at as guilty for the previous generations' crimes. She set out to learn "what really happened between 1933 and 1945." And then she concluded that being German meant that she had "special historic and moral responsibilities to assume." The moral outlook of Beate Klarsfeld and the other young Germans of whom we speak recognizes the truth that, even though personal guilt is lacking, they have nevertheless "inherited a dark legacy . . . from whose implications and consequences they are unable, if they are sensitive, to dissociate themselves."[25] The decisive words here are "if they are sensitive." And, in point of fact, the "dark legacy" will often adversely affect the younger generation even when sensitivity is lacking and the power of the past is not acknowledged. In this context, note the distinction between the absence of personal culpability and the presence of personal shame; the two are not necessarily equivalent.

5. *Some human beings bring themselves to accept a responsibility that, morally considered, is not directly theirs.*

Some individuals will to remember. The guilt they assume is borne vicariously. The memory they forge is an act of grace. This memory then helps determine their lives, for they incarnate their remembrance within deeds that cannot justly be demanded of them.

We think immediately here of the original purposes behind the founding of the German Reconciliation and Peace Service (Aktion Sühnezeichen/Friedensdienste). Begun in 1958 under the inspiration of two church leaders, Lothar Kreyssig and Franz von Hammerstein, the group started by bringing together teams of German young people who would surrender paid employment or formal education for a year or more in order to engage in volunteer work projects within different lands, including Israel. The initial intent of the organization included the quest for forgiveness and reconciliation, in light of the crimes against Jews and other reputed enemies of the Third Reich. Particularly in the earlier years, participants in this work specifically willed to take upon themselves the sins of their fathers.[26]

6. *One objective way to approach the subjective, psychomoral condition of a people is through an inquiry into the presence or absence among them of rectifying deeds.*

"You shall know them by their fruits" (Matt. 7:16). How can people legitimately forget their past until they come to terms with it by means of acts? In the measure that rectifying deeds are done, it may become right eventually to adjudge that the evil actions deeply rooted in socioreligious realities need to be mitigated by counteractions from within the same realities. Ceremonies, liturgies, and teaching of history offer means by which memory of a particular event becomes part of the collective consciousness in ways that make past and present continuous; they may help ensure against later generations succumbing to a similar evil. Other rectifying deeds also supply evidence that the past has been internalized, taken into the collective corpus. But insofar as the deeds are lacking, remembrance is a festering wound, and the nagging question remains: Who is entitled to forget?

In today's world, one decisive means of assessing the practical outlook and the moral condition of a people is through the actions of its government. We are permitted to speak here only of the democratic world; accordingly, East Germany is excluded from present consideration. Individual Germans and nonofficial groups in West Germany, including church bodies, do of course engage in many charitable and otherwise praiseworthy enterprises. Such acts can only impress and gratify the visitor. Again, the official program of *Wiedergutmachung* ("reparation") to Israel and individual Jews has done much to ease the collective conscience. Yet the truth persists that a primary test of the moral condition of a sovereign people is the continuing, contemporary policies of the govenment it elects. Within modern civilization, excepting such special times as emergencies brought by natural catastrophes, particular polities have dealings only with other polities.

The implication of the above truth is fairly obvious. A crucial and relatively precise means of applying our sixth proposition to the German condition today is through reference to official government policy toward Israel, for the latter polity comprises the one discriminate Jewish entity to which the German polity is now and can be related. In consequence, we are brought to ask if today's official German policy toward Israel is of such a nature as to justify the conclusion that the re-membrance of the Endlösung is morally decisive. As we consider the international scene, is it the case that German policy toward Israel dif-fers qualitatively from the policies of other states which recognizes the Jewish polity?[27] Was Chancellor Schmidt substantially justified in his judgment that his people have learned their lesson from the past?

There are serious differences of opinion on this subject. Our own persuasion is that contemporary German policy offers no special evi-dence to support affirmative answers to the questions just raised. The archbishop of Munich-Preising, Julius Cardinal Dopfner, declared shortly before his death that it is the duty of all Germans to support the Jewish people in the face of the latter's virtual isolation in world poli-tics, a duty that is rooted in "the full responsibility that [the Germans] must bear with regard to the Jews."[28] Where are the data to show, over subsequent years, that the Federal Republic of Germany has met or even approximated the test implied in Cardinal Dopfner's words? In what ways is Germany specially dedicated to the well-being and sur-vival of the State of Israel? Amidst continuing threats to the life of Is-rael, Germany's behavior has hardly manifested the distinctiveness that appears incumbent upon it because of its Holocaust past.

Should the rejoinder be forthcoming, perhaps in the name of Rein-hold Niebuhr and the theology of political realism, that nations do not repent, do not incarnate the altruistic spirituality that is sometimes at-tained by smaller groupings and particularly by individuals, we may respond that this is not the point at issue. Niebuhr's finding with respect to the morality or immorality of nations is essentially sound. However, we are not here involved in the question of how nations behave, but rather in the question of the ethical criteria to be adduced in order to judge whether *claims* concerning national moral health are convincing or truthful. It is overwhelmingly probable that West Germany will con-tinue to make decisions respecting Israel and the Middle East conflict on the basis of perceived self-interest. We simply inquire: What is the moral status and where is the moral convincingness in Schmidt's testi-mony, "We have learned our lesson from the past"? Nation-states and their representatives are probably not capable of choosing between perfection and imperfection. But they are never deprived of the choice between hypocrisy and ordinary decency. They always retain the choice of keeping silent. Had the German chancellor kept silent, he could hardly be accused of representative hypocrisy. But he did not do this. He spoke.

In our consideration of six moral-historical propositions we have focused on the nation and people of West Germany (having omitted East Germany for the reason already stated). What about Austria and its people?

Austria has claimed innocence of any of the Nazi crimes by virtue of having been an early victim of the Third Reich's expansionism. Despite evidence of the enthusiasm with which most Austrians greeted Hitler and his German troops in Vienna and his announcement of the *Anschluss* (annexation) in March 1938, the large membership in the Austrian National Socialist Party prior to that date (and ultimately more per capita then in Germany), the zeal with which Austrian mobs and local authorities went about despoiling its Jewish population, and the considerable role that Austrians later played in murdering Jews, Gypsies (Romanis), and communists,[29] Austria's stance has been endorsed by the United Nations allies of World War II[30] and the world community in general. Thus, Austria has been able to avoid paying reparations to slave laborers and Jewish survivors; it has escaped the opprobrium that Germany—and even Poland, a genuine victim nation—has had to bear; and its people have been enabled to forego any soul searching and repentance. Under these circumstances it was not surprising that in the country's presidential election of 1986 Kurt Waldheim was voted into office despite press revelations[31] of his being listed in the United Nations' archives of war criminals for having been an officer serving on headquarters staffs of several German combat groups in Yugoslavia and Greece, where thousands of suspected partisans, civilians, and Jews were killed or rounded up and deported to Auschwitz and other Nazi camps.

If blighted historical memory cannot be restored to health until its original inspiration is excised from the body politic, then the Austrian nation has revealed, not only by its voting record but also by its behavior since the election, that it has not yet sought for a healthy and restorative memory.[32]

Austria's responsibility and culpability for its Nazi past are being denied through a combination of evasion and defiance. Waldheim himself throughout his campaign flatly denied that he had done anything wrong, dismissing evidence as merely part of a slanderous attack and professing ignorance of events about which he had made his own notations at the time. He further argued that he and hundreds of thousands of other Austrians "only did their duty" while serving in the army of the Third Reich. A number of psychologists have theorized that many older Austrians voted for Waldheim because they subconsciously (or consciously?) identified with his denial of wrongdoing. As for those of the younger generation, their history books had told them Austria was Hitler's victim, and their postwar government had helped preserve the conspiracy of silence regarding reality.

The reaction of Waldheim's supporters to reports about his military service in the Balkans has been described as "so defiant, xenophobic, and ultimately antisemitic in tone that it was hard to avoid the conclusion that it was caused less by resentment over the rigorous scrutiny [of his personal history] than by a deep disquiet and defensiveness about the nation's own Nazi past."[33] Since responsibility has not been acknowledged, these people are unable to experience regret for past attitudes and actions or to feel compassion for those who suffered from such behavior.

Some six months after the election Austria's Chancellor Franz Vranitzky, who was only five years old at the time of the *Anschluss*, urged his countrymen to acknowledge what they, as a nation, "were guilty of in the past." "We must face our past squarely, accept our share of guilt and responsibility, and from that, deduce our standards for our actions in the future." The occasion for his remarks was a gathering of 350 veterans, former inmates of Nazi death camps, and former prisoners of war from forty countries. Vranitzky insisted that the past had to be discussed because the nation had become "the object of so much critical attention in the world."[34] Amnestia at the collective level is as unlikely to effectively suppress disturbing memories as psychological repression is at the individual level.

With President Waldheim refusing to take his chancellor's advice, one wonders how much effect Vranitzky's counsel will have elsewhere. Yet if the advice were acted upon only for reasons of expediency, it is doubtful that the long-term consequences would be significant. However, expediency plus accompanying changes in behavior have a way, sometimes, of producing unexpected positive results.

The question of the remembrance or amnestia of the Holocaust penetrates our entire study. For the present, two citations are offered. The first is from *Das Brandopfer* (*The Burnt Offering*) of Albrecht Goes: "Men have forgotten. And indeed one must forget, for how could one go on living if one could not forget. Yet at times there is need of one who remembers."[35] The second is from the Baal Shem Tov: "To forget is to prolong the exile; to remember is the beginning of redemption." These words are inscribed upon a wall at Yad Vashem.

3
SINGULARITY

This attempt to wipe Judaism from the face of the earth is
. . . the most historic event of our aeon, the decisive event which
cannot and may not ever become merely a bygone fact of the
past. It is and will remain a part of the consciousness of the
Christian Church, an event which puts all mankind on the
scales of judgment. Our society, our Church, was numbered
and weighed and found deficient. With this consciousness we
will have to live. . . . [It] would be a grave error if we would
consider the atrocities committed against the Jews as just another example of the power of universal evil. The Holocaust
was . . . a deliberate, coolly planned and technically perfected
challenge of all human values. As such it was a provocation
of God himself, a provocation to which the Church remained
silent.

Wolfgang Zucker, "30 Years After the Holocaust"

One compelling reaction to the Holocaust is the claim that the
event is unique. Our next task is to consider the force of this claim, together with some of its possible applications. The problem of uniqueness is shared by interpreters of the Holocaust who speak from all kinds
of viewpoints. Our analysis in chapter 1 of the meaning of the Final Solution has already pointed to the singularity of the event.

A friend has said, "I suppose it was the worst thing that ever happened."[1] A survivor of Auschwitz, testifying at the trial of Adolf Eich-
mann in Jerusalem, told of what he called "the history of the Auschwitz
planet."

The time there is not a concept as it is here in our planet. Every fraction of a
second passed there was at a different rate of time. And the inhabitants of
that planet had no names. They had no parents, and they had no children.
They were not clothed as we are clothed here. They were not born there and
they did not conceive there. They breathed and lived according to different
laws of Nature. They did not live according to the laws of this world of ours,
and they did not die.[2]

50

Among the reasons for the obscuring of the Holocaust and its distinctiveness is the omnipresence of human suffering and violence in our time. It is not that these realities are now so monstrous and all-pervasive that we have become obsessed with them. We suggest a much more radical interpretation. Hannah Arendt spoke of "the banality of evil." Emil Fackenheim is quite right that the risk in subscribing to this idea, as an overall historical interpretation, is that we fall into the trap set by the Nazis, who sought to make absolute evil into something routine and boring.[3] There is, nevertheless, an uncanny truth in Arendt's phrase. Evil becomes so terrible that it is no longer terrible. The incredible paradox is that final horror becomes trivial. Accordingly, it is no longer capable of gaining attention. It is boring. Or it is not even that. It is nothing at all.[4]

There is a universalism that is blind and even callous in the presence of particularity. There is particularism that does not see beyond one's own plight. We are called upon to take a dialectical approach here, to make evident a two-sided truth: each instance of human agony is at one and at the same time bound up with all other such cases, and yet it remains sui generis. Unless we maintain both these elements—the factor of continuity and the factor of discontinuity—we end up dishonoring the memory and the name of one or another human sufferer. The insistence that the misery of a single human being in any time or place is "equivalent to" the agony of six million Jews conveys the necessary recognition of the element of continuity. Taken in and of itself, there is nothing singular in the figure of six million. Out of five and a half million Russian prisoners of war in Germany, some four million were killed.

The insistence that the Holocaust carried out by the German Nazis "contains no historical or moral parallel" conveys the necessary recognition of the element of discontinuity. The two kinds of declaration must be made together, for the foundational reason that human suffering is not a quantitative matter subject to some form of objective measurement but is instead a qualitative condition to be apprehended in existential terms, through the faculty of sympathy. Whenever the stress on continuity is abandoned, the solidarity of all human beings in suffering is lost. Paradoxically, the special agony of the Jewish people is lost as well, for it is then deprived of its human reality. But whenever the stress on discontinuity is abandoned, the integrity of the Jewish sufferers is flouted and dissolved into something abstract. It is often pointed out that the greatest insult to the Jewish victims of the Nazis is to sub-

51

sume their plight under the generalizing category of mass agony, or, worse, of "war crimes."[5] To address the Holocaust survivor by reminding him of the horrors of, say, Vietnam is obscene. It dishonors his dignity. Yet the other side of the dialectic is possessed of undeniable and equal force. To separate the agony of the Endlösung from other sufferings would be to dishonor other victims within the unending tale of human misery.[6] Thus, there would be equal obscenity in reminding the Vietnamese sufferers about Auschwitz.

If we are to relate responsibly to human agony, we must adjudge that it is simply wrong to subject different forms and cases of suffering to competitive criteria. Individual and collective pain and agony are just that. They are to be received with unique tenderness and compassion—in sui generis ways, not in categorical or comparative ways. It is imperative that we do our best to individualize and humanize the figure of six million. Saul Friedman does precisely that when he says, "Sooner or later the Jewish child awakes screaming in the middle of the night with the spectre of the bones of his people before his eyes."[7] But to speak this way need not mean forgetting the other human beings in other times and other places who, each in his own way, have awakened screaming in the night. The one remembrance can feed the other remembrances.

We hope that the above dialectic will be kept in mind, in order that our own stress upon the singularity of Holocaust suffering will not be construed as implicit insensitivity to non-Holocaust sufferers.

FROM THE UNIQUE TO THE UNIQUELY UNIQUE

The question of the moral uniqueness of the Holocaust is at once complicated and refined by the question of extramoral uniqueness. Insofar as the Holocaust is a singular event, that fact can be made manifest through historical, philosophical, and theological reflection. Before we enter substantively into these areas, it may be helpful to distinguish alternative treatments of the concept "uniqueness." At least three interpretations vie for attention.

1. One interpretation emphasizes the kinship of all historical events, stressing the elements of continuity within the happenings of human life. From this standpoint, the Endlösung, for all its peculiar features, is

held to manifest essential continuity with other deeds of human genocide, such as the earlier Turkish slaughter of over one million Armenians during 1915 and 1916, or for that matter, the Nazi persecutions of the Gypsies (Romanis) contemporaneously with the Jews.[8] The late eminent historian Hermann G. Adler opposed the view that Nazism introduced an entirely new dimension into human destructiveness. In Adler's epigram, from the day of Original Sin, the Holocaust became possible.[9]

2. There are also undoubted elements of discontinuity (*Einmaligkeit*, "historical singularity") and discordance within the multitudinous events of history. In accord with this obvious fact, many interpreters of the Holocaust emphasize the unparalleled character of the obliteration of European Jewry. They single out such matters as the bureaucratization of murder, the combined technological and ideological "perfection" of the destructiveness, and the obsessive and even self-defeating character, from a military point of view, of the Nazi concentration upon the Jewish enemy. Within this same general category of interpretation falls the historical contention by a scholar in Darmstadt, West Germany that the Endlösung represents the singular culminating point of a denial of Jewish integrity prepared for centuries by those of the Christian world.[10] Again, historian Klaus Scholder of Tübingen identifies Nazism, not as a form of nihilism, but as a primitive dualistic system of absolute good and absolute evil, within which all of human history embodies a war of the two forces. Capitalizing upon the powerful presence of traditional antisemitism, National Socialism uniquely applied these two foundational categories to Germans ("good") and Jews ("evil"). The Nazis saw in the Jews a deadly bacillus threatening the very being of the healthy Aryan people. They had to be mercilessly objective and wipe out the death-bearing agents.[11] Here is a primary difference in the Nazi ideologies of Jews and of Gypsies, although, of course, the Germans considered the Gypsies highly inferior people (and peculiarly "asocial") and slaughtered one-half million of them. (In this book "ideology," following Karl Marx, is used in a more or less pejorative sense, to denote the use of ideas and arguments to serve collective self-interest.)

3. We may occasionally glimpse a transhistorical level for which, in English, the somewhat cumbersome expression "unique uniqueness" seems required (in German, perhaps *ganze Einzigartigkeit*, uniqueness in the connotation of "onlyness"). Now we are met not just with an unparalleled happening, or one discontinuous with other genocidal acts,

but instead with a truly transcending or metahistorical event, an event that twists our journey through space-time by 180 degrees.[12] It is an event that raises the question of *Heilsgeschichte* ("salvation history") or perhaps of the total eclipse of salvation history, an event that, if it is "comparable" at all, can only be compared with a very small number of other "incomparable" events, such as the Exodus and the giving of Torah or the Crucifixion and the Resurrection. Thus, in Elie Wiesel's *Beggar in Jerusalem*, it is testified that at Sinai the Torah was bestowed upon Israel, but then in the kingdom of night, in the flames of the Final Solution, the Torah was taken back.[13] Such radicalizing of uniqueness has the effect of placing the Holocaust within the same general frame of reference as certain traditionally sacred happenings or affirmations.

Presumably, one may reject this third understanding of uniqueness by, for example, rejecting all transcending, *heilsgeschichtliche* events. But once the rejection comes from a source that demands *heilsgeschichtliche* responses to alternative events (e.g., Exodus, Sinai, Calvary, Resurrection), we are obliged to answer, as a German saying has it, "ein Esel schimpft den andren Langohr" ("the one jackass is calling the other one 'Long-ears'").

Fresh dating procedures serve the function of recognizing and symbolizing watersheds of human history. Thus it is that in Christendom reference is made to "B.C." (Before Christ) and "A.D." (Anno Domini, "in the year of the Lord"). In recent years, however, some Jews and Christians have mutually agreed to a usage less ideologically tinged: "B.C.E." (Before the Common Era) and "C.E." (Common Era). In Islam, "A.H." stands for the all-decisive year of Muhammad's *Hijra* (Migration). The year 1941 is perhaps best identified as year 1 of the Holocaust. On this reckoning, 1990 is to be renumbered as the year 50. We propose the identifying initials "B.F.S." (Before the Final Solution) and "F.S." (in the year of the Final Solution). Accordingly, 1990 (A.D. or C.E.) becomes 50 F.S.[14]

Clearly, the altered symbology remains quite unconvincing unless one is persuaded that the advent of the Endlösung has meant an ontological redirecting of the course and fate of human history. On the basis of that persuasion, we now follow certain implications of this controversial persuasion, first from a philosophical and historical standpoint and then from a theological and moral one.

The philosophical issue of human nature and destiny and the theological issue of the divine nature and destiny converge under the power of the twofold question of responsibility (*Verantwortlichkeit*) and fate.

What·do we mean by human accountability–blameworthiness and its consequences? And what do we mean by divine accountability–blameworthiness and its consequences? Of course these questions have been raised and must be raised in any time and in any place. Yet, the philosophical and theological questions are here broached strictly within the frame of reference of a single event, the Holocaust. Wherein, then, lies the *historical existential* peculiarity of these questions?

All historical events are unique. History does not and cannot repeat itself. That various historical happenings appear to replicate other events is accountable in part through our temptation to be content with surface resemblances and in part through the powerful impulse within the human mind to subject successive happenings to generalizing categories. All too chillingly, the Holocaust contains its own peculiarities— such as the truth that never before in human history was systematic genocide conducted by a government in the name of a pseudoscientific doctrine of race and to the end of final blessedness.[15] Morality was transvaluated. Those who murdered were doing "the right thing."[16] Again, the *intent* of the Holocaust was unparalleled in human history, most especially the intent to eradicate human compassion.[17]

However, we must always keep in mind that uniqueness does not necessarily entail unique uniqueness. A kind of continuum impresses itself upon us. We move from the surface level of repetitive events (e.g., the births of thousands of kittens), to the deeper level of relative uniqueness (flavored by continuity and altered by discontinuity), and finally to an ultimate level transcending other levels: the level of incomparability or unique uniqueness (e.g., God, the Jewish people, the devil, or, for that matter, this particular dear and incredible little kitten in contrast to all other kittens.) There is a real sense in which every historical being participates in absolute uniqueness or "onlyness" because no other being can ever duplicate its exact history. We see, accordingly, how any such wording as "Is the Holocaust unique?" is exceedingly trivial. To answer yes to such a query is to make the same trite reply that is to be made respecting any happening in history.[18] Instead we have to ask, *in what senses* is the Holocaust unique? Is it indeed *uniquely* unique?

Before further pursuing questions such as these last, we may point out that the level of relative uniqueness is often able to assist in the understanding of uniquely unique events. Thus, in his introduction to *The Echo of the Nazi Holocaust in Rabbinic Literature*, H. J. Zimmels enumerates and then explains several factors that "made the persecution of the Jews by the Nazis unique in the history of mankind in general and in that of the Jews in particular":

1. the nature of the persecution;
2. the plan of the extermination of the whole Jewish race;
3. the number of countries affected and the number of their victims;
4. the use of modern methods of science and technology in the extermination of Jews;
5. the misuse of the victims and their bodies for forced labour, for medical, commercial and private purposes; and
6. the difficulties of finding places of refuge.[19]

Special attention is called to the second item in Zimmels's list. The question of the Endlösung is not that of the destruction of some or many Jews, but that of the total obliteration of Jewry as such. This latter, historically determined eventuality is to be balanced against the moral thesis set forth near the beginning of this chapter, where the qualitative, noncomparable character of humankind's miseries is emphasized. For the truth is that in the Endlösung the qualitative question of Jewish survival and life was so completely overpowered by the quantitative factor that the quantitative element became the all-decisive determinant of qualitative reality. The decision that there were to be no more Jews on Planet Earth constituted an absolute convergence of quantitative and qualitative reality. That decision points us, accordingly, in the direction of the uniquely unique character of the Holocaust. Here is the sense in which the singularity of the event is tied to the identity of the victims; it was the Jews, only the Jews, who were to be removed from human existence. Differently expressed, the *Einzigartigkeit* of the Holocaust rests in the fact that all Jewish babies and children were to die along with older people. At this point the varied forms of understanding (historical, philosophical, moral, and theological) begin to converge: there is a historical-phenomenological link between the Jewish people and the Creator and Judge of the world.

We are summoned to embark upon a journey that leads us beyond purely historical uniqueness into a land of paradox and mystery, of the heights and the depths of human experience and sin, of demonic forces and divine imponderabilities. If we are to gain understanding, we have no choice but to travel along that way.

A singular apprehension of the Endlösung appears attainable only if that event is itself sui generis—or, to put it more cautiously, only if, along with the evident continuities between the Holocaust and other acts of genocide and human destructiveness, there are qualitatively unique discontinuities. To the end of testing the assumption that the philosophical question of the nature and meaning of the Holocaust demands uniquely unique conceptualization, we proceed in what appears to be a self-contradictory fashion: we call to witness the phenomenon of antisemitism as such. A contradiction seems to enter here, for the simple and forcible reason that to place a particular event (for example, the Holocaust), or even a series of consanguine events, within a wider category (for example, antisemitism) appears to threaten the integrity of the event or events. However, in the present case this difficulty may not in fact intrude, provided that both the larger category of antisemitism is itself sui generis and the specific event, the Holocaust, is to be grasped as the uniquely unique climax-incarnation of antisemitism.

Once more, dialectical understanding is essential, where each integral side of a paradox points to the force and validity of the other side. For, if we were to treat the Holocaust as absolutely or transcendently unique, we would appear to suppress the long history of antisemitism of which the Endlösung is the culmination. Furthermore, were we to identify the Holocaust as absolutely different from all other events, we could not then find specific lessons in it.[20] On the other hand, in the very act of attending to the history of antisemitism, we are brought to the singularity of the Holocaust. No longer were sporadic persecution, various kinds of social denigration, and partial destruction the orders of the time; instead, every Jew had to be slaughtered as quickly as possible. Thus it is that, within the very frame of reference of the ongoing course of history, the *Shoah* manifests discontinuity as well as continuity with the past.

The decision to assign the Holocaust to the developing story of Christendom points to both the continuity and the discontinuity of the event. On the one hand, the Endlösung is enmeshed within a large, enduring structure of conviction and action. On the other hand, although the event constitutes the climax of a certain historical development and fate, the Final Solution nevertheless erupts beyond that structure since its specific acts had no precedential incarnation.

Sometimes the claimed uniqueness of the *Shoah* is derived from the claimed uniqueness of the Jewish people. There is much plausibility here, as is suggested at different places in these pages. Historically speaking, the peculiarity of an event, or composite of events, means nothing apart from the special subjects, the human individuals and groups involved. However, we again face a dialectical state of affairs. To point out that human events are made unique by their actors is to imply that the Holocaust has no greater distinctiveness than any comparable event involving a group of non-Jews. Yet here too we must move to the other side: those facts about the treatment of Jews that mark off the fortunes of these people from the fortunes of others become the ground for attesting to the distinctiveness of the Holocaust.

Reinhold Niebuhr stressed that the peculiarity and the persistence of antisemitism stems from the fact that the targets diverge from the hostile majority in two crucial ways, religiously and culturally. Niebuhr was addressing himself to the uniqueness of antisemitism, but he was not coming to terms with its uniquely unique character. Like others, he would refer as well to the condemning of Jews for their virtues as much as for their reputed vices. While in that, too, we are met by uniqueness, there is perhaps also a hint of unique uniqueness.

The world-shattering consideration behind such glimpses of truth is that the phenomenon of antisemitism is simply incomparable. There are no parallels to it. There simply is no historical analogue to antisemitism. It is not a question of "human prejudice" in a general sense. The practice of some social scientists of remanding antisemitism to the category of "human prejudice" is a temptation and a snare, whatever the superficial resemblance of antisemitism to ordinary prejudice. The incomparability of antisemitism is tied to that phenomenon's peculiar spatio-temporal character. Whether we speak of space or of time, the two primordial dimensions of human existence, no prejudice comes anywhere near antisemitism. No prejudice can approach antisemitism for either geopolitical pervasiveness or temporal enduringness. Other prejudices remain, by contrast, localized and fleeting; they are instances of spatial contingency and historical transience. In the last reckoning, and after their having been contrasted with antisemitism, they become slightly reminiscent of child's play.

In the history of Christendom only the Jewish people is charged with a world conspiracy against humankind. And the traditional Christian ideology has managed to nurture a variegated progeny. The centuries are awakened from the past to testify with a single voice to their having been permeated by *Judenfeindschaft*, enmity to Jews as Jews; for example, in the United Nations of recent years the international wrath reserved for the State of Israel finds no parallel in place or in time. The United Nations, the highest council of the world community, has become a center of antisemitism under the cloak of anti-Zionism and anti-Israelism.[21] At no time in the history of humanity has there been a counterpart to such a phenomenon. Thus, Saint John Chrysostom's allegation in fourth-century Antioch that the Jews are "a nation of assassins and hangmen" is duplicated word-for-word by Russian and Arab propagandists sixteen centuries later.

THE "NECESSITY" OF THE DEVIL

The philosophical-historical understanding of the unique uniqueness of the Holocaust may be aided by the concept of "the devil." This concept appears to be of seminal use in coming to grips with antisemitism and thence with the Endlösung. However, we introduce the concept with a certain diffidence. Our reference to the devil is hardly designed to disaffect readers, though the usage will doubtless have exactly that impact upon many, perhaps through their wariness of obscurantism and superstition.[22] One of our personal bafflements is that, despite the deliberate destructiveness that has permeated so much in human experience, many religious people still find it easier to go on believing in God than to consider the reality of the devil. We, the authors, are disturbed by those remnants of modern idealism, utopianism, and sentimentality that wish to decree, almost mechanically, the nonreality or even the inconceivability of the devil. If the abiding and omnipresent persecution of Jews raises fateful questions concerning the reality of God, certainly it ought to pose the question of the devil. (To seek to work out specifics of the relations of devilish action and human action presents no problems that are not equally present in the effort to reckon with the specifics of the divine and human relation.) Our simple persuasion is that it is extremely difficult to speak meaningfully of the hatred of Jews without speaking of a demonic force or a concatenation of such forces.

We should be among the last to sanction a "devil theory of history," for that view despoils the sovereignty of God, or at least the much more compelling affirmation of God's love. Nor should we ever agree that membership in the devil's work force frees human beings from responsibility or culpability. The protestation "I only obey orders" is no

59

valid defense. Human guilt persists, and it must be judged and punished. Furthermore, we do not suggest that there is no substitute for the word "devil"; we are willing to settle for such a term as "demonic power," provided only that the specificity and the other elements of the phenomenon in question, as discussed below, are not obviated. Above all, we should certainly not desire our theory of the distinctive character of antisemitism to stand or fall upon the usage of the concept "devil."

It is not our intention to offer an exhaustive clarification of, or "apology" for, the devil. Doubters would probably remain unconvinced, just as many persons remain wholly unimpressed by proofs for the existence of God. We may perhaps be permitted one literary and substantive gloss: the devil does not deserve a capital D. In point of truth, he deserves nothing. That the devil deserves nothing is related to his own nature. Although we appear to be referring at present to the reality of the devil, this is a manner of speaking. Strictly, and on the basis of the absolute ontological gulf between God and the devil, it is more accurate to speak of the devil's unreality. However, this consideration does not lessen in any way the usefulness and appropriateness of the concept of the devil within our current context.

We are the witnesses of a haunting combination of particularity and universality. The Jew is the particular victim, but for no particular reason. That is to say, the Jew is not to be destroyed because he has done something specific, committed some special crime. He is to be annihilated, not on the ground of doing, but on the ground of universal being—or, better, of nonbeing; he is presented as universal evil.[23] Accordingly his destruction is the inevitable and logical consequence of being the opposite of universal goodness.

The integrity of human beings has always been subject to attack by one or another foe. But we are dealing with the singling out of the Jew for denigration and death. What is the relation between the general and the specific attacks? Is antisemitism simply another technique within the devil's stratagems, just one more campaign within the eternal war upon man? Or is antisemitism of the very character of the devil? Is it a special malady that may eventually entice the divine-human creation back to a state of realized nonbeing? The daring assertion is sometimes made that the very edifice of our social libido, at least in the West, is somehow linked to antisemitism. For example, David Polish writes that "the truth of every cause is validated or found fraudulent in the way in which it confronts the Jewish people."[24]

The word "God" is our imperative symbol for the transcendent, persisting power of righteousness and creativity in the world. The word "devil" is the symbol of the transcendently unique and persisting power of evil and destructiveness, a concept marked, therefore, by a necessity comparable with that of God. The devil is not the reality of evil in any abstract or generalized sense; he (*sic*) is other than the power of evil as such (just as God is anything but abstract or generalized goodness or divineness). The devil is the totally unique power that concentrates upon totally unique evil. The meaning and force of this affirmation are contingent, obviously, upon the convincingness of the idea of "totally unique evil." Is there an evil in this world that is uniquely unique? Yes. We have already spoken of it. That evil is antisemitism.

The "devil" and "antisemitism" are correlative symbols: antisemitism is born of the devil, and the devil receives his sustenance from antisemitism. The elucidation or disclosure of the devil is required etiologically and existentially because the hatred of Jews is not, in essence, a matter of evil as such. It is *this* evil, an evil at once incomparable and incredible, as incomparable and incredible as the original election of Israel by God. Although incredibility is normally or linguistically the opposite of credibility, it is not necessarily the opponent of truth. To speak of the unbelievable destiny of the Jews is somehow to testify to God, for he is the unbelievably unique One. Were the divine election of the Jewish people comparable to other elections, we should have to settle for "the factor of the gods" or some other mundane accounting. In the same way, were the ongoing persecution of Jews comparable to other persecutions, we should have to settle for "the element of evil forces" or some equally profane explanation. But there is nothing like antisemitism. Accordingly, it is appropriate to speak of the devil.

Thus, it follows logically that, within one frame of reference, the devil may be denominated "god." He is the god of antisemitism. The devil seeks to emulate the real God. The kingdom of the true God extends to humankind, yet God sustains his chosen people. So, too, the devil covets a universal empire, yet he also retains his elected ones, his "faithful remnant," his special witnesses. These are the antisemites. Through the millennia and across all boundaries, the devil's faithful persist. The banality and the vapidity of the recent vogue of the devil in Hollywood and elsewhere lie in the ignorance of the truth that the devil does not work with just anybody. Satan's universality transcends his particularity, but it is implemented through the particularity. As we have observed, only the Jews are opposed without any limitations of

61

date or boundaries of place. The devil is universal, but he is very particular. The unique connection between the devil and antisemitism is authenticated through incarnating antisemitic depravity in so diverse and abiding a congeries of sources. The singularity of the devil is manifest in his tie with the world's one uniquely unique evil; the incomparability of the devil stands in horrible correlation with the incomparability of antisemitism. Men and nations who are normally foes always have the opportunity to join hands, in the devil's peace, against the one enemy, the Jew. Membership in the religion of antisemitism is ever open to all. It is the only universal faith. The language of antisemitism is the devil's native tongue; it quickly becomes the second language of the devil's disciples, and after a while it takes command of their original language.

We are beset by the unbelievable proposition that the devil acts to deceive the world into seeing in the Jew his own incarnation. The devil's final deed is to seek an appearance of coalescing with the Jew. This is the only possible masquerade for him. Who then could accuse him of being the real father of antisemitism? Here is the devil's uniquely unique work, for only the devil himself could "uncover" the devil in the Jew. Thus, while the Fourth Gospel was written down by a man who may have carried the name of John, the hidden source of John 8:42–47 may be understood as the devil himself. In that passage "the Jews"—note the indiscriminateness—are informed that they are not children of God but are children of the devil who willfully choose to fulfill his desires. The accusation of Jewish devilishness is an ultimate proof that the non-Jewish, antisemitic soul is invaded by Satan, for only the devil could demonically claim the Jew as his singular confrere. In sum, both psychoanalytically and spiritually speaking, the "Jewish world conspiracy" in fact comprises a world-wide conspiracy of demon-ridden Christians and other intriguers against Jews.[25]

Frequently "Auschwitz" (as a symbol for the Final Solution) and "Hiroshima" (incorporating Nagasaki and symbolically standing for the nuclear weaponry) are linked as comparable events. When the United States Air Force dropped the first atomic bomb (uranium-type) on Hiroshima on 6 August 1945 and a second one (plutonium-type) on Nagasaki three days later, some estimated 115,000 to 135,000 people were killed immediately, and many more were burned, maimed, and otherwise injured. After one year the total number of deaths had reached approximately 210,000. Forty years later bomb-related injuries and diseases accounted overall for some 315,000 to 340,000 deaths. And the final count is still incomplete. The physical pain, scars, and radiation sickness continue to torment thousands of those survivors. Shame and concern about being stigmatized and thus harming their children's and grandchildren's futures have kept many from acknowledging their disabilities. Guilt for surviving besets some. An overwhelming sense of loss and a feeling of having been abruptly cut off from the community that provided continuity and stability are prevalent aspects of these survivors' lives. The foregoing are evidence of some similarities of trauma and other after-effects suffered by these victims[26] and European Jews. Even so, can we equate the two catastrophes? There was no attempt or intent to degrade or dehumanize the Japanese people or to make them collaborators in their own deaths. But there is an even more fundamental disparity: The purpose of dropping an atomic bomb on two Japanese cities was not the annihilation of all Japanese people; the purpose was to end the war in the Pacific as quickly as possible, in order to avoid a protracted and bitter struggle that would have consumed unnumbered lives on all sides.[27]

What about the Cambodian massacres of the late 1970s? Under the Khmer Rouge government some two or possibly three million Cambodians out of a total of seven million are estimated to have been executed or killed by deliberate policies of starvation, expulsion from homes and land, or other conditions of life imposed on most of the population by the ruling party cadre. Brutal treatment was meted out even to children, and sometimes the tyrannized people—including children—were forced to participate in the killing (sometimes by decapitation) of one of their fellows for failure to meet some work standard or other arbitrary decree of the overseer. Disbelief, feelings of absolute helplessness and vulnerability, and gradual desensitization were experienced by those who have been willing and able to describe their ordeals. In this situation we find even more similarities to the *Shoah*: the large number and proportions of victims; the intense suffering and dehumanization; the methods which arbitrarily forced victims to become also victimizers; the targeting of specific groups (on ethnic, educational, religious, or political grounds) for annihilation; the methodical records kept by the murderers; and the traumas of survivors. But again we must note the fundamental difference: Not *all* Cambodians were intended to be killed. Khmer Rouge's goal of achieving a total social revolution and a "people's society" in democratic Kampuchea by getting rid of all those who could or would work against it can be recognized as strikingly similar to the National Socialist policies toward the non-Jewish subject peoples, especially in Eastern Europe.[28] In both cases no value per se was granted to any of these human lives. Their only value was a carefully calculated social one: to what extent would they serve the purposes of the power-holding group. These goals are not identical to those of the Endlösung, although they exhibit the same disregard for human life in the name of an abstract "ideal" (that is, ideology).

But how do these and other historical examples compare with the goal of antisemitism? Only the destruction of Jewry is subject to no purpose beyond itself, whatever rationalizations may be advanced to justify it. The war on Jewish existence that antisemitism embodies has but one intention: to create a world without Jews.[29] It is the end of all ends; it is at once the fulfillment (*telos*) and the conclusion (*finis*) of every end. To obliterate the Jewish people is the one goal of existence to which all other goals are subsidiary—or, more accurately, the one goal of nonexistence, the realization of nonbeing, for the destroyer as well as for the destroyed. It is, at one and the same time, sadism sui generis and masochism sui generis. To offer an aphorism for all this: in the categories of satanology, the Jew is the devil not because he is evil; he is the devil because he is the devil. Insofar as it may be felt that attention to the devil will have the effect of mystifying the identity of antisemitism, we suggest that so mysterious a phenomenon as antisemitism may well require consideration of a demonic force or forces if it is ever going to be reasonably comprehended.[30]

Any who doubt the singularity of the Endlösung may well reflect upon the current conspiracy to deny that it ever took place.[31] Such denials kill the sufferers a second time, by taking away the victims' first death. Thus do these devil's representatives offer a kind of grisly witness, if a self-contradictory one, to the distinctiveness of the Holocaust.[32] Moreover, the denial comes not from active participants in the mass murders, nor even from their compatriots or government, but from outside Germany—from France, Britain, Canada, Australia, and the United States. Here is a clear distinction from the case of the Turkish authorities and official historians who deny their own earlier government's massacre of Armenian fellow citizens. The unique uniqueness of the event is validated through the satanic pretense that it did not happen. Of what other comparably monstrous event in human history has there ever been a campaign contrived by reputedly civilized people to say that the thing never transpired? We are reminded forcibly of Arthur Hertzberg's observation that the antisemite invariably attacks Jews at "precisely that aspect of their current selves which is most uniquely

64

theirs, which most exactly expresses the specificness of their own life"[33] —be it their religion, their national homeland, or whatever. The antisemite always denies the reality or validity of whatever, in different periods, is the bearer of peculiarly existential meaning for the Jewish people. Today, accordingly, the slaughter of the six million and its remembrances must be taken away, must be obliterated.

How is this demonic denial promulgated, and how should it be countered? Lecturers are brought to university campuses by some student group under the spurious guise of freedom of speech and freedom to learn. Revisionist conventions are booked into university conference centers. Libraries are presented with free copies of some of the most respectable-appearing publications, and librarians are persuaded that these contain sound scholarly data. Books, journals, and articles are circulated widely, many earning their publishers financial profit as well as the satisfaction of having gained new converts to the antisemitic cause. In 1985 a court in Montreal found for the plaintiff, the government of Ontario, against the defendant, Ernst Zundel, who had written and distributed literature to disprove the Holocaust. The case was brought under Canada's law prohibiting the publication of false news detrimental to the public interest, specifically news likely to incite intolerance. The disturbing question remains whether such legal actions serve the purpose intended. Through extensive media coverage the defendant and his supporters were provided with a much wider audience for their "evidence" and antisemitic views than their own publications would normally reach. Is direct confrontation the most strategic approach? Yet if legal action is not brought, the law is useless and flouted openly.[34]

Another legal action was undertaken in California. Mel Mermelstein, a survivor of Auschwitz and Birkenau, sued the Institute for Historical Review for reneging on the Institute's offer to pay $50,000 to anyone who could prove that at least one Jew was gassed at Auschwitz. On 9 October 1981 Judge Thomas Johnson of the Superior Court of California issued a ruling that "judicial notice" is taken that "Jews were gassed to death at Auschwitz concentration camp" and that the Holocaust is not reasonably subject to dispute. In a later decision the Institute was ordered to pay Mermelstein the promised $50,000. However, it was never paid. The Institute was temporarily disbanded, but then reappeared. Was anything accomplished except a great deal of national publicity for the case of denial?[35] The rational view that the court's official ruling should put an end to any further questioning of the reality of the Final Solution does not meet the irrational mindset of those who *choose* to deny that particular reality because by so doing they add to the antisemitic arsenal.

We spoke above of the destruction of Jewry being an end in itself. Consider what Emil L. Fackenheim has written:

> While even the worst society is geared to life, the Holocaust Kingdom was geared to death. It would be quite wrong to say that is was a mere means, however depraved, to ends somehow bound up with life. As an enterprise subserving the Nazi war effort the murder camps were total failures, for the human and material "investment" far exceeded the "produce" of fertilizer, gold teeth and soap. The Holocaust Kingdom was an end in itself, having only one ultimate "produce," and that was death.

It is false to comprehend Nazism and the murder camps as only an extreme case of general technological dehumanization.

> In essence, Nazism was the murder camp. That a nihilistic, demonic celebration of death and destruction was its animating principle . . . [became] revealed in the end, when in the Berlin bunker Hitler and Goebbels . . . expressed ghoulish satisfaction at the prospect that their downfall might carry in train the doom, not only (or even at all) of their enemies, but rather of the "master race."

Fackenheim concludes:

> Even this does not exhaust the scandalous particularity of Nazism. The term "Aryan" had no clear connotation other than "non-Jew," and the Nazis were not anti-Semites because they were racists, but rather racists because they were anti-Semites. The exaltation of the "Aryan" had no positive significance. It had only the negative significance of degrading and murdering the "non-Aryan." Thus Adolf Eichmann passed beyond the limits of a merely "banal" evil when, with nothing left of the Third Reich, he declared with obvious sincerity that he would jump laughing into his grave in the knowledge of having dispatched six million Jews to their death. We must conclude, then, that the dead Jews of the murder camps (and all of the other innocent victims, as it were, as quasi-Jews, or by dint of innocent-guilt-by association) were not the "waste product" of the Nazi system. They were *the* product.[36]

Philosophically and historically speaking, we are now in a somewhat better position to reckon with the question, wherein lies the singularity of the Holocaust? Our answer is a simple one. (What are we saying? There could be no paradox more reason-defying than this: to propose a simple interpretation of the essence of the modern world's most impossible event, that event before which reasoned analysis seems so terribly helpless. Yet we contend that the truth is a simple one.) The Holocaust is the final act of a uniquely unique drama. It is the hour that follows logically, inexorably, and faithfully upon a particular history of conviction and behavior. It is a climax that succeeds the drawing up, over many centuries, of the requisite doctrinal formulations. It is the arrival of the "right time" (*kairos*) following upon all those dress rehearsals, those practice sessions of the Crusades, the Inquisition, and the like. The Holocaust is the consummation of all of them. Yet within this very simplicity, within this very paucity of originality, there implodes all the insane and demonic complexity. Only in our latter years could we finally ready ourselves for the eschatological deed, the Endlösung. Only the final destruction remained to be carried out. True, the labor would have to be back-breaking, but the consummation was nothing, really. All that remained to be done was to "manage" and to follow out the correct technical steps. Antisemitism "became professionalized and mass murder became an administrative process."[37] The German Nazis only lived out and applied a deep historical inevitability:[38] Here was the implementation of the dominant theological and moral conclusions of the Christian church, as well as the philosophical ideas of certain so-called great men of Western culture (Voltaire, Nietzsche, Fichte, and others), now aided by technological instrumentalities not previously marshaled or available. All in all, *we were following orders*—the remorseless, gathering commands of nineteen centuries.[39]

THE QUESTION ASKED
OF GOD

We move now into a more theological province.

The unique uniqueness of happenings summed up in words such as "Exodus" and "Sinai" is expressed theologically through a concept such as "positive revelatory significance," a revelation of life. By contrast, the Holocaust may be identified through the concept of "negative revelatory significance," as "anti-Sinai"[40]—that is, as a uniquely devilish event, a revelation of death itself. However, such an observation is not distinctively theological. It reflects a sharing by philosophy and theology: death is as much a philosophical as a theological theme.

Under the promptings of unique uniqueness, the theological province is entered through this inquiry: Is it or is it not the case that, in the shadow of the Holocaust, God and the relationship between God and his people ought to be apprehended in radically new and transcending ways? Is the poet Jacob Glatstein right that "above the gas chambers . . . Sinai, desolate, destroyed, has departed in smoke?"[41] Is it or is it not the case, theologically speaking, that F.S. is the polar opposite of B.F.S.? The question of the uniqueness of the Holocaust thus becomes the other side of the question of the intentions and behavior of the God of history. (We give this topic further attention in the next chapter when considering various theologians' and philosophers' efforts to address the God-question after the *Shoah*.)

The integral link between philosophical analysis ("the philosopher's task is the critical examination of our collective self-image"[42]) and theological analysis is conveyed in the title of Act 5 of Rolf Hochhuth's play *Der Stellvertreter (The Deputy)*: "Auschwitz, or Where are You, God?" Thus does the subject before us become more than a question of the devil and more than a question of human infamy: it also becomes a question of the divine fate. What is the life story of God? May it be that, in the end, God becomes the devil? In Hochhuth's drama the character known as the Doctor puts God, not man, on the stand of the accused (although Hochhuth never annuls human diabolism). True, we are brought to see that it is the Doctor, rather than God, who is dead, dead inside. (The Doctor has already confessed that he is the devil.)[43] But it is impossible to allow God to leave the courtroom because the question of Auschwitz is addressed, primordially, to him. And he must give an answer.

The Holocaust is a "trial" in the two major meanings of that word. It is a trial of singular agony and a trial of accusation: the former for Jews and certain quasi Jews, and the latter for the Christian and pagan world. But the Endlösung is also the trial of God. We do not refer to his suffering or his possible death there, although we are not here questioning those eventualities. We think rather of the second meaning, of God's being "on trial." In the Holocaust God is brought to trial as codefendant with men, as also with the devil. It is to no avail to seek to exonerate God by loading all the blame upon human beings. Men are culpable, of course. But the ultimate responsibility for the evil of this world is God's, for the plain reason that he made the world and he permits monstrous suffering to take place. "God is responsible for having created a world in which man is free to make history." Rubenstein and Roth carry this a step further, when they write: "God's establishment of that very freedom and responsibility, at least given the precise forms it has taken in history, rightly puts God on trial."[44]

Once upon a time, some Polish Hasidim conducted a court trial of God. The basis of their charge was dismay over the way Jews were suffering. The Hasidim decreed that God was guilty.[45] But in the presence of the Holocaust that earlier sentencing of God must remain relatively light. A special moral indictment is now entered against the Ruler of the Universe because, in the kingdom of night, his chosen ones were turned into vermin and worse than vermin, without his intervention. We are now met by the accusation of a most infamous crime: the complicity of God in the obliteration of the Six Million. (The capital letters are designed to stand for the coalescence of qualitative and quantitative reality.) The new charge against God is no less than one of implicit satanism. No plea of innocence is possible. No appeal is available. The only conceivable plea would have to be either weakness or absence from the scene, but these are hardly divine characteristics. The question stands: has the Lord of life and love become the Lord of death and hate? Has he been transmuted into the devil?

For the sakes of both the memory of the Polish Hasidim alluded to above, and all human sufferers in each time and place, we must reaffirm the sense in which the anguish and death of one human being, and particularly of a little child (without forgetting every bird and spider and deer and goat), are as terrible evils as the anguish and death of great numbers of people. But our real heartache arises from a different consideration: What is God to say or do now in self-defense? Or, rather, since there is no defense, what penance must God perform in order to escape a sentence of execution or at least to rectify the unspeakable injustices for which the Creator is plainly blameworthy?

The only penitential act we know for God is his expression of genuine sorrow for his place in the unparalleled agony of his people; he must promise that he will do his best never to sin again, never to have anything to do with such suffering in the future. Do any signs come now of the transmutation, the repentance of God? This brazen but inexpugnable question is grappled with at some length elsewhere in our study,[46] particularly in the next chapter. In these strange days, testimony (torah) sometimes comes to us from strange and fresh sources. For the present we adduce a single tale.

In Elie Wiesel's "*Ani Maamin*": *A Song Lost and Found Again*, God remains silent before the pleadings and denunciations by Abraham, Isaac, and Jacob, who protest and agonize over the unending sufferings of Jews. But when Abraham snatches a little girl from before the machine guns and runs like the wind to save her, and she tells him weakly that she believes in him, in Abraham, then at last a tear clouds God's eyes (though Abraham cannot see that). When Isaac beholds the mad Dayan singing "of his ancient and lost faith," of belief in God and the coming of the Messiah, God weeps a second time (though Isaac cannot see that). And when Jacob finds a camp inmate asserting that the Haggadah lies, that God will not come, that the wish to be in Jerusalem will never be granted, but that he will continue to recite the Haggadah as though he believes in it, and still await the prophet Elijah as he did long ago, even though Elijah disappoints him, then yet a third time (though Jacob cannot see that) God weeps, "this time without restraint, and with—yes—love. He weeps over his creation—and perhaps over much more than his creation."[47]

It may be that God is being saved now; through repentance and metanoia the Holy One is being made whole. If so, there is a sense in which B.F.S., the age until the Holocaust, is beginning to pass. In that case, the words *Ani ma'amin* ("I believe") may yet be repeated again in some small moment, down some out-of-the-way street.

FILLING THE CIRCLE
OF CULPABILITY

Thus far we have had much to say about the Jewish people, the German Nazis, the devil, and God; we have said little of the church and of Christians. The bearing of the latter identity upon the uniqueness of the Holocaust derives from the peculiar Christian contribution to that event. The singularity of the Endlösung is manifest, among other ways, through the role of Christendom and Christian teachings and behavior in helping to make possible the kingdom of night. Christianity created a social atmosphere of contempt for the Jewish people, which could be readily capitalized upon by secular antisemitic forces. Within the churches there was even some encouragement of Christians to believe that in the Holocaust, as in earlier persecutions, the Jews really had it coming to them.[48] It is scarcely necessary to point out that a great deal in Christian teaching and life has served to oppose antisemitism and the influences that issued in the Holocaust. Yet the essence of the Christian problem remains: its ambivalence toward the Jews and Judaism. Recent historiography has brought home the negativistic and hostile Christian influences. It is a significant and hopeful sign that many of these works are by Christian scholars.[49]

In relation to each other, the Jewish community and the Christian community tend to emphasize or to face different questions arising from the Holocaust. Among Jews, stress naturally falls upon problems of God, suffering, the covenant, and the land. (We may interject that in the measure Christians feel an affinity with Jewishness they ought to be concentrating on the same questions.) By contrast, in the Christian community the primary question is that of the culpability of Christians for the denigration and agony of Jews. Of course, such culpability is often denied. This question is not ignored by Jewish representatives,[50] but the difference remains. Thus the Jew tends to ask, "How can we continue to trust in God?"; the perplexed Christian tends to ask, "What has become of the credibility of Christianity? In the light of the Christian place in the Endlösung, how can the church ever regain its moral integrity?"

These latter two questions receive primary stress in the work of the United Methodist historian and churchman Franklin H. Littell.

> The cornerstone of Christian antisemitism is the superseding or displacement myth, which already rings with the genocidal note. This is the myth that the mission of the Jewish people was finished with the coming of Jesus Christ, that "the old Israel" was written off with the appearance of "the new Israel." To teach that a people's mission in God's providence is finished, that they have been relegated to the limbo of history, has murderous implications which murderers will in time spell out. The murder of six million Jews by baptized Christians, from whom membership in good standing was not (and has not been) withdrawn, raises the most insistent question about the credibility of Christianity. . . . Was Jesus a false messiah? No one can be a true messiah whose followers feel compelled to torture and destroy other human persons who think differently.[51]

Similar concern is expressed by the Canadian Catholic theologian Gregory G. Baum: "What Auschwitz has revealed to the Christian community is the deadly power of its own symbolism." The "anti-Jewish thrust of the church's preaching" is not just a historical, psychological, or sociological matter; "it touches the very formulation of the Christian gospel." Along with Littell, Baum concentrates upon the realities of Christian triumphalism and supersessionism in the presence of the Jews

71

and Judaism—what John Pawlikowski calls "the theology of substitution"—which "assigns the Jews to the darkness of history,"[52] rejected by
God and man, in ways that could only end in the murder camps. In the
Holocaust "the theological negation of Judaism and the vilification of
the Jewish people" within the Christian tradition were at last translated
into the genocide of the Jews.[53] And as the Protestant thinker Paul van
Buren points out, "the roots of Hitler's final solution are to be found . . .
in the proclamation of the very *kerygma* [message] of the early Christians"[54]—a message to be perpetuated and compounded in influence
across the centuries.

On the basis of these considerations, the Holocaust must be identified as a Christian event, of fateful significance, as much as a Jewish or
German event.

We do not mean to suggest that in the *Shoah* the church is confronted only with moral challenges and without specifically theological
questions. On the contrary, the entire Christological issue is reopened,[55]
as are the related questions of the Resurrection and of what it means to
speak of the church as "the Israel of God." The confluence of theological and moral issues is typified in an observation of Robert McAfee
Brown. The Jew laments: Since the world is so evil, why does the Messiah not come? The Christian wonders: Why, since the Messiah has
come, does the world remain so evil?[56]

In the course of our analysis of the Holocaust's singularity, we have
been required a number of times to reason in dialectical and paradoxical fashion. A final instance of this necessity is tied to the identity of the
human culprits in the suffering of Jews. Paradoxically, the Jewish people are supposed to have rejected God and yet also to represent him.
These two elements become unendurable to the world. On the one
hand, the Jews must be punished for their alleged repudiation of the
Christ. Yet, on the other hand, the pagan soul cannot bear the presence
of a transcendent Absence. As George Steiner affirms in his powerful
essay "A Season in Hell," "by killing the Jews, Western culture would
eradicate those who had 'invented' God, who had, however imper-
fectly, however restively, been the declarers of His unbearable Absence.
The Holocaust is a reflex, the more complete for being long-inhibited,
. . . of instinctual polytheistic and animist needs."

> Monotheism at Sinai, primitive Christianity, messianic socialism [which
> is directly rooted in messianic eschatology]: these are the three supreme
> moments in which Western culture is presented with what Ibsen termed

"the claims of the ideal." These are the three stages, profoundly interrelated, through which Western consciousness is forced to experience the blackmail of transcendence. "Surmount yourself. Surpass the opaque barriers of the mind to attain pure abstraction. Lose your life in order to gain it. Give up property, rank, worldly comfort. Love your neighbor as you do yourself— no, much more, for self-love is sin. Make any sacrifice, endure any insult, even self-denunciation, so that justice may prevail." . . .

. . . Three times, Judaism produced a summons to perfection and sought to impose it on the current and currency of Western life. Deep loathing built up in the social subconscious, murderous resentments. The mechanism is simple but primordial. *We hate most those who hold out to us a goal, an ideal, a visionary promise which, even though we have stretched our muscles to the utmost, we cannot reach, which slips, again and again, just out of range of our racked fingers—yet, and this is crucial, which remains profoundly desirable, which we cannot reject because we fully acknowledge its supreme value.* In his exasperating "strangeness," in his acceptance of suffering as part of a covenant with the absolute, the Jew became, as it were, the "bad conscience" of Western history.[57]

Christianity is disclosed (along with Judaism) as at once the effectuator and the crisis of Nazism. The phrase in parentheses here must be very carefully received. It does not at all mean that Jews, through their religion or anything else, are somehow to be blamed for antisemitism. What it does mean is that non-Jews, in their evil, resent and destroy Jews on the ground or pretext of Jewishness and/or the Jewish religion. Saul Friedländer makes clear that "whatever the Jews did or did not do, they could not alter the fact of antisemitism as such, and in particular the emergence of the murderous antisemitism of the Nazis which was fed by an element of true insanity on the one hand, and growing social disintegration on the other, both totally independent of the Jews themselves." Nazi antisemitism could attain its full power because "there were no strong countervailing forces in European society." Western society considered the Jews "undesirable elements which had to be excluded, whatever this would entail for the victims of exclusion."[58] But of course the undesirability was thoroughly Christian in its origins and largely Christian in its perpetuating motivations. The evidence from the churches of the Third Reich, of Hungary, and of Slovakia in particular—statements from leaders of both confessional communities, sermons, church publications—and much of what issued from official or semiofficial Vatican sources makes this abundantly clear.[59] Western society was a Christian society. The Lutheran scholar Wolfgang Zucker laments: "The Holocaust was a provocation of God himself . . . to which the Church remained silent. . . Our society, our Church, was numbered and weighed and found deficient. With this consciousness we will have to live."[60]

Historically speaking, the Holocaust, like all great events, was the outcome of multiple influences: German nationalism, conditions in Germany following World War I, Hitler and other leaders, international machinations, and the Christian and extra-Christian antisemitic traditions. Ismar Schorsch argues against assigning Christian prejudice a paramount place among Nazi antisemitism's roots and enabling forces; it is, for him, just one component in a complex matrix.[61] There is no necessary conflict of interpretation here. In historical analysis, differences between general causation—the creating of an atmosphere—and more specific causative factors must always be recognized and honored. A responsible interpreter will hardly restrict the Christian contribution to the Endlösung to the second of these categories. The Christian contribution fell primarily, though by no means exclusively, within the first category, the propagation and maintenance over many years of an atmosphere hostile to Jews.

To return to George Steiner: the effectuative elements killed the Jews, but the summons to perfection had the same consequence, for both elements were joined in the need to dispose of the Jews once and for all. Jesus was, after all, a Jew. In disposing of the Jew, we take vengeance upon our finiteness, yet being pagans beneath the baptized surface, we will fend off the gas and the flames.

Is there any real hope that Christian teachings and behavior respecting the Jewish people and Judaism may be altered in any morally telling way? This question is given much attention in subsequent pages. Our circle of culpability is, at any rate, now filled out: moral responsibility for the Final Solution clearly extends to the Christian community. For the Christian today, here is to be found the most singular quality and lesson of the Nazi Holocaust.

A consequence of the Christian condition as portrayed in this chapter is that every affirmation of faith and every moral judgment and hope become existentially problematic. So shattering an event as the Shoah has opened a crisis within every facet of Christian, Jewish, and other thinking. The singularity of the Final Solution connotes, at once, uniqueness, momentousness, revolution. Insofar as the Holocaust is a uniquely unique happening, this is because it is *metanoia*, a climactic turning around of the world (*eine Weltwende*). In the Endlösung, *die*

Stellvertreter ("the surrogates," the agents of the devil) bring Satan's nefarious work to consummation. And through the culpable acts of many people, the history of humankind reaches a fateful watershed. But so too does the history of God. *Metanoia* is now required of both. In the Chinese language the word for "crisis" contains two components: *wei* ("danger") and *chi* ("opportunity"). The *Shoah* is a crisis for man and God alike; for both, it is much more than a danger, but it need not be less than an opportunity.

4
DANGERS AND
OPPORTUNITIES

> The radical uniqueness of Auschwitz lies in its radical absurd-
> ity, in the fact that it is pure demonic evil. Jews were punished
> for having maintained fidelity to a covenant [that] promised
> survival to the Jewish people, and [that] identified that survival
> as a condition for the renewal of the world. Yet the more faith-
> ful Jews have been, the more has their survival been threat-
> ened.
>
> Lionel Rubinoff,
> "Auschwitz and the Pathology of Jew-Hatred"

In Chapter 3 we connected the singularity of the Holocaust to "the
question asked of God," the indictment and trial of the Ruler of the
Universe. The divine-human relation is fundamental to the entire question of the Endlösung; accordingly it requires painstaking and painful
reflection. Is it right to hold God accountable for human suffering? Is
the history of this world moving toward a meaningful climax, or is human history a meaningless flux? Is the voice of God somehow to be
heard from out of the hell of Auschwitz, or is there only silence, desolation, a "hiding of the Face"? Elie Wiesel writes that, on the level of
God, the Holocaust "will forever remain the most disturbing of myster-
ies."[1] There seems to be no way to explain it with God and no way to
explain it without him.[2]

We are confronted with two interrelated challenges: the issue of
theodicy, of the divine justice amidst the power of unique evil; and the
issue of the character and purposes of the covenant of God and his people. The Endlösung is inseparable from the covenant with Israel because the covenant was made, not with an individual and not with another people, but with the one people whose total extinction was
decreed by the Nazis. Moreover, the Nazis were also intent on eliminat-
ing all traces of the God whom Jews worshipped. This is what makes
possible the assertion that the uniqueness of the Holocaust is ultimately
theological in nature.[3]

On the one hand, we have to grapple with the question of meaning. Does life make sense, come what may, because it is finally ordered and blessed by a righteous and loving God, or is life "a tale/Told by an idiot, full of sound and fury,/Signifying nothing"? On the other hand, we must try to cope with the question of the will of God. Does God, essentially, make demands of his people, commanding them, especially, to suffer for his sake, or does he not do this? These two challenges are fused into one by their shared content: the murder of the Jews. As William Jay Peck has written, after Auschwitz, "the very being of God is . . . tied up with the problem of murder."[4]

THE RULER WHO IS
REALLY RULER

After the fact of the Holocaust, is it morally defensible to retain the traditional faith in God taught by Judaism and Christianity? Those who cannot answer this question affirmatively must nonetheless acknowledge that many Jews and others who went throught the agony of the Endlösung continued to live as believers, and died the same way. The Holocaust did not succeed, and has not succeeded, in destroying the faith of certain people. Even more astounding and paradoxical is the truth that some individuals *became* believers while in the kingdom of night.

For some, the rationale of faith is tied to the persuasion that puny and sinful men have neither the moral nor the spiritual right to question God. Who is man to think that he can indict the Ruler of the Universe and bring the Lord to trial? "My thoughts are not your thoughts, neither are your ways my ways, says the Lord" (Isa. 55:8). In the face of the divine query, "Where were you when I laid the foundation of the earth?" (Job 38:4), some believers will simply bow their heads in fearful humility and devout silence. It is told that a Rabbi Israel Shapiro of Grodzisk said to his people, as they were about to die at Treblinka, that their ashes would purify Israel and help to redeem the world.[5] "Though he slay me, yet will I trust in him" (Job 13:15).[6] For such believers, the Holocaust is, in effect, a nonevent—or at least it is no different in kind from other evils that have beset the people of God throughout history. Terrible as the happening was, it ought not be allowed to turn men to apostasy. Indeed, the argument has been put forth that were the Jews

77

of today to surrender their faith, they would be offering a posthumous victory to Hitler. This great numbers of them will not do.

Emil Fackenheim is particularly known for having emphasized that the "Voice of Auschwitz" has commanded that the "authentic Jew of today is forbidden to give Hitler another, posthumous victory" after his having succeeded in having six million Jews annihilated. For Fackenheim, this is, so to speak, a 614th commandment: It is a "divine commandment to recognize demonic forces such as the Rabbis did not have to suffer and face, and [it] bids us bear witness *against* these forces wherever they appear and whomever they threaten." Jews are commanded "to survive as Jews, lest the Jewish people perish, . . . to remember in our very guts and bones the martyrs of the Holocaust, lest their memory perish. [Jews] are forbidden . . . to deny or despair of God . . . lest Judaism perish, [and] to despair of the world . . . lest we make it a meaningless place in which God is dead or irrelevant and everything is permitted."

For Fackenheim the *Shoah* is a world-shaking event that cannot be absorbed into the earlier crises of Jewish history, although it fits the *pattern* of Jewish catastrophes of earlier centuries. It is certainly not a nonevent; in fact, it is just the opposite. It is a radical challenge of the most central affirmations of Jewish faith. Nevertheless, Fackenheim agrees with traditional Jews who refuse to grant Hitler a posthumous victory by surrendering either Jewish faith or Jewish identity.[7]

Michael Wyschogrod, however, objects to this emphasis on Hitler (negative though it is) because it places "Hitler's evil design at the heart of Jewish faith [where] only the message that God is a redeeming God belongs . . ." Despite Wyschogrod having been a child escapee of the *Shoah*, he insists on the destruction as being—theologically—a nonevent.[8]

LIFE AGAINST FAITH

For other persons, faith in God is no longer possible after Auschwitz. It was such a rupture in the history of the Jewish people that only radical rejection of the ancient faith tradition is possible. The human situation is devoid of transcendent meaning, and the very idea of the covenanting purposes of God is grisly, nonsensical, or both. Jakov Lind writes that when the Germans marched into Austria one Friday morning, "God lost his last chance to be recognized by me." In a more searing comment, Lind briefly summed up the Final Solution: The Jews who did not leave Europe in time Hitler "threw into the flames of God's ever burning love for his chosen people."[9] In Lind's story "Resurrection," a character named Sholom Weintraub responds to a religious outlook by saying:

> Frankly, Mr. Goldschmied, I have no sympathy for you. . . . You talk and talk. Religion, holiness, the Jews' mission. All a lot of phrases, slogans. Choice, dog, guilt. I don't give a shit about all that. In a few days they'll strangle me and burn me like a leper, and that's the end of Sholom Weintraub. They'll give me a number on a mass grave, colored with gold dust, and I'll never, never be alive again. Resurrection is nothing but Talmudic hair-splitting, mystery, smoke and sulphur, hocus-pocus, theological speculation. There is no second time, not before and not after the Messiah, and He doesn't exist anyway. I want to live, Mr. Goldschmied, I want to live and breathe, and I don't care how—like a dog or a frog or a bedbug, it's all the same to me. I want to live and breathe, to live.[10]

Sholom Weintraub was proved to be an optimist. In Bergen-Belsen we witnessed mass graves with single stones, erected long after the liberation, that read only, "Hier ruhen 5000 tote" (Here lie 5,000 dead). To be identified in death by one's number would have been *something*, a message of piteous spite for the darkness to read: "Here I am! I am only a number, but here I am!" Or here I was.

In *The Last of the Just*, André Schwarz-Bart, who as a young member of the Resistance was the only one of his family to survive, suggests that the presence of thirty-six Just Men (*Lamed-Vov*) in a generation will no longer suffice to preserve the world by absorbing its sufferings. Once it was enough. Not after the *Shoah*. For "a suffering so great leaves nothing to be redeemed, and precious little to forgive or be forgiven. It is not that God died after Auschwitz; it is that he is no longer needed. The covenant has been broken, not by the people but by their Lord."[11] The faithfulness of the people, and the unfaithfulness of God, or the futility of having faith in God's nourishing, saving, and resurrecting power is depicted in the prayer that ends Schwarz-Bart's book:

> And praised. *Auschwitz*. Be. *Maidanek*. The Lord. *Treblinka*. And praised. *Buchenwald*. Be. *Mauthausen*. The Lord. *Belzec*. And praised. *Sobibor*. Be. *Chelmno*. The Lord. *Ponary*. And praised. *Theresienstadt*. Be. *Warsaw*.

79

The Lord. *Vilna*. And praised. *Skarzysko*. Be. *Bergen-Belsen*. The Lord. *Janow*. And praised. *Dora*. Be. *Neuengamme*. The Lord. *Pustkow*. And praised . . .[12]

Another survivor, Alexander Donat, fought a raging typhus fever in the Warsaw ghetto in January 1943. His subconscious mind produced strange dreams and visions. In one of them a Jew who had converted to Christianity offered a prayer-indictment composed of portions of the "Our Father" prayer Jesus had taught his disciples, Jesus' last words on the cross, and the Jewish people's own crucifixion experiences:

Our Father in whom I do not believe
Hallowed by Thy name;
Thy Kingdom come,
Thy will be done, in earth as it is in heaven.
Give us this day our daily life,
Have mercy on the souls of murderers,
And forgive them their trespasses,
For we cannot.
Forgive them for they know not what they do,
And we can neither forgive nor forget.
We do not ask mercy, Lord, for ourselves,
Who were burned at the stake at Belzec
And gassed in the chambers of Treblinka,
Who died in the cauldrons of the ghettos,
Who perished of typhus and hunger,
For Thou has not granted us Thy mercy,
And Thou knowest not what Thou hast done.[13]

When Donat wrote his memoir of those times, he was no longer in the grip of typhus. But he continued to protest: In the ghettos and camps, day in and day out, "we cried for a sign" of God. But "God was not present at our indescribable predicament. We were alone, forsaken by God and men."[14]

Richard L. Rubenstein's point of view is among the most compelling revisions of traditional Jewish faith in light of the Holocaust. In his pioneering study *After Auschwitz*, Rubenstein tells of the radical change that occurred in his religious outlook following a conversation in 1961 with, paradoxically enough, one of the very few German Protestant pastors who had steadfastly risked his own life and the lives of his family by opposing the Nazis on Christian grounds and extending all possible aid and comfort to Hitler's victims. Various Christians in Germany had made the same point to Rubenstein, but hearing it from Heinrich Grüber, renowned provost of the Evangelical Church of East and West Berlin, gave it special force. According to Rubenstein, Grüber insisted upon the "very special providential relationship between Israel, what happened to it, and God's will," not just in biblical times but continuing to this very day. However, unlike other German clergy and churchmen who, when Rubenstein pressed them, seemed to back away from the conclusion that the Nazi slaughter of Jews was somehow God's will, Grüber responded quite assuredly. With openness and a complete lack of guile, he quoted Psalm 44:22, "for thy sake are we slaughtered every day," and continued: "For some reason, it was part of God's plan that the Jews died. God demands our death daily. He is the Lord, He is the Master, all is in His Keeping and ordering."

Rubenstein writes that Grüber

> dramatized the consequences of accepting the normative Judaeo-Christian theology of history in the light of the death camps. After my interview, I reached a theological point of no return—If I believed in God as the omnipotent author of the historical drama and Israel as His Chosen People, I had to accept Dean Grüber's conclusion that it was God's will that Hitler committed six million Jews to slaughter. I could not possibly believe in such a God nor could I believe in Israel as the chosen people of God after Auschwitz.[15]

Commenting further in a later source upon the same unforgettable episode with Heinrich Grüber, Rubenstein writes that if one is a traditional Jew,

> it is impossible to regard the sorrows of Jewish history as mere historical accidents. They must in some sense express the will of God as a just and righteous Creator. Either such a God is a sadist who inflicts pain because he enjoys it or he has a reason for the misfortune he inflicts. The only morally defensible motive for a superior to inflict pain on an inferior would be punitive chastisement which has as its purpose altering the victims's mode of behavior. If one takes Covenant Theology seriously, as did Dean Grüber, Auschwitz must be God's way of punishing the Jewish people in order that they might better see the light, the light of Christ if one is a Christian, the light of Torah if one is a traditional Jew.

Rubenstein is fully aware of the price to be paid for rejecting the God of the covenant.

81

If the God of history does not exist, then the Cosmos is ultimately absurd in origin and meaningless in purpose. . . . I have elected to accept what Camus has rightly called the courage of the absurd, the courage to live in a meaningless, purposeless Cosmos rather than believe in a God who inflicts Auschwitz on his people.

Rubenstein finds belief in such a God simply obscene.[16]

Rubenstein came to the realization that "as long as Jews are thought of as special and apart from mankind in general, they are going to be the object of both the abnormal demands and the decisive hatreds" of which Heinrich Grüber spoke, as well as of the kind of theology which holds that "because the Jews are God's Chosen People, God wanted Hitler to punish them." Accordingly, Rubenstein rejects all notions of special vocation or peculiar responsibility for the Jewish people. After Auschwitz, it is immoral to believe such things.[17]

Rubenstein is convinced that

the problem of God and the death camps is the central problem for Jewish theology in the twentieth century. . . . The catastrophe of 1939-45 represents a psychological and religious time bomb which has yet to explode fully in the midst of Jewish religious life. . . . God really died at Auschwitz. This does not mean that God is not the beginning and will not be the end. It does mean that nothing in human choice, decision, value, or meaning can any longer have vertical reference to transcendent standards. We are alone in a silent, unfeeling cosmos. . . . Morality and religion can no longer rest upon the conviction that divinely validated norms offer a measure against which what we do can be judged.

Yet, despite his avowal of cosmic emptiness, he has not given in to despair. "Death and rebirth are the greatest moments of religious experiences," and Jews have known both in this century.

[In Europe] we Jews have tasted the bitterest and most degrading of deaths. Yet death was not the last word. . . . Death in Europe was followed by resurrection in our ancestral home. We are free as no men before us have ever been. Having lost everything, we have nothing further to lose and no further fear of loss. . . . We have passed beyond all illusion and hope. We have learned . . . that we were totally and nakedly alone, that we could expect neither support nor succor from god or from our fellow creatures. . . . We have lost all hope and faith. We have also lost all possibility of disappointment.[18]

82

BEYOND THE OPPOSITES

Between unquestioning fealty to God and the abjuration or melancholy abandonment of God—in the name of life—other variations of existential argument and witness vie to be heard. Persons propounding these alternatives recognize that the Holocaust was and remains an event that challenges the central tenets of faith and theology in their own traditions and calls for some critical rethinking. For them the *Shoah* is, to use a concept we will develop in chapter 5, a partial event.

From an awareness of the pervasiveness of Christian antisemitism and its genocidal consequences, the Catholic theologian Gregory Baum has become convinced that the *Shoah*—that Awful Event, as he refers to it—must become a turning point for Christian theology. Because theology is fundamentally about God, how must the Final Solution affect our God-ideas? In Baum's *Man Becoming: God in Secular Experience*, he comments upon the aspect of traditional Christian thought that has insisted God is not responsible for evil and suffering. Despite such an insistence, the church's persuasion of God as Lord of history necessarily implied that human sins and crimes are somehow not out of accord with God's permissive will: God permits evil for the present, in order that a greater good will be achieved in the future. Thus, even Auschwitz fills a place in the divine providence. Yet is seems to Baum that this line of thinking makes a monster out of God. Accordingly, certain traditional understandings of the divine providence, omniscience, and omnipotence must be rejected.

> God is not provident . . . in the sense that as ruler of the world he has a master plan for human history by which he provides help for the people in need, especially those who ask him for it, and by which he guides the lives of men, even while acknowledging their freedom . . . [or] in which God has permitted evil and . . . calculated its damaging effects and compensated for them in the final outcome. . . . [Rather] God is provident in the sense that in whatever trap a man falls, a summons continues to address him and offer him new life that makes him more truly human.

Baum concludes that God is omniscient only "in the sense that there exists no human situation, however difficult, however obscure, however frightening, in which God remains silent or . . . in which a summons to greater insight is not available." Similarly, God is omnipotent only in the sense that there is "no earthly power oppressing man that is stronger than the divine grace that frees him to wrestle with it in some way and to become more human in the process." God is not master who rules from above, but from within—as "summons and vitality in people's lives," just as he summons the world to new life. Through this understanding, we are enabled to affirm "the radical opposition between God and evil." Evil is not permitted by him. Rather,

> God overcomes evil. God is constantly at work among men, summoning them and gracing them to discern the evil in human life, to wrestle against it, to be converted away from it, to correct their environment, to redirect history, to transform the human community. The death that destroys is never the will of God. On the contrary, God is the never-ending summons to life.[19]

The expression "this is God's will" must never be taken to mean that God wishes or even permits terrible calamities or injustices to happen. But it can mean, for a person of great faith, a continuing trust that God will summon forth new insights and create life out of death in unexpected ways. Baum writes: "Jewish men and women on the way to the extermination chambers may have said to themselves that this incomprehensible and groundless evil was in some mysterious way God's will—in the sense that they continued to trust in God. But on the lips of an observer such a statement would be dreadful blasphemy. . . . God's power over the world is not the miraculous action by which he makes things happen as he pleases, but the redemptive action by which he enables men to deal with their own problems." He calls people to "resist evil and find ways of conquering it."[20]

A Lutheran scholar, Franklin Sherman, carries forward Christian reasoning on the subject of how we may continue to speak of God after the Endlösung. Greatly influenced by Abraham Joshua Heschel's theology of the divine pathos, Sherman concentrates upon the divine suffering as a religious solution to the problem of theodicy in light of the Holocaust. Neither the conception of a God of judgment nor that of a God of moral education will do, as we confront Auschwitz. The same must be said, religiously and morally, of a reputedly self-limiting God. We may, however, speak of a suffering God, for "God participates in the suffering of men, and man is called to participate in the sufferings of God." And while it is true that the Christian will, accordingly, turn to the cross "as the symbol of the agonizing God," this cannot be allowed to mean any kind of triumphalism. "A God who suffers is the opposite of a God of Triumphalism. We can speak of God after Auschwitz only as the one who calls us to a new unity as beloved brothers—not only between Jews and Christians, but especially between Jews and Christians.[21]

Paul van Buren, an Episcopalian theologian, ties God's suffering to divine freedom—his "personal freedom to change and to suffer," a freedom surely "at least as great as our own." But in his "infinite freedom" God demonstrates his "power and majesty": for God is "free in the fullest power of personal love to hold back, to sit still and to suffer in agony as His children move so slowly to exercise in a personal and loving way the freedom which He has willed for them to have and exercise." In light of these assertions, van Buren then asks: "Was God involved in the blind and perverse slaughter of a third of His people?" Could such involvement somehow be consistent with a God "who has willed the free otherness of His creatures?" Van Buren thinks it is possible. God's "act of love [was] to suffer in solidarity with His people," for reasons we may only hesitantly suggest: "trying to awaken His creatures to their irresponsibility, [or] trying, by simply suffering with His people, to awaken His church to a new understanding of love and respect for them." The problem is, as van Buren concedes, that "the cost seems out of all proportion to the possible gain," even though we can see in Gentile Christians' responses that "at least something new has been started" by the *Shoah*, no matter if the response so far is minimal. Van Buren concludes that "God may be detected as being most present precisely when we have thought Him to have been most absent," as in the death camps or at the moment when Jesus on the cross cried out to ask why God had abandoned him.[22]

The suffering God theme is also part of the post-Holocaust interpretation of God by the Jewish philosopher Hans Jonas. While God suffered with all of creation from its inception, with the creation of humanity the divine cause and being became mutable and vulnerable to human actions: God not only experiences with the world, but he is also affected by what is done within the earthly realm. Although God is caring, he has left something for other agents to do and thereby made his care dependent on them. He is therefore also an endangered God, a God "who risks . . . the future of the divine adventure." Moreover, having "given Himself whole to the becoming world, God has no more to give. It is man's now to give to him." He can only "mutely" appeal to humankind to fulfill the divine aim.

Jonas "likes to believe" that when the children were gassed and burned, when women and men were turned into defaced and dehumanized phantoms in the camps, and when additional humans became victims of "the other man-made holocausts of our time," there was "weeping in the heights at the waste and despoilment of humanity; that a groan answered the rising shout of ignoble suffering and wrath—the terrible wrong done to the reality and possibility of each life thus wantonly victimized, each one a thwarted attempt of God." Over the world now hangs the "immense chorus" of these cries and the frown of wounded eternity, which may explain the "general malaise" and the "profound distemper of the contemporary mind." The impact humankind's deeds have on the Divine are reflected back onto humankind itself.[23]

Rabbi Arthur J. Lelyveld is prepared, with Gregory Baum, to raise questions about the divine omnipotence. According to him, we have no choice but to grant that gargantuan evil exists and is uncontrolled by God. "We cannot pretend to know why—we can only cling stubbornly to the conviction that there is meaning—*lam'rot hakol*, in spite of everything." However, Lelyveld refuses to forsake the demanding side of God. On the contrary, he divides the Christian and Jewish faiths precisely in that way. "The God of Christianity is the God who *gives*;[24] the God of Judaism is the God who *demands*." In the cosmic scope "there is that which is demanded of us." "The central stress of Judaism has been: 'Thou *shalt* be unto me a Kingdom of priests,' '*Choose life!*,' and 'Thus saith the Lord. . . .' The covenant obligation that is central in Judaism calls upon the Jew to be co-worker in perfecting the world—not to *be* saved but to *participate* in the redemption of mankind." Accordingly, as a Jew "I must interpret my responsibility as it is defined by the covenant task." As Lelyveld puts it, "the greater the evil, the more insistent and the more intense, even to the point of anguish, is the demand."[25]

However terrible the evil of the Final Solution, Lelyveld does not find it uniquely evil; Auschwitz was "a new phenomenon only in a quantitative and technological sense." The more efficient instruments for carrying out human destruction "give the nature of evil new dimensions," but they do "not change its essential nature." What, then, is to be said of God's demanding that Jews, and humankind in general, confront this ever-increasing efficiency of evil? Lelyveld responds by attesting to the sympathy that dwells "at the heart of the universe"—sympathy for the very creatures upon whom the divine demands are made. "In this sense, while I cannot say that God 'willed' Auschwitz, I can say that God 'wept' over Auschwitz." God also suffers from anguish. This divine sympathy "enables man to enter into 'partnership' with God." Thus, while Lelyveld, like Baum, finds it a "repelling, blasphemous idea" to adjudge that God willed the destruction of the six million, he insists that we cannot withdraw from the sufferers "the dignity that lies in recognition that there existed among them a willingness to die in fulfillment of a distinctive role." Some had the "incredible courage" to fight "despite the certainty of the futility of resistance"; others were sublimely ready to march, in defiance, "to the freight cars that were to carry them into Hell with the *Ani Ma-amin* on their lips." (The *Ani Ma-amin* is part of the Jewish liturgy: "I affirm, with unbroken firmness, that the Messiah will come. And even though He tarries, even so, I affirm it.") "We have said that Hitler's victims were offered no alternative. This is not wholly so. They had the alternative of dying as cravens, of cursing God and their identity. All the evidence says that in overwhelming numbers they died with dignity."[26]

All in all, Lelyveld believes that we can affirm general providence —that is, meaning and purpose in the whole and the trust of cosmic evolution "toward greater love, greater harmony, and greater justice." But we must reject special providence—that is, the juvenile notion of God as a personal protector and coddler. This is to ask "the impossible of the universe." In the relationship of genuine covenantal responsibility, "when God is the guarantor of value and the source of demand, then the confrontation of evil elicits not the plaintive 'Why did God do this?' but rather 'What does God ask of me?'"[27]

Viktor Frankl, a survivor, complements Gregory Baum's and Arthur Lelyveld's theological views through his experiential, psychiatrically oriented conclusions. Camp inmates had to stop asking about the meaning of life and instead think of themselves "as those who were being questioned by life—daily and hourly." The inmates' usual question had been, "If we don't survive, what meaning will all this suffering have?" Frankl turned the question around. If all this suffering and dying have no meaning, then what meaning has life itself? After all, a life whose meaning stands or falls upon the happenstance of one's own survival would not be, ultimately speaking, worth living at all. Frankl thus concluded that the very meaning of life extends to suffering and death. Potentially, therefore, we can supply meaning to our own lives by suffering as well as by creating and loving, "by the way and manner in which we face our fate, in which we take our suffering upon ourselves." In the last analysis, man ought to realize "that it is not up to him to question—it is he who *is* questioned, questioned by life; it is he

87

who has to answer, by answering for life. His role is to respond—to be responsible."[28]

The many attempts to sustain traditional faith in spite of the *Shoah* and to discover in its midst a continuity of revelation with, perhaps, a fresh understanding of the divine nature are praiseworthy. Yet all too often they seem to turn to ashes when exposed to the flames of the Final Solution. Can we be content with Ignaz Maybaum's affirmation that this "third churban" is a "severe decree" (*gezeirah*) that "reveals itself eventually as a messianic event"? Its messianic nature should be discerned in the fact that God "cuts out a past from the body of mankind and allows a new span of life to begin in revived health." By thrusting the history of mankind into a new chapter, progress can again be initiated because human "life has obtained atonement."[29] Can we understand or accept "progress" at such cost? Is the agony of six million innocents—and the enduring pain of any of their remaining relatives or friends—thereby justified or even mitigated? Can we relate positively to a God who would operate in such fashion? Is it sufficient to emphasize, as Leo Baeck did, that what is ultimately significant is how the person utilizes opportunities (regardless of the outcome) and how he finds meaning in death as he struggles for self-understanding? Can we, ought we, insist that a martyr is to be at peace "even with his enemy because his [own] life has been fashioned out of love"? Does the struggling to become "the realized ethical individual of the Jewish tradition," even in the distorted environment of Nazidom, meet the problems of helplessness, vulnerability, and degradation—not only of individuals but of a whole community faced with no choice but collective death?[30]

A variation upon the refusal to have one's faith destroyed while yet conceding that the object of our faith is also our enemy is found in Zvi Kolitz's reconstruction of the last thoughts of a pious Jew named Yossel Rakover, who was apparently murdered in the *Judenvernichtung*. Rakover addresses God:

> You may insult me, you may castigate me, you may take from me all that I cherish and hold dear in the world, you may torture me to death—I shall believe in you, I shall love you no matter what you do to test me!
> And these are my last words to you, my wrathful God: nothing will avail you in the least. You have done everything to make me renounce you, to make me lose my faith in you, but I die exactly as I have lived, a *believer*!

88

Eternally praised be the God of the dead, the God of vengeance, of truth and of law, who will soon show his face to the world again and shake its foundation with his almighty voice.

Hear, O Israel, the Lord our God the Lord is One.

Into your hands, O Lord, I consign my soul.[31]

Rakover's invective-prayer is highly paradoxical and dialectical. God seems to be the unquestioned superior of men, and yet his apparently sadistic wrath, in conjunction with the resoluteness of the believer's faith, almost seems to make the human being morally superior to God. The reader is left wondering who merits one's fealty: the One of Jewish tradition, or the man whose vituperation is washed by a holy assent. It is hard, psychologically speaking, to separate scorn, piety, and self-flagellation in Rakover's words.[32]

TOWARD CONCILIATION

Our ultimate challenge is to recognize fully the reality of evil for what it is, including human and divine responsibility for suffering, without at the same time betraying the foundational conviction that God is active in history, a conviction requisite to the belief that human life has meaning. In the words of Ulrich E. Simon, "nothing can be made of this mass dying if man is the measure of all things, except the message of an anthropology of despair: the only thing that matters is to be outside, and not inside, the cage."[33] Eliezer Berkovits helps, we submit, to reconcile the yes of faith in God with the no to God that is required for the sake of human dignity, the very image of God. Unlike many interpreters, Berkovits confronts head-on the ineluctable fact of the divine culpability for evil and suffering. Yet he does not finish by denying God.

Berkovits makes clear that he has no intention of explaining and certainly not of justifying the silence of God during the European Holocaust. This very caution enables him to speak existentially and forthrightly, yet not with impiety. ("The one [God] who is silent may be so-called only because he is present.") Unlike most Jews and Christians who use God's gift of freedom to humanity as a way of removing responsibility from God's shoulders (so to speak), Berkovits refuses to succumb to this temptation.[34] He emphasizes that nothing can exonerate God for the suffering of the innocent in history.

89

We may interject that while humans are sinful and blameworthy for their actions, this simply does not exculpate God. We have already cited Berkovits on this in chapter 3: "God is responsible for having created a world in which man is free to make history." Or, as Rubenstein and Roth put it: "To the extent that [humans] were born with the potential and power to be dirty, credit for the fact belongs elsewhere. 'Elsewhere' is God's address."[35] No human being ever had anything to do with his own birth into this world. In this sense we are required to declare the continuing innocence of people.

Now there simply is no justification for the tragedy and suffering of persons in the world. "God's dominion over the world is not a dominion of justice. In terms of justice, he is guilty. He is guilty of creation." There is no justification for the ways of God, the ways of providence. Within the dimension of time and history, such ways are simply unforgivable. Yet, asserts Berkovits, it is possible for us to accept these ways and hence to forgive. What is the moral basis of this acceptance, this forgiveness? There is the possibility of a trust in God, in a dimension beyond but fulfilling history, in which the tragedy of humankind will find a transformation.

> One of the teachers of the Talmud notes that when God asks Abraham to offer him his son Isaac as a sacrifice, the exact rendering of the biblical words reads: "Take, I pray thee, thy son." In the view of this teacher the "binding of Isaac" was not a command of God, but a request that Abraham take upon himself this most exacting of all God's impositions. In a sense we see in this a recognition that the sacrificial way of the innocent through history is not to be vindicated or justified! It remains unforgivable. God Himself has to ask an Abraham to favor Him by accepting the imposition of such a sacrifice. The divine request accompanies all those through history who suffer for the only reason that God created man, whom God Himself has to endure. Within time and history God remains indebted to His people; He may be long-suffering only at their expense. It was hardly ever as true as in our own days, after the Holocaust. Is it perhaps what God desires—a people, to whom he owes so much, who yet acknowledges Him: children, who have every reason to condemn His creation, yet accept the creator in the faith that in the fullness of time the divine indebtedness will be redeemed and the divine adventure with man will be approved even by its martyred victims?[36]

Perhaps we are a little better situated now to address the problem of the covenant. For the question remains searingly with us: Can the assertion continue to be made that central to the covenant is the obligation of the Jewish people to be "suffering servants" of the Lord? Can this assertion be defended morally today, after the Final Solution, or has it become an affront to the image of God in man? Does God really desire this self-abnegation?

An enigmatic passage in *A Beggar in Jerusalem* grasps us. We cited the end of the passage in chapter 3; its context is the ecstatic Jewish return to the Old City of Jerusalem.

> The crowd keeps getting larger. Military personnel and officials, celebrities and journalists, all are streaming by in one continuous procession, along with rabbis and students, gathered from all over the city, from every corner of the land. Men, women, and adolescents of every age, every origin and speaking every language, and I see them ascending toward the Wall, toward all that remains of the collective longing. Just like long ago, at Sinai, when they were given the Torah. Just like a generation ago, in the kingdom of night, when it was taken back.[37]

What did we witness in the Endlösung? Was it the recantation of the covenant? If so, to where was the covenant taken? To oblivion? If not to oblivion, then to what place? Could it be that the covenant was received back in order to be incarnated in a fresh form?

To some, the taking back of the covenant is as legendary as its bestowal. In consonance with this view, there was in fact no singular kingdom of night, for there never was a singular kingdom of day.

For others, God recanted because of the sins of his people. Israel betrayed the divine statutes and had to be judged. In response to this point of view, we cannot refrain from observing that there is much laughter in *A Beggar in Jerusalem*. For the most part, it is fearful, maniacal laughter. According to Rabbi Nachman of Bratzlav, somewhere in the world there is a certain city that encompasses all other cities. In the city is a street that contains all the other streets of the city; on that street is a house dominating all the other houses; it contains a room that comprises all the other rooms of the house. "And in that room there lives a man in whom all other men recognize themselves. And that man is laughing. That's all he ever does, ever did. He roars with laughter when seen by others, but also when alone."[38] Is there something special for him to laugh about now, F.S., in the shadow of the Final Solution? Yes, there is a special cause: The man is laughing because it was *in the kingdom of night* that the Torah was taken back.[39] This is an ultimate determinant that stands in judgment upon all lesser transformations of the covenant. We believe—we hope without falling into unkindness—that someone who identifies the Endlösung as an act of judgment by God upon his people makes himself subject to confinement in that room of laughter, where he will have to listen, without surcease, to the laughing man.

The teaching that the divine election of Israel requires the Jewish people to suffer distinctively and unendingly for the sake of God and his purposes was sent to perdition in the gas chambers and crematoria: "We received the Torah at Sinai / And in Lublin we gave it back / Dead men don't praise God. / The Torah was given to the living."[40] The symbolic declaration may be made that God recanted with reference to the Torah because he could no longer live with himself. The kingdom of night proved too much, even for him. Perhaps he foresaw the time when the six million reproofs would coalesce into one:

> One day they will assemble in the valley of bones—
> Ashes sifted out of furnaces, vapors from Luneburg,
> Parchments from some . . . books,
> Half-formed embryos, screams still heard in nightmares.
> God will breathe upon them. He will say: Be [persons].
> *But they will defy Him. We do not hear you. Did you hear us?*
> *There is no resurrection for us. In life it was a wondrous thing*
> *For each of us to be himself, to guide his limbs to do his will,*
> *But the many are now one. Our blood has flowed together.*
> *Our ashes are inseparable, our marrow commingled,*
> *Our voices poured together like water of the sea.*
> *We shall not surrender this greater self.*
> *We the Abrahams, Isaacs, Jacobs, Sarahs, Leahs, Rachels*
> *Are now forever Israel.*[41]

Elsewhere in *A Beggar in Jerusalem* a young madman, one of only three survivors who had escaped the deportation, asks: "How does God justify Himself in His own eyes, let alone in ours? If the real and the imaginary both culminate in the same scream, in the same laugh, what is creation's purpose, what is its stake?"[42]

Because of the torment carried by the "blasphemous" implication of the necessary penitence of God and the burden of the singular horror of the *Shoah*, some of us have no choice now but to range ourselves against the covenant of demand, the demand that Jews be ready to suffer, that they remain uniquely obligated. Rather, there must be some other form of covenant: of promise, of freedom, of defiance, of survival, of normality, of something, of anything, but *not of Auschwitz*, not a religious sanction to the murder of Jews.

That recognition, subconscious or conscious, motivated the remnant of Warsaw's ghetto population to rise up in a hopeless insurrection. Many Jews at that time and in the years following, along with some Christians, have perceived that in April and May 1943 a radical reversal occurred. As Manès Sperber put it, "the millennial epoch of the Jews' sanctifying of God and of themselves by submitting to violent death had . . . come to an end."[43] Testimony from the ghetto itself informs us that Rabbi Yizhak Nissenbaum acknowledged that the new enemy required a new response: Since "Hitler and his cohorts" want to destroy the Jewish body, not just the soul, the mitzvah of *kiddush haShem* (sanctifying God's name) now requires that the enemy be defeated by Jewish survival (instead of martyrdom). "This is the hour of *kiddush hahayyim* [sanctification through life]. . . . [I]t is incumbent upon every Jew to defend . . . his own life." One Rabbi reportedly concluded that active resistance to the German Nazis was essential on the ground that unless a portion of the Jewish people survived, the covenant would be abrogated. Since God apparently was not going to take the necessary action to prevent this possibility. Jews themselves must assume the responsibility of saving the covenant.[44]

Here morality and theology are welded together and made wholly one. The flame that fuses them thereby burns down our prison, and we are set free. How is the past to be redeemed? How is the Final Solution finally to be annihilated? There is no way, save through the radical transformation of the covenant. The covenant of demand means divine consent to Jewish oppression. The elect were informed that they were going to have to be "a kingdom of priests and a holy nation" (Exod. 19:6). Manès Sperber speaks of how he and other Jews became "victims of chosenness. . . . By making a covenant with us, God has cast the divine brick of His grace at us. Ever since then we bear the crushing burden of chosenness like a curse," yet we are supposed to praise it "as though it were a blessing" three times a day. And Irving Greenberg has observed that "not in their wildest dreams" could Jews imagine the kind of pain and destruction that would be the price.[45] There is no theological or moral way to answer the Endlösung unless we arrange a decent and fitting burial for this entire idea. There is no way to answer until we beat into the dust the myth of the Jew as "suffering servant." The gestalt beyond all covenantal demands, the forming of full Jewish humanity, is the birth of the epoch F.S., after the Final Solution.

Yes, the Torah was taken back in the kingdom of night. Does this mean that it will not be renewed? No. It is renewed. But it is also transformed. The covenant between God and his people no longer bears the stigma of demand—and not even, returning to Eliezer Berkovits's exposition, the character of a request. As Irving Greenberg has helped us to see, the covenant is resurrected as a wholly voluntary readiness on the part of Jews to continue to bear the yoke of Torah. They are in no way required to do so, nor even asked to do so. But they may will to do so, in service and therefore in joy. Here is the ever-potential incredibility of Jewish existence today: to honor the life that Torah is intended to sustain, after the death that Auschwitz was intended to finalize, and without having to do it. This, we dare to say, is today's revelation of God.[46] And it is left to each generation, to every Jew, to make the decision.

We spoke earlier about the man in a solitary room who laughs without surcease. There is another text regarding laughter. According to the Talmud, when God and man laugh *together*, both "attain a kind of triumph, a state of Grace [that] announces the coming of the Messiah.[47] When this mutual laughter is able to replace accusation or recrimination, joy can be unfettered rather than conditional.

The final and sublime logic in the avowal of total liberation is that the honoring of the life of Torah cannot be used as a weapon against those Jews who choose not to be "religious." Where freedom is truly reigning, it has to be indivisible. After the Holocaust, the sanctifying of the divine Name (*kiddush haShem*) is carried forward and accomplished in new ways through the sanctifying of human life as such (*kiddush hahayyim*). This unfolding of the covenant destroys any invidious judgments against the secular human being in contrast to the religious person. The flesh and the spirit are equals.

We fail to meet here the question of how the authentic witness for God and the truth is to identify itself and to be identified, through symbolization or other means, as against the witness for the devil and evil. What are the peculiar marks of those who will to be witnesses? The search for the answer to this question is among the most baffling and fateful challenges to face post-Holocaust theology.

FORGIVENESS

After the Endlösung, the question of the meaning of our human existence and the question of the will of God are brought together and given an existential, nontheoretical answer with the aid of rethinking the covenantal relation. When we speak of an "answer," we do not pretend to have attained ultimacy, for there are no ultimate human answers to the problems of life; at best, we may express fragmentary truths that simply help us to keep going, to get up in the morning and face another day. As Yehuda Aschkenasy of Holland has said, it is impossible to write a theology of suffering, because when you meet real suffering yourself, you won't get an answer through theology—though you may eventually learn to live with suffering.[48] The covenant is both transcended and fulfilled once the compassion of God stands in judgment upon the divine demand, once God, forgiving us, is also forgivable and forgiven. This kind of affirmation is fully post-Holocaust in character; that is to say, it takes the Endlösung with utter seriousness as a morally and theologically determinative event. Yet this view does not fall into cynicism or unbelief, for that would indeed grant a posthumous triumph to the Nazis as surrogates of the devil.

A passage from Reinhold Niebuhr, when given wider application than Niebuhr had in mind, conjoins him and Elie Wiesel. The passage brings as well a little focus to these poor midrashim upon the tale of that strange beggar who reaches out to us from the deep shadows of Jerusalem—no, from amid the sunshine of that city. The words are almost forty years old now. "Nothing that is worth doing can be achieved in a lifetime; therefore we must be saved by hope. Nothing which is true or beautiful or good makes complete sense in any immediate context of history; therefore we must be saved by faith. Nothing we do, however virtuous, can be accomplished alone. Therefore we are saved by love."[49]

One vital thrust of post-Holocaust theology, Jewish and Christian, is the asseveration that the "we" here must refer as much to God as to human beings.

5.
SERVITUDE
AND FREEDOM

It is useless to oppose antisemitism if the logic of one's belief
implies a prejudicial image of Judaism.
Alan T. Davies, *Anti-Semitism and the Christian Mind*

If the history of God and humans is afflicted radically by the Endlösung, a minimal Christian response ought to include alterations in
Christian dogma, just as Jewish response ought to include alterations in
Jewish dogma. However, at the end of Chapter 3 we raised the question
of whether there is any hope that Christian teachings and behavior will
change. In order to carry this question forward, we suggest a working
typology or continuum, with the usual proviso that different parties do
not always exactly fit one type and often cross the lines between types.

RESPONSES TO THE
HOLOCAUST

1. For some Christians, the Holocaust remains, morally speaking, a
   nonevent. (We speak of nonevent now in a quite different way from
   the spiritual refusal to permit the Holocaust to destroy one's faith,
   the way the term is applied in chapter 4.) Evaluatively stated, these
   Christians involved remain servants of the church's unholy past.
   Large numbers of persons, within Germany but also beyond, live
   and act in ways quite unaffected by the *Shoah*. They think and behave as if there had been no kingdom of night. Nothing essential is
   learned or changed.
2. For others, the Holocaust manages to gain the status of a partial
   event; it is partial in that it is able, objectively speaking, to exert a

greater or lesser impact upon Christian thinking and action. Evaluatively expressed, the door to freedom from the past is at least being
set ajar for Christians within this category. Some Christian, and Jewish, examples of this category have already been presented in chapter 4, although not from within the Federal Republic of Germany.

3. In a third model, *metanoia*—total revolution—is achieved both
within and through the Holocaust. Evaluatively put, Christians are
granted the power and joy of liberation. Liberation means not only
complete self-acceptance but also freedom from the idolatry of
triumphing over the other, the Jew. Once enabled to accept ourselves, we can begin to accept the other. Such deliverance may be
approximated collectively, as well as being realized individually.

In this chapter the first two of these models are explored; we give
greater attention to the second. The third possibility is given voice in
chapters 6 and 7; it is also represented through our critical comments
upon the other two types. Our examples for models one and two and
two examples of model three are taken from within the Christian community of West Germany. Because Christians of Germany were singu-
larly caught up in the Third Reich's "war against the Jews," and because all Christians cited here are drawn from among those who profess
to be keenly conscious of, or to have been influenced by, the Holocaust,
their utterances carry a fateful burden from which their authors cannot
escape and to which we must attend. Similar examples can be found
among Christian communities and churches of other nations, at least in
the West. However, few Christians among Asian, African, or other
Third World churches have given any thought to the Endlösung and its
implications for their own theology. Moreover, some deliberately insist
that the annihilation of European Jewry (even though carried out
within Christian Europe) has no relevancy for Christianity. Various
reasons are advanced for such a view—usually traditional theological
ones, but frequently a significant, even if unspoken, motivation is the
wish to invalidate the State of Israel. Those who speak from this persuasion insist that Israel was imposed on innocent Arabs[1] in order not only
to salve the guilty consciences of western Christians but also to enable
them to escape from accepting the survivor-refugees into their own
countries.

MODEL 1: THE PRE-HOLOCAUST PAST AS SLAVEHOLDER

From among many candidates, we choose one instance of recent Christian advocacy which proceeds, to all intents and purposes, as though there never was any such event as the Holocaust. This small book, *Die Judenfrage* (The Jewish Question), by the Christian writer Friedrich Gruenagel, is part of a series devoted to "the strengthening of biblical faith and Christian life." A major reason for our selection of the volume is that *Die Judenfrage* is popularly written and was designed to reach large audiences in the German churches.

Gruenagel's monograph initally prompts high expectations in its call for the reconciliation of Jews and Christians. At first the author appears to be directing us to a revolutionary position, a radical rethinking of Christianity, as the required moral reaction to the crimes against Jews. He emphasizes that the unparalleled events of the past remain unmastered (*eine unbewältigte Vergangenheit*). Satanic forces ever put us in their grasp, quite as readily as do divine powers. This truth lay incarnate in the dark events before 1945. Gruenagel laments the continuing and incorrigible antipathy to Jews, abetted as this is by the ideology of antisemitism, a pathological disease of the spirit that can break out in any time and in any land.

In addressing himself to the work of Vatican Council II, this Protestant writer praises Pope John XXIII's attempt to strike at the theological roots of antisemitism, and he regrets that the pope's effort was partly despoiled by Arab Christian interference. He identifies the human machinations that sought to undercut the council's striving to provide a statement on Judaism and the Jews. Regrettably, political interests interfered with the theological question. Gruenagel lauds Augustin Cardinal Bea's struggle against the "absurd Christian ideology" which teaches that the Jewish role or presence in the event of Golgotha meant God's damnation of the Jews. Vatican Council II clearly proclaimed the common origins of Jews and Christians and attained an outright condemnation of antisemitism.[2]

In light of these statements, how is it possible to link Gruenagel to the ideology of the Holocaust as nonevent? It seems astonishing, but immediately after his commendatory reference to the council's use of Holy Scripture, Gruenagel feels called upon to insert the traditionalistic contention that "the law" (*das Gesetz*) is the true and fateful cause of the woes of the Jewish people. He attributes to the apostle Paul an apprehension of a certain depravity (*Verworfenheit*) within his own people despite their acknowledged election by God, which prompts Gruenagel to refer to the "spiritual torment" in Heinrich Heine's conclusion that "the Jewish religion is not really a religion; it is a disaster." To be sure, this judgment did not make Heine an enemy of his people. Yet he "saw through" to the cause of their misfortune. In Gruenagel's words, "the pretension to the absoluteness of the law stood in the way."[3]

It is not long before Gruenagel explodes into anti-Jewish sentiments, cataloging many supposedly fundamental and lasting Jewish sins. At the center of these transgressions, he asserts, lie Jewish hardheartedness and nationalism. In fact, readers are advised that the German Nazi self-application of the idea of election, of being the chosen race, simply represented a reincarnating of the mentality of Jews. Today, Jews and Israelis maintain the threatening outlook of claiming a monopoly upon the blessedness of God, whom they utilize in order to make themselves victorious at the expense of other peoples. As Gruenagel's argument develops, it becomes clear that, as he sees it, the only basic fault of the Christian church in its entire relationship with the Jewish people is its failure to bring the Jews to Christ, as their solitary savior from "the law," nationalism, and other evils. Antisemitism becomes primarily a matter of Jewish culpability, the consequence of the Jewish hardness of heart. All in all, only when the Jews conquer their sins and "return" to Christ will antisemitism be overcome and Christians and Jews reconciled.[4]

Gruenagel's exposition brings forcibly to mind a concept or, better, an eventuality that is being argued over in some German church circles today: *eine geistliche Endlösung,* "a spiritual Final Solution." Among concerned Christian scholars in today's Germany stands Rudolf Pfisterer of Schwäbisch-Hall, who emphasizes that the Christian attempt to "save" Jews is, in his words, "nothing more than the continuing work of the Holocaust."[5] For, in the last resort, both "final solutions"—the attempts at physical and spiritual annihilation—see the Jewish presence as a "problem" to be solved and seek to put an end to it. The religious and human integrity of Jews is attacked just as surely in either case. There are, of course, other telling means of subverting Jewish rights and dignity—through, for example, Gruenagel's varied accusations against the Jewish people. As an alternative to the term nonevent, we may speak of the Endlösung as a "perpetuating event"—an event that serves to give continuing life to certain stereotypes and prejudices, which in turn nurture a spirit conducive to future Holocausts.[6]

Gruenagel and others of similar persuasion are living corporally in the years after the Holocaust, but their efforts and outlook are essentially pre-Holocaust in character. Christians such as these are unable to grant that such views contributed to a religious and social environment that helped make the *Shoah* possible. They cannot accept the judgment of Franklin H. Littell, who attests that the Endlösung is and will remain "the major event in recent church history," because it "called into question the whole fabric of Christendom." It exposed in the most awful measure the church's rebellion and betrayal, revealed "the final blasphemy of the baptized gentiles," their "open revolt against the God of Abraham, Isaac, and Jacob," and showed the thinness of the veneer with which a sham Christianity covered "the actual devotion of the European tribes to other gods."[7] We should not wonder therefore, that Gruenagel and those who share his views are forced into a situation where, to all intents and purposes, the Holocaust did not really happen. That is to say, it is as if there never were any murder camps, nor any support for Hitler's other anti-Jewish decrees and actions by pastors, bishops, cardinals, or theologians.

MODEL 2: CRACKS IN
THE PRISON BARS

> This abomination before God and man alike . . . is fundamentally a religious problem, a festering wound in the spiritual body of Christianity that will continue making a mockery of the most solemn services of the Christian churches, unless. . . . Well, unless what?
>
> Wolfgang Zucker, "30 Years after the Holocaust"

Major exemplification of the second model, the Holocaust as a partial event, is found in an official pronouncement of the Council of the Protestant Church in Germany (EKD; Evangelische Kirche in Deutschland) entitled *Christen und Juden* (Christians and Jews). This document is the product of five years of discussion and study.

The EKD's declaration goes farther theologically and morally than that church has ever gone before or, for that matter, farther than any other church had gone to that date. The German churchmen and theologians who prepared the statement remain acutely aware of the Endlösung; plainly it is much on their conscience. They speak of the deep

100

trauma that the event created for Christians, of the church's latter-day rediscovery of its Jewish roots, and of the abiding integrity of the faith of Judaism. They confess the appalling role of the Christian world in the historic persecution of the Jewish people, including the causative power of Christian antisemitism in the annihilation of European Jews. The council emphasizes that a special obligation falls upon the Christians of Germany to oppose the new antisemitism that appears in the form of politically and socially motivated anti-Zionism. Christians have a particular duty to support the independence and security of Israel—not alone as a political reality or human achievement, but also within the very frame of reference of the history of the people of God.[8]

On the other side, these spokesmen are beset by a traditional and familiar Christian dilemma. The EKD pronouncement reflects the conflict over the *Judenmission,* the mission to the Jews, that continues to divide German Christians. The authors ask how the Christian is to bear witness to the Jew. Asserting that Christ is the "Savior of all men," they insist that while certain ongoing missionary practices have given Jews reason for mistrust, Christians cannot remain silent concerning the ground of their hope and faith. Indeed, they contend that, according to the newer Christian understanding, mission remains equal to dialogue as a dimension of the one Christian witness to Jews. Thus, in the end, the council is not totally prepared, so the evidence goes, to accept Jews simply as equal brothers and sisters.[9]

The dominating challenge faced by the EKD council is how to reconcile its call for unqualified justice and love for the Jewish people with its Christological and other theological assurances, as plainly and forcibly stated throughout *Christen und Juden,* according to which the Christian faith comprises the fulfilled truth of God, the real consummation of Jewish (as of human) hopes and expectations.[10] *Christen und Juden* thus typifies the unending and tragic plight of the Christian church in the presence of the Jewish people: human equality is compromised and threatened by a presupposed inequality of decision, behavior, and faith.

Finally *Christen und Juden* fails to surmount or exclude the ancient canard of Jewish responsibility, or coresponsibility with the Romans, for the execution of Jesus.[11] Even were such responsibility a reality, the moral and psychological question remains: What is the purpose of repeating this charge within a church statement devoted to Christian-Jewish reconciliation, and this in the land of the Final Solution? (Moreover, it implicitly encourages the Christian community to repeat

101

the canard each church year throughout the world, as is still the dreadful custom.) In a word, until the EKD council is able to overcome the heritage of the past in light of the consequences to which it so fearfully contributed, these churchmen will be living, simultaneously, a post-Holocaust life and a pre-Holocaust life.[12]

JÜRGEN MOLTMANN AND MODEL 2

Our second model is additionally represented in the developing point of view of Jürgen Moltmann of the University of Tübingen. In keeping with Moltmann's considerable influence and the centrality to traditional theology of the issues he emphasizes, we offer a more lengthy analysis of and response to his position. Significantly, the same analysis applies to many of the liberation theologians of Latin America, although they have not claimed to be influenced by the *Shoah* and, in fact, have ignored it.[13] The intensive discussion will also focus a number of moral and theological issues posed by the Holocaust. So far, the *Endlösung* has had limited impact upon theology in Germany except in selective small circles. Will German religious thought continue to live, as it were, before 1933? With special reference to New Testament theology, Charlotte Klein has shown that a pessimistic reply to the question still must prevail.

On the other hand, there are some signs of change, one of the most remarkable of which we will discuss under Model 3. Moltmann has explicitly stated that the Holocaust is a most important influence on his rethinking of Christian theology.[14]

We concentrate upon two of Moltmann's important works, *Der Gekreuzigte Gott* and *Kirche in der Kraft des Geistes*, published in translations, respectively, as *The Crucified God* and *The Church in the Power of the Spirit*. We have supplemented our study of these materials by considering a subsequent volume *The Trinity and the Kingdom*, his dialogue with Pinchas Lapide (*Jewish Monotheism and Christian Trinitarian Doctrine: A Dialogue*), and by personal conversations with their author. This in no way implies that he accepts our judgments of them. It is essential to stress, however, that the key issue at this juncture is not whether Moltmann provides a "valid" interpretation of the Christian faith, and certainly not whether we do, but instead

102

whether Moltmann's representation of the Christian gospel in fact confronts the destruction of the Jews of Europe without equivocation, in accordance with his own declaration.

Several areas of discussion are suggested by *The Crucified God*. We do not see any way to dissociate totally this title from the infamous charge of deicide, but we are convinced that Moltmann's usage is not intentionally prejudicial.

JESUS, "THE LAW," AND
JEWISH REJECTION

First, there is the morally decisive and even fateful question of Jesus, "the law" (*das Gesetz*), and his reputed rejection by "the Jews." Moltmann makes Jesus "a scandal to the devout," which becomes a fundamental reason for his being crucified. Jesus was sentenced to die by "the law." He was cursed and condemned by the "guardians of the law" and of faith and killed as a "blasphemer," having been "handed over to the Romans to be crucified." His "sufferings and humiliation" are linked to "his freedom towards the law." Jesus placed himself "above the limits of the contemporary understanding of the law," demonstrating through his forgiveness of sins "God's eschatological law of grace towards those without the law and the transgressors of the law." Moltmann discerns a clash between Jesus' gospel and "the law" which led to a legal trial. He underwent "a trial before the Sanhedrin" as well as before Pilate. At stake were "the righteousness of faith and the righteousness of works, . . . the justification of the godless and the justification of the righteous." The Jews "condemned Jesus and delivered him to crucifixion" out of ignorance and lawlessness, "against the will of God and therefore against the law," and as evil men. "The purpose of the sending of the son of God is liberation from slavery under the law for the freedom of the children of God." Through faith in Christ men become "free sons of God." The unconditional love of Jesus for the rejected "made the Pharisees his enemies and brought him to the cross."[15]

The heart of Moltmann's exegesis is found in this passage:

[Jesus'] execution must be seen as a necessary consequence of his conflict with the law. His trial by the guardians of the law was in the broader sense of the term a trial about the will of God, which the law claimed to have codified once for all. Here the conflict between Jesus and the law was not a dispute about a different will, or the will of a different God, but about the true will of God, which for Jesus was hidden and not revealed by the human con-

103

cept of the law. Jesus' claim to fulfill the law of the righteousness of God, the claim made in the Sermon on the Mount, and his freedom from the law should not be understood as contradictory. For Jesus the "radicalization of the *Torah*" and the "transgression of the *Torah*" basically both amount to the same thing, the freedom of God to show grace. Thus, the right which he claimed to forgive sins goes beyond the *Torah* and reveals a new righteousness of God in judgment, which could not be expected according to the traditions of the law.[16]

Moltmann's wording here represents the traditional Christian view that the Jews created "the law," thus attempting to entrap God and limit God's freedom. Nothing could be further from the Jewish perspective: Torah (as "Teaching" rather than "law") was delivered to humans by God; it was a divine gift, and it is not a human creation at all. In it are to be found the treasures of God's wisdom applicable to the human and earthly situation. The role humans—Jews, in this instance —have is to study, understand, interpret, and apply Torah's guidelines to all of life. Interpretation and application are especially important as the conditions under which people live change. Through this living of Torah, the Jewish people are understood to be God's active partners, working to complete and perfect the unfinished work of creation in accord with God's will for redemption.

Furthermore, Moltmann does not take sufficiently into account the insistence within much contemporary scholarship that, very largely, the conflicts and happenings he describes do not reflect historical truth. Minimally speaking, his interpretations are off balance. They fail even to acknowledge, much less to respond to, the massive historical work that maintains the precise opposite of his claims. Given this other increasingly accepted conclusion, it is just incorrect to say that Jesus stood in opposition to contemporary Judaism, its representatives and its teachers. He did not come into conflict with "the law" or with his people. He lived and died a faithful Jew, standing indeed for the best in the tradition of the Pharisees. Pharisaism sought fundamentally to keep "the law" alert to human needs; Jesus and the Pharisees were in this respect reformers, against the Sadducees.[17]

Moltmann is well aware of the general historical question: "Is the preaching of the church in continuity and harmony with Jesus and his history?" He acknowledges the place and the use of historical criticism. Yet he then writes that critical scholarship must "ask what the testimonies have to say about those to whom they bear witness, and what faith has to say about the one who is the object of faith, and whether it [faith] is in accordance with him.[18] We respond that surely critical scholarship must also ask whether elements or data that are allegedly "in accordance with him" are also in accordance with the truth.

To refer to a most grave subject, is it possible or the case that Jesus could have been condemned in the manner Moltmann reports? There is simply no way around or through the formidable conflict between New Testament claims of what Jesus said and did and what he may actually have said and done. Fundamental and responsible historical scholarship requires that we continually look behind the New Testament documents, and indeed that we study these documents with full attention to independent knowledge of first-century Judaism and Palestine. In this latter context, particular attention is called to the charge of blasphemy reputedly leveled against Jesus.[19] On grounds at once juridical and historical, Justice Haim Cohn of the Supreme Court of Israel argues convincingly against the possibility of this charge. He also corrects certain other errors. Thus, the whole notion that Jesus was given a Jewish trial on a charge of blasphemy, that he was found guilty of blasphemy on his own confession, and that he then received a capital sentence through the Sanhedrin runs hard against no less than seven well-established provisions of Jewish law.[20]

Jürgen Moltmann argues that the charge of "blasphemer" brought against Jesus must have been based on a type of blasphemy made by a "false Messiah . . . intervening in a matter where rights are reserved for God alone"—that is, in showing mercy, an act seen as self-deification.[21] He finds it entirely likely that Jesus would have been called a blasphemer "in view of the whole of his scandalous message."[22] But it is most debatable whether Jesus' teaching, religiously, was in fact "scandalous." More significantly, even extreme messianic claims were not received as blasphemous: There is no biblical or rabbinic law on the subject. We do not discuss the controversial issue of whether Jesus in truth claimed to be "messiah"; it appears that he did not. Finally, were Jesus in fact found guilty of blasphemy, why was he not stoned to death, as required by the religious law? Moltmann fails to meet these all-decisive difficulties.

Why need we be concerned with Christians', and specifically in our present context Moltmann's, emphasis on and presentation of "the law"? Its bearing upon a concern with the Holocaust is weighty. We know that Nazi ideologists and the Deutsche Christen (the German Christian Movement) outdid each other in insisting that the Jewish "law" meant evil and slavery. Of course, it cannot be overstressed that the Nazis were equally intent on liberating Christians from "Jewish conscience" and from Christianity's own "higher law" given by and through the Jew Jesus. Conversely, the genuine liberation that Christian faith can provide is the archenemy of Nazi "liberation." Yet the unhappy truth remains that persisting Christian negativism toward the Jewish "law," including that found among today's liberation theologians, offers, however unintentionally, a negative form of alliance with National Socialist ideology and thus helps to perpetuate pre-Holocaust influences. Moltmann asks, "Does inhuman legalism triumph over the crucified Christ, or does God's law of grace triumph over the works of the law and of power?[23] This question is posed on the same page where he refers to "the cries for righteousness of those who are murdered and gassed." Moltmann's query and his subsequent reference, when put together, form an added, fateful question: Did not the charge of "inhuman legalism" against Judaism and the Jewish people contribute to the murdering and the gassing?[24] Irving Greenberg declares: "Since even God should be resisted [were he to order a Holocaust], we are called to challenge such a central *sancta* as the Gospels, the Church Fathers, and other sources for their contributions to the sustenance of hate."[25] How can Moltmann escape Greenberg's indictment once he has made the "guardians of the law" into the enemies of Jesus? In this crucial respect, his interpretation of the New Testament appears to be, at one and the same time, pre-Holocaust and precritical.

Jürgen Moltmann is concerned to show as convincingly as possible the absoluteness of the rejection of Jesus, for this total rejection, including God's abandonment of him, is at the heart of Moltmann's theological argument and system.[26] For that very reason Moltmann *must* make Jesus the victim of his religion, of the "guardians of the law," as well as of society and the state, regardless of the reality that recent historical scholarship has disclosed?[27] If this is the case, Moltmann is as much subject to the perils of ideology as were the writers of the early Christian movement.[28] As the British historian James Parkes has often asked, how can true theology ever be grounded in false history?

JUDAISM AND THE JEWS

We consider next the related question of Jürgen Moltmann's description of, and attitude to, Judaism and the Jews, especially as given voice in *The Crucified God*. The affirmation, expressed by Moltmann, that God's grace is revealed in sinners and his righteousness in the unrighteous, hardly originated with Christianity. For untold numbers of Jews, not "this faith" (Christianity) but Judaism is fully capable of setting them "free from their cultural illusions, releasing them from the involvements which blind them, and confronting them with the truth of their existence and their society." In addition, to identify the Judaism of Jesus' day as a matter of works-righteousness is a basic misinterpretation, one that echoes prevailing German biblical scholarship before and since 1933.[29] Judaism is being misread through the eyes of Pauline and Lutheran thought. (Moltmann is Reformed, but as Wilhelm Pauck once remarked, it is very hard for German theologians to sever the umbilical cord that ties them to Martin Luther.) The New Testament scholar Krister Stendahl identifies the theological model of "law" versus "gospel" as a subtle and powerful form of anti-Jewishness in Christian theology, particularly in Protestantism and most prominently in Lutheranism. The issue falsely becomes one of free divine grace versus the self-justifying acts of humans. In fact, the anti-Judaism in the dichotomy is really not so subtle, as Stendahl's own analysis shows:

> According to this model, this habit-forming structure of theological thinking, Jewish attitudes and Jewish piety are by definition the example of the wrong attitude to God. The Christian proposition in the teachings of Jesus, Paul, John, and all the rest, is always described in contrast to Jewish "legalism," "casuistry," "particularism," ideas of "merit," etc. This whole system of thinking . . . treats Jewish piety as the black background which makes Christian piety the more shining. In such a state of affairs, it is hard to engender respect for Judaism and the Jews. And the theological system *requires* the retention of such an understanding of Judaism, whether true or not.[30]

Significantly, when it comes to Jesus' last words on the cross as reported in the Gospels of Luke and John, Moltmann refuses to be bound by these reports as accurate. He explains that these words have been substituted for Jesus' actual words (the cry of abandonment, "My God, my God, why hast thou forsaken me?") in order to fit the particular theological perspective of the gospel writer. In the case of Luke, confidence in God is shown instead: "Father, into thy hands I commit my spirit" (Lu. 23:46, and Ps. 31:6). In John's Gospel, "It is finished" (Jn. 19:30) represents the end of his struggle "with his victory and glorification on the cross." But when it comes to the Jews, "the law," and such other tenuous claims as the one that Jesus forgave sins, Moltmann remains wedded to the text and unwilling to apply the same historical methods of analysis.[31]

In truth, according to the historic and prevailing Jewish view, "the law" (better, Torah/Teaching) means liberation. It is indeed, "sweeter than honey" (Ps. 19:10). We think of the daily prayer of the Jew: "Our Father, our King, be gracious unto us for we have no works. Save us according to thy grace." This prayer is only made possible by the Torah. Among many Christian faults is the failure to recognize that the whole Jewish attitude to Torah and to God's grace found its source and origin well before Christianity was born. Unhappily, Christians have been conditioned to misrepresent first-century Judaism, and thence later Judaism. In the traditional Jewish viewpoint, Torah constitutes God's gift of undeserved grace and freedom, of hope for the future, and of guidance for everyday life. Moltmann makes much of the ecstasy of freedom in Christ, but he has nothing to say about the ecstasy that generations of Jews have experienced in following a pattern of life established by God's teaching. Moreover, what does it mean to say, practically and in real life, that Christians are free and Jews are not? In what concrete way is the Christian "set free" more than the Jew? And what does it ever mean to include Jews among the "godless"?[32]

Moltmann also speaks of the positive effect that the Resurrection of Jesus may have on people "who are open to the world and to the future," by whom he means those who understand Christ's death on the cross as "representative suffering and sacrifice 'for them.'" Those who are "closed to the future and without hope—those who do not understand Christ's death in this way—cannot benefit from the promise the Resurrection provides.[33] Yet surely Jews and Judaism are widely and abidingly marked by openness to the world and the future. One does not honor the dignity and self-identity of Jews, or of others who do not profess the Resurrection, by implying otherwise.

When as Christians we claim that the unrighteous are made righteous through Christ's atoning death, are we being morally insensitive? We neither quarrel with the note of universalism in Moltmann's denial that the unrighteous are punished with eternal condemnation, nor do we deny that "in the end the victims will not triumph over their executioners." But unless we allow a place for some form of essential condemnation, we deprive ourselves of theological and moral criteria for distinguishing between the exploiters and the exploited, between the Nazis and their victims. The problem here is the perennial temptation

108

within the Christian community, especially within modern Christendom, to be deficient, in principle, at the point of justice. This is a fault against which Judaism has always retained safeguards. More seriously expressed, does not the Christian proclivity to stress the divine foregiveness constitute an ideological transgression against the victims of unrighteousness, a transgression that comes, ironically, from within the very circle of those who have been, historically, the victors, the powerful? Moltmann himself may be called to witness here: "Indifference towards justice and injustice would be a retreat on the part of God from the covenant."[34]

It is important that there be a greater and more concrete stress upon the truth that the crucified man to whom Moltmann bears witness was a Jew. Moltmann attests that God became "the kind of man that we do not want to be: an outcast, accursed, crucified."[35] But we must avoid the abstraction of "a" man who is then also taken to be the Christ/Messiah of God. It is essential to emphasize here that it was *this Jewish man* who was put to death; this declaration, in addition to its other necessities, also helps to point to the singularity of antisemitism in time and place. Lastly, Moltmann contends that the Jewish answer to the question of redemption "could be described by saying that God forces Israel to repent through suffering." What is the ground of this allegation? Moltmann seeks support for the judgment in Emil L. Fackenheim, but this is not licit. To Fackenheim God is anything but a coercive presence.[36]

THE CHRISTIAN IMPERIUM

A third issue for discussion raised by Jürgen Moltmann's work is the crucial matter of Christian absolutism and triumphalism. Moltmann attests that "*only* the crucified Christ can bring the freedom which changes the world because it is no longer afraid of death." The church of the crucified Messiah can liberate all persons, including Jews. The preaching of the cross "is the *only* adequate access which the godless have" to the God who was crucified. "In the face of Jesus' death-cry to God, theology either becomes impossible or becomes possible *only* as specifically Christian theology." "*Only* from him [Jesus] and through him does the resurrection hope then extend to the living and dead." The way through judgment and Godforsakenness "is *only* passable for men in his company." Moltmann does concede that Israel demonstrates to the church "that the redemption of the world is still to come," yet earlier he denies any such function to Israel, holding that the church and the gospel meet the problem. Now, however, he explains the lack of redemption by adjudging that "the church of Christ is not yet perfect and the kingdom of God has not achieved full revelation as long as these two communities of hope, Israel and the church, continue to exist side by side.[37] This appears to imply that the absence of redemption centers essentially in the incompleteness of the church. Yet how is this anything but the traditional conversionist position and eventual Christian triumphalism, despite the consideration that elsewhere the "success" of the church and the redemption of the world are distinguished?

Again, while Moltmann asks for "an openness on the part of Christians to the existential basis of Judaism," his pages in many respects also mirror an opaqueness to the Jewish apprehension of Judaism and of faith. Thus, he declares that

> when we have spoken of the conflict into which Jesus came with the "law," this does not refer to the Old Testament *Torah* as instruction in the covenant of promise [to Abraham]. The more the understanding of the *Torah* became remote from the promise, the more violent became the conflict with the gospel. The closer the understanding of the *Torah* draws to the original promise and election of Israel [through Abraham], the greater the possibility of an understanding for the law of grace, of the gospel and for the hope which it gives to the hopeless and to the gentiles.

Here it seems that Moltmann is either cutting the ground from under the uniqueness he has earlier insisted upon respecting the Christ-event, for he is telling the Jew, in effect, what he ought to believe respecting the essential nature of faith—namely that faith is a matter of "promise" in contradistinction to any specific revealed guidelines for living in society (Torah/"law"/Teaching). In the passage quoted above, and in the preceding sentences from *The Crucified God*, the latter process certainly seems to be in force. For Moltmann claims that "the struggle between the gospel of Jesus and the understanding of the law which prevailed at [that] time [is to be] related [to] the promise of Abraham, the promise of life. . . . [T]hrough the gospel this promise was liberated from the shadow of a legalist understanding of the law and given universal force for everyone who believes, whether Jew or Gentile." He insists that this emphasis does not invalidate "the promises of Israel [or] the election of Israel": in fact, it "reminds [the convinced Jew] of his best traditions." But who is to define the "best traditions" of Judaism?

110

And what becomes of the Exodus-Sinai revelation? And of the Jew who holds to this as the existential basis of his life and faith? He must remain in some way unregenerate, upon Moltmann's own reasoning; and the "root experience" of the Jewish people is banished or implicitly relegated to "the shadow of a legalistic understanding" of Israel's election. We are left with the question whether, within the bounds of *The Crucified God*, there is any ground for asserting that Israel "rightfully exists alongside the church" and in consequence "cannot be abolished."[38]

Triumphalism is a serious enough problem for Christians when it is being explicitly avowed. However, certain passages in *The Crucified God*—inadvertently, we believe—fall into a more serious condition: triumphalism in the guise of antitriumphalism. We have just considered one example, wherein the supposed conflict of Jesus and Paul with the existing understanding of "the law" is said *not* to negate Israel's election but rather to universalize it. This interpretation, made as early as the first century C.E., nevertheless obliterates Judaism's main foundation: God's gift of Torah. A second example follows:

> The proclamation of the cross is "Christianity" for all the world (Blumhardt), and may not erect any new distinctions between men, say between Christians and non-Christians, the pious and the godless. Its first recognition leads to self-knowledge: to the knowledge that one is a sinner in a solidarity with all men under the power of corruption. Therefore *the theology of the cross is the true Christian universalism*. There is no distinction here, and all will be made righteous without any merit on their part by his grace which has come to pass in Christ Jesus. (Rom. 3:24)[39]

Alas, what Moltmann does here is precisely to erect distinctions between Christians, who "know" and "agree" with what he says, and Jews, the essence of whose faith is, for him, only grasped through the advantage of the true Christian gospel. And this result occurs in the very course of denying that any distinctions or divisions between humans are being erected. Here is moral and theological irony in its most dire form.

Traditional Christian triumphalism is unfortunate enough, but it is not as unfortunate as the triumphalism that denies, or does not see, the truth that it is being triumphalist. It is very painful for us who are Christians, but we cannot escape from the judgment made by a participant at the Hamburg Holocaust Conference (1975): there is a crying need for an unqualified relativization of absolute claims and loyalties of the kind that made the Endlösung possible.

111

Part of the famous episode in Elie Wiesel's *Night,* where a young boy is murdered at a death camp before the assembled prisoners and a voice whispers that God is hanging there on the gallows, is reproduced toward the conclusion of *The Crucified God.* Moltmann declares that any other response than the whispered one "would be blasphemy. There cannot be any other Christian answer to the question of this torment." But why has "Christian" been inserted here? None of the alternative answers that are possible to the question—"Where is God?"—are outside the realm of Jewish responses. And practically all Jews would agree with Moltmann's rejection of them: that is, a God who could not suffer, an absolute or an indifferent God. Furthermore, the sufferer and the reluctant witnesses, fellow sufferers, were Jews. Moreover, the context in which the episode is introduced into *The Crucified God* is a consideration of a *Jewish* interpretation of the history of God and of his people, particularly Abraham Joshua Heschel's theology of the suffering, the pathos, of God. God suffers *with* his and her people *because of* intense interest in and concern for them; conversely, the Holy One experiences redemption when Israel is redeemed. Yet Moltmann moves directly from Heschel's analysis to the selection from *Night* by identifying the episode as "a shattering expression of the *theologia crucis*" (theology of the cross).[40] Should this dreadful happening—only one of countless equivalent atrocities—be utilized to understand a Christian theology of the cross? Is it licit to, as it were, christologize the Jewish martyrs by making them "dumb sacrifices" of whom it can be said "in a real, transferred sense, that God himself hung on the gallows . . ."?[41] Must it not be left strictly within the Jewish frame of reference in which it occurred? After the *Shoah,* are we Christians not obliged to *listen*—listen to Jews? Must we not hear and give consideration to Jewish protests, even directed to or against God, and to Jewish theology about God's suffering?

Wiesel himself has said that when he wrote that account he was very careful about what he said. Of course it was a protest; that is clear from the entire narrative to this point. In answer to a student's question about what he meant, he has explained succinctly:

> I felt that the Covenant was broken. I had to tell God of my anger. . . . We had to say to God, "Ribbono Shel Olam, I . . . want You for a *din torah*! I have the right to call You to judgment. I have the right as a human being, I have the duty as a Jew to tell You that something is wrong in Your Creation." . . . Even when I wrote it, I was very careful. I was afraid of commen-

taries. What I said is that . . . I heard a voice saying. Well, whose voice was it? I did not say it was mine. And what if it was God's? So I left it ambiguous on purpose. I like clarity except when it comes to certain very dangerous topics.[42]

A more shattering consideration is involved when we see that the final section of *The Crucified God,* "The fullness of life in the trinitarian history of God," immediately follows consideration of the story from *Night.* The very juxtaposition necessarily implies a spiritual impotence and even emptiness with regard to the faith of Judaism, an implication that does not, we fear, observe the command of love for the sufferers, or of honor for one's parents (in faith). Moltmann grants that the covenant provides Israel with "immediacy" in the relationship with God and creates a "direct correspondence" between the pathos of God and the sympathy of humans, which Christians, especially Gentile Christians, cannot experience. The latter's relationship with God must be within a trinitarian framework, for only through Christ can a "dialogical relationship with God" be opened up for them. Yet in the glowing description that follows regarding the communion that God makes possible "through his self-humiliation in the death of the crucified Christ and through his exaltation of man in the resurrection of Christ," and "the gracious presuppositionless and universal . . . community of God with all men in their common misery," one loses sight of the Jewish community and wonders whether any of this is meant to apply to it. In fact, Moltmann specifically asks if the sphere of God that is opened up in Christ is "comparable to . . . the field of force of God's *pathos*" (that is, as Judaism knows it). In Christ is found "the final and complete self-humiliation of God in man. . . . He does not merely become the covenant partner of an elect people so that men must belong to this people through circumcision and obedience to the covenant in order to enter into this fellowship. . . . God does not become a law, so that man participates in him through obedience to a law."[43] It is sad that Moltmann should say these things at this place in his study. Whatever potentially positive value he may find in Judaism for Jews is not made explicit enough. And it is overwhelmed by his traditional Christology. We plead for nothing more than respect for the dead children, women, and men who could never accept propositions such as those just cited. Let us enable the sufferers of Auschwitz and of the other hells to have their moment alone with God, or without him; let us not intrude with our theological caveats, however much these may stem from conscience and conviction. The six million who were systematically murdered in the camps, willingly or unwillingly, did not represent the Christian view Moltmann proclaims. Would it not be infinitely more fitting just to honor these persons as human beings, and let things stand that way?

Moltmann confesses that "a 'theology after Auschwitz' may seem an impossibility or blasphemy." His own presentation is surely not blasphemous in any sense implied in that passage, but it is in another way. It moves, in all inadvertence to be sure, against the God who dwelt in the destroyed Jews. The author testifies: "Even Auschwitz is taken up into the grief of the Father, the surrender of the Son, and the power of the Spirit. . . . God in Auschwitz, and Auschwitz in the crucified God . . . is the basis for a real hope."[44] Again Christian triumphalism intrudes itself in the guise of its very opposite. For what could be more uncompassionate than the trinitarianization, the Christianization, of Auschwitz, of those poor souls who, had they been allowed the choice, would have in many instances willingly inhaled the gas and entered the flames rather than accede to any trinity of the Christian God? Had Moltmann taken Christians who died in the camps and argued in a parallel way, our reaction would be entirely inappropriate. But these are Jews of whom he speaks.

THE FATE OF GOLGOTHA

An appraisal of *The Crucified God* cannot very well avoid a fourth issue, that of the cross. We are confronted by a two-sided question: the historical-moral fate of the cross as a Christian symbol, taken in the context of the fortunes of the Jewish people; and the moral and theological difficulty posed by Moltmann's linkage of the cross with ultimate horribleness. We must not pass over Moltmann's testimony that the crucified Christ is a powerful counterforce to Christianity as "an accomplice of oppression."[45] Full acknowledgment also must be made of the beauty and the strength of Moltmann's call for identifying the Christian gospel with the alienated, the poor, the rejected, and the godless. Nevertheless, we must comment critically upon certain additional passages in *The Crucified God*.

We read that Christ's "death is the death of the one who redeems men from death, which is evil." Yet in the Nazi time the cross assisted in bringing death, the polar contrary of the "pains of love." The "crucified Christ" simply cannot be separated from what has happened to the cross. Moltmann insists that "the cross does not divide Christians from

Jews."[46] In truth, countless Jews of our world will never be able to distinguish the cross from the swastika, nor ought they be expected to do so. After the Holocaust a Jewish woman, catching sight of a huge cross displayed in New York City each year at Christmastime, said to her walking companion, Father Edward H. Flannery, "That cross makes me shudder. It is like an evil presence."[47] Although the cross had already been the dread symbol of murdering crusaders, inquisitors, and pogromists, in and through the Endlösung it became ultimately corrupted by devilishness. When asked by two bishops in 1933 what he was going to do about the Jews, Adolf Hitler replied that he would do to them exactly what the Christian church had been advocating and practicing for almost two thousand years,[48] and there is no evidence that the bishops made any kind of rebuttal, then or later.

Moltmann further writes: "The poverty and sufferings of Christ are experienced and understood only by participation in his mission and in imitating the task he carried out. Thus the more the poor understand the cross . . . as the cross of *Christ*, the more they are liberated from their submission to fate and apathy in suffering." No, in stark truth the six million Jews—including those Jewish Christians whom the Final Solution did not exempt—were not liberated, from death or from other suffering. They were not liberated at all, through "understanding" or anything else. "'Resurrection, life and righteousness' come through the death of this one man in favor of those who have been delivered over to death through their unrighteousness." In actuality, the Jews did not really qualify either as unrighteous or, for that matter, as righteous. They were just murdered. And they were murdered just because they were Jews—not good Jews or bad Jews or any other kind of Jews, but just Jews. What does it mean to say to the Jews of Buchenwald or Belzec that "through his suffering and death, the risen Christ brings righteousness and life to the unrighteous and the dying"?[49]

Much further along in *The Crucified God* we are advised that

in becoming weak, impotent, vulnerable and mortal, he [the crucified God] frees man from the quest for powerful idols and protective compulsions and makes him ready to accept his humanity, his freedom and his mortality. In the situation of the human God the pattern formations of repressions become unnecessary. The limitations of apathy fall away. Man can open himself to suffering and to love. In *sympatheia* with the *pathos* of God he becomes open to what is other and new. The symbols which show him the situation of the human and crucified God give him protection as a result of which he can allow his own self-protection to fall.[50]

Moltmann may be right in asserting that some gentiles can still speak in these terms; many, of course, have done so. But the utterly disarming fact is that before, within, and beyond Auschwitz, many Jews have been able to do the very same thing, and this without faith in Christ. To insinuate that the power of a "hidden Christ" is present there would be to fall into a deus ex machina. The God of these Jews has long since freed them from all kinds of idolatries. However, the truly decisive consideration is that in the presence of the kingdom of night, the claims Moltmann makes for both Christian and Jewish symbols and virtues ("weakness," "impotence," "vulnerability," "mortality," "repressions," "openness to suffering and love") have come to have the very opposite meanings and consequences from those he indicates. For within our shared history they have been transubstantiated into demonic structures. As Irving Greenberg observes, in our world suffering only helps to "strengthen rampant evil and to collaborate in the enthronement of the devil."

The American theologian William R. Jones reaches a similar conclusion: The acceptance of suffering as having a redemptive function that works against evil and therefore is an essential part of one's faith and life leads to quietism and simple endurance. It tends to justify the evil of suffering. There is no basis for working to counteract that evil.[51] The endlessly woeful consequence is that the Crucifixion is robbed of its redemptiveness. All that survives upon the hill of Golgotha is unmitigated evil. After Auschwitz, the Crucifixion cannot be accepted as a determinative symbol of redemptive suffering. From the point of view of the Holocaust, God is not met on the cross, even in his "Godforsakenness." Once upon a time he may have been met there, but he is no longer met there. As we seek to behold Golgotha now, our sight is blocked by huge mounds of torn bodies and ashes.

In Moltmann's own reasoning, the only two allowable possibilities appear to be that the Jews of the death camps were either redeemed or remained in some way unregenerate or perverse. If we opt for the first possibility, what does the redemption of these Jews mean? They were piled into heaps of corpses and either buried or burned. With respect to the second possibility, they did not identify with the suffering Christ, and this at the very boundary of their lives. Therefore, are we to conclude that they deserved their suffering? When we consider the atrocities that the Jews of the death camps and elsewhere in Europe had to suffer, even before the finality of inappropriate death, it is morally revolting to suggest, amelioratively, that they were somehow redeemed.

116

And it would be outrageous to suggest that they were perverse for not identifying with the suffering Christ. Another German theologian, Roman Catholic Johann-Baptist Metz, has forcefully addressed this issue quite differently: If we Christians are "to come to terms with Auschwitz," we will have to "forgo the temptation to interpret the suffering of the Jewish people from our standpoint in terms of saving history. Under no circumstances is it *our* task to mystify this suffering! We encounter in this suffering first of all only the riddle of our own lack of feeling, the mystery of our own apathy, [but] not . . . the traces of God."[52]

The measure of our disquietude here is tied to the ironic truth that Jürgen Moltmann's ideals are the very highest: he struggles against blasphemy, against hopelessness, against exploitation. Reinhold Niebuhr taught that the most formidable temptations of man assail him not at his lowest moments, but at his highest. There is at this place in Moltmann's work a temptation to the greatest blasphemy of all, as he himself uses that concept. For it was the very faith he identifies as offering the ultimate assurance to man which itself played a major role in bringing the Jews to the Endlösung to their state of horror and forsakenness. Accordingly, Moltmann's theory turns out to be, at this precise point, one not of assurance and hope but of hopelessness. It purports to deliver people, but it does the opposite: it helps to subject certain human beings to the most terrible suffering and degradation, and for the sole reason that they do not or cannot accept "the faith." Any faith capable of this evil outcome will have to be radically regenerated, along with the blasphemous and hopeless faiths Moltmann so admirably and rightly condemns.

THE CHURCH IN THE POWER
OF THE SPIRIT

A number of welcome changes and advances appear in Moltmann's later study, *The Church in the Power of the Spirit (Kirche in der Kraft des Geistes)*, and in the volume that comprises his dialogue with Pinchas Lapide, *Jewish Monotheism and Christian Trinitarian Doctrine*. We refer primarily to the chapter "The Church of the Kingdom of God" and especially to the sections concerned with the church and Israel/the Jewish people. Especially commendable are Moltmann's new emphases upon unique Christian solidarity with Israel, upon the Christian relation to Israel as being preeminent over and determinative

117

of the other salient relations he considers (to the world religions, to human society, and to the world of nature), and upon the need for the church's return to its foundations in Israel. Moltmann pays serious attention to the views of Franz Rosenzweig, Abraham Joshua Heschel, Gershom Scholem, and Jewish mysticism. Israel is fully acknowledged as the Christian's abiding source, his brother in hope. For centuries, anti-Judaism has meant the paganization of the Christian church. Moltmann now most effectively laments and criticizes the centuries-long triumphalism of the church, in which the church has sought to represent itself as the uniquely sovereign authority of God upon the earth, with its consequent separation from the history of Israel. Such absolutism not only "cuts the church off from its origin" but also from its future.[53]

Fundamental and requisite presuppositions for the end of Christian triumphalism include the rediscovery of the relevance and truth of the Old Testament (Torah), a new discovery of the unfulfilled elements within the messianic hope, and the placing of Israel in a partnership with the Christian church. Israel retains her sacred calling, alongside the church, until the End-time. Particularly noteworthy is Moltmann's assertion that hatred of the "obdurate" Jews is ultimately grounded within Christians' self-hatred. Noteworthy as well is his observation that the refounding of the State of Israel, whose integrity he honors, has put the relation of Christians to Jews upon a completely new plane: Jews now meet Christians not just as "the synagogue," but as citizens of a sovereign state. Moltmann manifests an entirely fresh attitude to Torah and to Jewish obedience to it, in marked contrast to many assertions and implications in *The Crucified God*. His condemnation of Christian supersessionism is a high point of *The Church in the Power of the Spirit*.[54]

Are we to conclude that the point of view of Moltmann's earlier study has been surmounted? Unfortunately, no. We comment upon two decisive points: the issue we discussed in chapter 4 of the perpetuating of special demands upon Israel; and the nagging question of the Christian imperium.

First, for Moltmann, the special calling of Israel remains the sanctification of the divine Name, and "obedience to the will of God according to the Torah—that is to say, living commitment to the service of righteousness . . ."[55] We must acknowledge, to Moltmann as to the Jewish community, that many Jews will continue to insist upon this role. Insofar as the Jewish people, or some among them, desire to perpetuate

118

a special calling or task, that is their business or at least their right. For Christians to deny that right out of hand is to fail to honor Jewish integrity. But we must also suggest that Christians are forbidden to make any special demands upon Jews. Here abides a serious shortcoming in Moltmann's continuing work. Christians have no right to inflict spiritual and moral requirements upon the Jewish people that may perpetuate or compound Jewish suffering.

The tragic irony is that had Christians centuries ago acknowledged the high calling of the Jewish people, and their living testimony to the righteousness that God hopes will prevail in creation, historically there is every reason to believe that Jewish existence would not have become marginal and vulnerable, nor would it have involved so much suffering. Jews would have been free to follow Torah or not—in the freedom God has bestowed on all persons and peoples. Under such circumstances Christians could have spoken prophetically to Israel in order to remind it of its responsibilities, if this seemed necessary and if they had adhered to their own responsibilities, without such words leading to inquisition, crusade, expulsion, or massacre. But that has not been the history of Christians and Jews. Nineteen hundred years of denunciation and denigration, of oppression and rejection, of Christian antisemitism, culminating in the Holocaust have canceled any such prophetic role for Christians. Now the situation is such that as long as the Christian community tries to make Israel something special, to trumpet forth that Israel has obligations greater than or different from those of other human beings, the burden of the Christian past will not be lifted. Christians will continue to share in God's original sin (so to speak), namely, God's insinuation of divine powerlessness and perfection into the life of ordinary mortals. As a matter of fact, Jürgen Moltmann may be called to witness against himself at this very point: he states again and again that the life and character of God entail divine suffering, not the making of demands.

The problem of making demands upon Jews is revealed especially sharply in Moltmann's section on the land of Israel.[56] Granted that his allotting of a special and positive role for Israel overturns erstwhile Christian condemnations of Judaism and the Jewish community, the special requirements he amasses for Israel nevertheless flout his assertions in *The Crucified God* that human beings should be accepted in all their individual and collective dignity, without any conditions.

Second, although Moltmann deplores Christian triumphalism in his later volume, he does not in fact surmount it. He maintains, or at least

119

reports, the view that the second advent of Christ will bring to fulfillment not only the Christian but also the Jewish hope. And he himself asserts that at the Parousia, the Second Coming, Christ will manifest himself as the Messiah of Israel. Moltmann contends that this modern millenarian view of the culmination of Christian salvation history, held by Reformed federal theology, pietist theology, and the Erlangen school, succeeded in overcoming anti-Judaism. However, in truth it did not have this consequence, and neither does Moltmann's point of view. He testifies that through their "rejection" of Christ, the Jews become the "last" to "come in" after the gentiles. Yet such testimony is made possible only through denying that the Jews are, in Franz Rosenzweig's phrase, "already with God," thus denying that God remains faithful to his promise. Hence, the anti-Judaism of *The Crucified God* is only tempered in the second volume, not really vanquished.[57] We must remember in this frame of reference that the actual replacing of the Jews by the gentiles within the church is what made possible the entire anti-Jewish development of Christianity. From the standpoint of the relevant pages in *The Church in the Power of the Spirit*, the Christian church does constitute the practical replacement of Israel in the work of salvation. The church remains, in Moltmann's view, the roundabout instrument of the salvation of Israel. The conclusion one must draw from this is that Jewish fate is tied to the success of the church in converting the nations. In view of Jews' experiences with Christianity, such a conclusion would hardly offer hope.

For all the changes between the two studies under review, Moltmann remains impaled upon the dilemmas of the apostle Paul and subject to all of the latter's ambivalence respecting Israel and his fellow Jews. We simply do not understand what it means for Moltmann (following Paul, as the evidence has it) to aver that Israel remains the hope of the Church.[58] The fact is that, according to the Pauline outlook, original Israel betrayed its soteriological calling, its place in salvation history (see Rom. 9–11). For all Paul's eschatological insistence that "the whole of Israel will be saved" and that "God's choice stands" (Rom. 11:26, 28), there is no way to avoid concluding that the apostle's own persuasion was that the church has effectively replaced original Israel and inherited the divine election.[59] There is no denying that for Paul, Jews as well as gentiles are justified in God's sight only by coming to Jesus Christ (Rom. 10:9–17). Within this context, the only substantive difference between *The Crucified God* and *The Church in the Power of the Spirit* is that the latter propounds what might be called postponed

120

triumphalism or proleptic triumphalism, in partial distinction from pure triumphalism. Moltmann may now be fighting anti-Judaism at the essential point of opposing churchly triumphalism as a present historical evil. But his own absolutism and triumphalism have not been overcome at the all-decisive point of living human relations with Jews today.[60] The knowledgeable Jew will simply ask, how does your new position differ in substance from the old view you now appear to be criticizing? For there is really no difference between saying that Jesus Christ is the one whom Jews must accept now and saying in the final reckoning it is Jesus Christ who will redeem them. In truth, from a moral standpoint the second position may be identified as more lamentable because it acts to subject the Jewish future to a fate over which the Jewish people are deprived of any say or control. Their dignity as human beings is impugned as much as or more than ever. Moreover, the spiritual pride of the Christian believer remains as a corrupting influence.

ASSESSMENT FROM WITHIN

To conclude our exposition and evaluation of Jürgen Moltmann's work, we suggest that the version of Christian faith this theologian advances is not to be criticized upon arbitrary or external grounds; instead, it deserves to be approached as though from within—that is, upon the moral foundation that he himself provides. Certain of his own presuppositions and reasoning combine to offer the foremost argumentation against his conclusions. Moltmann is struggling courageously to create a post-Holocaust theology. Yet he cannot escape the fact that *The Crucified God* comprises, in essence, pre-Holocaust thinking, and that the same is the case, in somewhat qualified measure, with *The Church in the Power in the Spirit*.[61] In fact, Moltmann explicitly insisted to us that his later volume involves no shift within his theological point of view.[62]

Specifically, the problem centers in the nature and genuineness of human liberation. It is our conviction that Christianity's history and its consequences, considered especially from the standpoint of that world-transforming event called the Endlösung, have seriously called into question many dogmatic Christian affirmations and claims. In social, psychological, and political terms, the plight of the Christian faith is that it has been taken prisoner by ideology, an ideology pervaded by a terrible irony because it seems deprived of any means to transcend itself and to learn thereby the truth of its own entrapment. The Christian faith, which is supposed to bring freedom, is transmuted into an apologetic weapon while identifying itself as transapologetic. Christians are reputedly enabled, with the aid of the gospel, to expose the falsehoods, evils, and wiles of those who do not assent to or benefit from the gospel of liberation. But a grim specter stands over the world Christian community. What of the dreadful eventuality that many of those whom Christians seek to identify as slaves may in truth be free men and women, those they endeavor to portray as free (namely, themselves) are in truth slaves—for example, slaves to both a pre-Holocaust and a Holocaust-preparing past that extends back through Martin Luther to Chrysostom and to Paul, to the fate-bearing and enslaving dichotomization of "gospel" and "law"?

Is there any exit from this moral plight, a means whereby the Endlösung itself is transfigured? At the close of chapter 3 we spoke of the Holocaust as *metanoia*, a turning around of the world. Can a comparable revolutionary ferment somehow invade the church? Can Christians come under the power of *metanoia*, total revolution, genuine liberation, under "the power of the Spirit," to resort to Moltmann's Pauline terminology? We shall have more to say concerning this possibility, this hope, but for the present there may be some positive relevances in the judgments of two Catholic theologians.

Rebecca Chopp asserts that the Scriptures "must go through a process of deideologisation in two senses." First, the "concrete socio-political context" must be utilized as we interpret any text. Second, deideologisation requires us to examine and recognize the "systematic distortions, or the false consciousness, within the text itself. . . . Christians cannot purge the text, but by remembering the horrors resulting from the text and this suffering in the past and present, Christians may be able to live their faith as witness that such distortion and persecution shall never again occur. The New Testament prejudice against the Jews must be rendered explicit and accepted as a real distortion within Christianity."[63]

More radically, Rosemary Ruether finds the resolution of the Christian moral-theological problem only in the church's unqualified repudiation of its antithetical theology (*gegensätzliche Theologie*) and its "realized eschatology." Ruether asks, "Is it possible to say 'Jesus is Messiah' without, implicitly or explicitly, saying at the same time 'and the Jews be damned'?" She answers, only if the Christian affirmation is relativized into a "theology of hope," which will free it of anti-Jewish imperialism, and indeed of all religious imperialism. The "theology of hope" is, of course, linked to the name of Jürgen Moltmann. But, as we have seen, much appears hopeless in this theorization. Since his theology is so much a part of and so typical of the mainstream of the churches' teaching, must we conclude that Christian thought is, of necessity, marked with moral hopelessness? Or can there be a theology that sustains genuine hope, the joy of liberation?

Ruether further states: "The self-infinitizing of the messianic sect that empowers itself to conquer all mankind in the name of the universal" is essentially "a false messianism. What Christianity has in Jesus is not the Messiah but a Jew who hoped for the coming of the Kingdom of God and who died in that hope."[64] Short of this kind of judgment, is there any way to acknowledge the double crisis of Christian relevance and Christian identity as emphasized by Moltmann himself?[65] And, of incalculably greater importance, is there any other way to receive ultimate Christian liberation from complicity in the Final Solution? In alternative terminology, is there any resolution of our problem apart from the total humanization of theology? Perhaps Jürgen Moltmann's developing thought may yet complete a journey along such possibly saving roads, and one day it may become, accordingly, a true theology of hope.[66]

6

LIBERATION :
MODEL 3

No Christian theology, teaching, or symbol can be true which
has the effect of systematically devaluing and denying the existence, authenticity, and rights to interpretation of others.
Mary Knutsen, "The Holocaust in Theology and Philosophy"

We have considered two responses to the Holocaust: the Endlösung
as effectively a nonevent, and the Endlösung as a partially influential
event. In the former the Christian church's unholy past is perpetuated.
In the latter deliverance from that past is initiated. Chapters 6 and 7 are
written on behalf of a third possibility, the Holocaust as determinative
of theological and moral revolution.

From the Roman Catholic side, Gregory Baum declares:

The message of the Holocaust to Christian theology . . . is that *at whatever
cost* to its own self-understanding, the church must be willing to confront
the ideologies implicit in its doctrinal tradition. We must be willing to sever
ourselves from the ideological deformations, whatever they may be, *even if*
we do not know as yet how to formulate the positive content of God's revelation in Jesus Christ. . . . We cannot afford, at this time, to be afraid. And in
my mind, *this ongoing conversion of the church to truth* includes the
correction of *all* its implicit ideologies, not just the anti-Jewish trend.[1]

And, from the Protestant side, Paul van Buren adjudges:

Having begun by taking Jews into account in a way not known before in the
history of Christianity, at least a few Christians have begun to realize that a
reconsideration of what Christians have been saying about Judaism and of
Christian-Jewish relations must lead to a reconsideration of Christianity itself. . . . Theology can shut its eyes and pretend that the Holocaust never
happened and that Israel doesn't exist. Theology has shown itself capable of
such blindness before! But if there are prospects for serious theology, for a
theology not hopelessly blind to matters that pertain to the heart of its task,

124

then the time has come for a reconsideration of the whole theological and Christian enterprise of the most radical sort. . . . [The command out of Auschwitz] is that we accept a judgment on something false lying close to the very heart of our tradition, and that like Abraham, we have to set out on a journey of radical reconstruction not knowing the final destination. If theology does not hear that voice of command to go, if it shuts its ears to the voice of Auschwitz, then I see no reason to bother ourselves or anyone else with a discussion of the prospects for theology.[2]

From France, Catholic priest Bernard Dupuy adds:

Little by little . . . the representatives of the Churches agree that Christian responsibility [in the events which led to the Nazi genocide] was not limited to faults committed by individual Christians but emerged from the age-old teaching of the Church on Judaism and Jews. [Therefore] the task of contemporary Christianity must be to replace the teaching of contempt by the teaching of esteem. After having ejected Israel from its thinking, the Christian world must today restore Israel to its proper theological place. . . . If, after all that happened, the Church refuses to remember and to listen to the voices calling out to her from Auschwitz, if she does not examine her conscience and does not commit herself to this ongoing task of strengthening the link between the Church and the Jewish people, if she remains silent, then she will indeed be increasing her guilt, thus bearing a heavy responsibility for the future. For let us not delude ourselves: *all this could happen again*.[3]

The Christian churches and Christian thinking are challenged by two inseparable questions. How seriously are they going to treat the singular event of the rediscovered Holocaust? How seriously are they going to take the moral consequences of the traditional Christian teachings concerning the Jewish people and Judaism? Emil L. Fackenheim suggests that the link between Christian affirmation and Christian antisemitism has become *the* question for contemporary Christianity.[4]

As a means to the end of Christian *metanoia*, we shall be dealing with selected areas of the church's teaching and experience in the light of several compelling norms: the dictates of historical truth; the consensual standards of Jewish and Christian morality; the loving faithfulness of God; the subjecting of certain affirmations of faith to judgment at the hands of historical events; the challenges of existential rationality; and the indispensableness of political power and political values.

THE OBJECTIVITY
OF GUILT

It is imperative that we first dissociate ourselves from a particular form of subjective fixation upon Christian "guilt feelings" respecting antisemitism. This judgment is harmonious, we suggest, with James Parkes's persistent stress upon the critical, all-decisive character of objective historical truth and its lessons. In making the point, we in no way turn our backs upon the new historiography, with its finding of the massive Christian contribution to the Holocaust. A singular pioneer in this very historiography, Parkes himself has nonetheless always avoided a fixation on guilt.

The indefatigable editor of *Encounter Today*, Sister Marie-Thérèse de Sion of Paris, has lamented what she calls "certain masochistic trends" among today's Christians who, finding their lives darkened by the shadows of Auschwitz, "burden themselves" with guilt feelings for a presumed collective guilt. Such Christians, she contends, only "surprise their Jewish friends who detect here a pathological 'lack of dignity.'"[5] Sister Marie-Thérèse, who has labored tirelessly and even heroically for Jewish-Christian reconciliation, nevertheless utters here only a partial truth. Were she speaking of certain parties, she would be presenting the whole truth, but she is alluding to Rosemary Ruether and her *Faith and Fratricide*. That work is surely not above criticism, but it is not properly subject to the particular criticism Sister Marie-Thérèse makes. As a matter of fact, in *Liberation Theology*, Ruether herself rightly insists that no reconciliation with a person who exploits and defames others is possible, until and unless the humanity of the evildoer is somehow acknowledged together with the humanity of those he has oppressed.[6] The difficulty with Sister Marie-Thérèse's appraisal is that she does not distinguish between subjective guilt feelings and the objective pathology of the Christian world, as the latter is chronicled by Ruether.

Will D. Campbell, in reckoning with American racism, observes that this phenomenon is not a mere subjective attitude or prejudice; it is the condition, the objective structure in which the American people live and move and have their being. In consequence, so Campbell attests, if we are white, we are racist.[7] This applies not only to all American gentiles, but also to all American Jews, except, of course, Jews who are also blacks. So, too, with those of us who are Christians, and this by no means excludes black Christians: to be a part of the Christian domain is to participate in that objective demonic structure called antisemitism.

126

Accordingly, although we must not display subjective guilt feelings or in any way abide masochism, truthfully Christians are enmeshed within a special objective condition. They are assailed by an ontology of guilt, by the being of guilt, a condition inexorably bound to a particular story, to certain given historical facts. Nevertheless, a partial qualification is necessary. Not all of the Christian world has been entangled with the objective condition of antisemitism. Some Christians have been spared the moral culpability and fate of Roman Catholic, Eastern Orthodox, and Protestant Christians within the western world. We cannot rightfully impute to other Christians our own historic hostilities to the Jewish people. Thus, many Christians in the Third World have not even known of the Christian contribution to Nazism; they have been kept rather free of the antisemitic influences associated with and made politically inevitable by the entrenched social and cultural power of western Christendom. However, at least two facts point to the solidarity in sin of all Christians: contemporary antipathies toward the Jewish people of the State of Israel within Christian segments of the Third World; and the universal Christian possession of and allegiance to the New Testament, with its antisemitic proclivities, as a decisive spiritual authority. It is impossible to overcome Christian enmity toward Jews without vanquishing the absolutism of the Christian gospel.[8] All Christians face the challenge to reconcile the reputed Word of God in the New Testament with justice and understanding for Jews.

From the foregoing analysis it follows that the responsibility of Christians, as against beating their breasts in self-hatred and self-agonizing, is to turn away from their subjectivities and fight for the objective transformation of the relevant teachings and moral condition of modern Christianity. If it is the case that the German Nazi Endlösung comprises an ultimate incarnation of the church's teaching of contempt for the Jews and Judaism, the only way to wage effective war upon this consequence is through a pervasive revolution in Christian doctrine and behavior, involving the most radical surgery and the most radical theological reconstruction. Without such a revolution, the church and its adherents will quite possibly contribute to future attempts to obliterate the Jewish people. The one thing Christians of today can do about the Holocaust is to work against its repetition.

What revolutionary Christian responses must be advised? What steps must the Christian community take, along the frontier, along the pathway to human liberation? We shall be speaking ideally, in large measure, although in truth certain signs of hope have already manifested themselves within the Christian world.

127

The exposition to follow in part offers proposals not yet made in this book and in part summarizes and reviews affirmations already given voice. The section "The Jews and Jesus Christ" responds to the traditional Christian charge of Jewish unfaithfulness. "The Faithfulness of God" respresents God's fidelity to his people, in opposition to Christian supersessionism. "Theology of the Cross" proposes a post-Holocaust understanding of the cross of Jesus. "The Issue of the Resurrection" addresses the most serious of all theological problems in the Christian-Jewish relationship. "Reaffirmations" refers briefly to two proposals made in earlier pages—a post-Holocaust determination to abolish the making of special demands of Jews, by any party including God—and further assesses the morality of the "trial of God." And "Political Power and the People Israel," endeavors to apply the lessons of the Holocaust to the morality of political sovereignty. Throughout, we try to honor Irving Greenberg's principle that no statement, theological or other, can be made "that would not be credible in the presence of the burning children."[9]

THE JEWS AND
JESUS CHRIST

The claim that the Jewish people are deservedly chastised by God for rejecting the one true faith is among the most socially fateful Christian traditions. The Christian revolutionary will identify this allegation for what it is, a calumny.

Every year the defamation gains a renewed lease on life during so-called Holy Week, more correctly identifiable as Unholy Week. Historian and Anglican clergyman James Parkes attested that his Christian conscience no longer permitted him to enter a church during Holy Week, and the Christian educator Heinz Kremers of the University of Duisburg observes that the Passion story remains "the most dangerous root of anti-Jewish emotions among German school-children."[10] The calumny is aided and abetted all across the United States by television films, including Franco Zeffirelli's much-touted *Jesus of Nazareth*, that reach far more people than church services do. Adding fuel to the fire are the many productions of Passion plays, generally not viewed as ordinary theatrical dramas with allowance for dramatic license or questionable elements but as sacred drama to be accorded reverence and

128

acceptance as the truth.[11] The blame is not, however, exclusively that of filmmakers, play producers, or even succeeding generations of clergy. Such people are simply carrying forward the falsehoods of the New Testament and of the ecclesiastical tradition.

There are two sides to the matter: the reputed spurning of Jesus as the Messiah, the Christ, on the part of "the Jews"; and alleged Jewish blameworthiness in the Crucifixion of the "Son of God."

On the first side, the Jewish community cannot and will not accept Jesus as the Christ. An all-decisive reason for this is that our world remains unredeemed. Hence, Jesus could not be the promised Messiah. Although this is not to imply that Jewish teaching treats the Messiah as a divine savior,[12] yet the coming of the Messiah is peculiarly linked in Jewish thought to an objective transformation of life wrought by God. Jewish insistence upon the fact that Jesus cannot have been the Messiah, sustained as it is by almost two full millennia of experience, received climactic vindication in the Endlösung, the ultimate act of unredemptiveness. Here lies the source of the lament that with the Holocaust it is "too late for the Messiah to come."[13] Theologically and positively speaking, the Jewish nonacceptance of Jesus as the expected or promised Christ is a case of Israel's persisting faithfulness to the covenant. David Tracy recognizes this when he points out that Christians need to "retrieve, theologically, the eschatological reality of the not yet [of Messianic times] as a historical reality" as well as the "radical not yet in our age disclosed . . . in the Holocaust." Then Christians can "recall that the concept Messiah cannot (by being spiritualized) be divorced from the reality of Messianic times."[14]

On the question of the Jews and the fate of Jesus—an issue that rates only summary treatment at most—the fact is that they and their leaders would have had nothing to do with any betrayal of one of their countrymen to the hated Roman occupying power. This consideration is discussed in the important but predictably ignored study by Haim Cohn, *The Trial and Death of Jesus*. We earlier alluded to Cohn's analysis of the impossibility of any Jewish legal or religious condemnation of Jesus. When we keep in mind the numerous provisions of Jewish law that would rule out any capital sentencing of Jesus through a "Jewish trial" on the charge of blasphemy (see n. 20, chap. 5, as well as such other factors as the falsity of the tradition that the Romans were accustomed to release malefactors at Jewish festival times (see the account of Barabbas; Mark 15:6–15), we are enabled to recognize the massive speciousness of the New Testament on the subject of Jesus' trial and death. Haim Cohn concludes his work with these words:

129

Hundreds of generations of Jews, throughout the Christian world, have been indiscriminately mulcted for a crime which neither they nor their ancestors committed. Worse still, they have for centuries, for millennia, been made to suffer all manner of torment, persecution, and degradation for the alleged part of their forefathers in the trial and crucifixion of Jesus, when, in solemn truth, their forefathers took no part in them but did all they possibly and humanly could to save Jesus . . . from his tragic end at the hands of the Roman oppressor. If there can be found a grain of consolation for this perversion of justice, it is in the words of Jesus himself: "Blessed are they which are persecuted for righteousness' sake: for theirs is the kingdom of heaven. Blessed are ye, when men shall revile you, and persecute you, and shall say all manner of evil against you falsely, for my sake. Rejoice, and be exceeding glad: for great is your reward in heaven" (Matt. 5:10–12).[15]

It is necessary to insert a caveat in the name of realism. Regrettably, historical analysis is a highly limited weapon in making wholesome the emotional commitments of human beings and in counteracting their volitional prejudices. The New Testament documents are not objective history; they are polemical, evangelical tracts. But this datum cuts two ways: On the one hand, it reflects the fact that the records cannot be finally received as bearers of objective truth; on the other hand, it also points up the consideration that the Christian world is wedded to these documents. Scholarly analysis is severely restricted in its function of redeeming the human bias derived from and perpetuated by them. As the Christian scholar Ulrich Simon of King's College, London, points out, the defamation of the Jewish people in the Gospel of John, that New Testament book most dear to Christian piety, constitutes in and of itself an incitement to corporate murder.[16] It is wrong to maintain that the New Testament as such is antisemitic; but to shut our eyes to the antisemitic elements in the New Testament is equally foolish and irresponsible.

The Christian reformer has his work cut out. His chances of exerting creative influence are not great if he limits himself to the idealistic notion that disseminating the truth about history will bring about changes in human behavior. It is essential, therefore, that he not hamstring himself by espousing one method alone.

In a single sentence, Ignaz Maybaum points up the necessity for extrahistorical strategies and also authenticates our judgment that the alleged Jewish responsibility for the death of Jesus deserves no more than cursory treatment: "The ancient tradition that 'the Jews killed Christ' . . . has its origin in the twilight between myth and history and is therefore not accessible to historical research."[17]

Both the Christian and Jewish realist recognizes that antisemitism is seldom overcome by logical arguments or proofs of the falsehoods involved; it is a matter of conversion. One is only *converted* into becoming an opponent of hatred of Jews.

THE FAITHFULNESS
OF GOD

Christian supersessionism is the notion that the Christian community of faith has replaced the people Israel as the divine instrument of salvation. The view has as its corollary that Jews must be missionized if they are to be brought to the truth, the Christian gospel. What may the Christian revolutionary say to this?

Is not the persuasion that the Christian church has superseded Israel an affront to the Ruler of the Universe, who has promised that he will be forever true to the people of Abraham, Isaac, and Jacob (Gen. 17:13, 19; Lev. 24:8; 2 Sam. 23:5; 1 Chron. 16:17; Ezek. 37:26; and so on)? The General Synod of the Reformed Church of Holland has declared that the election of Israel is continued in the Jewish people today because the faithfulness of God does not falter or come to an end.[18] Accordingly, any assault upon the ongoing integrity of original Israel, the chosen of God, is an assault upon God for daring to remain faithful to this people. The Dutch Christians do not make the point, but Christian conversionism is forbidden because the effort to change the Jewish community into a part of the Christian church is a veiled attack, often unknowing, upon the foundation of the church and hence upon the Christian faith itself. The foundation of the church is the Israel of God. If the Jewish people are not the elder brothers and sisters within the family of God, it follows that the gentiles as reputedly adopted younger brothers and sisters actually remain lost and without hope (see Eph. 2: 12). The covenant into which they are ostensibly led by means of the event of Jesus the Jew becomes a delusion. Conversionism aimed at Jews reverses the true course of the history of salvation and turns upside down the structure of salvation history. Such conversionism implicitly assails Christianity. It is a Christian impossibility—not for pragmatic reasons, so dear to some religious thinkers, but for reasons of theological principles.[19]

Some of West Germany's churchmen are ready to be even more radical in their reasons for rejecting efforts to convert Jews. Reinhold Mayer of the University of Tübingen, although a member of the study commission that produced the EKD statement *Christen und Juden*, writes that the mission to Jews in whatever form, is, "anachronistic and degrading," a kind of behavior that Jews "in faithfulness to their calling cannot take seriously." Two other members of the EKD commission speak in the same way. Rolf Rendtorff insists that Jews are not to be treated as potential Christians; they possess their own inner integrity. And Heinz Kremers believes that Christians are called, as Pope John XXIII said, simply to accept Jews as equal brothers.[20]

In 1980 the Synod of the Protestant Church of the Rhineland, the largest synod in West Germany, issued a document of singular importance. Relevant to the present discussion, it insisted on the permanent election of the Jewish people, their continuing significance for salvation history, the recognition that through Jesus Christ the church is taken into the covenant of God *with* His people, and especially the following: "We believe that in their calling Jews and Christians are always witnesses of God in the presence of the world and before each other. Therefore, we are convinced that *the church may not express its witness toward the Jewish people as it* does its mission to the peoples of the world."[21]

Although the Holocaust does not motivate the Christian reformer's struggle against conversionism, as evident from the foregoing paragraphs, that event has served nonetheless to bring home the consequences of the erstwhile Christian program to convert Jews. We referred in chapter 5 to the interpretation of the missionary stance toward Jews as a form of spiritual Final Solution. Here is a terrible reminder that the Christian supersessionism and triumphalism which helped ensure the Endlösung also serve today, in effect, to sustain the German Nazi program. Supersessionist theology is a carrier, it carries the germs of genocide, but the genocide only of Jews.

THEOLOGY OF THE CROSS

Johann-Baptist Metz tells his theology students, "Never again . . . do theology in such a way that its construction remains unaffected, or could remain unaffected, by Auschwitz. . . . Ask yourself if the theology you are learning is such that it could remain unchanged before and after Auschwitz. If this is the case, be on your guard!" This is an "apparently very simple, but, in fact, extremely demanding criterion."[22]

When we apply this criterion to the Christian theology of the cross/ the Crucifixion, where are we led? The Christian revolutionary will strive to rethink certain understandings of the cross of Jesus, and particularly the assertion that the cross represents the ultimate in human Godforsakenness. In chapter 5's "The Fate of Golgotha" we considered some aspects of Christian interpretation of that event that cannot pass Metz's test. Now we have the temerity to envisage a post-Holocaust affirmation/confession that may do so: the crucifixion of the nonresurrecting Christ and the nonresurrection (as yet) of the crucified Jesus.

This potential interpretation may be formulated in at least two alternative ways: (1) absolute Godforsakenness, until the still future resurrection, which means the future resurrection of Jesus, as of others; or (2) the pure faith of Christian Judaism, not to be confused with Jewish Christianity, which is the faith of Jews and not of gentiles. However, we here comment only upon the former alternative.

First, let us remember, as Franklin Sherman reminds us, that the cross was a Jewish reality of suffering and martyrdom long before Jesus and for several centuries after. On occasion, thousands were crucified at a time. Behind the Christian "interpretations surrounding this man who suffered as a Jew is the Jewish reality that should make Christians the first to identify with the sufferings of any Jews."[23] Jesus remains, in this sense and in reality, a representative, a *Stellvertreter*, of his people.

When asked, or even challenged, by Christians about why the Jewish people are unwilling to let the past be the past, to bury the memories and get on with the present, Elie Wiesel has gently but pointedly reminded them: You Christians have been remembering the death of one Jew for almost 2,000 years and making it the pivotal point of your faith. Are we not to remember the death of six million Jews in our own time and anguish over the implications?

The question Christians must face is whether there is an "absolute Godforsakenness" that transcends and overcomes the Christian claim regarding Jesus' experience. Jürgen Moltmann adjudges that due to Jesus' "full consciousness that God is close at hand in his grace," his total abandonment and deliverance up to death, as one rejected, are the very torment of hell and put at stake the very deity of Jesus' God and Father.[24] How is that different from the conviction of many pious Jews during the *Shoah* that God (Ribbono Shel Olam) was with them and would somehow, miraculously, save their community? We suggest that this particular "abomination of desolation" simply does not stand up as the absolute horror upon which Christian faith can and should, dialectically, build its hope. We contend that in comparison with certain other sufferings, Jesus' agony and death become relatively nondecisive. Here is a description of the disposal of Jewish children in Auschwitz in the late summer of 1944:

> When the Hungarian Jews arrived we used a music camouflage. At the time the children were burned on big piles of wood. The crematoria could not work at the time, and therefore the people were just burned in open fields with those grills, and also children were burned among them. Children were crying helplessly and that is why the camp administration ordered that an orchestra be assembled of a hundred inmates and should play. They played very loud all the time. They played the Blue Danube or Rosamunde; so that even the people in the city of Auschwitz could not hear the screams. Without the orchestra they would have heard the screams of horror; they would have been horrible screams. The people two kilometers from there could even hear those screams, namely, the ones that came from the transports of children. The children were separated from their parents, and then they were put in Section III camp. Maybe the number of children was several thousand.
>
> And then on one special day they started burning them to death. The gas chambers at the time were out of order, at least one of them was out of order, namely the one near the crematorium; it was destroyed by mutiny in a special commando operation in August, 1944. The other three gas chambers were full of the adults and therefore the children were not gassed, but just burned alive.
>
> When one of the SS people sort of had pity with the children, he would take a child and beat the head against a stone before putting it on the pile of fire and wood, so that the child lost consciousness. However, the regular way they did it was just throwing the children on the pile.
>
> They used to put a sheet of wood, then the whole thing was sprinkled with petrol, then wood again, and petrol—and then people were placed there. Then the whole thing was lighted.[25]

A woman prisoner in Auschwitz remembers all too vividly the quiet night in the summer of 1944 (quiet only because the backlog of corpses to be dealt with had put a tempory halt on arriving transports) when their somber consideration of the night sky reddened by the gigantic flames of the burning pits was suddenly shattered by the screaming of children. It was "as if a single scream had been torn out of hundreds of mouths, a single scream of fear and unusual pain, a scream repeated a thousand times in the single word, 'Mama,' a scream that increased in intensity every second enveloping the whole camp and every inmate." Without even being aware of their own actions, the women joined their own screams of despair to those of the unknown children. Not until the next day did they learn from some of the men prisoners what had been happening: The SS had loaded the children into wheelbarrows and dumped them into the fiery ravines.[26]

The Galilean was at least a grown man; a mature man, a man with a mission, and by all the evidence a courageous man, who set his face steadfastly to go up to Jerusalem (Lu. 9:5). In contrast, there has occurred within this world and within the present epoch an evil that is more terrible than other evils, a Godforsakenness that is worse by an infinity of infinities. This is the evil and Godforsakenness of little children witnessing the murder of other little children while knowing that they also are to be murdered in the same way, being aware absolutely that they face the identical fate. Before this kind of event, the death of Jesus upon the cross is lost in relative moral nonsignificance. The Godforsakenness of Jesus has proved to be nonabsolute, if it ever were absolute. The Godforsakenness of the Jewish children is a final horror that bears within itself an ultimate *Einzigartigkeit* (unique uniqueness): Their passion stands in judgment upon making Jesus' passion the foundation of Christian faith.[27] At most, the continuing representation of Jesus' crucifixion in this way reflects pre-Holocaust theology; it is not theology "after Auschwitz."

In adducing the present point we do not renege upon the judgment put forth in chapter 3 that any and every instance of human agony must be received in equal and qualitative terms, rather than comparatively or competitively. We submit, however, that there is a moral and existential difference between human suffering as such and the suffering of children, due to such factors as innocence and, above all, the uncomprehending quality of the anguish of these little creatures of God. Moreover, the adult sufferer has at least had a chance to realize some kind of personal fulfillment.

THE ISSUE OF THE RESURRECTION

The Christian revolutionary will insist upon a genuine reaffirmation of Jewishness, which entails radical historicalness. It is not correct to say that Jewish thinking unexceptionably takes history and historical events seriously; many in the Orthodox community do not. Nevertheless, historicalness as a norm within Jewry is supported by a long and weighty religious and moral tradition. Eugene Borowitz has referred to history as "the laboratory of Jewish theology."[28]

We must make clear at the beginning of this most decisive of all our steps that the avowal of Jewish historicalness is not to be confused with the efforts of so-called Judaizers, or with Jewish Christianity.[29] We speak in behalf of Christian Jewishness, with the accent always on the adjective. The rediscovery of Jewishness as the bedrock of the Christian faith does not and cannot be permitted to mean reductionism. Against all reductionist temptations, the Christian reformer will assert the integrity of his faith: "In Christ [the Jew] God was reconciling the world [kosmos] to himself" (2 Cor. 5:19). There is a universe of difference between this Pauline affirmation and the idolatrous notion that Christ was God, reconciling the world to himself. We must stress *the world* in contradistinction to Israel, God's firstborn, for Israel already lives in his presence, as Franz Rosenzweig put the matter.[30]

The event of Jesus is the joy that ends the desolation of those who have been without hope. Jesus became, in a way unforeseen by himself in his lifetime, a second Abraham, the Abraham of the gentiles, patriarch to the pagans. We who are gentiles must somehow be rescued from religion, from all pitiful gods that tempt us, from all our idolatries. When Jesus is turned into an idol[31]—seven words that form a most fitting single title for the whole story of Christendom—we are only returned to our pagan sins, our idolatries, our hopelessness. The Christian is given the chance to live out a unique and independently valid challenge to be an adopted child of God, within the covenant of promise. In the course of his pilgrimage from time to eternity, the Christian must never leave the bedrock of Jewish historicalness. It gives meaning to his life, ever helping him to separate truth from heresy.

We cannot lose sight of the stubborn truth that a nonconversionist viewpoint respecting Jews, however much it may aid reconciliation between Christians and Jews, does not in itself reduce obstacles to solidarity with peoples of other faiths. On the contrary, the very affirmation that, through Jesus, we who are gentiles are enabled to become part of the Israel of God, serves to point up an unhappy division within humanity, the division between Israel (Jews and Christians) and all those who remain beyond the covenant of promise. The only way to counteract possible hostility to these other peoples is through relativization, the unqualified acknowledgment that our way is not the only possible way to salvation or the good life.[32] It cannot be overstressed that this acknowledgment accords with major emphases within the Jewish tradition. Through his very participation in Jewishness, the Christian is helped to surmount exclusivism and intolerance.

The fact stands that a widely accepted theological schema gnaws at the vitals of the Christian church, a schema according to which the Cross-Resurrection-Parousia is effectively made into a solely decisive series of events for salvation. More precisely, as Heinz Kremers comments critically, in the thinking of many Christians such a series of events transcends the ordinary realm of history, forever taking precedence over all historical happenings.[33] Thus, Alan T. Davies speaks of the Crucifixion and the Resurrection, which for him lie along "the margin of history," as qualifying "the extent to which Christian faith can accept new revelatory moments."[34] A ready consequence of this schema is that Christianity itself becomes a wholly transcendent "reality," moving in entirely "spiritual" ways above the flux of history. History is no longer open to God's presence, in direct contrast to a dominant emphasis within Judaism. This Christian outlook easily turns into forms of absolutism and triumphalism, or of particularism wearing a camouflage of universal truth. As we have seen, by equating the suffering and death of Jesus with the very torment of hell, Jürgen Moltmann in effect denies any crucial theological significance to the Holocaust. At most, the latter event can possess only ancillary significance because the very hell of Godforsakenness preceded it and, indeed, furnishes prototypical substance for the Holocaust itself.

If we are to be human beings without reservation, that is, fully historical beings, how can we remain bound by certain original salvational processes, which, through dogmatic presentment, rule out the moral and theological decisiveness of other happenings? However, it is not alone as "fully human beings" that we must assert the significance of historical events. We face a strange but fundamental paradox: The Jewish and Christian traditions themselves call us to this assertion. Irving Greenberg writes: "For traditional Jews to ignore or deny all significance to this event [the *Shoah*] would be to repudiate the fundamental belief and affirmations of the Sinai covenant: that history is meaning-ful, and that ultimate liberation and relationship to God will take place in the realm of human events."[35] Once the Christian casts aside this in-sistence upon historicalness, he abandons the biblical *Weltanschauung*. Again, whatever else is meant by the "third person" of the Trinity, that person points out the significance of post-New Testament *historical* life. In the worldly unfolding of events, a crucial acting out of the di-vine-human drama is to be found and with it fresh apprehensions of God herself.

It must be asserted, however, that when we turn to the question of the Resurrection of Jesus Christ, our problem is seen to be infinitely sharper than the potential denial of the religious significance of various historical events. True, the effort is sometimes made to establish a posi-tive relation between the allegedly saving event of the Resurrection and the devilish event of the Holocaust. Ulrich E. Simon, for example, testi-fies that without the Resurrection the Endlösung is nothing other than pure hell.[36] Beyond the fact that alternative human experiences can be described as hellish, there remains no comparison between the Cruci-fixion and the Resurrection at the point of theological and moral deci-sion making. A simple but crucial reason is that, although there is no doubt at all that the Crucifixion occurred (granting that the interpreta-tions of the event are legion), there are grave questions respecting what it means to talk about the reality of the Resurrection.

We have cited Emil L. Fackenheim's query of whether the link be-tween Christian affirmation and Christian antisemitism is today the central moral issue for the church. As a means of facing up to this query some Christian theologians have called for a recovery of Jewish-ness within the church. But what is that recovery to mean? Many times these days we read or hear Christian representatives saying that the persisting presence of Christian antisemitism demands a wholehearted rethinking of the church's teachings. Yet it soon becomes apparent that many such people have no intention of surrendering or even of refor-mulating major doctrines of their faith, even though these very teach-ings cause the trouble.

The ultimate test case is the Resurrection, for two reasons. First, the faith of countless Christians has at its center the consummated Resur-rection of Jesus Christ. "If Christ has not been raised, . . . your faith is vain"—so writes the apostle Paul (1 Cor. 15:14).[37] Second, the one place for the reaffirmation of Jewishness to happen, if it is to happen at all, is in connection with the momentous and all-determining tenet of the

Resurrection. *A genuine rediscovery of Jewishness has to mean the taking of historical fact with utter seriousness,* in contrast to the negations of Greek and Manichean spirituality. Jewishness means a denial of any consummated resurrection, until the present time in history and beyond today.

The church traditionally asserts that with the Resurrection the eschatological or messianic era began, for in that event Jesus Christ "is exalted to be Lord of the dawning *kingdom* of God; and he is transfigured into the Lord of the coming *glory* of God. . . . God the Father glorifies Christ the Son through his resurrection. . . ."[38] The End-time is thus brought into the present world; the eschatological future is historicized. But that is not all. Through the continuous and contemporaneous asserted truth that in Jesus Christ the eschatological domain entered into human history in definitive, salvational form, Christianity has legitimized historically-theologically its supersessionism and triumphalism over Judaism and the Jewish people, as well as its exclusivism toward other faiths. As Rosemary Ruether has shown in *Faith and Fratricide* and elsewhere, with massive historical support and authentication, this Christological eschatology is the root of Christian negation of and antipathy toward Jews and Judaism. Yet the church feels no guilt and reassures itself because dogma teaches that the Resurrection is not a mere human idea or human spiritual experience but is exclusively a deed of God. It is God who, through a special sacred-historical act, vindicates the Christian faith in the face of its denial by the overwhelming majority of Jews.

The Christian moral plight is epitomized most explicitly in the combination of theological ideas presented by Wolfhart Pannenberg (although they are hardly unique to him): (1)"Through the cross of Jesus, the Jewish legal tradition as a whole has been set aside in its claim to contain the eternal will of God in its final formulation." (2)"The law" is consummated, fulfilled in Jesus. (3)Jesus himself stood in opposition to a hardened Jewish "law" and came into fundamental conflict with that "positive Israelite legal tradition which had become calcified as 'the law' after the exile." (4)Jesus' "claim to authority through which he put himself in God's place, was . . . blasphemous for Jewish ears" and accordingly he was "slandered by the Jews before the Roman governor as a rebel." (5)Through the Resurrection of Jesus the God of Israel confirmed Jesus' position against "the law," from which he sought to liberate his fellow Jews, and his claim of divine authority. Pannenberg has again and again repeated these statements with particular emphasis on

139

the last point. Thus, in an interfaith colloquium at Harvard University, he reiterated that the Resurrection "obviously means the divine confirmation of Jesus' claim . . . that the eschatological reality of the Kingdom of God was already present in his life and work . . . that in Jesus the future of the divine Kingdom has already become a present reality. This phenomenon lies behind the later dogmatic concepts of the incarnation."[39]

If it is correct that the Christian historicizing of eschatological reality is the foundation of Christian antisemitism, and if it is correct that the center and proof of Christianity is the event of the Resurrection, then any continued advocacy of the Resurrection appears to represent in clear and authoritative form the fateful, culpable union of the Christian message and the murder camps. It also contains the Christian ideological contribution to a potential *future* Holocaust of the Jewish people. Furthermore, in the dispensation F.S., Christians cannot plead innocent to the charge of complicity, for the evidence is all too clear. Nevertheless, the advocacy of the Resurrection goes on, along with all its implicit or explicit anti-Jewish component, year in and year out, in church after church—perhaps even without full awareness of the antisemitic poison that is being absorbed in the process of worshipping the God of Truth and Love.

What are we to do?

At this juncture we need to recall the warning of the Catholic theologian quoted at the opening of the section "Theology of the Cross": "Never again . . . do theology in such a way that its construction remains unaffected, or could remain unaffected, by Auschwitz." Let us try to apply this caveat to the present pivotal issue.

One revisionist alternative is to shift the foundation of Christian teaching from the supersessionism of Christology and Resurrection to something else—something such as an emphasis on the inclusion of Christians within the covenantal life of Israel.

A second revisionist alternative is to retain Jesus' Resurrection as a divine event that has happened but to strive to redeem it of its triumphalist and replacement connotations. Jacobus (Coos) Schoneveld, a Dutch Protestant who lived and worked in Israel thirteen years as representative of the Netherlands Reformed Church and who now resides in West Germany as General Secretary of the International Council of Christians and Jews, sees the need to return the Resurrection to its original context: the sacred history of Israel. As he puts it:

The Resurrection means the vindication of Jesus as a Jew, as a person who was faithful to the Torah, as a martyr who participated in Jewish martyrdom for the sanctification of God's Name. What else can this mean than the validation of the Torah and vindication of the Jewish people as God's beloved people? The Resurrection of Jesus confirms God's promises as well as God's commandments to the Jewish people. . . . [By contrast to the Christian accusation of Jews as Christ killers or a deicide people], I see the Jewish people's survival throughout the centuries in the light of what the Resurrection means: the affirmation of the Torah, of the people of Israel, and of Jewish existence. Therefore, Christian affirmation of the Jewish people ought to belong to the very center of the Christian faith. And if in the present the Jewish people get a new chance to survive and revive, particularly through the State of Israel, I see this in the light of the Resurrection. . . .

It is not true that the church has replaced Israel or taken over its vocation. Both Israel and the church await the fulfillment of the Torah, when the image of God will be visible in the whole of humanity. The Jews await this final Day incorporated in the people of Israel, the Christians incorporated in the body of Christ. . . . Jews have expressed their faithfulness in a "no" to Jesus as his church tried to take the Torah away from them. Christians may express their faithfulness in their "yes" to Jesus who embodies the Torah, and therefore also in a "yes" to his brothers and sisters, the Jewish people.[40]

Upon the reasoning of Schoneveld, the Resurrection is legitimately and morally restored to Christianity because the poison of victimization has been drained away from it.

A third alternative to our moral dilemma is not revisionist but revolutionary: to affirm, negatively speaking, that the Resurrection of Jesus has not in fact occurred, or, positively speaking, that it is a still-future event.

Another insight of Johann-Baptist Metz is appropriate as we consider this third option; the application is our own and not his. "We Christians can never again go back behind Auschwitz. To go beyond Auschwitz is . . . impossible for us of ourselves; it is possible only together with the victims of Auschwitz."[41] This is relevant to an observation made above: a genuine rediscovery of Jewishness means taking historical fact with utter seriousness. Within the bounds of this kind of thoroughgoing historicalness, not monopolized by Jewry, there are two alternatives respecting the first Easter Sunday: the somatic (bodily) resurrection of Jesus and the nonresurrection of Jesus.

Paul van Buren, representing an influential strain within recent theology, opts for a third alternative, an extrabodily Resurrection.[42]

From the standpoint of Jewish historicalness, not to mention ordinary common sense, such a declaration is not an authentic possibility because the avowal of an extrabodily resurrection is not convincingly allowable apart from Greek presuppositions and conditioning. Such a declaration does not really become meaningful except on the ground of the Hellenist divorce of spirit and matter. Accordingly, van Buren and others at this point dissociate themselves from Christian Jewishness, Jewish historicalness. Affirming an extrabodily Resurrection tacitly disavows resurrection as such. As Rosemary Ruether writes, the anthropology of body-soul dualism contradicts the biblical understanding of humanity and creation. The messianic hope of redemption entails the redeeming of life in the body, not flight from the body.[43]

In this context, Christian fundamentalism remains in the biblical historical tradition. That is to say, with its literalist teaching of the somatic resurrection of Jesus, fundamentalism is at least being faithful to Jewish categories of thinking and life, not to mention the attestations of some of the first Christians. For all his triumphalist protestation, Wolfhart Pannenberg can hardly endear himself to those who insist upon a literal bodily resurrection, for he explicitly denies that the understanding of the first Christians was a revivification of a corpse. Pannenberg strives hard to believe in the Resurrection, and yet he does not afford it its full somatic identity.[44] In point of truth, the original Christian declaration of the event of the Resurrection—before the time of the "appearance" to Paul of the resurrected Lord (1 Cor. 15:8)—made no allowance at all for Paul's distinction between the body that is sown and the body that is raised (1 Cor. 15:35–50). To many in the original Christian community, as reported in the Gospels, Jesus was raised from the dead —neither his spirit nor his spiritual body, but Jesus himself. Thus, for the writer of Luke's gospel—which may be the earliest, in spite of the traditional holding among scholars that Mark precedes it[45]—and for the Christians whose convictions Luke reports, the risen one was Jesus of Nazareth. Either Luke's account represents the truth, or Jesus has not been raised. We are not permitted the option of an extrabodily spiritual Resurrection.

Biblical fundamentalism is the one unflagging foe of all things Greek—that is, all things dualistic and abstract. Yet it pays an enormous and fateful price: it violates historicalness, surrenders existential reasonableness, and falls into superstition. With the first Christians, fundamentalists obliterate the harsh distinction between hopefulness and consummated event. They fail to comprehend, or refuse to accept, the nature of historical fate, that is, of physical death. This permits them to fashion the Resurrection of Jesus into an accomplished fact. And this, in turn, makes them susceptible to the same "theology of replacement" in relation to Judaism and Jews as the less literalistic forms of Christianity.[46]

Moreover, the fundamentalists' affirmation of the Resurrection includes the attestation that the messianic age entered history at that time —a view far removed from the Jewish insistence that there are no signs that the world has been redeemed or that the messianic age has begun. Their own experiences in this century make this an irrefutable conclusion. The error of the literalist notion of the somatic Resurrection of Jesus is its prematurity.

In summary, most tragically, the new rethinking of Christian doctrine, the very movement that insists justice be brought to the Jewish people at long last, is, with few exceptions, engaged in a balancing act. It is *Christian triumphalism with guilt feelings*. The new theology fancies that it can overcome anti-Jewishness while holding onto, among other doctrines, the consummated Resurrection of Jesus Christ. But that dogma is essentially antihistorical and anti-Jewish. The salient moral question, therefore, is not do we or do we not believe in the Resurrection of Jesus, but instead, do we who are calling for a Christianity purged of antisemitic elements and proclivities and a reaffirmation of Jewishness mean what we say? Are we prepared to follow out to their full conclusion the consequences of our summons, or are we fooling ourselves and others? It is neither theologically correct nor morally right to maintain, as Pannenberg does, that God has acted to vindicate the Christian cause as against the Jewish people and faith. But there may be only one possible ground for denying Pannenberg's vindication —by testifying that Jesus has not yet been raised from the dead. Thus does the Christian revolutionary work, at the very heart of traditional Christian affirmation, to sever the link between the church's teaching and the convictions that led to the *Shoah*.[47]

REAFFIRMATIONS

In the course of our analysis we have already introduced two additional and essential elements in the work of Christian revolution, and we discuss them as "Reaffirmations."

143

1. The Christian revolutionary will oppose that aspect of the asserted religious covenant that makes abnormal demands upon the Jewish people, a psychology helpfully identified by Rabbi N. Peter Levinsohn of Heidelberg as the "suffering servant syndrome."[48]

The Christian who has read the saga of Jewish vulnerability and torment over the centuries, culminating in Hitler's Final Solution, will rebel. He will ask, how long must this one people be the vicarious victim for God's long-suffering with the evil-doers of the world? Is there no alternative between the ongoing victimization of the people of the covenant, that God may stay His anger with the evil-doers, and the destruction of human history, that God may at last enact divine justice?[49] The Christian revolutionary will be joined by some Jews, not all from a revolutionary perspective. One example is the protest of a survivor: "Let us not create a new Jewish post-Holocaust theology of the suffering servant. It is blasphemy to ascribe such radical evil and the unspeakable suffering it caused any divine purpose. . . . Let us not let the perpetrators of evil define us as holy victims. That would be the final triumph of antisemitism. Let us not hold onto suffering as a yellow badge of Judaism."[50] Even so, we Christians must be cautious not to assume a new imperialistic stance toward Jews.

We earlier conceded that Christian negation of a Jewish resolve to perpetuate a special calling would dishonor Jewish integrity. That calling could well involve a readiness to suffer in obedience to the apprehended will of God, Holocaust or no Holocaust. Even in the Warsaw ghetto, with the brutal round-ups for deportation in full operation, many religious Jews rejected any form of violent resistance as a desecration of the "majesty of martyrdom" to sanctify the Lord's name. One even argued that if Jesus, on his way to death on Golgotha, had picked up a stone and hurled it at a Roman soldier, he could never have become the Christ.[51]

Accordingly, a great deal depends upon the intent and the content of the Christian opposition to Jewish martyrdom. Is the message from the Christian side the counsel of friends, or is it a fresh, if inverted, form of yet another demand upon Jews? There is an added complication; however the Christian community may behave, special demands upon the Jewish people will continue to be made from various quarters. These demands are particularly apparent when one surveys the criticisms of Israel for engaging in—or not engaging in—certain actions that generally are accepted if undertaken—or not undertaken—by other nations. And a further temptation can enter: Christians may not wish the Jew to be singled out for abnormal obligations because secretly they themselves, although heirs of the Jew Jesus, desire to escape from special responsibilities. There is no human deliverance from this entire psychology. All in all, we do not here claim that Jews of a transformed covenant will be spared all unusual suffering.

But we do say that, after Auschwitz, such suffering must be opposed and repented of by God himself and herself; if this is so, the next question concerns what obligations are given us, and especially to those of us who are Christians? Alan T. Davies of Canada has given one answer: The voice of Auschwitz that commands Jews not to surrender their Jewish identity commands Christians that they must never again, through silence, speech, or act "involve themselves in a second Auschwitz as they did in the first Auschwitz." Implicit in this command is the special responsibility for Christians to resist and eliminate antisemitism and to preserve the State of Israel.[52] Although today's need for theological reconstruction applies as much to the Jewish community as to the Christian church, the question of what obligations the faithful now have retains a particular focus for Christians, for the all-important reason that Christians historically have stood in the forefront of leveling special demands upon Jews. Nevertheless, note a serious consequence, deriving from our own opposition to those demands. Unavoidably, we are trespassing upon an intra-Jewish conflict. In expressing our own conviction, we inevitably take the side of those Jewish representatives who subscribe to a position paralleling ours, in opposition to those for whom the sanctification of the divine Name through suffering, whenever required, will remain an abiding commandment, until the very "end of days."

Requiring special behavior from the Jewish people continues to be found even among Christians who evince a new solidarity with Jews. Thus, in *The Burden of Freedom* Paul van Buren avows that the Jewish people "do not possess freedom as their own treasure, to enjoy for themselves," but rather for serving mankind's freedom and allowing that God's freedom "might be Israel's consuming passion." Israel "is no more free to be other than God's people."[53] Doubtless without intention, van Buren here reflects an ideology that has beset the Christian church for hundreds of years—or, more accurately, one-half of an ambivalent ideology which, on the one hand, fabricates abnormal obligations for Jews and, on the other hand, with glaring inconsistency faults them for "always" behaving in sub-Christian fashion. Jews are expected to be both angels and devils—everything but ordinary human beings. The reply to the first of the two aspects of this ideology may well be Emil L. Fackenheim's admonition that the Jew today "is commanded to descend from the cross and, in so doing, not only to reiterate his ancient rejection of an ancient Christian view but also to suspend the time-honored exaltation of [Jewish] martyrdom."[54]

The import of Fackenheim's wholly post-Holocaust counsel can be directed equally to would-be taskmasters in the Christian world, to a type of Jewish traditionalist, to those other persons and collectivities who have become apostles of the perfectionism in question, and, if need be, even to God himself. To all these eligible parties we believe the response must be, "You have entered your last demand against us"; to such parties as need an added word, the judgment is forthcoming that "in the name of reputed freedom and divine opportunity for the Israel of the past—the life of 'holy obligation'—you have only made certain that succeeding generations of Jews would be brought to degradation and agony and death." The one immorality that equals the visiting of the iniquity of the fathers upon the children and the children's children, to the third and the fourth generation" (Exod. 34:7) is that of visiting the presumed covenantal obligations of the fathers upon generation after generation of their children, independently of the children's consent. The Jewish children of the murder camps rise in silent refutation of both these forms of immorality. The myth of the Jew as "suffering servant" will be relieved of its horrible force only as the victims of the myth say no to it, they will be aided in their determination by the efforts of Christians who refuse to be a party to such an illicit requirement.

A widely shared objection to our denial of the covenant of demand is that this viewpoint flouts the will of God. But the objector himself has a problem. That problem involves the arbitrariness as against the morality of God. If the objector bases his complaint upon the sovereign arbitrariness of God, we can no longer carry on the discussion because there is no common ground. If the objector argues that God has already determined the demand and provided the only alternative through His Son Jesus Christ, God is being denied the freedom to change, which the objector claims for himself, and other humans.[55] But if the objector seeks to retain a moral deity, then the challenge to him is to show that it is not morally wrong to take requirements once imposed upon the fathers and to impose them upon succeeding generations, even at the cost of the latter's safety and security. The objector is asked: in which epoch are you living, B.F.S. or F.S.?

146

Today a plea is often made for the secularity of theology. Within the context of relations with Jews, Christians may honor that plea by receiving Jews simply as people, ordinary people. Any other stance helps to perpetuate a pre-Holocaust outlook. To annul the covenant of demand is to witness against Jewish suffering from the human side. But this does not resolve the problem of God and Jewish suffering. We are brought to a further step.

2. The Christian revolutionary will appear as a witness, together with numbers of his Jewish brothers and sisters, before a special tribunal where a special trial is being conducted: the trial of God. We have referred to such a trial in chapter 3, but the "blasphemy" of post-Holocaust thinking is nowhere made more necessary than in this chapter. We have celebrated God's faithfulness to her people; now we are so brazen as to join in his trial, to covet the Lord's penitence. Yet the reader is asked: Is there a choice? The fatefulness of history must be consummated. Of moral necessity, B.F.S. is to be succeeded by F.S., for the sake of truth and goodness. After all, God has the highest stake in these virtues, much higher than ours.

Many persons are doubtless shocked and offended by the very thought that human beings have a right to put God "on trial," but we call attention to Scripture. There are biblical grounds for human protagonism before God: for example, Abraham's contention with God and our patriarch's question, "Shall not the Judge of all the earth do right?" (Gen. 18:22–33); the protests before God throughout the Book of Job; and, for the Christian especially, Jesus' cry of abandonment on the cross. Of course, we are not permitted to ignore God's accusations against his human creatures in the name of her justice. In fact, in the voices of some of God's children accusing others in the human family for imposing suffering and degradation on them we must hear the reverberations of *divine* protest. Elie Wiesel reminds us of a Jewish legend in which God points out to the "evil spirit" that the basic difference between a group of pure people and a group of impure people was that the pure ones had protested. The others *should* have protested: "against Me, against Man, against everything wrong. Because protest in itself contains a spark of truth, a spark of holiness, a spark of God."[56]

In the name of holy protest, there has to be, at the very least, a total revolution in the doctrine of election. That teaching has made the agony of Israel an unceasing sentence and has turned God into the devil's equivalent. If the doctrine of election is to be retained, this can only occur through its radical humanization. Chosenness will become election

147

to life. For this first time in the story of the people of God their existence will become an unqualifiedly normal reality.

A "commandment" can mean opposite things. There is the command to sacrifice oneself, and there is the command to live. When using the concept of "demand," we mean the first of these; it stretches things unduly to apply that category to survival. Normally, the human will to live does not require prodding. The saving experience at the Red Sea that the Jewish people have known requires no demand in order for it to be remembered and celebrated. The commanding experience at Sinai, the other "archetypal" or "root" event of Jewish history and faith, is of a quite different nature. Yet the two are inextricably linked. Can these two types of experiences be found in the *Shoah*? Emil Fackenheim writes: "If one tries to hear a redeeming voice at Auschwitz, there is only silence. But a commanding voice speaks to those willing to listen: A Jew is forbidden to give Hitler a posthumous victory, and to consent to despair is to give that victory. The moral-religious contradiction can be resolved only by affirmation that *there can be no second Holocaust*."[57] The contradiction is to be resolved, Fackenheim implies, only by the interrelatedness of salvation and command being retained. After Auschwitz, no command is legitimate that does not save, and there is no salvation without honoring the command to live. The command of collective self-sacrifice is terminated, and the command to survive takes its place.

The original covenant is transformed but nevertheless honored through what Fackenheim calls the 614th commandment, the command to live.[58] This commandment is nothing more nor less than the free choice and right of Jewish existence as such, another way of saying that it is not a commandment. But it is the commandment that ends or fulfills all others; it is a proclamation of independence, a testimony to the utter sanctity of Jewish life.[59] B.F.S. became total dehumanization; F.S. is life with no strings attached. The dehumanization was to be final; the humanization must be final. The dispensation of the first Torah is ended, for Torah is now embodied, in a definitive sense, within the Jew himself. The Jew is the incarnation of the word, the teaching. F.S. is the era of the incarnation of the Jewish people.

For all time, any human being, not excluding the Jew, can resolve to become a martyr. But after the Holocaust, martyrdom cannot be a collective ideal for the Jewish people.[60] As one survivor has insisted, with the uprisings of the Warsaw, Bialystok, and other ghettos "the mil-

lennial epoch of the Jews' sanctifying of God and of themselves by submitting to a violent death" came to an end.[61] The Endlösung is the eschatological judgment upon a double-standard God and upon all double-standard theology. The Holocaust remains the rational climax of the
unholy split between Jewishness and humanity. The holy nation became excrement.[62] In alternate terminology, the dispensation F.S. is the
victory of God as love over the devil as hate.

Yet the nagging question persists: can the command to survive be
wholly set free from the element of demand? If the Jewish people will
to survive, but to survive only as human beings, and not as Jews, do
they not betray their own integrity and fall prey to an abstract existence? And yet, if they will to survive as *Jews*, do they not continue to
subject themselves to the arbitrary and impossible demands of others,
not excluding God?

We are unable to supply an answer that will finally resolve or silence this question. But we are required to respond to it. Fackenheim
has been cited as pleading, not for one command but for two: Jews
must "descend from the cross," and they must survive as Jews; otherwise a posthumous victory will be handed to Hitler. But how is it possible to call, at one and the same time, for an end to martyrdom and for
Jewish survival? One way in which it may be done is through the gaining and retaining of political freedom and power. Today, F.S., the command to live as Jews can be moral only where the Jewish people have
sovereign power.[63] Otherwise that command is immoral. Fackenheim
asks: "Is not, after Auschwitz, any Jewish willingness to suffer martyrdom, instead of an inspiration to potential saints, much rather an encouragement to potential criminals? After Auschwitz, is not even the
saintliest Jew driven to the inexorable conclusion that he owes the moral
obligation to the antisemites of the world not to encourage them by his
own powerlessness?"[64] We find that the antisemites of the world are
owed nothing at all, any more than is their master the devil, but Emil
Fackenheim is surely correct in affirming that Jewish martyrdom can
no longer be sustained. That is to say, if in the epoch B.F.S. the martyrdom of Jews was empowered to sanctify the divine Name, in the dispensation F.S. such martyrdom will only blacken God's name. It will,
indeed, threaten his salvation. We must conclude that as a Jewish option the theology of victimization, that terrible but natural child of the
covenant of demand, was put to death in the murder camps.[65]

149

POLITICAL POWER AND
ThE PEOPLE ISRAEL

Thomas A. Idinopulos and Roy Bowen Ward point out, in an otherwise faulty appraisal of a work by Rosemary Ruether, that "doctrinal formulations (or reformulations) will not end anti-Judaism, much less antisemitism because history shows both to be complex phenomena which depend heavily on political, social, and economic factors, as well as on the intellectual and theological developments which gave expression to them."[66] This passage reflects the importance of a theology of politics.

The phrase "theology of politics" stands for the responsible application of theological and moral principles to the political domain, the domain of power. A theology lacking relevance to the political realm is worthless. As Alistair Kee writes, the "question is not whether political theology is still theology, but whether anything that is *without* political significance deserves the name 'theology.'"[67] A purely theoretical or academic theology is a form of idolatry and even blasphemy, because it takes the name of God and subjects it to the imaginings of the human mind and the ideological self-deifications of the human spirit.

As so often, Irving Greenberg contributes positively to the rethinking of theology in the era after the Holocaust, in this instance through his commentary upon a Jewish woman and her child. The scene is Auschwitz, following upon a horrifying train journey.

> In this state, when she suddenly understood where she was, when she smelled the stench of the burning bodies—perhaps heard the cries of the living in the flames—she abandoned her child and ran.
>
> Out of this wells up the cry: Surely here is where the cross is smashed. There has been a terrible misunderstanding of the symbol of the crucifixion. Surely, we understand now that the point of the account is the cry: "My lord, my lord, why have you abandoned me?"[68] Never again should anyone be exposed to such one-sided power on the side of evil—for in such extremes not only does evil triumph, but the Suffering Servant now breaks and betrays herself. Out of the Holocaust experience comes the demand for redistribution of power. The principle is simple. No one should ever have to depend again on anyone else's goodwill or respect for their basic security and right to exist. The Jews of Europe needed that goodwill and these good offices desperately—and the democracies and the church and Communists and their fellow-Jews failed them. No one should ever be equipped with less power than is necessary to assure one's dignity. To argue dependence on

law, or human goodness, or universal equality is to join the ranks of those who would like to repeat the Holocaust.[69]

The worst fate that can befall any people is to be bereft of political sovereignty. As Richard L. Rubenstein says, "theologians or moralists may argue that all men possess some God-given irreducible measure of dignity, but such talk will neither deter future emulators of the Nazis nor comfort realistically their victims. . . . Human rights and dignity can only be attained by membership in a community that has the *power* to guarantee those rights."[70] It is, indeed, a moral responsibility for a people not to be weak. This duty is owed, not only to themselves but also in a sense to their foes and detractors, lest the others be tempted into aggressive acts against them. Significantly, the Black leader Eldridge Cleaver, who often speaks in these terms, emphasizes that the Holocaust has taught him that if you go along, or have to go along, with tyranny, you simply cannot live. He concludes that there must be "Black power" in order to encourage the white brethren to be and to behave like decent human beings.[71] The most significant way for the Christian community to relate to Jews today is from the standpoint of a theology of politics rather than from that of religion, for the erstwhile political powerlessness of Jews has only guaranteed their persecution and suffering, as religious ideas justified it.

If Exodus and Sinai are understood as decisive signs of a beginning of redemption within history, a beginning that was to expand through the cooperative efforts of God and humans, then the *Shoah* was the most decisive counteroffensive by forces opposing redemption. Irving Greenberg insists that in all of Jewish history, "the peak of enslavement and moral chaos was achieved in the Holocaust. Surely this was the climax of the rollback of redemption—threatening to destroy redemption itself." However, rather than yield to nihilism and despair, the Jewish people "created a new, indeed unparalleled, beachhead of redemption, the reborn State of Israel."[72]

The creation of the State of Israel in the immediate aftermath of the Final Solution, in the year 8 F.S., is the collective equivalent of the individual decisions of Jewish parents, including survivors above all, to have children. It represented not only defiance of all antisemites but also a defiant affirmation—perhaps directed at God—of a will to live despite the worst that could be done to a people. Israel represents a response to radical evil that exists in the world, against which we all have an obligation to fight. It is the Jewish people's recognition that "exis-

151

tence precedes ethics" and that "power is of the essence when we dare to exist."[73]

The Jewish people have at last gained the power that can help keep their enemies at bay, their human foes and their divine protagonist. True, the theology of politics cannot be permitted to mean the theologizing of politics. That is to say, theology cannot rightly subject the political domain to the dictates of religion—for example, by claiming absolute rights, in the name of God or Allah or the Marxist revolution, for a particular people to any given land or by claiming absolute right, in the name of God or Allah or anything else, for a particular ruler to govern as he will. There are no absolute human rights to anything. All human rights are limited and partial. Nevertheless, through Israel, Jews are enabled to fight for their lives. This, as Pinchas Peli attests, is the very "essence of Israel's meaning."[74] It is as simple, as complicated, and as painful as that. Men do not live by bread and bullets alone, but without them they can become either ravening wolves or helpless victims. In fighting for the nation's right to exist and survive, Jews are saying, in effect, "We are here to live. We are going to defend our right to do so, if necessary by fighting for our lives. And if we have to die, we are going to die in battle, not in crematoria."[75]

Those who are bothered by a stress upon sovereignty as the central meaning of the State of Israel have failed to take to heart the Jewish story. *Eretz Yisrael* forms the answer to almost two thousand years of Jewish defenselessness. As Manès Sperber puts it, "Israel is a state like any other; it is not the state of chosen people; it must not be so, for it must live. For the heirs of Belzec, Maidanek, and Auschwitz have no right to be lambs."[76] It is the only restitution of power—the ability to determine one's fate, at least to some degree—in an effective form. In that sense Israel is "the major creative response to the Holocaust" and the "only serious attempt to challenge . . . the possible eventuality of a second Holocaust."[77] Israel embodies the most effective reply to those who talk glibly of spiritual force—the "power of the Cross" or of *Satyagraha*—as the answer to physical force and armed aggression or exclusionary immigration policies when lives are at stake. These persons are not simply wrong in an empirical or political sense. They are, objectively speaking, immoral; that is to say, they are threats to the human creation of God. There is a parallel in the pacifism advocated by some Christians—pacifism in the sense of a political instrument, in contrast to the vocational pacifism of individuals—and the Christian effort tacitly to abolish Jewry through missions. If the latter represents a "spiritual Final Solution," pacifism as an advocated policy directed to Jews reestablishes the threat of a physical Final Solution. Auschwitz throws into clear relief, and once and for all, the demonic character of much Christian spirituality, a type of spirituality that, when applied to Jews, is best summed up in a certain cynic's definition: Christianity is that religion which teaches that the Jewish people are to turn the other cheek.

A perfect illustration of double-standard Christian morality is a piece by Quaker professor Calvin Keene. Having sought to dispose of those Christians who related the reestablishing of the State of Israel to the will of God, Keene introduces his own version of a covenant of demand by declaring that Israel is to be "evaluated" and "the future of this new state" is to be "determined" by "its practice or lack of practice of justice, mercy, and righteousness."[78] The revealing element is not so much what he tries to demand of Israel as what he fails to ask of the Arabs. Evidently the latter's hostile policies toward Israel are acceptable. That Keene should refuse to apply his Quaker-pacifist demands to the Arabs suggests that his purpose is not in fact the making of peace but that of an Israel turned into defenselessness through the implementing of his brand of "Christian" perfectionism. This type of double standard applied to Israel is by no means limited to pacifists or Quakers. The Rev. Peter R. Powell, Jr., asserted that he was quite "comfortable calling [the Jews in Israel] to live by a morality greater than that of their neighbors. . . . If [Israel] becomes just another nation, then it has lost its birthright."[79]

Of course, we must not be oblivious to the universal temptations of power. Due to the ontological status of human statehood as a creation of God and not God himself, political sovereignty may never be exalted into an absolute.[80] Nor can we ignore the incapacity of power to resolve problems of ultimate human meaning and the purposes of life. Power is to be lived with in ways advocated by Reinhold Niebuhr.[81] It is neither to be idealized into some kind of messiah nor disdained as some kind of devil. Power is to be used as an instrument for restraining human sin and channeling human creativity in a world that will never be perfect.

Even though the Christian church has, overall, partly corrupted the Jewish doctrine of God, the church has, overall, contributed much to the doctrine of man, thereby helping to chasten Jewish anthropology. Much of the Christian insight into human social and political life teaches us to be suspicious of people and their motives, particularly of ourselves. The French Christian scholar Fadiey Lovsky writes that the Holocaust comprised the most striking historical demonstration of "the

153

hereditary reality of human sin."[82] Although the symbolism of sin as a "hereditary" taint wrongly obscures human responsibility for evil, it does have the virtue of pointing out human proclivity and solidarity in sin.

Power has the best chance to achieve relative responsibility under a system of political democracy: in that system the destructive dangers and the constructive opportunities of power are each taken into account. Democracy is a creative alternative to two extreme political views, absolutism and anarchism. Political absolutists, whether of the older kingly and historically tyrannical sort or of the newer totalitarian type, pretend that the masses of humanity are either too evil or too stupid to govern themselves. At the other extreme stand the idealistic anarchists of history who teach that governmental rule is really not required because human beings are, in essence, too good to have to be subjected to arbitrary and artificial political restraints. Against both views Reinhold Niebuhr affirms that "man's capacity for justice makes democracy possible; but man's inclination to injustice makes democracy necessary."[83]

In theological language, man is made in the image of God, yet he is also a sinner. He is capable of honoring and achieving a certain measure of justice; hence, the masses of men can rule themselves. But rule and government are necessary because men also seek to exercise power over their fellows. Accordingly, a political structure of "checks and balances" is required to protect us from others and to protect others from us. Absolutism is unduly pessimistic about man; anarchism is unduly optimistic. Alone among political systems, democracy takes seriously both the heights of human constructiveness and the depths of human sin. None of this is to suggest that there is any such thing as *the* Christian—or Jewish—political system. All human systems stand under the judgment of God. Democracy is more a method than a doctrinaire claim.

In the frame of reference of international affairs, the challenge of justice is to render every nation its due, to ensure it of whatever it can legitimately claim simply by virtue of being a nation—a minimal standard of living, the capacity to defend itself, the right to participate in the counsels of nations, and so on. The prime question of international relations remains: How can power be utilized to contribute to justice among the nation-states? The general answer must be not through annulling power, which would be to turn away from the exigencies and responsibilities of the real world, and not through uncontrolled power, which would mean imperialism and international anarchy, but rather through manifold structures of balanced or mutually trammeled power. With the aid of these structures, human collectivities are able to maintain a tolerable coexistence. In sum, the key to relative justice among the nations must always remain the art of compromise.

Because the prevailing emphasis in this book is upon a theological way of looking at life, it is appropriate to include a word about the relation between the ultimate resources and promises of faith and the sphere of political action. There are two polar types of religious believers: some stay aloof from the world and remain "pure" but thereby commit the sin of irresponsibility; and others plunge into the world and inevitably, therefore, take upon themselves the dirtiness and nasty compromises of the political scene. The difficulty with many religious people, as Arnold Nash used to say, is that they are always committing the wrong sins rather than the right ones.

Martin Luther offered a curious word of advice to his fellow Christians: "Sin bravely, if also you have brave faith." All persons sin. The question is whether we are going to be irresponsible sinners sinning not bravely, or responsible sinners sinning bravely. In our time F.S. the Jewish people, with the least reason to retain any faith, had the audacious faith to begin again, to recreate a nation state moribund for almost two millennia. The Jewish emergence from powerlessness and return to history "was a testimony to the Jewish ability, spiritual as well as physical, to perform the deed and live with its results"[84]—in Luther's words, to "sin bravely." There is a grandeur here that is obscured for most people by constant media attention to the crises and ordinary problems of that new nation in one of the most strife-torn areas of the world. There is also courage—the courage of a people who "dared to embody 2,000 years of hope in the fragile vessel of a state."[85]

There is a final mercy that God in his grace makes available in the realm of human power relations. The political man of faith lives with an uneasy but easy conscience—uneasy because he inexorably falls short of every ideal, but easy because he is assured that the Ruler of the Universe accepts him nonetheless. To those who take on political obligations, a strange assurance comes. Perhaps it can best be called "the peace that passes all understanding." In a word, the ultimate resource behind sustained political action is the divine forgiveness.[86] But is this not the hidden resource behind all that we say and do, the final power that enables life to go on? If so, there is some hope for all, even for those who unintentionally betray the truths of God.

Irving Greenberg refers to the ghastly idea that we try telling the burning children in the pits of Auschwitz that they are burning for their sins.[87] Likewise we may say: try informing the children that they are chastised by the Lord as Jews who have spurned the one true faith and crucified the "Son of God." That they are superseded by the Christian church in God's economy. That the cross of Jesus comprises the ultimate in human Godforsakenness. That they are the suffering servants of the Lord. That God is not to be called to account for their fate. That the Resurrection has taken place and is able to save them. And that political and military power are not for the people of God.

Try it.

7

TURN TO THE
KINGDOM OF DAY

Yom haShoah, . . . this day of mourning is going to have to be
one of . . . our most sacred holy days along with Christmas and
Easter. Christmas and Easter remind Christians all over the
world that life is precious. Yom HaShoah reminds Christians
what can happen when life becomes expendable.

> John W. Bressler, "I Can't Laugh Anymore"

There is no truth for me which I could defend with my back
turned to Auschwitz.

> Johann-Baptist Metz, "Facing the Jews"

We have told of the attack upon an old man as found in "To the
Mound of Corpses in the Snow." Very soon night came. The old man
had died. His body was but one of many corpses in "the endless field of
the Gentiles." Then at once, from a wholly other realm, there appeared
a holy seraph. It was Rabbi Uri of Strelisk, come to mourn the father's
murder. From the mound of corpses crept a little grandson to ask why
the seraph had not sent thousands of angels and seraphim to defend
them. But Rabbi Uri was himself kneeling frozen in the field, and the
snow kept falling.[1]

It was but a few moments from the officer's attack upon the father
until the death of the holy man. For this book, the space-time between
has been but a few fragile chapters. But perhaps it is better to count up
to a lifetime: nineteen hundred years of the Christian church. William
Jay Peck testifies that in a "structural sense, the whole of Christianity
was responsible for the death camps"; accordingly, any "denial of such
involvement will doom the message of the church to remain at the level
of shallow and impotent argumentation." Arthur A. Cohen observes
that the "failure of Christian *caritas* as an efficacious sacrificial ethic,
the inability of Christians in the breach to take up the cross of martyrdom, is dramatic (albeit polemical) proof that triumphalism has left the

157

muscle of Christian moral resolution flaccid and unserviceable in historical crisis." For Stefan Zeroniski, "the crime itself never dies, regardless of when it was committed—a thousand years ago or early this morning." Yet it seems to this Polish writer that one must also "keep a second ear open to catch the sound of any bells from a new tower, from a temple of the future."[2]

Is there a new temple under construction somewhere? In this study we have returned to the kingdom of night. We have focused upon the remembrance of the Holocaust, the terrible singularity of that event, and the consummate need for a revolutionary transformation of Christian moral and theological teaching and action respecting Judaism and the Jewish people. We have also given some attention to Jewish attempts to come to grips with old and new realities in creative and responsive ways, ways which Christians may want to take to heart and mind for their ultimate well-being. In conclusion, we direct our thoughts to the future, applying the category of hope to, successively, the people Israel, the Christian church, and the world of eschatology.

For Christians to say anything at all about hope and the Jewish people, they must be engaged in their own form of hoping, the hope that they are somehow part of that same people. Some Christians today have set out upon a strange road, a journey of *metanoia* from the epoch B.F.S. to that of F.S., a long night's journey into day. The Exodus from Egypt has become their Exodus, as Sinai has become their Sinai. And now the same is to be said of the Holocaust. To these Christians belong, in an extraordinary way, the murder center of Belzec and the uprising of Vilna. And to these Christians is given the task of addressing others within and beyond the church. Will you not stand with the children of Theresienstadt, the women of Birkenau, the men of Treblinka? Will you not enter within their struggle, their hell? Will you not honor the State of Israel, fighting its afflictions and rejoicing in its blessings? Together with the Jew Jesus, the authentic Christian is conjoined with the unending story of Israel, the people of God, a tale that is pierced by, but then prevails over, "the Final Solution of the question of Jews." Johann-Baptist Metz speaks not only for himself but also for these new Christian pilgrims when he says that then will "'Auschwitz as an end' [mean] an end of that kind of Christianity which refuses to form its identity in the face of and together with the Jews."[3]

HOPE AND THE
PEOPLE ISRAEL

Jewish tradition bids that every discourse end on a note of hope. Yet it appears necessary to break this rule in the case of the *Shoah* and mix hope with uncertainty and even a sense of foreboding.

The kingdom of night is hopelessness. Ours is the time after the kingdom of night—F.S. All idealism has been put to the torch: God will watch after his own, as he did in Auschwitz. By identical reasoning, to enter the kingdom of day is to persist in hope. Yet even the kingdom of day is not the kingdom of heaven: here is the crux of our human problem. No perfection is possible within human affairs, and there will be no perfection within the bounds of this world. Just as the kingdom of night could not succeed in vanquishing all goodness, so too, the kingdom of day cannot vanquish all evil. Yet this does not make the kingdom of day unattainable; it can come, and it does come in a fragmentary but promising sense.

If the kingdom of night is absolute dehumanization, absolute death, the kingdom of day is simply humanization resought, life regained. The kingdom of night is the slaughter of Jewish infants and children; the kindgom of day is the birth of Jewish babies and the raising of youngsters. Such birth as an act of courage and faith is never without risk, for what if these little ones should one day be obliterated? Emil Fackenheim has pointed out the fateful and irremedial predicament of Jewish parents in the era F.S. They cannot but be aware that, if they raise their children as Jews, they may be exposing them, or their grandchildren, to a future Final Solution. Yet if they cease to be Jews, their children or grandchildren could be among the future murderers.[4] What an intolerable dilemma! Yet the choice must be made—and is. And what are the choices Christian parents face? When the opportunity presented itself for following Jesus' example of bearing the cross of suffering for others, very few chose to emulate him. Thus, we Christians and Gentiles are eternally indebted to that "faithful remnant" of Christians or secularists whose commitment to righteousness and compassion led them to risk their lives and sometimes to give their lives in the effort to help the victims of the omnipresent Nazi apparatus. It was all too easy to merge into the anonymous mass and escape the test, especially because the churches, by and large, did not challenge their parishioners to act as the Good Samaritan of Jesus' parable did. Do Christian parents today prepare their children to make their Christianity a basis for standing along-

159

side the persecuted or threatened, including especially the Jewish people in their being singled out for suffering? Or are these parents preparing, either implicitly or explicitly, their children to be ready to move into the murderers' company?[5]

Are we not confined to the hope that our hopes will prove authentic ones, consonant with reality? These hopes have to keep struggling against the force of a betraying hope, for, as Manès Sperber teaches, there is the hope that guides and the hope that misguides. The second kind leads man "in chains to his death." Sperber cites the lamentation of the young Polish poet Tadeusz Borowski, not a Jew, who killed himself at the age of twenty-nine. Borowski said of himself and the other inmates of Auschwitz, "It is hope that provokes men to march indifferently to the gas chamber, and keeps them from conceiving of an insurrection; hope makes them dumb and causes them to resemble corpses. . . . Never has hope provoked so much ill as in this war, as in this camp. We were never taught how to rid ourselves of hope. And that is why we are dying in the gas chambers." Sperber notes that, in contrast with almost all the other insurrections, the revolt of the Warsaw ghetto was not inspired by any hope at all.[6]

But still the resisters fought. Why? Was theirs a postponed, future-oriented trust that after all there would be a future, with Jews as part of it, even if they themselves would not be alive to see it? Why did they fight? They fought to regain dignity. Then bystanders of later years would not be able to ask, "Why didn't the Jews resist?" But tragically this expectation was unfulfilled.[7] They fought to send a message to future Jewish generations: Take your fate in your own hands; do not let others determine it for you. And they fought to end almost two millennia of powerless vulnerability. Although we must be vigilant against the hope that misguides, the resort to armed power is not always bereft of genuine hope. It may foster such hope because it sometimes works to sustain life. Political sovereignty for the people Israel, as we have understood it, is an essential of the kingdom of day.

The Jewish poet Paul Celan concluded that only one thing was still attainable during the horror of the Holocaust; language remained undefeated despite "a thousand nights of death-dealing speech."[8] We should be the last to hold that the poetic/linguistic calling cannot be a heroic form of struggle against the enemy. We honor Celan, who created the single most powerful poem to come out of the Endlösung: "Todesfuge" (Fugue of Death).[9] Nevertheless, we must disagree with his conclusion. We must speak in behalf of another war, a war for life, humanity, and justice, a struggle at whose heart was the killing of the killers. We have noted the Jewish resistance even in Auschwitz and Treblinka. The integrity of power was never wholly annihilated, even among Jews under sentence of death. Here is the partial truth in T. W. Adorno's famous aphorism that no poetry is possible after Auschwitz. For all its cathartic and testimonial value, poetry was snuffed out in the fires. The fires themselves were finally extinguished, but only by shells and bombs. As Manès Sperber has so forcefully reminded us, since 1945 and beyond 1948 to the present, Palestinian/Israeli Jews have sought to "teach the world that the long hunting season" is over forever; that people may "no longer kill Jews easily or with impunity. The soldiers of this new army are fighting to deliver their people from a degradation that threatened to encourage exterminators, . . . as well as their innumerable silent accomplices the world over."[10]

Today's free State of Israel, among its many other achievements, reproduces and perpetuates this *Widerstand*, this *Résistance*. In essence, Israel constitutes the dowry brought to a new marriage, a new covenant of promise and life. Israel is the rainbow set again in the clouds—but not only for the Jewish people. Just as the rainbow seen after the recession of the floodwaters signified the divine covenant with all living creatures (Gen. 9:9-17), so the restoration of sovereignty to this long-suffering people can be a sign of hope for other oppressed and minority peoples of the world.

David Wolf Silvermann asks: Dare we not say today that the founding and preservation of Israel is God's gesture of faith in the midst of His silence?[11] Bound together as they are, Holocaust and State of Israel create a shattering dialectic for any faith that posits the decisiveness of historical events, an assumption that itself precludes any separation of the transpolitical and political realms. The Holocaust inquires: How can you still believe in the God who delivers Israel? The State of Israel replies: How can you not believe in the God who delivers Israel? On the cross the Palestinian/Galilean Jew Jesus cried out, with the psalmist, "My God, my God, why have you forsaken me?" In our time the Israeli poet Yehuda Amichai asks: "My God, my God / Why have you not forsaken me?"

The unbearable, relentless logic endures that God, the one who does not deliver Israel, is yet the one who does deliver her. Having faith, we are sent into despair; and in despair, we are lifted back into faith. Can we believe in God? No, it is impossible. *Can* we believe in God? Yes, for a fleeting moment.

Many (most?) of us find that such "moment-faith" is the most we can count on. The times may be such that anyone who can confess to "untroubled theism" after confronting the Holocaust is *not* religious.[12]

In the dialectic of Holocaust and State of Israel, each focus takes its opposite into itself.

> . . . The smell of our land is like the smell of our strong wine.
> Our slaughtered dead children come here to rest and play,
> Near to us, face to face with us,
> Cooling their faces, no longer wandering homeless, astray.[13]

On 4 April 1976, we attended a service in the Yad Vashem Memorial, Jerusalem, in honor of Joseph S. Cammerer of Germany, one of the "Righteous of the Nations" who, during the Nazi time, had aided Jews at peril to his life. A cantor was singing. At that moment fighter aircraft of the Israel Defense Forces were suddenly heard. The singing stood for the powerlessness of the Jewish victims; the aircraft represented the power of the State of Israel. To Ilse Aichinger, whose question is inscribed at the beginning of this book the answer may now be sent with love: Here is where the children are, some of them.[14] The tension between despair and hope forces us to add: Yet even here the children are the deliberate targets of those who would destroy the State that sustains Jewish life—and hope. Terrorists are well aware that, even more than most societies, Israelis link hope and the future with children.

If our dialectic of despair and faith is not nonsense, we are granted an alternative to both utopianism and cynicism. We are emboldened to struggle along, not because any final answers have come, but because our plight has been comprehended, the plight that God and Israel share, a condition that makes them friends forever. Mutual understanding is anointed by mutual compassion. The choice of future courses of action becomes one of responsibility resting upon reality. Yizhak Orpaz tells of the man who is conscious that no way out of his condition is open. "His hope, and if you like, his salvation, lies in the question: How do I live with this? He does not tire, because he bears with him a kind of ancient memory of a blessing and a breaking. In his quest he makes a flawed world meaningful."[15]

The threat is always bursting into a promise, yet the promise is ever being held back by a threat. On the one hand, strange deliverances emerged out of the very kingdom of night.

I am Gyorgy Kemeny. Live in Budapest as a graphic designer. I work like everybody does. Thirty years ago I was a Jewish boy of nine. My parents put me to an asylum to keep my life saved. There I was once shot at, but the bullet missed to kill me. Next I was taken to a mass execution at the River Danube. But an air raid dispersed my were-to-be murderers. When liberation came, I weighed 34 pounds. My mother still starts crying, when remembering all this. Today I live in Budapest. I am a graphic designer, work like everybody else.[16]

On the other hand, a menacing shadow casts itself across the promise, a shadow of the kind that, in consonance with the above reasoning, we must ever expect yet ever work to efface: Will the kingdom of night reappear?[17]

The people of today's State of Israel have been described as "a concentrated example of siege and dread." Aharon Megged writes that the Yom Kippur War of 1973

re-linked the Zionist period of the last two or three generations, to the old long chain of Jewish history; a history of people living as a minority—this time within an ocean of Arab hostility—isolated, with no allies to depend upon, and continuously struggling for its very survival. All our life in Israel, which seemed to be a departure from that history, has now apparently come back to it.[18]

Elie Wiesel speaks from a similar point of view.

For the first time in my adult life I am afraid that the nightmare may start all over again, or that it has never ended, that since 1945 we have lived in parentheses. . . .

Could the Holocaust happen again? Over the years I have put the question to my young students. And they, consistently, have answered yes, while I said no. . . . I was somehow convinced that—paradoxically—man would be shielded, protected by the awesome mystery of the Event.

I was wrong. . . . All of a sudden, I am too much reminded of past experiences. The enemy growing more and more powerful, more and more popular. The aggressiveness of the blackmailers, the permissiveness of some leaders and the total submissiveness of others. The overt threats. The complacency and diffidence of the bystanders. I feel as my father must have felt when he was my age. . . .

And so I look at my young students and tremble for their future; I see myself at their age surrounded by ruins. What am I to tell them?

I remember and I am afraid.[19]

A Christian scholar in Germany shifts the focus somewhat. He refers to the veil draped over the *Sonderbehandlung* ("special treatment") of the three million Jews of today's Soviet Union.[20] *Sonderbehandlung* was the Nazi code word for the extinction of the Jews. Genocide need not take place overnight or even within a decade. It can be a drawn-out business.

Are there any signs of promise from within the threat, and despite it?

Let us admit the worst into conscious analysis. Let us grant—on the basis of very weighty but not absolutely certain evidence—that the unchanged and unchanging position of the overwhelming majority of the Arab states is that Israel has no right to independent and sovereign nationhood in Palestine, and, accordingly, that she must be destroyed as quickly as time and opportunity will permit with the aid of, or despite the necessary prudence of, interim agreements, settlements, and even peace treaties. Let us concede that the Arab conflict with the Jews of Israel has nothing to do, in its essence, with territorial withdrawals or border adjustments; therefore, Israel could pull back to the pre-1967 armistice lines, or to the 1947 partition lines, or, for that matter, to a single beachhead on the Mediterranean coast and yet remain as "guilty" as she has always been and as liable to obliteration, on "moral" grounds.

In this study we have distinguished two fundamental components of the Endlösung: the dehumanization of Jews and Jewish resistance. The difference between resistance in the Nazi time and Israeli Jewish resistance today is that the latter is not doomed. It is representative of the kingdom of day because it is made possible by a humanized Jewish society, it reflects the regaining of life, and futhermore it will possibly succeed.

Today there are formidable obstacles to the success of a potential Arab or other Holocaust of the Jews. A number of nations other than Jews and their destroyers are potentially involved. The question—"Are you prepared to support, through silence or in other ways, a *Judenvernichtung?*"—is quite different today than it was in 1933. Now the potentiality of betraying Jewish lives, although never before a disconcerting matter in the history of the West, has been invaded by international self-concern. The same Elie Wiesel who fears that the nightmare may start all over again properly pointed out—four years earlier than he wrote of fear of remembering—that "for the first time man's fate and the Jewish fate have converged. That means it is impossible to try another Holocaust again without committing the collective suicide of the whole world.[21] Herein lies a most encouraging consideration. A threatened Israel may well take the position (we ought to say, is morally obligated to take the position) that it will not allow a second Holocaust, although the primary decision, either one way or the other, will have been the responsibility of its foes. Two thousand years of antisemitic annihilationism would appear sufficient.

The ideology of the disposable Jew met its nemesis in the 1940s in the almost coincident invention of nuclear weapons and the reestablishment of the Jewish state—a very interesting juxtaposition (compare Ps. 2:4: "He who sits in the heavens laughs; the Lord has them in derision"). The world will simply have to learn that it can no longer dispense Jewish fate. Following Emil Fackenheim, we have alluded to the requirement that Hitler not be permitted a posthumous victory. It is instructive to substitute "the world" for "Hitler."

An analogue from recent history is very relevant. When in 1973 the Soviet Union threatened to dispatch its own troops to join the Syrian Army during the fourth war against Israel, the United States officials said no, you will not do that, because if you do, you will be met by American forces armed with tactical nuclear weapons.[22] It is hardly necessary to record that the Soviet Union drew back. As Louis Halle of the University of Geneva points out, thermonuclear weaponry, with the aid of effective espionage satellites, has become a powerful force over a full generation contributing to world peace.[23] There is every reason to expect that this technology will continue to perform a like function in the years ahead. It is possible, of course, that the Arab nations will decide to consummate their death wish for the Jews through their own self-destruction. Adolf Hitler was perfectly ready to destroy Germany and the entire German people in the course of the Endlösung. However, the price of a new Holocaust is escalating rapidly.[24] A nuclear deterrent can be made to work—not that it ever guarantees anything. We do not speak here of the kingdom of heaven; rather, we speak of the kingdom of day. The reminder of John Maynard Keynes is at once apt and gratuitous: "In the long run we shall all be dead."

Yet a dread implication of our analysis remains. Despite appearances, the real tragedy of, and threat to, the Jewish people today centers not alone in the Middle East but also in the Soviet Union and such places as Argentina and Eastern Europe, where national sovereignty, often a functional good, is manifest as a moral peril. Truly, as long as Israel exists, the Jews of the Soviet captivity are granted a measure of hope. But is this authentic hope, or is it the kind of hope that cannot deliver? The problem is met in only a most minimal way through those Jews who manage to escape from the ever-so-gradual Soviet way of eradicating Jewish existence.[25]

Perhaps we need to fulfill the Jewish tradition after all and end this discussion on a note of hope. David Roskies, in his monumental study of responses to catastrophe in modern Jewish culture, finds that Samuel Bak's "midrash" on Jewish history, as conveyed in his paintings, says that "to live as Jews means to uphold the covenant even as it is desecrated, to exist both in the shadow of eternity and on the brink of destruction." One can return to the Decalogue only through Vilna and Ponar. "The tablets have been broken—*in order that they may be pieced together again.*" One can build only on ruins, and the "sacred symbols, though defiled, are the only ones left." In the closing words of his book, Roskies writes that "the great *imitatio Dei* of the modern period has been [the Jews'] ability in the midst and in the wake of the apocalypse, to know the apocalypse, express it, mourn it, and transcend it; for if catastrophe is the presumption of man acting as destroyer, then the fashioning of catastrophe into a new set of tablets is the primal act of creation carried out in the image of God."[26]

HOPE AND THE
CHRISTIAN CHURCH

Would not the Jewish people, as perhaps the world itself, be better off without the church, without Christianity? Those who speak from within the Christian community cannot avoid this question, just as the detractors of Christian faith will not permit them to avoid it. For example, it is argued that one fundamental reason why antisemitism is at a nadir in certain parts of the world is that Christians in those places have, to all intents and purposes, subdued their faith-claims under the impact of secularization, the norms of religious pluralism, and simple humanitarianism. There is much comfort, for Jews and for others, in the fact of a post-Christian era in which hosts of the church no longer wreak persecution and destruction upon humankind.

However, a moral desire that the Christian church continue, maintaining its integrity and independence, is forcibly expressed not only by Christians but also by some Jews. A parable in Matthew tells of an unclean spirit "gone out of a man" which then "brings with him seven other spirits more evil than himself, and they enter and dwell there; and the last state of that man becomes worse than the first" (12:43, 45). Even if Christianity has brought great harm to Jews, as to other peoples, would not the church's abolition or demise open the door to equally sinister or more evil spirits? A gentile world freed from the moral constraints provided by the Christian faith may very well, so the argument goes, visit upon us even greater hells than the original Holocaust. Anthropotheism, the effectual divinization of man,[27] can only let loose an infinity of horrors. Nazism was itself an embodiment of a devilish/religious impulse, not only to control human beings absolutely but also to make man God.[28] Does not the Christian church, at least ideally and potentially, provide a brake upon such self-idolatry? A colleague in Strasbourg writes: "It is regrettable that the virus of dechristianization is rife in the world."[29] It is worth noting that this speaker is a Jew whose father was murdered in Auschwitz.

Our question revolves itself into another question. What kinds of Christianity are possible? It is clear that the world and especially the Jewish people, not to mention Christians themselves, will be infinitely better off if *triumphalist* Christianity can be overcome. For there is no escape from exclusivism and intolerance as long as humankind is divided into "the elect and the reprobate."[30] Although this sounds like an equal criticism of Judaism as of Christianity, as indeed Rubenstein doubtless intended, no truth is of greater importance: The faith of Judaism has always been massively free of the idolatries that have pervaded Christendom.[31] We are required to conclude from this that it is false, in principle, to claim that only through the religion of Christianity can the all-decisive human struggle against idolatry be waged. But we can also help to implement this truth by giving ourselves to the restoration of Jewishness within a Christianity infected by seven unclean spirits. In this direction are to be found wholeness and justice and love. Thus, we are enabled to address both groups of friends referred to above—those who fear for the end of Christianity, and those who are sickened by the sins of the church.

Because of faith that God did not intend that what he was doing "in Jesus Christ" should lead to Christian domination of others, we are enabled to question and challenge traditional teachings and to live with whatever unresolved problems that may create.[32] We are persuaded that a reformed Christian faith—one empowered by revolutionary ferment and chastened by relativization but not subjected to reductionism —can be a great ally of the Jewish people, as of human beings everywhere. Simultaneously it can be an ally of the suffering, penitent, compassionate God, who yearns over the world and its people who seemingly want to destroy each other in the name of one or another salvational ideology.

When all is said and done, there is no equal to the steadfast, vital spirituality that bears as its fruit compassion and a zeal for justice. We refer as an example to an individual who lives this kind of faith. In Denmark today the name of Finn Henning Lauridsen stands out: He is the founder of the agency For Israels ret til at besta (For Israel's Right to Exist). An earnest Christian, Lauridsen devotes himself to arousing public opinion within and beyond his own country in behalf of the Israelis' right to live a free life. Outstanding artists contribute to the publicizing of Lauridsen's effort. He is much distraught over the possibility of a new *Vernichtung* of the Jewish people and insists upon the moral obligation of Christians and others to act to prevent a second Holocaust.[33]

A Dutch pastor has said, "Only by understanding Auschwitz can we be Christians again."[34]

HOPE BEYOND HOPE

The Israeli poet Abba Kovner would show visitors how the hut in which he worked on his kibbutz lies halfway between the children's playground and the cemetery. Is this not where all of us carry on our work? Robert McAfee Brown writes that unless our future is also God's future, the scenario for our future "is too threatening to entertain."[35] The apostle Paul declares, "If in this life we who are in Christ have only hope, we are of all men most to be pitied." (1 Cor. 15:19).

Inexorably, human memory fades, as does human resolve. This will be true of the Holocaust, as of earlier afflictions of the people of God. For this reason above all others it is imperative that Christian congregations incorporate the memory of the *Shoah* into their liturgies and calendars. Only in this way will the past live meaningfully in the present. Only in this way will this rupture in history, this cataclysm that must shatter all equanimity and shallow optimism, become part of the common store of memory of the two peoples and a perpetual challenge to work against any repetition. Only in this way can we hope to build up a deposit of moral reserve on which we may draw when other ideologies attempt to subvert the proclaimed ethics of our communities or when dangers tempt us to abandon our morality.[36] We can only trust that our remembrances and intentions will somehow be gathered into the strange work of the Ruler of the Universe. May it be that the Holy One is answering, in imponderable ways, our wretched petitions for freedom, our case against the divine indifference, against the demonic powers, against, most of all, ourselves? Should the Lord fail to give heed —if there is no response, no revolution in God as in us, no new bell tower, no temple of the future—then the final message of the Endlö-sung will remain a bleakness that rolls on and on and on.

The rebellious, religious, realistic Jewish believer may be the one who dares to approach the abyss and to reach back over it in search of meaning, language, and song as she continues to live with the God of the covenant.[37]

The Christian revolutionary is the eschatological human being who sets his face, in faith, to the end-time. We have cited Ulrich Simon's judgment that without the Resurrection, the Holocaust is simply hell. He is right, in principle. But for the sufferers, as for the survivors and their descendants, hell can be defeated only through the hope of a future resurrection, when God will be victorious over every satanic and evil power, including death itself. *No past event, however holy, or divine, can ever redeem the terror of the present. Only a future event can finally do this.* A past event can only point toward such a messianic event in the time still to come.

There is the assurance of the fully eschatological character of the Resurrection. Redemption comes; redemption is coming. "The creation waits with eager longing for the revealing of the sons of God. . . . [T]he whole creation has been groaning in travail until now" (Rom. 8:19, 22). Our day remains, as it were, Holy Saturday, the strange in-between time, that day when we, along with God and God's people, enter the precincts of hell—a hell far more real than visionaries have ever depicted. Our Holy Saturday is that day, that shabbat, when we stop and when we are stopped, when we face up to and when we are faced by, the end-time. We who voluntarily and vicariously approach the whirlwind of the *Shoah*, along with those who were caught in its vortex, see the two sides of Sinai: the luminous face of Scripture and promise and the dark face revealed in the kingdom of night.[38]

There is great cause for despair; there is no cause for despair. There is much need for anxiety; there is no need for anxiety. The veil of sadness spread upon all things and all people, upon utopian humanists as upon hopeless humanists, shall be taken up. That young Jewish prophet

169

from the Galilee sleeps now. He sleeps with the other Jewish dead, with all the disconsolate and scattered ones of the murder camps and with the unnumbered dead of the human and the nonhuman family. But Jesus of Nazereth shall be raised.[39] So, too, shall the small Hungarian children of Auschwitz. Once upon a time, they shall again play, and they shall again laugh. The little one of Terezin shall see another butterfly. We shall all sing, and we shall all dance. And we shall love one another. "The wolf shall dwell with the lamb, and the leopard shall lie down with the kid, and the calf and the lion, and the fatling together. . . . They shall not hurt nor destroy in all my holy mountain; for the earth shall be full of the knowledge of the Lord as the waters cover the sea" (Isa. 11:6, 9). The last enemy, death, shall be *sentenced* to death (1 Cor. 15:16; Rev. 21:3, 4). "He who keeps Israel will neither slumber nor sleep" (Ps. 121:4). "Do not be anxious" (Matt. 6:25). Everything will come right. Ani maamin—"I believe in the coming of the Messiah, though he tarry, yet I believe."

APPENDIX 1

THE CHRISTIAN WORLD
GOES TO BITBURG

One must have a good memory to be able to keep the promises
one has given.
—Nietzsche, *Menschliches, Allzumenschliches*

President Richard von Weizsäcker of the Federal Republic of Germany praised President Ronald Reagan of the United States for his "courage" in persisting in his promise to take part in a memorial visit at the cemetery of Bitburg. And West German Chancellor Helmut Kohl thanked Mr. Reagan for sending "a very powerful message" in determining to go on with the visit.[1] But whose brand of courage was the American president manifesting? And what kind of message did he in fact send?

One salient means of grappling with these questions is recourse to the history of Christendom in its relation to the Jewish people and Judaism. The subject before us is anything but a restrictedly "Jewish issue"; it is a Christian and a world-moral issue.

I

A large number of contemporary scholars advance the finding that the Christian church's traditional anti-Jewish teaching conjoined with the Christian world to help make inevitable the Holocaust of the Jews of Europe. The finding has even become something of a truism. Be it noted that many of these historiographers are themselves Christians.[2]

The causative phenomenon here identified suggests a certain perspective for comprehending and assessing President Reagan's resolution to go to Bitburg.

A. Roy Eckardt, "The Christian World Goes to Bitburg" from *Bitburg in Moral and Political Perspective*, ed. Geoffrey H. Hartman (Bloomington: Indiana University Press), 80–89. Copyright © 1986 by Indiana University Press. Reprinted by permission.

There is no question of Mr. Reagan's sympathy toward the victims of the Holocaust, his commitment to the prevention of another such terrible event, and his strong support of the State of Israel. It would be wholly unfair to number him among the many leaders of the Christian world who have failed to understand the moral implications of the Holocaust or remanded it merely to the history of the Jews. Nevertheless, it was as supreme representative of a land largely composed of Christians that the president traveled to that other, even more explicitly Christian land, the one that had consumed itself in Nazism. The American people are heirs of a religious tradition that has for centuries taught contempt for Jews, yet vast numbers of Americans are sympathetic to Jews, to Judaism, and to the State of Israel. The American problem is one of ambivalence. The president's refusal to cancel the Bitburg visit, despite the hue and cry against it, reflected this ambivalence. In addition, as pointed out by the Rev. Robert Huston of the United Methodist Church, such errors of judgment provide implicit support for anti-Semitism. Again, and of the highest significance, how ironically concordant it is that Mr. Reagan should be presiding over the very nation that, as David S. Wyman and others have reminded us, was in the 1930s and 1940s responsible for "the abandonment of the Jews" to what would be for most of them certain death.[3] By resolving to honor, among others, fallen members of the Waffen SS who may have carried out the murders of Jews, President Reagan and his advisors were recapitulating symbolically both the hostilities of the long Christian tradition and the more recent American abandonment of the Jewish people.

The president's action reincarnated the historic Christian acceptance of, and alliance with, the enemies of Jews. Bitburg was and will remain an event of celebration for all Nazis and neo-Nazis. It was to be expected that as soon as they heard the news of Mr. Reagan's visit, numbers of Waffen SS veterans in Germany would rejoice in the assurance that they had been "rehabilitated." One of them said: "The Zionists stop at nothing. But the President is an honest man. He made his decision, and he sticks to it."[4] The visit could thus also reembody the long-familiar utilization and prostitution of the Christian teaching of forgiveness in the service of anti-Semitism.

In such ways as these the Christian world, past and present, was standing at the side of the American president as he journeyed to Bitburg.

II

We shall be referring to the morality and hopefulness in the opposition by Christians to the memorial visit. The fact remains that this body of protest is of little if any immediate ethical or practical help in addressing the relation of Bitburg to Christian teachings and traditional behavior. Such protests simply pose highly moot questions: Were the objectors honoring integral Christian teachings or were they somehow managing to escape and surmount those teachings? More profoundly, just which teachings are to be identified as intrinsically Christian? The applicable and compelling datum, accordingly, is the failure of the Bitburg visit substantially to jeopardize Ronald Reagan's long-run high approval rating among the American populace.[5]

Of still greater moral significance is the split that invariably obtains between Christians and Jews—it surfaced once again at Bitburg[6]—respecting the praxis of "forgiveness." In light of highly divergent historical experiences as between Christians and Jews, the fact that the "forgiveness of one's enemies" plays a more conspicuous verbal and at least professed role in Christian circles than it does in Jewish circles opens the fateful question of the presence of Christian ideology (= rationalization at the collective level) or what is often denominated false consciousness. The reason for saying this is that on purely objective moral grounds, Christians, as past and present victimizers of Jews,[7] ought to be infinitely wary of propagating the idea of forgiveness for anti-Semitism, especially for wholesale murder of Jews. Whenever the victimizers of our world preach to the victims such ideals as love and forgiveness, we do well to adopt a "hermeneutic of suspicion" (Paul Ricoeur). The element of self-serving on the part of the victimizers enters in as an extremely destructive eventuality, as against any analogous situations among the victims.

A. C. J. Phillips, chaplain of St. John's College, Oxford, used the occasion of Mr. Reagan's Bitburg cemetery visit to call upon the Jewish community to forgive the perpetrators of the Holocaust. Phillips concluded his summons with the unbelievable statement: "In remembering the Holocaust, Jews hope to prevent its recurrence; by declining to forgive, I fear that they unwittingly invite it."[8]

Here was a typical instance of the capture of Christian faith by an ideological taint and false consciousness. The truth that as a Christian clergyman, *Stellvertreter* of the church catholic, Anthony Phillips carries upon his hands (as do many of the rest of us) the blood of the Chris-

tian ages ought at least to have compelled him to refrain from such imperialistic moralizing directed to the Jewish people respecting how they
ought to have responded to Ronald Reagan's act.

Even though I write as a Christian, I believe that condemnations of
the Bitburg memorial visit from within the Jewish community embody
a much higher level of morality than do Christian preachments upon
the virtues of love and forgiveness. For there can be neither love nor
forgiveness without repentance and righteousness on the part of the
guilty: this is a main pillar of the biblical witness (see, e.g., Matt.
5:23–24), so often negated by the ideological drives and pious sentimen-
talities that beset the Christian community.

III

Let us return to our epigraph from Friedrich Nietzsche. The Christian memory is an afflicted memory. Christians of America bear a dual
psycho-moral burden: the more recent culpability of their country's
abandonment of the Jewish people, and the much more archetypal and
more deeply repressed, never-ending destructiveness of their religious
community vis-à-vis Jews. Because the American nation's abandonment of the Jews only a generation ago has never been gathered up, internalized, and grappled with in a life-and-death way as an abidingly
accusing fact of life for the American collective conscience, our representatives can go about dispensing the cheap grace of forgiveness for
those German Nazis who committed murder. Cheap grace is the kind
that is "sold on the market like cheapjack's wares." The forgiveness of
sin is distributed at cut prices.[9] In quite sincere fashion Ronald Reagan
could act to shower the German people with these pretensions of grace
while turning his back upon the horrendous record of the United States
respecting the Jews in the Nazi time.[10] And Mr. Reagan could go even
further. Shortly before departing for Bitburg, he declared to a group of
foreign journalists: "All of those in that cemetery have long since met
the Supreme Judge of right and wrong, and whatever punishment was
needed has been rendered by one who is above us all."[11]

The "good memory" that induced President Reagan to "keep the
promise" he gave Chancellor Kohl to visit Bitburg bore no relationship
to any imaginable existential memory of the Holocaust. For the latter
memory would have compelled him and his advisors to do something
entirely different: to honor instead Elie Wiesel's counsel, "Your place,
Mr. President, is with the victims." No, Mr. Reagan's "good memory"

174

arose out of his participation in the collective unconscious of Christendom: a company comprising the crusading legions, theologians, and ecclesiastics of the imperialist Christian church, the historic calumniators and destroyers of Jews and Judaism.[12] Friedrich Nietzsche rejected the Christian virtues of love, pity, and forgiveness. The affinities between Nietzsche and Nazism are well known. Yet, irony of ironies, Bitburg has pointed up the element of moral convincingness in Nietzsche's antipathy to the Christian virtues. For once human forgiveness gets transubstantiated into ammunition for the devil's own cause; i.e., anti-Semitism, the perniciousness that perennially lurks within the Christian ethic, comes to reveal itself in finally destructive form.

Thus, while Nietzsche's aphorism upon the essentiality of memory in the keeping of promises applies strikingly to Ronald Reagan's promise to go to Bitburg, it does not do so at the level of conscious memory. For at the conscious level Mr. Reagan comes across as the well-intentioned though ignorant grandfather,[13] whose awareness of the recent history of Germany is, with that of countless other Americans, either selected or deficient or distorted, or all three. (At one point Mr. Reagan presented the astounding historical datum that very few Germans living today were old enough to remember the Nazi times.) But in the murky world of the unconscious, everything is different; our president was largely acting out the collective memory of 1900 years of Christian history. In Mr. Reagan's particular case, and with Bitburg especially upon our minds, the evil could be actualized and compounded by his special obsession—identical to the one that inspired the Vatican to make its peace with the Hitlerites—the obsessive fear of Bolshevism. Most portentous of the visit to Bitburg was Ronald Reagan's declaration shortly before becoming president: "The Soviet Union is behind everything that is going on in the world." At this juncture, the unconscious and the conscious domains tend to be mutually supportive.

The ongoing character of collective Christian culpability for the Holocaust is demonstrated in the truth that the Christian crime goes on. Any who today support the central Christian doctrines of supersessionism and triumphalism vis-à-vis Judaism and the Jewish people thereby act to keep alive the *Anschauung* that helped make inevitable the death camps of Europe. In keeping with this truth, the head of a nation made up mostly of Christians had in fact only one choice that could be deemed righteous: to stay away from the Bitburg cemetery.

But President Reagan and his advisors also aggravated the psychomoral plight of persecutors and perpetrators within Germany, those "countless ones who were in some fashion accessory, as well as the standard-bearers of the perverted racist world view." Among these people,

> their beloved objects—the Nazi ideology and the delusion of chosenness—continue to survive. No loss has occurred; at worst they were "robbed" by the enemy. The libido has not been required to relinquish its objects. This means that no loss, no demise has taken place—and thus, in turn, that no mourning work could be or needs to be performed. Substitutes were not acceptable. By incessant rationalization and the use of other multiple, convoluted, out-of-the-way defense strategies, a liberating result was achieved that led to a rehabilitation of the old Nazi *Weltanschauung*. Perpetrators became innocent victims. They felt doubly confirmed in their paranoia, for the war was lost—"as we all know"—due to treachery and sabotage, while the victorious Allies were incited and led by "World Jewry."[14]

To this frightening condition—as described by a psychoanalyst in the Germany of today—our president has now added his own contribution. Instead of fostering the reconciliation that he claimed for his act, Mr. Reagan helped to compound human alienation.

The inability to mourn (*die Unfähigheit zu trauern*)[15] is dialectically-existentially linked with the inability to repent (*die Unfähigkeit zu bereuen*).

The future may do its best to obscure or obliterate these truths. But this will not prevent them from crashing down upon the human sphere. History, symbol, and morality are all inseparable.

The etiology of the Bitburg event is, in sum, closely tied to the ethos of vast numbers of church people. Inevitably but revealingly, one such individual found the president's action "to be the most Christian act of his administration." Untold numbers of church people will keep on preaching and supporting a self-righteous, "high morality" of forgiveness for enemies of Jews because they have never repented of their own enmities toward Jews. They have instead been able to justify their own anti-Semitisms on the ground of the Jewish "sin" of "rejecting" the Christian claim. Thus is Jewish suffering transmuted into deserved suffering. Here is the fundamental reason we Christians can turn our backs upon Jewish suffering. Because Christians fail to see the log in their own eye, they are prevented from seeing a log of comparable size in the eye of foes of the Jewish people. Were they themselves Christianly penitent, they would not be so ready to parcel out for the enemies of Jews the cheap grace of forgiveness, any more than would the president whom they had elected. Redemption for acts of cheap grace takes place only when it is made to cost dearly. Mr. Reagan's appearance at Bitburg revealed once more the modern transformation of the original Christian gospel into an ideology of "forgive and forget"—a comfortingly pleasant notion but no less an effectively anti-Jewish and immoral one.

IV

And yet, a deep paradox is present. Something incommensurable, something impertinent, something daring, enters in to break the depressing spell. Amidst the gloom of Bitburg a strange kind of hopefulness intrudes—and this from within the Christian community itself.[16] In point of redeeming truth, some persons of the Christian church immediately grasped and made public the morally intolerable quality of Ronald Reagan's "good memory." To the group of foreign journalists mentioned above, Mr. Reagan had argued that his visit would symbolize "the great reconciliation that has taken place" between the United States and Germany. Therefore, he insisted, it was "morally right" for him to go to Bitburg. But to a considerable number of Christians the president's visit was morally wrong. Thus, the Christian Study Group on Judaism and the Jewish People, a body of American theologians and scholars, found Reagan's "intention to put the past behind us and not to remind the German people of the crimes of the Nazi regime [to be] an affront to many in the new Germany who have been struggling again to become a member of a community of civilized nations by accepting the shame of the past and not denying it." This group further identified the Reagan decision as an offense to Jews and to other victims of the Nazi crimes. Again, some 150 American Protestants and Catholics asserted in an open letter to Mr. Reagan:

We are shocked by the insensitivity and inaccuracy of your explanation that the German soldiers buried [in Bitburg] "were victims, just as surely as the victims in the concentration camps."

The failure to distinguish between perpetrators and victims, between the death of combatants in battle and the slaughter of innocents in the Nazi concentration camps does injustice not only to the memory of the dead but to the most basic tenets of Jewish and Christian morality.[17]

The signatories included the president and general secretary of the National Council of Churches; Baptist, Presbyterian, Episcopalian, Lutheran, Methodist, Congregationalist, United Church of Christ, and Roman Catholic officials; heads of theological seminaries and academic institutions; noted theologians and scholars; and clergy, nuns, and lay leaders.

These persons were not only evidently unimpressed by the president's reputedly inside knowledge of the divine procedures; they also found his "moral" position to be perfidious. But how could such protests ever become possible? Other protests were made, in Germany as in America. *How could it be that certain Christians, heirs as they equally are with Ronald Reagan of the very same collective memory that ensures the denigration of Jews, should rise above all such conditioning?*

The aphorism of Nietzsche requires a corollary: One must have a replacement memory if one is to gain the courage to expunge the evil in promises previously given. These protesting Christians have come under the power of just such an antithetic memory. They remember the small Hungarian children of Auschwitz being burned alive in the presence of other Jewish children who *knew* that in the next moment they would be murdered in the same way (this for the "crime" of being Jewish). Here is a memory that sentences to perdition the collective anti-Jewish memory of the Christian church. It is this new memory that gives life and meaning to a faithful remnant of Christians who will never abandon the Jewish people. Had he wished to do so, or had he possessed the courage, Ronald Reagan could have confronted himself with this other memory. And thereby he could have used the unspeakable occasion of Bitburg in order to represent—or at least to plead for—the remorse of the American people for their part in the abandonment of the Jewish people.[18] Thus could Bitburg itself have been transfigured into a world-decisive act of authentic reconciliation—*with* the people of Germany, *with* the Jewish community, and, incredibly, even *with* possible penitents within the Waffen SS as with other Nazis, the living dead of today's Europe.

A personal observation may be allowed. Perhaps it is the writer's roots in the land of Germany that motivate part of his sorrow over acts of cheap grace directed to—more accurately, directed *against*—the German people. Only costly grace can redeem. The act of the American president and his counselors was, descriptively speaking, a snare and a perversion: this judgment must be entered by one American who perforce lives as though next to the people of Germany. The contention concerning grace is made in the very name of the persecutors and their children, who must otherwise remain lost souls.[19]

178

As matters stand, the name of Bitburg will ever bear the stigma of human alienation instead of human reconciliation. Nevertheless, this fact may itself be treated heuristically. President Reagan claims to be privy to the fact of divine punishment. Let us at the end venture to implement his own reasoning: One day he too may be summoned to judgment and asked how he could ever have acted to memorialize the killers. Yet the action by him and his administration must remain a relatively lesser episode within the larger, unending, and much more infamous tale. It is the entire Christian corpus that will be brought to judgment for its role in creating the victimizers. Once this takes place, the War Between the Memories will have reached its denouement.

APPENDIX 2

WE ARE CALLED TO
REMEMBER IN WORSHIP:
CREATING CHRISTIAN
YOM HASHOAH LITURGIES

While Jewish observance of Yom HaShoah is an unambiguous "family" affair, Christian observance is far more problematical. The Holocaust was a Christian event and is a Christian problem in an almost opposite way to that in which it was a Jewish event and is a Jewish problem. While Jews were the certain victims, Christians were the murderers, accomplices, indifferent bystanders and only in minuscule numbers, helpers or rescuers.[1] But the problem goes even deeper than this. We are faced with far more than the apostasy of a generation. Roy Eckardt states the Christian condition unequivocally.

> There is a dimension to the *Endlösung* that the Christian must know, and from which the Jew is spared . . . The dark night that surrounds the Christian soul is the night of objective guilt . . . because here, in this event, . . . "the theological negation of Judaism and the vilification of the Jewish people" within the Christian tradition were, at the last, translated into the genocide of the Jews. . . . The annihilation of the Jews expresses, on the one side of the coin, an ultimate resolve on the part of the Nazis, and, on the other side of the coin, the final logic and application of nineteen hundred years of Christian teaching respecting the Jewish people.[2]

A Christian liturgy for Yom HaShoah[3] must bear this burden, and in some way prepare the way for this acknowledgment.

Alice L. Eckardt, "We Are Called to Remember in Worship: Creating Christian Yom HaShoah Liturgies" reprinted with emendations from *Liturgies on the Holocaust*, ed. Marcia Sachs Littell (Lewiston, N.Y.: The Edwin Mellen Press), 11–17. Copyright © 1986 by Marcia Sachs Littell. An earlier version of this article appeared in *Shoah* 1, no. 4 (1979): 1–4. © 1979 by Zachor and the National Jewish Conference Center. Reprinted by permission.

One function of corporate worship is to make the past live in the present in a meaningful way so that each generation experiences those events that help to give meaning to its own existence: acts of heroism, sacrifice, courage, suffering, redemption and rebirth, moments of doubt, faith, and insight. Religious ceremony (liturgy and ritual) creates and keeps alive a common store of memory. Not only does public worship perpetuate the orienting events of faith history in new times and circumstances, but it should—if properly informed by responsible theology—build up "a significant deposit of moral reserves" on which its participants may draw when other ideologies attempt to subvert the proclaimed ethics of the community.[4]

Many of us are convinced that in this century events have occurred that must be seen and understood as new faith-orienting experiences—experiences that challenge much that we have professed and on which we have placed our trust. Therefore, even without a clear consensus about the full religious significance of these events, they must become part of the common store of memory through inclusion in the liturgical services of the churches as well as the synagogues. A new and surer "deposit of moral reserves" must be accumulated that will not evaporate when most needed, that will not include a self-destruct mechanism such as the dogmatic arrogance of the traditional Christian claim that presumed the right to destroy error.[5] These events are the Nazi Holocaust of European Jews, and the rebirth of the State of Israel.

The primary task of any Holocaust memorial service is to engage the worshippers existentially in the plight of the Jewish families and communities trapped within the German Nazi state and its willing accomplices. Within my own congregation I have attempted to make meaningful the progressive denial of rights, human status, and life to the Jews of Europe by relating such denials to the congregation's own lives. Barriers of abstraction, of "foreignness," and of either overt or latent antisemitism must be overcome by the weight of the overwhelming human tragedy.

Unless it is an unusual congregation, a good deal of preparatory educational work should be done before the observance. If that is not feasible, the service should include a considerable amount of information. Even now, after the showing of the television program "Holocaust," and quite a number of other dramatic representations, most gentile Christians know little about the Nazi "Final Solution," and even less about why Christians should concern themselves about it. The more informed a congregation is about the factual aspects, the more time and attention can be directed to other dimensions of the subject.

Planners of a Holocaust service must be clear in their own minds regarding its purpose and the ends to be achieved, since this will determine the form of the service and the choice of liturgical materials. This is particularly essential for this service because of the complexity of goals[6] and the psychological factors. I am convinced that no Christian service should be without a penitential confession of Christian failings and culpability. Since confession of sin and repentance are part of every Christian worship, to omit a specific confession on this occasion would be a continuation of the earlier sin. However, as Donald McEvoy insists, the intent of a Christian Holocaust observance is not "to lay a 'guilt trip'" on the congregants but through "acute awareness of the realities of that era [to] sensitize the Christian conscience and fortify the resolution that the mistakes of the past never be repeated."[7]

A great deal of learning and engagement come about through a congregational committee planning its own service. There are now some very helpful sources for both Christian and Jewish or interfaith groups to utilize. A particularly useful one is the collection of twenty services and/or sermons published by the Anne Frank Institute of Philadelphia. A number of other materials can be found at the end of this essay.

There are certain stipulations for a Christian observance of the *Shoah* that I believe must be insisted upon.

1. *Do not "Christianize" the Holocaust.* Hitler's "war against the Jews" was only incidentally an attack on the churches, an attack which depended on their willingness, or unwillingness, to accept Hitler's authority. The relatively small number of Christians who suffered or died on behalf of their faith and/or because of aiding the Nazis' primary victims must not be exaggerated, as if the church did not fail its test. Many Christian victims were imprisoned or killed for factors unrelated to their religious convictions or behavior. Polish clerics, for example, were often seized because they were perceived as symbols and potential leaders of Polish nationalism. Those Righteous Among the Gentiles (in this case, Among the Christians) are to be venerated and celebrated. The Dutch family of Corrie ten Boom with her father and sister, the French priests Péres Marie-Benoît and Roger Braun, the German Catholics Father Bernhard Lichtenberg and laywoman Gertrud Luckner, the Dutch Adventist John Weidner, the German Protestant Pastors Paul Schneider, Hermann Mass, and Heinrich Grüber, and the French Protestant congregation of Le Chambon led by Pastor André Trocmé—these are the true saints of the twentieth century. But they were the all

too tiny faithful remnant. We dare not try to rewrite history to exonerate that which cannot be exonerated.

2. *Do not turn the Holocaust experience into a triumphalist demonstration of the truth of the Christian gospel.* This most monstrously evil event must *raise questions*, not support traditional answers, especially traditional answers that represent negation of Jewish existence and faith! An article in *The Church Herald* exemplifies Christian triumphalism applied to the Holocaust. After describing the hell that Auschwitz represented, and the "psychological ploys" which inmates used to "escape the situation," the author points to "the members of one small group, Christians, [who] distinguished themselves by their refusal to turn inward. Rather they accepted the reality of their situation and lived for Christ by ministering to others." The author further asserts (as if proudly) that "in Auschwitz Protestant as well as Catholic clerics were singled out for special abuse," without any mention of the "special abuse" meted out to *all* Jewish arrivals. The author's intention is further revealed by his assertion that the martyr priest Maximilian Kolbe, who offered himself for execution in place of a fellow prisoner, did so with the words, "I'm a Christian and I'm not afraid to die." Yet Rolf Hochhuth, who dedicated his play *The Deputy/Der Stellvertreter* to Father Kolbe, reports simply that the priest gave the reason that he was no longer fit for work.[8]

The love, courage, and faith of this band of Christians in Auschwitz is not being challenged here. What is being rejected is the audacity which would usurp "the Auschwitz experience"—that event most obsessionally fixated on Jews—and claim it as a validation of the Christian gospel and a demonstration of the superiority of the Christian faith: "When all else perished, Christ remained. And Christ was sufficient. The Auschwitz experience gives meaning to Paul's words to the Galatians: 'I have been crucified with Christ; it is no longer I who live, but Christ who lives in me' (Gal. 2:20). Christ lives, even in the fires of Auschwitz."[9]

By contrast to this triumphalist misuse of the Christ figure we can offer worshippers other thoughts on which to meditate:

• Had Jesus lived—or had he returned—during the Nazi era, he, too, would have been shot at the edge of a huge pit or been sent in the cattle cars to a death camp and gas chamber.[10] Just as crucifixion was the method of mass executions of Jews under the Romans, and Jesus suffered it with his countrymen, so shooting and gassing were the methods under the Nazi Germans, and he would not have been spared that death either.

• "The Christ-Messiah was in Auschwitz. With His brethren He suffered the Holocaust, once again on the Cross, as Marc Chagall has painted Him with tallith and tefillin. And we in the . . . so-called Christian world were the onlookers."[11] Even worse, baptized and communing Christians sent Him and His people there. "Is this nothing to you, all you who pass by?" (Lamentations 1:12)

• "The word did not become flesh; the numbers did."[12]

• "When the body of Christ is discovered at Auschwitz, it will be raised from among the victims, not hidden among the Catholic and Protestant and Orthodox guards and administrators."[13]

• A Jewish poet of Vilna also links the crucified Christ to Jewish suffering:

> Close to the walls of the ghetto at Vilna there stands, blood-soaked, a wooden cross.
>
> . . . .
>
> Endlessly suffering, the crucified Christ cries out:
> "Forgive the murderers, O Father: arouse those who are silent!"
> And as the wings of death brush by, he softly whispers in bliss:
> "Hear, O Israel . . ." Whitefaced, the Mother sinks to her knees:
> "O Father in heaven, you take our children, you lead us unto death;
> but if you leave some to give witness—speak then O God, speak out of their mouths."[14]

3. *Do not use readings from Jewish sources and then criticize, refute, or reinterpret them to fit Christian views.* Because we are the outsiders to the *Shoah*, we are particularly dependent on the testimony of the witnesses. The words, and art, and music of those who perished or survived the experience have an authenticity that must not be made the subject of disputation. Their power to disturb our consciences and awaken our spirits lies inescapably in their coming to us from out of the whirlwind.

Of the many eloquent testimonies of varying types, one of the most challenging is "Yossel Rakover's Appeal to God" by Zvi Kolitz.[15] This defiant affirmation of faith to the God whom the Hasid Rakover can only view as having veiled His countenance from the world and decided to sacrifice mankind to its wild instincts exceeds the Book of Job in both its accusations and its refusal to abandon belief. After Rakover's last words—the Sh'ma and a committing of his soul into the hands of the Lord (Ps. 31:4)—only awed silence is appropriate. We *must* reject the kind of false reading that accuses Rakover of having "the illusion that he can bang his fist on the table of the Almighty and demand answers to his complaint," the judging that faults him for desiring vengeance, or the nitpicking introduction of irrelevancies. But above all, we Christians are forbidden to do what the German Catholic editors did when they published this modern-day Job, namely, empty it of its power and undercut its challenge by a Christian apologetic that remains unchanged by the *Shoah*: "No, the angry God of the fathers . . . , the God of Jesus Christ . . . is not an 'angry God,' even though He is Just. He is the God of incomprehensible love . . . God's last and definitive word to the world and to history is not a word of vengeance but of love, . . . spoken . . . through the passion and death of His only-begotten, his beloved Son."[16]

Too long now has Christianity taken the words of Hebrew Scripture and twisted them to fit Christian convictions. It is time we read that Scripture in its own right and for its own revelations. How much more is this true with regard to the new Torah written and being written in our own day! It is time for us to listen and to remain silent.

4. *Do not attempt to strip the Holocaust of its terrifying and awesome character.* Do not take refuge in circumlocution or abstract language. We are called to face the reality in its stark horror and in its betrayal of humanity, for only in so doing will we be forced to recoil from any kind of "explanations" or excuses. Only then will we realize that the Holocaust must be so etched in the collective as well as individual consciousness that it will become "a plumb line by which we [will] measure our response to every denial of human rights and every circumstance of tyranny . . ."[17]

Numbers are abstractions: "six million" can become too remote to have meaning. Yet the numbers do have significance. At some indeterminate point the accumulation of numbers is indicative of a qualitative change. The murder of one person is still murder and a crime against humanity. But the murder of six million people becomes something more. To give it a name, "genocide," is even more abstract. And so we must resort to two strategies. First, make the number of six million relevant by comparing it to the population of a certain number of towns or cities with which the congregation can relate. Secondly, use the building blocks of $1 + 1 + 1 + \ldots$: tell the stories of *this* girl Eva Heyman, *this* boy Moshe Flinker, *this* father Shlomo Wiesel, *this* mother Lena Donat, *this* grandmother and grandfather Racz. "I don't want to die, because I've hardly lived."[18] The cry of a 13-year old girl wondering if she will meet the fate her closest friend had already met breaks through the walls we try to build around the Holocaust to shield ourselves from its terror and accusation.

5. *Remember the total abandonment Jews experienced.* The lack of simple and ordinary gestures of sympathy or kindness was more devastating to the victims' spirits than the cruelty of the officials and guards. We, the fortunate, must not close ourselves off from suffering wherever it is felt. The role of indifferent bystander has been revealed all too closely as the accomplice of those with evil intentions. We are reminded most vividly of Jesus' own words on this subject:

> "I was hungry and you gave me no food, I was thirsty and you gave me no drink, I was a stranger and you did not welcome me, naked and you did not clothe me, sick and in prison and you did not visit me. . . . Truly I say to you, as you did it not to one of the least of these my brethren, you did it not to me." (Matthew 25:42–45)

In this account we have a compelling reason for Christian liturgies centering on the Holocaust. We dare not ignore or forget those six million lives or the meaning they have for our own.

6. *Finally, do not allow a Yom HaShoah service to become a one-time occurrence.* We are building a common store of memory, and that is accomplished only through repetition and emphasis. Every year we observe the death of one Jew almost 2,000 years ago. Should we not each year remember the death of six million of his people and ask what that says to us? Should we relate the two observances? In Claremont, California, alongside the annual service of Good Friday an ecumenical prayer vigil was held as "A Christian Witness to the Memory of the Holocaust of Six Million Jews." A Statement was also issued by the participants.[19]

Do not make this service the only time during the year when the entire realm of Christian-Jewish relations is considered. A Holocaust memorial service should be the *beginning* of new awareness and sensitivity, and of efforts to build new bridges of understanding and support across the lines of faith, so that as Christians we will never again send others down the bloody path to Ponar and Auschwitz, Babi Yar and Chelmno, Buchenwald and Belzec, Terezin and Treblinka, Dachau and Sobibor, Mauthausen and Maidanek.

Having considered carefully the guidelines and goals, the components of the service can then be marked out. Words can be very powerful, and are central to most worship services. But they should be reinforced and brought to life by the use of other means of communication. Silence as a counterpoise is not only effective but at times almost obligatory. Appropriate music, particularly some of the songs written in the ghettos, can sometimes have an impact far beyond the spoken word. Visual images—enlarged pictures, slides, films and filmstrips—are invaluable aids, and there are many good resources. Ritual acts such as candle-lighting and candle-extinguishing can be given a new meaning in the setting of a memorial service for the six million through creative imagination: Extinguishing six out of eleven candles can demonstrate the proportion of European Jews murdered; lighting six candles in memory of each of the six million can accompany six readings or a recital of names of the major killing centers or the countries of origin; the lighting of a seventh candle for the State of Israel as a symbol of the new hope and new existence/resurrection of the Jewish people would be most appropriate. The wearing of a Star of David armband by all participants in the service may give an immediacy of relationship that can be most significant. Liturgical dance offers a new dimension of expression. The use of art and poetry produced by Jews during or after the Holocaust may help us to rediscover the inner meaning of some traditional imagery which Christianity has torn out of its original Jewish setting. Abraham Rattner's artistic renditions of Moses, Job, and Jesus reveal the continuity of their anguish and their grasping for the truth. The poetry of Hermann Adler (quoted briefly earlier) links Jewish suffering in the Holocaust to the suffering of Jesus, as it also links the bereft mother of Jesus with a Christian heroine of the *Shoah* who is called "a new madonna."[20]

In a way that many find strange, and yet is not, Christian Holocaust services can enrich the life of a congregation in a most unique and significant way, by wresting theology from dogma and opening it up to existential re-evaluation (a re-evaluation shared at certain levels with our Jewish friends), by making the faithful more aware of the necessity of examining moral decisions more fully than ever before, and by sensitizing the worshippers to the experiences and responses in the Holocaust of the people from whose midst their own faith initially sprang and onto whose roots their own community claims to be engrafted.

LITURGICAL
RESOURCE MATERIALS

Cargas, Harry James. *A Holocaust Commemoration for Days of Remembrance: For Communities, Churches, Centers, and for Home Use.* Washington, D.C.: Holocaust Remembrance Foundation, 1982.

_____. "A Holocaust Liturgy," (based on the Catholic Mass for the Dead), *Modern Liturgy* [California], September 1984; reprinted in *Christian Jewish Relations* 18, 1 (1985): 34–40.

Commemorations for Yom HaShoah, Holocaust Remembrance Day. (Two services: one at a Reform synagogue, one at an Episcopal Church). National Conference of Christians and Jews, n.d. (about 1983).

Fisher, Eugene J., and Klenicki, Leon. *From Death to Hope.* 15 pages, New York: Stimulus Foundation, 1983.

"A Litany of Remembrance for the Victims of the Holocaust" (prepared for the Washington Cathedral, 29 April 1979). Printed in *Interreligious Currents* [UAHC] 6, 2–3 (Winter/Spring 1987): 4–5.

Littell, Marcia Sachs, ed. *Liturgies on the Holocaust: An Interfaith Anthology.* Lewiston, N.Y.: The Edwin Mellen Press, 1986.

McEvoy, Donald, ed. *Christians Confront the Holocaust: A Collection of Sermons.* New York: National Conference of Christians and Jews, 1979.

"The Miracle of Denmark: A Christian Service and Commemoration of the Rescue of the Danish Jews." (5-page leaflet; adapted from a Jewish service created by Rabbi Maurice Davis, 1973). National Conference of Christians and Jews, n.d. (about 1979).

Roskies, David. *Night Words: A Midrash on the Holocaust.* Washington, D.C.: B'nai B'rith Hillel Foundation, 1975.

Szonyi, David, ed. *The Holocaust: An Annotated Bibliography and Resource Guide.* New York: Ktav for The National Jewish Resource Center (CLAL), 1985. See sections IB, II, III, X.

"This Shall Tell All Ages: Art, Music, and Writings on the Holocaust." New York: United Jewish Appeal, 1981.

Alice L. Eckardt

NOTES

Complete bibliographical details for most works cited may be found in the Selected Bibliography. Citations from any work not so listed include this information in the relevant note.

PREFACE

1. Joan Arnold Romero, "The Protestant Principle: A Woman's Eye View," in Rosemary Ruether, ed., *Religion and Sexism* (New York: Simon and Schuster, 1974), p. 335.

2. Emil Fackenheim, "Concerning Authentic and Inauthentic Responses to the Holocaust" (Unpublished paper prepared for International Scholars Conference on the Holocaust, New York, 3–6 March 1975).

3. Robert McAfee Brown, "Foreword," *Long Night's Journey into Day: Life and Faith after the Holocaust* (Detroit: Wayne State University Press, 1982), pp. 9–10.

4. When Count Eberhard of Württemberg established the University of Tübingen in 1477, he specified in the charter that the university was to remain *judenrein* ("Jew-free"). A delegation sent by the pope confirmed the founding and its charter. In 1492 Duke Eberhard extended the stipulation to all of Württemberg as he expelled those Jews then living in the Duchy. The Holy Roman Emperor, Charles V, "reconfirmed the 'privileges' of Württemberg, which [remained] 'unburdened' by protective rights for Jews" (Heiko A. Oberman, *The Roots of Anti-Semitism*, pp. 3, 53n.28, 62n.107, 96). In the Hitler period, Gerhard Kittel, a noted Protestant New Testament scholar and authority on ancient Judaism, held forth at Tübingen, and gave the Nazi regime intellectual rationale for all of its actions against Jews except its final one: mass murder. By that stage, Kittel had no say in the matter, and had given away all ground on which he could have protested.

1. RETURN TO THE KINGDOM OF NIGHT

1. To our knowledge, Elie Wiesel was the first to apply the phrase "kingdom of night" to the Holocaust; see his *Night*. This is his most explicitly confessional work, with the possible exception of the much later *A Jew Today*. An authoritative history of the Holocaust years is Lucy S. Dawidowicz, *The War Against the Jews, 1933–1945*. The title is not sufficiently discriminating: Dawidowicz is concerned with the destruction of Jews

in Germany, Austria, Poland, the Baltic countries, and, to a very limited extent, western Russia. Other areas with a prewar Jewish population of no less than 2.5 million—Czechoslovakia, Hungary, Rumania, Bulgaria, Yugoslavia, Greece, Italy, and western and northern Europe—are only briefly considered in an appendix. Nora Levin's *The Holocaust* includes a country-by-country account following lengthy consideration of the preparatory phases of the Final Solution. The most thorough-going study of the *Judenvernichtung*, based on German records and documentation, remains Raul Hilberg's *The Destruction of European Jews*. Hilberg has added much additional data and has further refined the interpretation of the evidence in his "revised and definitive" three-volume edition of 1985; citations, however, are to the original volume. The most recent comprehensive work is Martin Gilbert's *The Holocaust: A History of the Jews of Europe During World War II*. Gilbert approaches the subject from the perspective of the victims, thus balancing Hilberg's work. For an informative survey of Hitlerism and Nazi Germany, with sections on the persecution of Jews, the SS and the ideological basis of its mentality and command structure, the concentration and death camps, and the mass executions of Russian war prisoners, see Helmut Krausnick et al., *Anatomy of the SS State*. For a thorough study of the deportation of Jews from Germany, with emphasis upon the kind of bureaucracy that reduces human beings to virtual robots, see Hermann G. Adler, *Der Verwaltete Mensch* (Managerial Mankind). A volume put forth by a Christian scholar in East Germany is Heinrich Fink, ed., *Stärker als die Angst* (Violence as Anxiety/Dread); the most significant contribution to it is H. David Leuner, "Versagen und Bewährung der Christen in der Solidarität" (Failure and Testing of Christians in Solidarity). See also Terrence Des Pres, *The Survivor*; Saul Friedlander, *L'Antisemitisme Nazi*; Sebastian Haffner, *The Meaning of Hitler*; Yehuda Bauer, *A History of the Holocaust*; Léon Poliakov, *Harvest of Hate*; Gerald Reitlinger, *The Final Solution*. For a fine collection of testimonial literature from during and after the Holocaust, see Albert H. Friedlander, ed., *Out of the Whirlwind*. Yaffa Eliach has provided an incomparable book in her *Hasidic Tales of the Holocaust*.

2. Jules Isaac, *The Teaching of Contempt*.

3. Uri Zvi Greenberg, from "To the Mound of Corpses in the Snow," trans. A. C. Jacobs, in *Anthology of Modern Hebrew Poetry* 2: 259.

4. On the problematic character of the term "Holocaust," see Alice and Roy Eckardt, "Studying the Holocaust's Impact Today: Some Dilemmas of Language and Method," pp. 224–26.

One way of summing up the *Shoah* is to list its most significant aspects. It was: —an uninterrupted progression—of steadily more stringent anti-Jewish decrees and actions—toward increasingly radicalized objectives—and brutality of methods—in constantly expanding territories—with ever-greater speed—to the accompaniment of increasingly virulent anti-Jewish propaganda; while the marked victims found themselves faced with: —rapidly accumulating deprivations—in repeatedly diminished space—with ever fewer options—until no choice or space was left.

5. So Gerald Reitlinger argues in *The Final Solution*, p. 102. Raul Hilberg speaks of the fateful step across the "dividing line" that inaugurated the "killing phase," and he refers, in *The Destruction of the European Jews*, pp. 177ff., to two all-decisive orders by Hitler in 1941 that were to doom all European Jewry.

6. The figure of eleven million estimated (incorrectly) by the Nazi bureaucrats included Jews of European countries that the Third Reich never succeeded in dominating:

Great Britain, Ireland, Portugal, Spain, Sweden, Switzerland, and Turkey. Of the eleven million, the Nazis succeeded in destroying about six million. It is not possible to furnish exact figures. The *Encyclopaedia Judaica* estimates 5,820,960.

7. Abel J. Herzberg illustrates this aspect of the truth in his essays on Bergen-Belsen in *Amor Fati*.

8. See Terrence Des Pres's chapter "Excremental Assault" in *The Survivor*.

9. Abba Kovner, "A First Attempt to Tell"; Elie Wiesel, *Legends of Our Time*, p. 229; Cynthia Haft, *The Theme of Nazi Concentration Camps in French Literature*, p. 133.

10. Haft, *Theme of Concentration Camps*, p. 153.

11. *Yad Vashem* means "lasting memorial" (literally, "a monument and a name"; cf. Isa. 56:5).

12. See Léon Poliakov, *Auschwitz*, pp. 127–36.

13. In October 1943, the Germans razed what was left of the camp. They plowed the area and created a farm, using bricks from the gas chambers for a farmhouse. Areas not being used for farming were sowed with lupin seed or turned into pine woods. Thus they hoped to hide Treblinka from the world. See Alexander Donat, *Treblinka*; Yitzhak Arad, *Belzec, Sobibor, Treblinka*; Yuri Suhl, ed. and trans., *They Fought Back*, pp. 150–55; Wassilij Grossman, *Die Hölle von Treblinka* (The Hell of Treblinka), pp. 45–48; Jean-Francois Steiner, *Treblinka*. A serious fault in Steiner's work, a one-time best-seller, is his failure to acknowledge his sources. He is also sensationalistic; see the critical remarks by Haft, *Theme of Concentration Camps*, pp. 190–91, and by Israel Gutman, "Remarks on the Literature of the Holocaust," p. 133.

A revolt in Sobibor in October 1943 is described by one of the escapees, Richard Rashke, in *Escape from Sobibor*. A television dramatization based on this book was first shown in Spring 1987. Other accounts can be found in Arad, *Belzec, Sobibor, Treblinka*, and in Novitch, *Sobibor* (especially pp. 30–31, 43–45, 89–99, 112–13, 156–63). As with Treblinka, Sobibor was levelled soon after the uprising, and a farm was erected on the site.

14. "Tuchin."

15. The most comprehensive and authoritative single volume on this issue remains *Jewish Resistance During the Holocaust*. However, there is an increasing number of books dealing with revolts in the ghettos and camps, and with partisan fighters: Reuben Ainsztein, *The Warsaw Ghetto Revolt*; Yitzhak Arad, *Ghetto in Flames* and *The Partisan*; Yehuda Bauer, *They Chose Life*: Shalom Cholawski, *Soldiers from the Ghetto*; Lester Eckman and Chaim Lazar, *The Jewish Resistance: The History of the Jewish Partisans in Lithuania and White Russia During the Nazi Occupation, 1940–1945*; Michael Elkins, *Forged in Fury*; Philip Friedman, ed., *Martyrs and Fighters*; Chaika Grossman, *The Underground Army: Fighters of the Bialystok Ghetto*; Moshe Kaganovich, *Jewish Partisans of Eastern Europe*; Isaac Kowalski, ed., *Anthology on Armed Jewish Resistance, 1939–1945*; Shmuel Krakowski, *The War of the Doomed: Jewish Armed Resistance in Poland, 1942–1944*; Dan Kurzman, *The Bravest Battle: The Twenty-eight Days of the Warsaw Ghetto Uprising*; Amy Latour, *The Jewish Resistance in France (1940–1944)*; Dov Levin, *Fighting Back: Lithuanian Jewry's Armed Resistance to the Nazis, 1941–1945*; Zivia Lubetkin, *In the Days of the Destruction and Revolt*; Ber Mark, *Uprising in the Warsaw Ghetto*; Henri Michel, *The Shadow War: Resistance in Europe, 1939–1945*; Miriam Novitch, *Sobibor: Martyrdom and Revolt: Documents and Testimo-*

191

nies; Marie Syrkin, *Blessed Is the Match: The Story of Jewish Resistance*; Yuri Suhl, *They Fought Back: The Story of the Jewish Resistance in Nazi Europe.*

16. Raul Hilberg's *Destruction of the European Jews*, which is restricted to the Holocaust as such, is often singled out as an illustration of this outlook. Although Hilberg approaches the Endlösung as though from the standpoint of its perpetrators rather than of its victims, this is necessary for realizing his purpose. He is the foe of everything Nazi, and his brilliant work remains authoritative.

17. A. Roy Eckardt, *Christianity and the Children of Israel.* This volume is based on a doctoral dissertation supervised by Reinhold Niebuhr.

18. Jacob Robinson, assisted by Mrs. Philip Friedman, *The Holocaust and After*, p. 323.

19. Elie Wiesel, "Jewish Values in the Post-Holocaust Future," p. 283.

20. Immanuel Kant taught that the noumenal world forever eludes us, in contrast to the world of phenomena.

21. Haft, *Theme of Concentration Camps*, p. 11.

22. Compare a critical comment regarding a public school curriculum on the Holocaust written by one of the five members of a panel of review appointed by the U. S. Education Department: "The program gives no evidence of balance or objectivity. The Nazi point of view, however unpopular, is still a point of view, and it is not presented; nor is that of the Ku Klux Klan" (*Together* 2, 3 [October 1987]: 1, 14).

23. Lawrence L. Langer, *The Holocaust and the Literary Imagination*, p. xiii. The issue we raise is not quite the same as that of literary quality, although related to it. Cynthia Haft is entirely correct that the phenomenon of the concentration camps can penetrate the individual and collective consciousness of our time only through literature which manifests "the power of language . . . to contain and transmute all passions, all human experiences." As she observes, the mere fact of having been through a concentration camp, or, for that matter, of having learned what happened to others there, hardly bestows literary talent or creates a work of art. *Theme of Concentration Camps*, pp. 10–11, 189.

24. Cynthia Ozick, "The Uses of Legend: Elie Wiesel as Tsaddick," p. 19. Cf. Wilfred Owen, referring to World War I: "My subject is war, and the pity of war. The poetry is in the pity."

25. Elias Canetti wrote this before the reconstitution of the State of Israel. However, he never indicated a change in his point of view after 1948. *The Human Province* (London: Andre Deutsch, 1985), as quoted in *The Times* [London], 27 July 1985, p. 8.

26. See Alice L. Eckardt, Appendix 2. See also Franklin H. Littell, *The Crucifixion of the Jews*, Appendix; Marcia Sachs Littell, ed., *Liturgies on the Holocaust.*

27. While Irving Greenberg does not go this far, he is yet taken by the baffling nature of the event, arguing that no final or definitive lessons can be learned from the Holocaust. "The event in itself is so radical a surd, it breaks so many limits and accepted norms, that its implications are more often paradoxical, dialectic, and baffling. Most attempts to give definitive or single meanings to Holocaust implications usually bespeak lack of knowledge of what happened or, what is worse, propaganda or use of the victims for selfish advantage" ("Lessons to Be Learned from the Holocaust"). In another place he speaks more positively respecting the Holocaust and its moral and spiritual lessons ("Cloud of Smoke, Pillar of Fire: Judaism, Christianity, and Modernity after the Holocaust").

Adi Ophir protests against the sanctifying of the Holocaust, which he sees resulting from focusing exclusively on the Jewish aspect of that event, and making it a holy source of reference. In particular he is concerned about the tendencies in this approach that make the Divine into Absolute Evil with this concept then becoming the center of a new religion. By contrast, Ophir holds that a focus on the human aspects, that is, analyzing the enabling conditions and other factors that made the Holocaust possible, allows us to identify the *Shoah* as Absolute Evil whose revelation was in the past but whose possibility is also in the present. We are thus liberated from a Holocaust mythology that discards the biblical God of Israel on the basis of his being Absolute Evil, and are freed to cope with the human possibilities of other atrocities ("On Sanctifying the Holocaust: An Anti-Theological Treatise" in *Rethinking the Holocaust*).

28. Probably no other modern event has produced a comparable mass of writing. The single bibliography entitled *The Holocaust and After* (see n. 17 above) reflects the vast number of publications that bear in one or another way upon our present concerns. The annotated volume contains 6,637 items. However, it was published in 1973, the journal materials it lists are largely limited to Jewish periodicals, and the entries are restricted to literature in English, although much of this comprises translations from such other languages as Hebrew, Yiddish, Polish, and German. We estimate that at this writing the number of published items relating substantially to the Holocaust and its aftermath total more than fifty thousand.

29. We should not overlook the fact that similar legal and illegal actions against Jews were being simultaneously undertaken by the Polish government and many of its people and institutions.

30. William Jay Peck points to God's unfairly forgiving Cain for his brother's murder, thus refusing "to close the door on that appalling fratricide. The sign leaves the future open" to a history of fratricide ("From Cain to the Death Camps," p. 159). Elie Wiesel concludes his meditation on that first murder with the observation that had Cain "chosen to bear witness [against God's unfairness either in preferring Abel's gift *or* in creating a world in which death existed] rather than to shed blood, his fate would have been our example and our ideal, and not the symbol of our malediction" (*Messenger of God*, p. 64).

2. REMEMBERING

1. Langer, *Holocaust and the Literary Imagination*, p. 270.

2. Wiesel, "Jewish Values in the Post-Holocaust Future," p. 282.

3. Konrad Kellen, '*Seven Beauties:* Auschwitz—The Ultimate Joke?"; also Alvin Rosenfeld, "The Holocaust According to William Styron," *Midstream* 25, 10 (December 1979): 43–49, and *Imagining Hitler*.

4. The opposite reaction to despising the victims is that of glorifying them. John Cardinal O'Connor expressed this latter view as he sought to answer journalists' questions about his visit to Yad Vashem in January 1987: "it might well be that the Holocaust may be an enormous gift that Judaism has given to the world," for the suffering taught the world about the "sacredness and dignity of every human person" (*New York Times*, 3 January, 1987). Apart from the question of whether the Jewish suffering has taught the

world about individual worth, the viewpoint expressed by the cardinal may be rejected by many people on other grounds.

5. Elias Canetti observed in 1945 that "the lust of the presumptuous man . . . infects others, who would like to be just as presumptuous as the presumptuous Nazis." *The Human Province*, (London: Andre Deutsch, 1985), as quoted in *The Times* [London], 27 July 1985, p. 8.

6. Dan Diner, "The Historians' Controversy," in "Rethinking the Holocaust," p. 76. See Appendix 1 for one analysis of Reagan's decision to go to Bitburg.

7. Metz, *The Emergent Church*, pp. 29–30. The television dramatization "Holocaust," written by Gerald Green for U.S. television, was shown in West Germany in spring 1979, but only by regional stations rather than as part of the national network. East Germany has not shown it at all, although some East Germans living close enough were able to tune in. Although a mass audience watched the program and responded with many telephone calls, there has been little continuing interest.

8. Rotenstreich, *Reflections on the Contemporary Jewish Tradition*, p. 13.

9. Golo Mann, as cited in *Newsweek*, 26 May 1975.

10. Abraham Zvie Bar-On, consultation, Jerusalem, 24 May 1976.

11. Harvey Cox, *Feast of Fools*, pp. 12, 13.

12. Hilel Klein, consultation, Jerusalem, 2 June 1976.

13. Jürgen Moltmann, consultation, Tübingen, 14 August 1975; Alexander and Margarete Mitscherlich, *Die Unfähigkeit zu trauern, Grundlagen kollektiven Verhaltens*; Dieter Hartmann, "Compliance and Oblivion: Impaired Compassion in Germany for the Victims of the Holocaust"; Abba Kovner, "Threnody for a Movement."

14. Robinson and Friedman, *Holocaust and After*, p. 310; Hartmann, "Compliance and Oblivion," p. 198.

15. Abel J. Herzberg, consultation, Amsterdam, 20 January 1976; H. David Leuner, "Versagen und Bewährung—Die Welt und das Brandopfer der Juden," p. 5. President Roosevelt's "no" on this occasion is only one example of the narrow and mean-spirited attitudes that prevailed in circles that determined the policies regarding Jewish refugees in the United States, Great Britain, Canada, Australia, and New Zealand from 1933 through the end of the war *and after*. Responsibility cannot be assigned simply to the national leadership, at least in the United States, but this is not to remove the culpability of officials not exercising their leadership positions in order to change the situation. Polls taken repeatedly during these years revealed a high level of antisemitism that worked against action to admit or rescue European Jews. See: Irving Abella and Harold Troper, *None Is Too Many*; Paul Bartrop, "Indifference and Inconvenience: Australian Government Policy Towards Refugees from Nazi Persecution, 1933–39"; Henry Feingold, *Politics of Rescue*; Saul Friedman, *No Haven for the Oppressed*; Martin Gilbert, *Auschwitz and the Allies*; Walter Laqueur, *The Terrible Secret*; Robert Morse, *While Six Million Died*; Monty Penkower, *The Jews were Expendable*; David Wyman, *Paper Walls*, and *The Abandonment of the Jews, 1941–1945*.

16. It is estimated that some 32,000 non-Jewish German civilians were executed between 1933 and 1945 for various "political" offenses. These included Conservatives, Socialists, Communists, Catholics, Protestants, writers, journalists, and teachers. Martin Gilbert, *The Holocaust: Maps and Photographs* (London: Board of Deputies of British Jews, 1978), p. 20.

17. Carol Rittner and Sondra Myers, eds., *The Courage to Care*; H. David Leuner, *When Compassion Was a Crime.*

18. Alphons Silbermann, "Antisemitismus in der Bundesrepublik Deutschland." The study was commissioned by the German Research Society. This criticism appears to be the judgment of the noted German public opinion analyst, Elisabeth Noelle-Neumann, as reported in *Deutschland Berichte* (Bonn-Holzlar) 12, 10 (Oct. 1976): 25–26.

19. Cf. Sarah Gordon, *Hitler, Germany and the "Jewish Question."*

20. Bethge, Address at the Annual Scholars Conference on the Church Struggle and the Holocaust, Chicago, 9 March 1986. Johann N. Schmidt of the University of Hamburg believes that Nazi ideology as such is not highly regarded in his country. The "actual scandal lies in thoughtlessness and opportunism . . . , in playing down the unimaginable . . . , in a readiness to belittle the crimes of the past." The phrases used to refer to the Nazi past evade the real horrors: "the bad years," "that dreadful time," "the dark times." The desire to forget rather than acknowledge all the moral demands that remembering would require was made more evident in the internal German debate during 1985–1986 over staging Rainer Werner Fassbinder's play *Garbage, The City and Death* than in the subsequent Bitburg affair. Schmidt, "'Those Unfortunate Years': Nazism in the Public Debate of Post-War Germany" (Lecture delivered 15 Oct. 1986 at Indiana University and published by The Jewish Studies Program), pp. 1, 11, and passim.

21. Gisela Hommel, "Anti-Semitic Tendencies in Christian Feminist Theology in Germany," pp. 43–44.

22. Jürgen Neven-du Mont, *After Hitler.*

23. See, for example, Arthur R. Butz, *The Hoax of the Twentieth Century* (Richmond, Surrey: Historical Review Press, n.d. [but probably 1976]), and *The Journal of Historical Review*, a slick paper revisionist journal presented as a respectable, scholarly publication and widely distributed to libraries and American academics. The earliest of these denials of the Endlösung were written by Paul Rassinier and published in France and West Germany between 1959 and 1965. Similar publications then appeared in the United Kingdom under the pseudonym Richard Harwood as *The Myth of the Six Million* and *Did the Six Million Really Die?* From these sources the accusatory falsifications moved on to the United States and Canada where the British version continued to be printed and circulated; as well, many new offshoots appeared. It is becoming impossible to keep track of the numbers of worldwide publications, in many languages, that continue to proliferate. One recent book (1979) was found to have been written by a State Department-registered Saudi Arabian agent. In the United States there is a close link between antisemitic/Holocaust revisionism and White Power/anti-Black movements and literature. See pages 64–66 for additional comments on the denial phenomenon.

24. Dan Diner, "The Historians' Controversy,", pp. 76–77. While the failure of today's German historians to come to grips with the scandal of National Socialism and its Final Solution may be explained as a failure of nerve or of will, it may also be the case that the very conceptual and intellectual tools historians use, along with other political and social scientists, to comprehend the conflicts and cruelties of society are inappropriate for understanding the Holocaust. Arthur A. Cohen, *The Tremendum*, as paraphrased by Rubenstein and Roth, *Approaches to the Holocaust*, p. 330.

25. Langer, *Holocaust and the Literary Imagination*, pp. 248–49; and Klarsfeld, in an address in Allentown, Pennsylvania. Klarsfeld said, "I think as a German I have a duty to show that Germany can represent something else besides the Nazis. Being German, I

think it's our duty to help the Jews. It's important for a German to change the image of Germany" (*The Globe Times*, Bethlehem, Pa., 30 March 1987).

26. A. Roy Eckardt, *Your People, My People*, pp. 253, 254. In recent years the outlook of many of the young people who take part in Aktion Sühnezeichen/Friedensdienste has differed from that of their predecessors. It is now possible for German youth who are conscientious objectors to satisfy the requirement of alternate service through work in this group. Some of the participants in the program have no idea of voluntarily bearing "the sins of the fathers," despite the fact that the officially stated purposes of the movement have not been altered. Michael Krupp, consultation, Jerusalem, 22 March 1976; consultation with AS/F volunteers in Jerusalem, 30 May 1976. From the beginning, Poland and Russia were designated as recipients for works of reconciliation, along with Israel, but the USSR has not permitted West German youth to carry on any reconciliation functions within its borders. Other nations such as France and the United Kingdom have also been locations for AS/F projects.

27. In early 1984 when West Germany was proposing to sell an extensive array of sophisticated weaponry to Saudi Arabia, a letter of appeal sent to the Bundesrepublik's government by the National Christian Leadership Conference for Israel (U.S.A.) made exactly this point: that the BRD (The Federal Republic of Germany) has a special reason for refraining from the sale of such arms to Israel's enemies, even when other democracies, including the United States, fail to follow similar policies of restraint.

28. Julius Cardinal Döpfner, as cited in the *Münchener Katholische Kirchen-Zeitung*, 6 Jan. 1975. Cardinal Dopfner died in 1976.

29. George Jahn, Associated Press release, in *Philadelphia Inquirer*, 5 December 1986.

30. In October 1943 the foreign ministers of the Soviet Union and Great Britain and the American secretary of state issued a communique following their meeting in Moscow stating that "Austria, the first free country to fall victim to Hitlerite aggression, shall be liberated from German domination."

31. An Austrian journalist and paper originally published the first revelations about a past that Waldheim had kept secret and lied about. The World Jewish Congress then had a group of researchers try to find out the whole story. This enabled those who did not want to believe what was uncovered to accuse Jews, specifically the World Jewish Congress, of fabrication. On 2 June 1986 the congress published a report of its findings to that date: *Kurt Waldheim's Hidden Past: An Interim Report to the President, World Jewish Congress.*

32. On the Friday evening, 4 July 1986, preceding the formal installation of Kurt Waldheim as president, five Americans—Sister Rose Thering (OP) and Father David Bossman, both of Seton Hall University, together with Rabbi Avraham Weiss, Glen Richter, and Bobby Brown—began a five day public "vigil of conscience" in Vienna. Commencing with an "open Shabbat" on the property adjacent to the only synagogue remaining of the city's forty-three before November 1938, the five sought to make a testimony regarding the need for an international investigation of the criminal charges against Mr. Waldheim. Although a few Austrians expressed appreciation, a large portion of those who approached the group "vented a deep-seated antisemitism" that included shouts of hatred for Jews (and their Christian friends) and regrets that they had not all been gassed. Despite the peaceful nature of the vigil and their having secured all the required police permits, Sister Thering was subjected to a strip-search at the airport on departure. *New American* 1, 7/8 (1986): 7–10.

33. Gordon Craig, *The Philadelphia Inquirer*, Book Review, 9 October 1986, p. 3.

34. *The Philadelphia Inquirer*, 5 December 1986.

35. Goes, *The Burnt Offering*, p. 7. A slightly different translation appears as an epigraph in Jacob Presser, *The Destruction of the Dutch Jews*.

3. SINGULARITY

1. Dorothea Dier, consultation, Summit, N.J., 14 March 1975.

2. As cited in "Auschwitz."

3. Emil L. Fackenheim, as cited in the *Baltimore Jewish Times*, 10 June 1977, p. 40.

4. Compare Vincent Canby: "As pop music is now being magnified to the point where we can barely hear it, the volume of screen violence is being raised close to the point where we no longer see it. . . . The same graphic scenes of violence that penetrate dull brains, make those brains duller, more impervious to shock, so that succeeding films must go even further. The volume of screen violence must continue to be raised." *New York Times*, 17 Oct. 1976.

5. A special variation of the moral problem here is associated with the argument sometimes proffered that Hitler intended, ultimately, a "Final Solution" for the churches as well as for Jewry. Any reputed connection here is wholly misplaced. All Christians always had the "opportunity" to turn their backs on their faith. The Nazis themselves came largely out of the Christian community. There was no parallel with the Jews. A Jew who became a rabid antisemite or sought to swear fealty to the Führer would meet the same fate as every other Jew. Only rarely did the Nazis preserve a Jew who was especially useful to them.

6. In a discussion of global hunger, Joseph Holland includes the factor of discontinuity between that phenomenon and the Holocaust, but he also refers to a fundamental element of continuity in the two, namely, Christianity. "Before it was the gas ovens; today it is the slow and painful process of *starvation*. Despite the differences, the new holocaust shares one shattering fact with its predecessor. It is the powers, structures, and policies of the nations where Christianity is strongest which oversee the extermination." "Hunger: Global Holocaust Exodus?," p. 17. The oil-rich Muslim Arab states must now be assigned responsibility along with the Christian nations. For analysis of the links among the Holocaust, modern technology and bureaucracy, demographic trends, and the future disposal of "surplus" populations, see Richard L. Rubenstein, *The Cunning of History*; and Isidor Wallimann and Michael N. Dobkowski, eds., *Genocide and the Modern Age: Etiology and Case Studies of Mass Death*. For brief but helpful analyses of German civil servants, industrialists, army officers, police and SS, see Section 5 of Alex Grobman and Daniel Landes, eds., *Genocide: Critical Issues of the Holocaust*.

7. Saul S. Friedman, "Arab Complicity in the Holocaust," p. 9.

8. For accounts of the Armenian massacres, see *A Crime of Silence: The Armenian Genocide*; Richard Hovannisian, ed., *The Armenian Genocide in Perspective*; Henry Morgenthau, *The Murder of a Nation*; Howard Sachar, *The Emergence of the Middle East, 1914–1924*, chap. 4; Marjorie Housepian, "The Unremembered Genocide." Housepian emphasizes that the event has been glossed over by historians. The Turkish

government has consistently denied the massacre. Vigen Guroian's, "A Comparison of the Armenian and Jewish Genocides: Some Common Features" considers a number of similarities. James J. Reid examines the Turkish racial myth and the expressed need to purge Turkish society of impure elements and "cancers" ("The Armenian Massacres in Ottoman and Turkish Historiography"). For a work on the Gypsies, see Donald Kenrick and Gratten Puxon, *The Destiny of Europe's Gypsies*.

9. Hermann G. Adler, consultation, London, 18 Feb. 1976.

10. Hans-Joachim Gamm, written communication, 23 Sept. 1975.

11. Klaus Scholder, consultations, Tübingen, 9 Aug. 1975, 27 Sept. 1975, 21 Dec. 1975; and "Judentum und Christentum in der Ideologies und Politik des Nationalsocialismus 1919–1945" (Judaism and Christianity in the Ideology and Politics of National Socialism 1919–1945).

12. The "metahistorical uniqueness" of the *Shoah* for Uriel Tal emerges in the transformation of values and symbols applied to the Jew. The symbol is transformed into the substance and consequently the negation of Judaism had to be transformed into the annihilation of all Jews physically. "On the Study of the Holocaust and Genocide," p. 45.

13. Elie Wiesel, *A Beggar in Jerusalem*, p. 200.

14. There are moot questions here. Alternative choices for year 1 include 1939, the year World War II began, and 1942, for it was early in the latter year that the resolve to implement the Endlösung was officially made. The date 1941 is based upon the "killing phase" of the program against the Jews (see chap. 1, n. 5 above). Any advocated symbology faces the criticism that it is either arbitrary or contrived. One alternative is "B.A." and "A.A.," "Before Auschwitz" and "After Auschwitz." There are substantive and moral objections to singling out this one murder camp, despite its horribleness and dominance. Yet there is no doubt that this name has become the single most powerful symbol of the Holocaust.

15. "To the Fascists [the Nazis], the Jews are not a minority but the enemy race, the Negative Principle as such. The good fortune of the world is dependent upon their extermination"; M. Horkeimer and T. W. Adorno, *Dialektik der Aufklärung* (Dialectics of the Enlightenment), as cited in Manfred Franke, *Morderläufe* 9./10.XI 1938, p. 7. Among the more famous Nazi slogans was "Die Juden sind unser Unglück" (The Jews are our disaster).

16. This phrasing was used by Dietrich Goldschmidt, consultation, Berlin, 19 Nov. 1975.

17. Zacharia Shuster, consultation, Paris, 29 Jan. 1976. Hitler spoke frequently of his desire to create a "new" German youth that would be hard as Krupp steel and without pity. In a speech of 22 Aug. 1939 concerning the "destruction of Poland," he counselled that one would have to be "hard and ruthless" and would have to "harden oneself against all considerations of mercy." He also said, "One must not have mercy with people who are determined by fate to perish" (April 1942, cited in Hilberg, p. 662). Himmler made this point in addressing a group of SS-*Gruppenführer* on 4 Oct. 1943: "Most of you must know what it means to see a hundred corpses lie side by side, or five hundred, or a thousand. To have stuck this out and . . . to have kept our integrity, this is what has made us hard. In our history, this is an unwritten and never-to-be-written page of glory." Dawidowicz, *The War Against the Jews*, p. 149.

18. A. Roy Eckardt's "Is the Holocaust Unique?" was submitted to *Worldview* with the title "In What Senses is the Holocaust Unique?"; in changing the title for publication,

the editors showed a lack of familiarity with the contents of the essay, but in their error they also pointed up a fundamental conflict in the reading of events.

19. H. J. Zimmels, *The Echo of the Nazi Holocaust in Rabbinic Literature*, pp. xv–xxiii. The bare listing obviously requires amplification. Important specifics must include the assiduous utilizing of Jews as instruments of their own betrayal and destruction.

20. Abraham Zvie Bar-on, consultation, Jerusalem, 24 May 1976.

21. Just before his premature death, Robert Alden described the anti-Israeli tone within the United Nations. He saw the expressed anti-Jewishness as reflective of a seething hostility that had been brewing for many years. Before the packed chamber of the Security Council, Yakov Malik of the Soviet Union spoke of the Israelis as "murderers and international gangsters"—whereupon the room exploded into prolonged applause. The date of the meeting was four days after the Arabs launched the Yom Kippur War (*New York Times*, 11 Oct. 1973). It is one bizarre irony of history that the headquarters of world antisemitism should come to be located in an American city containing the world's largest Jewish population.

22. James Parkes was disturbed by our associating the concept of the devil with antisemitism. "I am particularly distressed at the introduction of the devil now that Rosemary Ruether's book *Faith and Fratricide* has at last opened the way to a discussion of the Christian liturgy as the real root of antisemitism. If you read the New Testament in church as the 'Word of God' for two thousand years, I think it is enough explanation of the subconscious and instinctive hostility which is the 'abnormal' part of antisemitism." However, he had no objection to the phrasing "demonic forces"; his distress evidently centered in the suggestion of a "personal" devil; Parkes, written communication, 26 May 1976, slightly emended. In light of the traditional Christian stress upon the devil, in marked contrast to Jewish theology, it is noteworthy that, among others, the contemporary Jewish philosopher Emil L. Fackenheim is prepared to consider seriously the concept of the devil; "The Nazi Holocaust as a Persisting Trauma for the Non-Jewish Mind," pp. 375–76. John T. Pawlikowski argues that A. Roy Eckardt's effort to link the devil to antisemitism and the Holocaust wrongly calls human culpability into question and leaves human dignity intact; *The Challenge of the Holocaust for Christian Theology*, pp. 18–19. We seek to meet this criticism in the course of this and succeeding chapters.

23. The analysis at this point is aided by a consultation with Bernard Dupuy, Paris, 28 Jan. 1976.

24. David Polish, "The Tasks of Israel and Galut," p. 10; Eckardt, *Your People, My People*, p. 83.

25. Eckardt, *Your People, My People*, pp. 87–90. Those who equate Jews with the devil may have assured themselves that they are furnishing fresh, creative wisdom. In truth the equation erupts from a collective unconscious formed by a centuries-long history. If the charge did not itself have devilish consequences, it could be dismissed as simply dull. More than a thousand years is a long time for men in otherwise disparate places of the globe to mouth the identical words. For additional discussion of the devil in the context of antisemitism, see A. Roy Eckardt, "The Devil and Yom Kippur," esp. pp. 70–74.

26. About 50,000 Koreans, who had been brought to work in Japanese industries in place of Japanese men who were serving in the Armed Forces, were in Hiroshima at the time of the dropping of the bomb. Of these, 20,000 survived, and most of this number re-

turned to Korea. Very few of these victims have access to the medical and social services supplied by the Japanese government to holders of A-bomb cards, for they have been unable to meet the conditions for receiving the cards (i.e., a Japanese witness to testify to their presence in Japan at the time). The South Korean government has not undertaken similar care of these people. In addition to Koreans, there were Chinese, Malayans, Germans, Russians, more than 3,000 Americans of Japanese descent (trapped in Japan by the outbreak of war), and some Dutch and American prisoners of war in Hiroshima on 6 August 1945.

27. Needless to say, President Truman and his military advisers were mostly concerned about American casualties. "Truman understood, as a political leader, that his decision responded to the moral imperatives of a nation at war in the present rather than to those of a world civilization in the future"; Lansing Lamont, *New York Times Book Review*, 5 Jan. 1986, p. 31.

28. A similar decision to sacrifice millions of human lives in order to achieve a socio-politico-economic end was made by Josef Stalin in 1932–1933. In the process of forcing the kulaks to accept collectivization of agriculture, a "terror famine" wiped out about fifteen million lives, seven million of them in the Ukraine.

29. Karl Marx, himself born a Jew though converted at age six by his father's decision, first used this phrase. He was not thinking of physical elimination but of an end to Jewish religion and all the characteristics he associated with the traditional Jewish community—an aim ironically similar to that of the Christian church, for which Marx had little use.

30. Emil Fackenheim has been struggling with the philosophical and theological problems of the Holocaust since 1970; "The People Israel Lives." In one discussion of the uniqueness of the Nazi Endlösung, he emphasizes that it was "evil for evil's sake, or, to put it otherwise, the diabolical. The Nazi revolution has been called the 'revolution of nihilism,' which means destruction for destruction's sake. And if you ask, 'why should anybody want to do destruction for destruction's sake?' I think the closest I can come . . . is to think of the devil"; "Commanded to Hope," p. 157.

31. See chap. 2, n. 21.

32. They avow that the event never occurred, yet the rationale of that event is the very thing that impels their efforts, the same rationale that impelled the first Nazis. As one of these reincarnations of the Nazis has said, "All the stories about Auschwitz aren't true, but I wish they were."

33. Arthur Hertzberg, "Response to Uriel Tal," p. 373.

34. A more bizarre and troubling case involves a high school history teacher of Eckville, Alberta, Canada. For fourteen years he not only denied the Holocaust but also taught his students that a world Jewish conspiracy exists and was responsible for such events as the French Revolution, the American Civil War, World War I, and the Bolshevik Revolution. The lack of community response to such distortions of history and the poisoning of the minds of the young students calls to mind Elie Wiesel's statement, "The opposite of love is not hate but indifference." Jigs Gardner, "The Keegstra Affair," *Midstream* 31, 9 (November 1985): 7–9.

35. In 1981 Mermelstein initiated a suit against a Swedish publisher, Ditlieb Felderer, for libel and intentional inflicting of emotional distress. Beginning in 1980 Felderer had sent Mermelstein, whose mother and sister were gassed and father and brother perished in Nazi work camps, pamphlets entitled the Jewish Information Bulletin in which

Mermelstein was accused of "peddling the exterminationist hoax." An accompanying letter called him a "racist and exterminationist." In 1986 a Los Angeles jury awarded Mermelstein $500,000 in compensatory damages and $4.75 million in punitive damages, although it was doubtful whether Felderer, who had not even answered the complaint, could be made to pay these damages; *New York Times*, 18 January 1986. Mermelstein is not concerned with receiving the money; his efforts in both cases have been to get a legal ruling on the revisionists' allegations that the Holocaust is nothing but a deliberate falsification of history, and he seeks to make publishing such material financially counterproductive.

36. Emil L. Fackenheim, "The Human Condition after Auschwitz: A Jewish Testimony a Generation After," pp. 9, 10.

37. Levin, *Holocaust*, p. 91.

38. "It is true that, since Auschwitz, the calendar does not follow a new time reckoning. Yet there has taken place in our mentality—rarely consciously, but unavoidably unconsciously—something like a new way of measuring time. . . . Although the mechanism of destruction had always existed, it was only its perfection that made it into a category. The new, unprecedented element was not the frightful cruelty of individual people, but the anonymous effortlessness of desk work carried out conscientiously and without a flaw"; Günter Grass, as cited and translated in Eva Fleischner, *Judaism in German Christian Theology since 1945*, pp. 20–21. Grass's piece originally appeared in the *Frankfurter Allgemeine Zeitung*, 2 June 1970.

39. See John T. Pawlikowski, "The Dialogue Agenda," p. 2. For an interpretation quite different from ours, one that emphasizes independently causative elements of specifically twentieth-century history, see Rubenstein, *Cunning of History*. According to Rubenstein, the Holocaust must be placed "within the context of the phenomenon of twentieth-century mass death. Never before have human beings been so expendable." The Holocaust is "an expression *of some of the most profound tendencies of Western civilization in the twentieth century*. Given Britain's imperial commitments, Europe's Jews were as much a superfluous population for Great Britain as they were for Germany. . . . From a purely bureaucratic perspective, the extermination of the Jews of Europe was the 'final solution' for the British as well as the Germans"; pp. 12, 20. Rubenstein of course also takes seriously the elements of historical uniqueness in the Holocaust.

40. Elie Wiesel, in Abrahamson, *Against Silence*, 3: 312. Wiesel also refers to "the dark kingdom" as representing "the other side of Sinai, the dark side of Sinai"; ibid. 1: 28, 29, 246.

41. Glatstein, cited in Manès Sperber, . . . *than a Tear in the Sea*, p. xv.

42. Fackenheim, "Human Condition after Auschwitz," p. 7.

43. See A. Roy Eckardt, ed., *The Theologian at Work*, pp. 129–30, and *The Deputy*, act 5, sc. 2, reproduced ibid., pp. 136–46, or pp. 241–53 of *The Deputy*.

44. Eliezer Berkovits, "The Hiding God of History," in Yisrael Gutman and Livia Rothkirchen, eds., *The Catastrophe of European Jewry*, p. 704; Rubenstein and Roth, *Approaches to Auschwitz*, p. 299.

45. Samuel Sandmel, "The New Movement," p. 13.

46. See pp. 91–92, 145–147.

47. Elie Wiesel, "*Ani Maamin*," pp. 89–103.

48. Wilm Sanders of Germany reports the following as a typical judgment of "simple Catholic Christians": "The Jews are accursed. In the moment that they crucified

Christ, the Lord God repudiated them. And ask of him what they will it is of no use—see what they have endured in the concentration camps. The Jews are accursed. The Lord God will refuse them a favorable hearing. They have no dwelling-place in the world. They crucified the Christ. And they refuse to be converted. They do not believe in Christ"; *Antisemitismus bei den Christen?*, (Antisemitism Among Christians?), pp. 7–8. A scholar in West Germany contended that in spite of this prevalent theological view the vast majority of Christians in that country today remain unaware that the Holocaust had anything to do with religious influences; Rolf Rendtorff, consultation, Heidelberg, 30 Oct. 1975. Compare a statement made in 1936 by the Lutheran bishop of Baden: "When the Jews crucified Jesus, they crucified themselves, their revelation, and their history. Thus the curse came upon them. Since then that curse works itself out from one generation to another. This people has, therefore, become a fearful and divinely ordained scourge for all nations, leading to hatred and persecution"; cited in Gutteridge, *Open Thy Mouth for the Dumb*, p. 71.

Each of these phenomena is to be found among Christians of the United States, Britain, and elsewhere. In January 1980 a Protestant minister in Minneapolis, Minnesota, asserted, in a series of sermons, that the Jews were slaughtered during the Holocaust because they had lost favor with God. "God has made them really a scandal in the world. And you can't change that. And it's not due to just antisemitic feeling [or] to people charging them with being the Christ crucifiers. It's due to their rejection of God. And the fact that God has rejected them . . . as a nation"; *Minneapolis Tribune*, 2 March 1980, cited in *Christian-Jewish Relations* [London] 72 (September 1980): 46–47. An Assemblies of God education text in 1972 explained the persecution of Jews throughout history as "the price Jews paid for their rejection of Christ"; *Time*, 18 December 1972. When Father Edward Flannery wrote *The Anguish of the Jews* (1965), he hoped to acquaint Christians with the immense suffering undergone by Jews at the hands of Christians over many centuries. Twenty years later (1985) his book was republished, and he conceded with sorrow that his objective had not been realized in the interim: "The vast majority of Christians, even well educated, are all but totally ignorant of what happened to Jews in history, and of the culpable involvement of the Church" (p. 1). Moreover, the task of eradicating antisemitism is one to which "the generality of Christian clergy and laity is indifferent" (p. 295).

49. Relevant works include: Jeremy Cohen, *The Friars and the Jews*; Alan T. Davies, *Anti-Semitism and the Christian Mind*; Eckardt, *Christianity and the Children of Israel* and *Your People, My People*; Edward Flannery, *The Anguish of the Jews*; Malcolm Hay, *The Roots of Christian Anti-Semitism* (also as *Thy Brother's Blood* [1975] and *The Foot of Pride* [1950]); Friedrich Heer, *God's First Love*; Jules Isaac, *Teaching of Contempt*; Charlotte Klein, *Anti-Judaism in Christian Theology*; Pinchas E. Lapide, "Vom 'Gottesmorde' zum Völkermord" (From the Murder of God to the Murder of Peoples); Franklin H. Littell, *The Crucifixion of the Jews*; Franklin H. Littell and Hubert G. Locke, eds., *The German Church Struggle and the Holocaust*; Haim Maccoby, *The Sacred Executioner*: Heiko A. Oberman, *The Roots of Anti-Semitism*; the following works of James Parkes: *Antisemitism*; *The Conflict of the Church and the Synagogue*; *A History of the Jewish People*; *The Jew in the Medieval Community*; *Judaism and Christianity*; Rudolf Pfisterer, *Im Schatten des Kreuzes* (In the Shadow of the Cross); Léon Poliakov, *The Aryan Myth* and *The History of Anti-Semitism* (4 volumes); Richard L. Rubenstein, *After Auschwitz*; Rosemary Radford Ruether, *Faith and Fratricide*;

Frederick M. Schweitzer, *A History of the Jews Since the First Century A.D.*; Kenneth R. Stow, *Catholic Thought and Papal Jewry Policy, 1555–1593*; Uriel Tal, *Christians and Jews in Germany*; Joshua Trachtenberg, *The Devil and the Jews*; Robert L. Wilken, *Judaism and the Early Christian Mind*.

50. Manès Sperber, the celebrated Jewish novelist and former psychiatrist said to us: "The seed of the Holocaust is Christianity, fertilized by other factors. The bankruptcy of Christian messianism is in my eyes"; consultation, Paris, 29 Jan. 1976.

51. Littell, *Crucifixion of the Jews*, pp. 2, 17.

52. Gregory G. Baum, *Christian Theology After Auschwitz*, pp. 8, 9, 11.

53. Gregory G. Baum, Introduction to Ruether, *Faith and Fratricide*, p. 8.

54. Paul van Buren, "The Status and Prospects for Theology," p. 3. Van Buren's article is based on a paper read before the annual meeting of the American Academy of Religion, Chicago, Nov. 1975.

55. Had Jesus been alive at the time of the Endlösung, he would not have been put to death for deliberately making an issue of himself, as seems to have been the case in his own lifetime (see Luke 9:51), but instead with absolute fatefulness. He was one of those *Untermenschen*. On the Christological question, see Michael B. McGarry. *Christology after Auschwitz*; Eugene B. Borowitz, *Contemporary Christologies*; and John Pawlikowski, *Christ in the Light of the Jewish-Christian Dialogue*.

56. Robert McAfee Brown, "The Holocaust: The Crisis of Indifference," pp. 18–19.

57. George Steiner, *In Bluebeard's Castle*, pp. 41, 44, 45. For a much earlier effort to link antisemitism with the attack upon God, but one that is somewhat paralleled by Steiner, see Eckardt, *Christianity and the Children of Israel*, chap. 2. One may object to Steiner's representation of monotheism at Sinai as a call for perfection. Rather, the Torah that emerged from Sinai may be seen as a fairly realistic way of creating a society that could live responsibly with its own members as well as with neighbors (as individuals and nations). If one wants to stress perfectionism in the Tanakh, one would be on surer ground with the biblical prophets. At least, this would be the case if the prophets were taken literally rather than within their historical contexts or rather than as warning messages presented in hyperbolic style in order to gain the attention of the people.

58. Saul Friedlander, "Some Aspects of the Historical Significance of the Holocaust."

59. See, e.g., John S. Conway, "The Churches, The Slovak State and the Jews, 1939–1945," *The Slavonic and East European Review* 52 (1974) pp. 85–112; Richard Gutteridge, *Open Thy Mouth for the Dumb; Judaism and Christianity Under the Impact of National Socialism (1919–1945)*; Yeshayahu Jelinek, "The Vatican, the Catholic Church, The Catholics, and the Persecution of the Jews during World War II: The Case of Slovakia," in Bela Vago and George L. Mosse, ed., *Jews and Non-Jews in Eastern Europe, 1918–1945*; Charlotte Klein, "The Vatican and German-Italian Antisemitism in the Nineteen Thirties" (unpublished paper), "Vatican View of Jewry, 1939–1962," and "The Vatican and Zionism, 1897–1967"; Robert Major, "The Churches and the Jews in Hungary," *Continuum* 4, 3 (1966): 371–81; John Morley, *Vatican Diplomacy and the Jews During the Holocaust 1939–1943*; Livia Rothkirchen, "The Stand of the Churches vis-à-vis the Persecution of the Jews of Slovakia," in *Judaism and Christianity Under the Impact of National Socialism (1919–1945)*, pp. 273–86; Johan Snoek, *The Grey Book*.

60. Zucker, "30 Years after Holocaust," p. 10.

61. Ismar Schorsch, "German Anti-Semitism in the Light of Post-War Historiography."

4. DANGERS AND OPPORTUNITIES

1. Wiesel, *Legends of our Time*, p. 20. But Wiesel contends that today it is harder to live with than without God. "Can you compare today the tragedy of the believer to that of the nonbeliever? The real tragedy, the real drama, is the drama of the believer"; "Talking and Writing and Keeping Silent," in Littell and Locke, eds., *The German Church Struggle and the Holocaust*, p. 274.

2. Elie Wiesel, in Irving Abrahamson, ed., *Against Silence*, 1: 250.

3. Cf. Rubinoff: "The Messianic covenant is essentially a promise to exist between revelation and redemption and to work toward redemption through witness and 'through the sweat of one's brow' . . . as well as one's body"; "Auschwitz and the Pathology of Jew-Hatred," p. 348.

4. William Jay Peck, "From Cain to the Death Camps: An Essay on Bonhoeffer and Judaism," pp. 159–60.

5. Fackenheim, "Nazi Holocaust," p. 376.

6. This rendering in the King James version is the most familiar to religious people. Other versions present a quite different meaning, e.g., "Behold he will slay me; I have no hope" (Revised Standard Version).

7. Fackenheim, "Jewish Values in the Post-Holocaust Future," pp. 272, 273, 29.

8. Michael Wyschogrod protests that the Holocaust must not be permitted to mute or silence the basic Jewish message of a faithful, redeeming God; "Some Theological Reflections on the Holocaust," in Lucy Y. Steinitz and David M. Szonyi, ed., *Living After the Holocaust*, pp. 66–67.

9. Jakov Lind, *Counting My Steps*, pp. 54, 205.

10. Jakov Lind, "Resurrection," in *Soul of Wood and Other Stories*, p. 154.

11. Tom Idinopulos, "Art and the Inhuman: A Reflection on the Holocaust," *The Christian Century* 91, 35 (16 October 1974): 955.

12. Ibid., and Schwarz-Bart, *The Last of the Just*, p. 374.

13. Donat, *Holocaust Kingdom*, p. 119. In another fever dream Donat was faced with accusers who denounced him for the fact that he, his wife, and his child were still living. One of the accusers sentenced him to banishment from his people: "Henceforward he shall walk the lonely path of the man who has no people" (p. 118).

14. Alexander Donat, "The Voice of the Ashes."

15. Rubenstein, *After Auschwitz*, pp. 46, 52–54. See also Richard L. Rubenstein and John K. Roth, *Approaches to Auschwitz*, pp. 308–11, for a full account of the conditions under which that conversation took place and of Rubenstein's admiration for Grüber. Dean Grüber denied ever having said what Rubenstein ascribed to him; *Christianity and Crisis* 24, 2 (28 December 1964).

16. Rubenstein, "Some Perspectives on Religious Faith after Auschwitz," in Littell and Locke eds., *German Church Struggle and the Holocaust*, pp. 261, 262.

17. Rubenstein, *After Auschwitz*, pp. 56, 58, 69.

18. Ibid., pp. x, 128, 223, 224–25. Rubenstein may be asked whether the Jewish people, having regained the land of Israel and national sovereignty, have not also become vulnerable again. Have they not reappropriated hope and hence exposed themselves to the possibility of greater disappointment, even unto despair? See Alice L. Eckardt, "The Holocaust: Christian and Jewish Responses," p. 463. See also Richard L. Rubenstein, "Jewish Theology and the Current World Situation." Since then Rubenstein has acknowledged Israel's fragility, and changed his view that the goal of Jewish history had been reached with the State of Israel's reestablishment; Rubenstein and Roth, *Approaches to Auschwitz*, p. 314.

In his most recent writing Rubenstein continues to deny both the notion that the Jewish people are either chosen or rejected by God, and the biblical-rabbinic version of the God who acts in history. However, he no longer sees the cosmos as totally "cold, silent, unfeeling"; rather it is full of life of which the source is divine life. God is "the ground and source of all existence" and is spoken of as *Holy Nothingness* to communicate "the mystery of divinity." Nevertheless, apart from his own beliefs, he is convinced that most religious Jews eventually will retain faith in the biblical God of history, even if it means regarding Auschwitz as divine punishment, and in the divine election of Jews, even if this has its difficulties, for it has given Jews a sense of hope and meaning; Rubenstein and Roth, *Approaches to Auschwitz*, pp. 312, 315, 311, 314–15.

19. Gregory Baum, *Man Becoming*. The quotations in this paragraph are taken from pp. 242–46 (passim) and from "Christian Theology After Auschwitz." Baum's view that God enables the individual to draw on an offered inner strength to meet the most destructive situations and thereby to become more human finds its counterpart in Leo Baeck: "Only when the self can be so free of vagaries of situation . . . that in the face of suffering and even death he can actualize true love in himself, only then is he a free individual. . . . Baeck insists that this becoming a person is . . . part of the cycle of mystery and commandment which derive from the hidden and revealed aspects of divinity"; S. Daniel Breslauer, "Martyrdom and Charisma," *Encounter* [Indianapolis] 42, 2 (Spring 1981): 139, 140.

20. Baum, *Man Becoming*, pp. 248–49. Cf. this post-Holocaust interpretation of God by the Jewish philosopher Hans Jonas: God is a suffering, becoming, caring God, who is not omnipotent. Omnipotence is "a self-contradictory, self-destructive, indeed senseless concept." For a time, God "has divested Himself of any power to interfere with the physical course of things" and "responds to the impact on His being of worldly events." A consequence is that we humans "literally hold in our faltering hands the future of the divine adventure and must not fail Him, even if we would fail ourselves"; "The Concept of God after Auschwitz," pp. 465–76.

21. Franklin Sherman, "Speaking of God after Auschwitz."

22. Paul van Buren, *Discerning the Way*, pp. 115, 116, 117. Rubenstein and Roth find that van Buren takes God off the hook too easily, as no "credible Christian theology in a post-Holocaust world" should do. They observe that "God is not bound by human freedom unless God chooses to be. And if God wants to be, so that the divine presence at Auschwitz is that of suffering with the victims and not interceding on their behalf, then that is a problem for us all—God, Christians, Jews, and everybody else"; Rubenstein and Roth, *Approaches to Auschwitz*, pp. 298–99.

23. Hans Jonas, "The Concept of God After Auschwitz," pp. 468–75 passim.

24. This is one way of looking at the God of Christianity. Another is to see God as *demanding* that Christians accept the way of the cross as the Christians' own road—a way of self-sacrifice that they may have to emulate. For the psychological consequences of such a perceived demand in connection with antisemitism, see A. Roy Eckardt, *Christianity and the Children of Israel*, pp. 52–61; *Elder and Younger Brothers*, pp. 22–25; *Your People, My People*, pp. 79–80, 86.

25. Arthur J. Lelyveld, *Atheism is Dead*, pp. 158–76, 177.

26. Ibid., pp. 172–83 passim.

27. Ibid., pp. 182–83, 184.

28. Viktor Frankl, *From Death Camp to Existentialism*, pp. 77, 105, 107.

29. Ignaz Maybaum sees the "third churban" as ending the Middle Ages, in which both Christianity and Judaism sought to enclose its own people in a world sedulously isolated from contact with all other faith communities and societies; *The Face of God after Auschwitz*, p. 61.

30. Baeck, in Breslauer, "Martyrdom and Charisma," pp. 137, 138.

31. Zvi Kolitz, "Yossel Rakover's Appeal to God," in Friedlander, ed., *Out of the Whirlwind*, p. 399. Cf. the Rebbe in a tale of Elie Wiesel: "There is joy as well as fury in the *hasid's* dancing. It's his way of proclaiming, 'You don't want me to dance; too bad, I'll dance anyhow. You've taken away every reason for singing, but I shall sing. I shall sing of the deceit that walks by day and the truth that walks by night, yes and of the silence of dusk as well. You didn't expect my joy, but here it is; yes, my joy will rise up; it will submerge you'"; *The Gates of the Forest*, p. 196. Elsewhere the character Michael declaims: "I go up against Him. I shake my fist, I froth with rage, but it's still a way of telling Him that He's there, that He exists, that He's never the same twice, that denial itself is an offering to His grandeur"; Elie Wiesel, *The Town Beyond the Wall*, p. 123.

32. A most powerful castigation of God on the ground of the Holocaust is Uri Zvi Greenberg, "To God in Europe," trans. Robert Friend, in *Anthology of Modern Hebrew Poetry* 2: 264–78.

33. Ulrich E. Simon, *A Theology of Auschwitz*, p. 82.

34. Cf. van Buren: To say that God was not in the death camps "because He did not act . . . assumes that God should have done what He could not have done without ceasing to be the God of love and freedom . . ."; *Discerning the Way*, pp. 18–19.

35. Rubenstein and Roth, *Approaches to Auschwitz*, p. 299.

36. Eliezer Berkovits, "The Hiding God of History," in Gutman and Rothkirchen, eds., *Catastrophe of European Jewry*, pp. 694, 704; *Faith after the Holocaust*, pp. 99, 131. "God took a risk with man and he cannot divest himself of responsibility for man. If man is not to perish at the hand of man, . . . God must not withdraw his providence from his creation. . . . That man may be, God must absent himself; that man may not perish in the tragic absurdity of his own making, God must remain present. . . .

He is present without being indubitably manifest; he is absent without being hopelessly inaccessible. Thus, many find him even in his 'absence'; many miss him even in his presence. Because of the necessity of his absence, there is the 'Hiding of the Face' and suffering of the innocent; because of the necessity of his presence, evil will not ultimately triumph; because of it, there is hope for man"; *Faith after the Holocaust*, p. 107.

We find it noteworthy that "The Hiding God of History," although it is the only explicitly theological study among a large number of contributions in *Catastrophe of European Jewry*, should nevertheless be placed at the end of the volume and form a kind of climax to the entire achievement. A full presentation of Berkovits's point of view is found in his *Faith after the Holocaust* and *With God in Hell*. For two, a Jew and a Christian, who reject the traditional Jewish and Christian view that the acceptance of suffering has a redemptive function that works against evil, see p. 116.

37. Wiesel, *Beggar in Jerusalem*, pp. 199–200.

38. Ibid., p. 30.

39. What are we to make of this? We recall that in Psalm 2 God laughs in derision at human attempts to defy the divine will, especially with regard to God's people. If we view Rabbi Bratzlav's tale F.S., we may find the biblical situation reversed. God's demand that the Jewish people abide by the covenant and testify on behalf of God to the world was transformed into a devilish demand through the will and actions of the very people of the world God was seeking to help. Hence God was forced *by humans* to take back the gift of the Torah. Now it is a human who laughs at God; maniacally, if he is aware of the bitter irony of God's plight; derisively, if he perceives that God has been all but defeated by those he created with freedom to choose good or evil.

40. Jacob Glatstein, "Dead Men Don't Praise God," in *Selected Poems of Jacob Glatstein*.

41. David Polish, "The Resurrection—An Elegy for the Six Million," in *High Holiday Prayer Book*, eds. Mordecai Kaplan, Eugene Kohn, Ira Eisenstein (New York: Reconstructionist Foundation, 1948) 2: 404. Also reprinted in Franklin H. Littell, *The Crucifixion of the Jews*, Appendix B, p. 152.

42. Wiesel, *Beggar in Jerusalem*, p. 28.

43. Manès Sperber, . . . *than a Tear in the Sea*, p. xiv.

44. Hirsh Jakob Zimmels, *The Echo of the Holocaust in Rabbinic Literature*, pp. 63–64; and Michael Chernick, consultation and unpublished correspondence, May and October 1977.

45. Manès Sperber, as cited in a book review by Jakob J. Petuchowski, *Conservative Judaism* 31, 1–2 (Fall–Winter 1976–1977): 96; Irving Greenberg, "Voluntary Covenant," p. 17.

46. Irving Greenberg, consultation, Southampton, England, 21 July 1977. We are indebted to Greenberg for this insight. In October 1982 Greenberg published a fuller development of his thinking on the subject in "Voluntary Covenant." In it he submits that the authority of the covenant was broken and the Jewish people were released from its obligations. Moreover, God was no longer in a position to command. But "the Jewish people was so in love with the dream of redemption that it volunteered to carry on its mission." (p. 17).

47. Elie Wiesel, in *Teachers' Study Guide: Jewish Legends*, Joseph Mersand, ed. (New York: Archdiocese of New York and the Anti-Defamation League of B'nai B'rith, n.d.), p. 8.

48. Yehuda Aschkenasy, consultation, Hilversum, Holland, 16 Jan. 1976. Nora Levin reminds us that incompleteness "is of a piece with the Jewish religious tradition"— a tradition that across the centuries has not only contended with God but even dared to entertain the idea that God can sin. Generally, Judaism has refrained from pursuing "the unknowable and the limitless," and it "does not insist on answers when there are none" ("Life over Death," pp. 22–23). There is a vital lesson here that Christian theologians might well take seriously. To seek an accounting from God must be consistent with the divine intent, for at stake is our dignity as free human beings created in the image of the divine.

49. Reinhold Niebuhr, Frontispiece to Ursula M. Niebuhr, ed., *Justice and Mercy*.

5. SERVITUDE
AND FREEDOM

1. The role of Arabs in opposing admission of Jewish refugees to Palestine during the critical years of the late 1930s and the 1940s, and in influencing the British government to so alter its admission policies that a maximum of 75,000 Jews were to be granted certificates of entry from May 1939 to May 1944, is probably better known than other active collaboration with the Axis partners. The German and Italian governments found ready allies in a number of Arab personages and countries. Hajj Muhammed el-Huseini, Grand Mufti of Jerusalem, was welcomed in Berlin when he had to flee from British authorities seeking to arrest him for inciting revolt in Palestine. Rashid Ali el-Kilani, prime minister of Iraq, led an unsuccessful pro-Axis coup d'état and armed resistance to British forces in the country in April–May 1941 and then fled to Berlin. El-Huseini and el-Kilani played a major role in persuading the Reich to reject a Red Cross–British proposal to evacuate 70,000 Jewish children from Rumania to Palestine. Anti-British military officers in Egypt, who in 1952 overthrew King Farouk's government, were also anxious to receive Italian and German support. See Lukasz Hirszowicz, *The Third Reich and the Arab East*; and Malcolm Hay, *The Roots of Christian Anti-Semitism*, p. 7.

2. Friedrich Gruenagel, *Die Judenfrage (The Jewish Question)*, pp. 7, 8, 16, 19, 20. In fact, Gruenagel idealizes Cardinal Bea's contribution and correspondingly distorts the cardinal's actual point of view. See Augustin Cardinal Bea, *The Church and the Jewish People* and the critical commentary on that volume in Eckardt, *Your People, My People*, pp. 52–56. The latter study analyzes the historical fate of the Vatican schema *De Judaeis* (pp.42–56; cf. pp. 189–93).

3. Gruenagel, *Judenfrage*, p. 23.

4. Ibid., pp. 23. 40–46. Space forbids attention to Gruenagel's defense in chapter 3 of Martin Luther's position on the Jews.

5. Rudolf Pfisterer, consultation, Schwäbisch-Hall, 24 Sept. 1975.

6. F.S. assertions by Christians that the Holocaust was God's judgment on and punishment of the Jewish people—for whatever reasons—perpetuate the churches' centuries-old theology about God's rejection of the "children of Israel." Another way in which the Endlösung acts to perpetuate itself can be found in the accusations that Israelis are today's Nazis, as they are regularly depicted in Soviet and Arab political cartoons and writings. The Western press is hardly guiltless in this regard either. After the Six Day War of 1967 news media in the United States, Britain, France, and elsewhere moved progressively toward a more negative and hostile presentation of Israel in its news stories, columns of comment, and political cartoons. With the Israeli invasion of Lebanon in 1982 the floodgates of abuse were opened, quite as if no other nation had ever invaded a neighbor's territory in order to do what it thought necessary to protect itself. Whether the PLO's forces posed a serious enough threat may be and is debated. But this was hardly the first time a government may have acted unwisely. The overwhelmingly denunciatory tone found in so much of the Western press seemed to suggest that editors, writers, reporters, and cartoonists had been waiting for the opportunity to blast Israel. The same phenomenon was manifested regarding the Israeli handling of the riots by Arabs in the Administered Territories in December 1987. One political cartoonist likened Israeli treatment of the Arab population of those territories to the apartheid police methods of South Africa as well as to the Nazi Brown Shirts. See Stephen Karetzky, and Peter Goldman, eds., *The Media's War Against Israel* (New York, Jerusalem, Tel Aviv: Steimatsky, 1986).

7. Franklin H. Littell, "Particularism and Universalism in Religious Perspective." Emil L. Fackenheim writes in similar vein: "If [it were recognized that] Nazi antisemitism was not *simply* anti-Christian but rather the nemesis of a bi-millennial disease within Christianity *itself*, transmuted . . . , [then] Auschwitz would be *the* central theological event of this century not only for the Jewish but also for the Christian faith"; "Nazi Holocaust," p. 373.

8. Rat der Evangelischen Kirche in Deutschland, *Christen und Juden*, pp. 25, 28–31.

9. Ibid., pp. 33–35.

10. So, for example, pp. 9, 15, 16, 17–24. Thus, we are reminded that the early church saw in Jesus' life, death, and resurrection the realization of the divine promises for Israel and the nations. In consequence, the Christian community knew itself to be obliged to testify to Jews and gentiles of its faith, love, and hope. The fact that a great deal of the exposition in *Christen und Juden* is couched in the form of historical-phenomenological analysis cannot hide the truth that Christian claims lie behind and motivate the presentation. Furthermore, the historical materials themselves are not always balanced. A grievous defect is that the authors fail to stress sufficiently that the enmity that developed and was perpetuated between the Jewish and Christian communities has been predominantly a matter of Christian culpability.

11. Ibid., pp. 17–18.

12. The Study Commission "Church and Judaism" that produced the statement included such noted figures as Otto Betz, Helmut Gollwitzer, Franz von Hammerstein, Martin Hengel, Heinz Kremers, Friedrich Wilhelm Marquardt, Reinhold Mayer, Peter-Christian von der Osten-Sacken, Rolf Rendtorff, and Martin Stöhr. Not all of the document's assertions can be assigned to any one of these individuals because a majority vote determined the result. Some of these persons have indicated their disagreement with particular passages. Others on the commission found parts of the document too far-reaching. A very full study that has been prepared for the use of churches and students as part of the implementation of the statement marks a very significant change in the EKD's theology regarding Judaism and the Jewish people and incorporates much more thoroughgoing consideration of the complex issues.

The conversionist problem is further exemplified in another church pronouncement stemming from an international consultation held in Oslo in August 1975. The predicament of the formulators of its report is revealed most vividly in these words of introduction by Paul D. Opsahl and Arne Sovik: "It is to be hoped that this report conveys to all readers the capacity to regard Jewish people with high honor, love, and a sense of eschatological wonder, as well as a clear witness to the name and honor of Jesus Christ, and the centrality of his crucifixion and resurrection"; "Christian Witness and the Jewish People: The Report of a Consultation Held under the Auspices of the Lutheran World Federation, Department of Studies," in World Council of Churches, *The Church and the Jewish People*, newsletter no. 4 (1975), pp. 10–18.

13. For more on liberation theologies viewed from the perspective of Christian-Jewish relations and post-Holocaust theology, see John Pawlikowski, *Christ in the Light of the Christian-Jewish Dialogue*, pp. 59–75; Michael D. Ryan, "Liberation Theology: Implications for Christian-Jewish Relations" (Unpublished paper, delivered to Christian Study Group on Judaism and the Jewish People, February 1981); Clark M. Williamson, "Christ Against the Jews: A Review of Jon Sobrino's Christology," *Encounter*

[Indianapolis] 40 (1979): 403–41: Dan Cohn-Sherbok, *On Earth As It Is In Heaven: Jews, Christians, and Liberation Theology*.

14. Klein, *Anti-Judaism in Christian Theology*; Jürgen Moltmann, written communication, 3 Apr. 1975.

15. Jürgen Moltmann, *The Crucified God*, pp. 24, 33, 51, 68, 99, 125, 128, 133, 187, 190, 191, 248, 297.

16. Moltmann, *Crucified God*, p. 132.

17. Presenting a series of theses dealing with the emergence of Christianity from Judaism, David Flusser places this item first on the list: "Jesus was a Jew. He lived in accordance with the Jewish law, and died for it. He was 'born under the law' (Gal. 4:4) and did not wish to become a reformer of Judaism" (Thèses sur l'émergence du christianisme à partir du judaïsme," p. 4). Among historical studies, a thoroughly documented work, written in a semipopular way, is Jules Isaac, *Jesus and Israel*, esp. pts. 1–3, on the wholly positive relation of Jesus of Nazareth to Judaism, Torah, and his own Jewish people. See also Ben Zion Bokser, *Judaism and the Christian Predicament*, esp. pp. 181–209; David Flusser, *Jesus*, esp. pp. 44–64; Joseph B. Tyson, *A Study of Early Christianity*, pp. 373–80; John Koenig, *Jews and Christians in Dialogue*, chap. 1; E. P. Sanders, *Jesus and Judaism*; Gerard S. Sloyan, *Is Christ the End of the Law?*, chap. 2; Clark M. Williamson, *Has God Rejected His People?*, chaps. 1, 2. Geza Vermes's several studies (which are continuing) offer many new insights: *The Gospel of Jesus the Jew; Jesus the Jew; Jesus and the World of Judaism*. Harvey Falk's *Jesus the Pharisee: A New Look at the Jewishness of Jesus* presents a new thesis regarding the disputes which the gospels portray Jesus as having with other Jews of his day.

18. Moltmann, *Crucified God*, p. 114, 115.

19. Cf. ibid., pp. 128–35.

20. Haim Cohn, *The Trial and Death of Jesus*, pp. 53, 95–98, 101, 102, 105. The seven provisions of Jewish law are: 1) no Sanhedrin was permitted to try criminal cases outside the temple precincts, in any private home; 2) no criminal case could be conducted at night; 3) no one could be tried on criminal charges or on the eve of a festival; 4) no one could be convicted on his own testimony or on the basis of his own confession; 5) a person could be convicted of a capital offense only on the testimony of two lawfully qualified eyewitnesses; 6) the eyewitnesses were required to have warned the accused of the criminality of his intended act and the legal penalties for it; 7) the meaning of "blasphemy" is the pronouncing of the name of God, and it is irrelevant what alleged "blasphemies" are uttered as long as the divine name is not expressed. See also Cohn, "Reflections of the Trial and Death of Jesus," p. 17.

In *Revolution in Judaea* Haim Maccoby uses the Gospel materials along with recent discoveries and scholarship about the Jewish milieu of Jesus' time to arrive at a nontraditional view of how and why Jesus ended on the cross at Golgotha.

21. Moltmann, *Crucified God*, p. 129.

22. Ibid., p. 128.

23. Ibid., p. 175.

24. Cf. Jules Isaac, *Genèse de l'antisémitisme*; *Teaching of Contempt*. Jules Isaac examined the views of the great Protestant reformers in the hope that the Reformation's return to "the purest sources—the Word of Christ" might have moved these Christian leaders away from the traditional views about Jews. He found his hope to be in vain. After reading the terrible things that Luther wrote *about* Jews and the actions he advised

secular rulers to take *against* Jews, Isaac wrote: "Patience, Luther, Hitler will come. Your wishes will be granted, and more!" To his readers, Isaac enjoined, "Let us recognize here the family ties, the blood ties, uniting two great Germans, and let us place Luther in the place he deserves, in the first row of Christian precursors—of Auschwitz"; *Jesus and Israel*, p. 249. See also: Jeremy Cohen, *The Friars and the Jews*; Heiko Oberman, *The Roots of Anti-Semitism*; Kenneth Stow, *Catholic Thought and Papal Jewry Policy, 1555–1593*.

25. Greenberg, "Lessons to be Learned."

26. Cf. Moltmann, *Crucified God*, pp. 40, 51, 276. Moltmann develops this theme also in *The Trinity and the Kingdom*, pp. 76–83, and in Lapide and Moltmann, *Jewish Monotheism and Christian Trinitarian Doctrine*, pp. 51–55. We consider this subject again in chapter 6.

The author of Mark's gospel presents all segments of the Jewish people and nation as rejecting or opposing Jesus, including his mother and the rest of his family. See S. G. F. Brandon, *Jesus and the Zealots*, pp. 274–76, and *The Fall of Jerusalem*, pp. 50–51; also Rosemary Radford Reuther, *Mary—The Feminine Face of the Church* (Philadelphia: Westminster Press, 1977), pp. 37, 38, 47. By contrast, Luke's gospel presents Jesus' mother Mary as faithful to her son from the moment when the angel Gabriel told her of her holy conception (Lu. 1:26–55), and John's gospel, from the earliest days of his ministry—even though she did not understand fully (Jn. 2: 3–5)—to his bitter end on the cross (Jn. 19: 25–27).

27. See notes 17 and 20 of this chapter for some of these sources.

28. By ideology we mean a "set of teachings or symbols unconsciously generated by a society to protect itself against others, legitimate its power, and defend its privileges"; Gregory Baum, as cited by Arne Siirala, p. 141. Once theology is determined by ideology, there is no reason not to conclude, as did the early Christians and church fathers, that the Jewish catastrophes of the first and second centuries of the Common Era were divine punishment. At the same time, the early Christians could interpret the persecution and martyrdom of their own community, including the demise of the "mother church" in Jerusalem, as holy suffering that demonstrated Christian faithfulness to God.

29. Moltmann, *Crucified God*, pp. 27, 39, 69, 140–41. See Klein, *Anti-Judaism in Christian Theology*, chaps. 3, 4.

30. "Even when the seriousness of Jewish piety is commended, it is done with faint praise: it may be admirable in its sincerity but just for that reason, it is more off the mark"; Krister Stendahl, "Judaism on Christianity: Christianity on Judaism," in Frank Ephraim Talmage, ed., *Disputation and Dialogue*, p. 355; italics added.

31. Cf. Moltmann, *Crucified God*, p. 147.

32. Ibid., p. 73.

33. Ibid., p. 186.

34. Ibid., 176, 177, 272.

35. Ibid., p. 205.

36. Ibid., p. 102. See the reference in chap. 6, p. 146, to Fackenheim's post-Holocaust call for a suspension of the ideal of Jewish martyrdom.

37. Moltmann, *Crucified God*, p. 1, 52, 75, 153, 163, 263, 134; emphases added.

38. Ibid., pp. 135, 134.

39. Ibid., pp. 194–95; italics added.

40. Ibid., pp. 273–74.

41. Ibid., p. 278.
42. Wiesel, in Abrahamson, *Against Silence* 3: 246.
43. Where does Judaism teach this?
44. Ibid., pp. 277–78.
45. Ibid., p. 3.
46. Ibid., pp. 51, 134.
47. As cited in Edward H. Flannery, *The Anguish of the Jews*, 1965 ed., p. xi. The silence and complicity of the churches during the Hitler years has been quite thoroughly documented, although there is still need for additional research, especially in churches of Eastern Europe and the Balkan countries. We cannot deal with that massive subject in this volume. However, many pertinent studies will be found in our Bibliography.
48. Guenter Lewy, *The Catholic Church and Nazi Germany*, pp. 274–75.
49. Moltmann, *Crucified God*, p. 52, 185.
50. Ibid., p. 303.
51. Greenberg, "Lessons to Be Learned"; William R. Jones, *Is God a White Racist?* (Garden City: Anchor Press/Doubleday, 1973); pp. 16–17, 18. Jones insists that only the non-acceptance of—the fight against—suffering is a positive step toward its eradication. For another consideration of this topic, see pp. 87ff. in this volume.
52. Johann-Baptist Metz, *The Emergent Church*, p. 19.
53. Jürgen Moltmann, *The Church in the Power of the Spirit*, p. 136.
54. Ibid., pp. 137, 138ff.
55. Ibid., p. 147.
56. Ibid., pp. 149–50.
57. Ibid., pp. 138–40, 141–44.
58. Ibid., p. 144.
59. Cf. A. Roy Eckardt, *Elder and Younger Brothers*, pp. 55–58. Our interpretation of Paul in 1967 is sustained by E. P. Sanders, who in *Paul and Palestinian Judaism* shows the impossibility of trying to make Paul a support for Christian "acceptance" of Judaism. See also Sanders, "Given the Christian Claims . . . How Should Christians Think of Themselves and of the Jews in Light of the Continuation of the Jewish People?," in Josephine Knopp, ed., *International Theological Symposium on the Holocaust*, October 15–17, 1978, pp. 51–63.
60. Moltmann's triumphalism in the guise of opposition to triumphalism is subsequently embodied in a declaration that "the ecumenical movement will not . . . be complete without Israel." Alluding to the present organizational arrangement in the World Council of Churches of the working group called "Consultation on the Church and the Jewish People," Moltmann argues that it "would be a great step forward for the ecumenical movement if the churches' conversation with Israel were conducted in the framework of Faith and Order rather than in their 'Dialogue with Other Living Faiths and Ideologies'"; Address on the occasion of the fiftieth anniversary of Faith and Order, Lausanne, Pentecost 1977, as reported in *The Church and the Jewish People*, newsletter no. 2 p. 15. True dialogue means accepting the partner in his own self-understanding. The last thing that the Jewish community could tolerate would be identification as part of the Christian ecumenical movement, for this would mean being drawn into the Christian church. Christians who want to affirm the integrity of Judaism and the Jewish community have to avoid many pitfalls; this is one of them. Johann-Baptist Metz speaks of "an ecumenism between Christians and Jews, in accepting which the Jews would not be compelled to

deny their own identity." But any such theological reconciliation can succeed only if it puts down deep roots within church and society, which requires "touching the soul of the people"; *The Emergent Church*, pp. 28–29.

61. In 1976 Gregory Baum reached a similar conclusion with regard to another volume of Moltmann's, *The Experiment Hope*, a conclusion he found relevant to most Christian theologians: After Moltmann said very beautiful things about Jewish existence before and after he proceeded to speak of Jews and Christians being united in a common waiting for the promised fulfillment, he then turned "to such a definitive and unqualified affirmation of Christ's unique mediatorship that the positive things said about Jews in earlier paragraphs are quickly forgotten. . . . Apart from Christ and his preaching, it would seem, there is no salvation. Even though Moltmann writes his theological tracts with great sensitivity to the Jewish Holocaust, *it appears that the theology of substitution emerges whenever Christians reflect on the central dogmas of their faith.*" That, he added, is "a very disturbing discovery"; "Christian Theology After Auschwitz," p. 11; emphasis added.

62. Jürgen Moltmann, consultation, Tübingen, 29 Dec. 1975.

63. Rebecca Chopp, "The Interruption of the Forgotten," p. 24.

64. Ruether, *Faith and Fratricide*, p. 246; "Christian-Jewish Dialogue: New Interpretations," p. 4.

65. Cf. Moltmann, *Crucified God*, p. 7.

66. Moltmann is not alone in his predicament respecting the Jewish people and Judaism. His problem is paralleled in the works of, among other German theologians, Hans Küng and Wolfhart Pannenberg. See, e.g., Küng, *On Being a Christian*, pp. 166–74, 202–12, 259–60, 273–74, 357, 541–44; Pannenberg, *Jesus—God and Man*, pp. 246, 247, 252, 263. In a second English edition of the latter, published in 1977 (a translation of the fifth German edition), Pannenberg's strictures against "the Jewish law" and Judaism remain.

6. LIBERATION

1. Baum, *Christian Theology after Auschwitz*, p. 12. Baum defines "ideology" as "the deformation of truth for the sake of social interest."

2. Van Buren, "Status and Prospects for Theology."

3. Bernard Dupuy, "The Ethical Imperatives for Concern for Human Rights and Holocaust" (Unpublished paper, International Council of Christians and Jews Conference, New York City, June 1979). With regard to the need to "restore Israel to its proper theological place," we are reminded of the concluding remarks of Yosef Hayim Yerushalmi in responding to a paper by Rosemary Ruether: "not by your ancestors, but by your actions, will you be judged. For my people, now as in the past, is in grave peril of its life. And it simply cannot wait until you have completed a new *Summa Theologia*" (in Fleischner, *Auschwitz*, p. 107).

4. Fackenheim, "Nazi Holocaust," p. 375.

5. Marie-Thérèse Hoch, *Encounter Today* 11, no. 4 (1976): 65. Lamentably, *Encounter Today* ceased publication in 1980.

6. Rosemary Radford Ruether, *Liberation Theology*, pp. 136–37.

7. Will D. Campbell, "The World of the Redneck," in Paul T. Jersild and Dale A. Johnson, eds., *Moral Issues and Christian Response*, p. 158.

8. Cf. Helmut Gollwitzer, "Christen Begegnen Juden Heute in Deutschland" (Christians Face Jews in Today's Germany), in Helmut Gollwitzer and Eleonore Sterling, eds. *Das gespaltene Gottesvolk* (The Ruptured People of God), pp. 115–16. But how can the New Testament serve to correct antisemitism and anti-Judaism—as Gollwitzer claims for it—when the New Testament documents themselves are parts of the problem?

9. Greenberg, "Cloud of Smoke," p. 23.

10. James Parkes, consultation, Iwerne Minster, 1 Mar. 1976; Heinz Kremers, "Das Judentum in Theologie und Religionbuchern, aus christlicher Sicht," (Judaism in Theology and Religious Books, from Christian Perspective), in *Stimmt Unser Bild vom Judentum?* (Is Our Image of Judaism Correct?), p. 44.

11. The Oberammergau play, the most widely known, has been the center of much controversy in recent years. See Saul S. Friedman, *The Oberammergau Play: A Lance Against Civilization* for a history of this religious drama and its repercussions; also, "Oberammergau: Christian Folk Religion and Anti-Judaism," *Face to Face* 12 (Winter 1985); Judith Hershcopf Banki, *What Viewers Should Know About the Oberammergau Passion Play, 1980* (New York: American Jewish Committee, 1980); John J. Kelley, "Christian Strategy on Passion Plays," *The Ecumenist* 24, 3 (March/April 1986): 38–44; Marc H. Tanenbaum, "The Role of the Passion Play in Fostering Anti-Semitism throughout History," *Good Friday Worship* (Detroit: The Ecumenical Institute for Jewish-Christian Studies, 1983), 6–21; Leonard Swidler, *Guidelines for the Oberammergau Passionsspiel and Other Passion Plays* (New York: Anti-Defamation League of B'nai B'rith, 1980).

In the United States a number of major productions are also regularly performed, and many more locally produced amateur variations exist. Most present the same problems as the Oberammergau play regarding historical inaccuracies and reinforcement of anti-Jewish attitudes. It should be noted that there are a few exceptions, where the producers have begun to show sensitivity to these issues and to attempt corrective treatment of the subject.

12. Cf. Arthur A. Cohen, "Messianism and Sabbatai Zevi," pp. 30–49, esp. p. 49; see also Joseph Klausner, "The Jewish and the Christian Messiah," in *The Messianic Idea in Israel*, pp. 519–31.

13. Emil Fackenheim asks, "Can the coming of a Messiah be counted on when, at the time of most desperate need, he failed to come? And if and when he does come, will the Jewish people live to see him?"; "Reflections on Aliyah," p. 26. A Messiah "that can come yet at Auschwitz did not come is . . . inaccessible"; *To Mend the World*, p. 328. Elie Wiesel has chided and confessed: "The only response after [the *Shoah*] would have been the coming of the Messiah, but nothing else. If the Messiah had come in 1945, I would have said, 'Well, OK, I am grateful'—not to forgive him but somehow to make up. But nothing less"; in Irving Abrahamson, *Against Silence* 3: 313.

14. David Tracy, "Religious Values after the Holocaust: A Catholic View," p. 99.

15. Cohn, *Trial and Death of Jesus*, p. 331. For a full discussion of this book, see Eckardt, *Your People, My People*, chap. 3.

16. Ulrich E. Simon, consultation, London, 20 Feb. 1976. See Eckardt, *Your People, My People*, pp. 8–13.

17. Ignaz Maybaum, *The Face of God after Auschwitz*, p. 11.

18. Eckardt, *Your People, My People*, p. 58.

19. Ibid., p. 226; Eckardt, *Elder and Younger Brothers*, pp. 157–58. For a fuller discussion of the missionary question, see the latter work, pp. 61–66, 73–74, 76–80, 86–88, 93–94, 152–58.

20. Mayer, *Judentum und Christentum* (Judaism and Christianity), p. 162; Rolf Rendtorff, "Juden sind keine potentiellen Christen" (Jews Are Not Potential Christians), pp. 358–60; Kremers, "Judentum in Theologie und Religionsbuchern," p. 48.

21. "Toward Renovation of the Relationship of Christians and Jews," in Helga Croner, ed., *More Stepping Stones to Jewish-Christian Relations*, pp. 207–9; italics added.

22. Johann-Baptist Metz, *The Emergent Church*, p. 28.

23. Franklin Sherman, "Speaking of God After Auschwitz," p. 30.

24. Moltmann, *Crucified God*, pp. 148–51.

25. This description is reproduced, with minor changes, from an account cited in Greenberg, "Lessons to Be Learned."

26. Sara Nomberg-Przytyk, *Auschwitz: Tales from a Grotesque Land*, pp. 81–82.

27. Yet, the Roman Catholic author Elisabeth Orsten finds the agonies of these burning children no challenge to the pre-Holocaust theology of the cross: "God's last and definitive word to the world and to history [is] a word of love, . . . spoken . . . through the passion and death of His only-begotten, His beloved Son"; "Light in the Darkness," in *The Bridge*, III, John M. Oesterreicher, ed. (South Orange, N.J.: Institute of Judaeo-Christian Studies, Seton Hall University, by Pantheon Books, 1958), p. 337.

28. Dov Marmur, consultation, London, 16 Feb. 1976; Eugene Borowitz, *How Can a Jew Speak of Faith Today?*, p. 25.

29. For a consideration of the question of Jewish Christianity, see Eckardt, *Elder and Younger Brothers*, pp. 138–40, 155–57.

30. Ibid., pp. 159–60.

31. See, e.g., John A. T. Robinson, "Our Image of Christ Must Change," *The Christian Century* 90, 12 (21 March 1973): 339–42.

32. An additional insight is appropriate here, namely, the contention that Christians must move beyond and outside a christocentric theology in order to recognize that God's action is not, and never has been, exclusively concentrated or finalized in Jesus Christ. Paul Knitter's *No Other Name?* (Maryknoll, N.Y.: Orbis Books, 1985) surveys a number of Christian theologians who are seriously challenging the finality or "definitive normality" of Christ and Christianity. Tom Driver, in a review article, commented that he was grateful to Knitter for showing him that he was not alone in his "christological radicalism." A theocentric theology must "recognize alternative ways by which people may authentically worship God and experience liberation. Accordingly, it must reconsider traditional Christian positions on such central issues as incarnation, resurrection, revelation, exclusiveness, and universalist claims"; "Toward a Theocentric Christology," *Christianity and Crisis* 45, 18 (11 Nov. 1985): 449–52. See also Deane William Ferm, "Honest to Jesus," *The Christian Century* 89, 12 (22 Mar. 1972): 332–35. Johann-Baptist Metz insists (as did Karl Barth) that there is "only one great ecumenical task" for Christianity: its relationship with Jews. Only when Christians have resolved "their identity . . . in front of and together with the history of the beliefs of the Jews" will they be able to develop Christian unity and "contribute productively to an ecumenism of the great religions as a whole"; "Facing the Jews," pp. 33, 28, 33.

33. Heinz Kremers, written communication, 19 Nov. 1975.

34. Alan T. Davies, "Response to Irving Greenberg," in Fleischner, ed., *Auschwitz*, pp. 61–62.

35. Greenberg, "Cloud of Smoke," p. 24.

36. Ulrich E. Simon, consultation, London, 20 Feb. 1976. The "conquest of death by the One who acts for the many . . . enables us at last to say that the dead are not dead because they have been gassed and their bodies burnt in crematoria"; Simon, *Theology of Auschwitz*, pp. 109–10.

37. The preceding verse (13) and the two following verses (15, 16) usually receive little mention even though in the English translations they seem to raise questions. The Hebrew construction states Paul's conviction unambiguously: "*if* there is no resurrection of the dead, then Christ has not been raised. . . . We are even found to be misrepresenting God, because we testified of God that he raised Christ, whom he did not raise, *if* it is true that the dead are not raised. For *if* the dead are not raised, then Christ has not been raised." To be sure, Paul goes on in verse 20ff to assert that "in fact Christ has been raised from the dead" and to argue that he was "the first fruits of those who have fallen asleep" and that others will be raised each "in his own order." Paul then further modifies the statement regarding the raising of the dead: "at this coming, those who belong to Christ" will be raised, before he delivers the kingdom to God.

38. Moltmann, *The Trinity and the Kingdom*, pp. 122, 124.

39. Pannenberg, *Jesus—God and Man*, pp. 67, 257, 258; and "Christianity and the God of Israel" (Unpublished paper, Harvard Divinity School Colloquium, October 1966).

40. Jacobus (Coos) Schoneveld, "The Jewish 'No' to Jesus and the Christian 'Yes' to Jews," *Quarterly Review* [Nashville], 4 (1984): 60, 63; slightly emended.

41. Metz, *The Emergent Church*, pp. 19, 32.

42. Paul van Buren, *The Burden of Freedom*, pp. 90ff. Although van Buren nowhere uses the term "extra-bodily," he here argues that the Resurrection "was not, apparently, a case of resuscitation," and he speaks on behalf of a "strange variation on embodiment." For a later but similar exposition, see Paul M. van Buren, *Discerning the Way*, pp. 79, 82, 87, 190, 195, 196.

43. Ruether, *Liberation Theology*, pp. 62–63.

44. Pannenberg, *Jesus—God and Man*, pp. 75, 77.

45. On the basis of careful linguistic and translational analysis, Robert L. Lindsey argues the primacy of Luke (see, e.g., "A New Approach to the Synoptic Gospels"). Lindsey is supported by David Flusser (see, e.g., "The Crucified One and the Jews").

46. Although most nonfundamentalist Christians—Protestant, Roman Catholic, and Eastern Orthodox—do not espouse biblical literalism, most of them are still guilty of a "fundamentalism of the spirit." That is to say, although they are willing to engage in critical study of the texts and the sources and to take account of historical context and circumstances, they are not ready to move far from the center of tradition or to consider the radical implications of a thoroughgoing historical view.

47. The theological and moral question of Jesus' Resurrection is more intensively analyzed in A. Roy Eckardt, "Toward A Critical Assessment of Christian Theology in the Aftermath of the Holocaust." In a critique of a preliminary commentary by Eckardt upon the Resurrection, John Carroll White identifies "the experience of a resurrection event" as "not nearly the obstacle to the reconstruction of Christian theology that A. Roy Eckardt makes it out to be." White confuses the issue, which is solely one of the reality or nonreality of the Resurrection event itself, and not one of "experience." John Carroll

White, "Resurrection, Pluralism, and Dialogue: A Response to A. Roy Eckardt," in Josephine Knopp, ed., *Proceedings of the Second Philadelphia Conference on the Holocaust*, pp. 140–48.

48. N. Peter Levinsohn, address at the colloquium on "Antisemitism and Other Forms of Group Prejudice," University of Southampton, England, 20 July 1977. For more discussion of this subject, see "Toward Conciliation" in chapter 4, "Political Power and the People of God" and "Hope and the People of God" in this volume. Also see Alice L. Eckardt, "Power and Powerlessness."

49. Alice L. Eckardt, "Power and Powerlessness," p. 191; cf. Eliezer Berkovits, *Faith After the Holocaust*.

50. Heidi M. Ravven, letter to *Midstream* 27, 6 (June/July 1981): 62, 63.

51. The person continued: "For two thousand years we have served mankind with the Word, with the Book. Are we now to try to convince mankind that we are warriors? We shall never outdo them at that game"; cited by Alexander Donat, *The Holocaust Kingdom*, p. 103. See earlier brief reference to Leo Baeck and martyrdom.

52. Davies, "The Contemporary Encounter of Christians and Jews," p. 58.

53. Van Buren, *The Burden of Freedom*, pp. 14, 68, 74.

54. Emil L. Fackenheim, *God's Presence in History*, p. 87.

55. A perfect example is to be found in Willard Oxtoby's skepticism that the Exodus-God would act again in the history of the present era, and Oxtoby is especially skeptical that He would do so in the State of Israel: We Christians "as outsiders can [not] honestly accept the Jewish interpretation of the 1967 war as 'divine rescue.'" Cited by Alan Davies, "The Contemporary Encounter of Christians and Jews," p. 57.

56. Wiesel, *Jewish Legends*, p. 8. Has Christian history failed because Christians have *not* protested against what it believed (or chose to believe) God had ordained regarding Jews and others outside the church?

57. Emil L. Fackenheim, (Unpublished paper prepared for the symposium on the Holocaust, Cathedral of St. John the Divine, New York, 3–6 June 1974). See earlier reference to the commanding "Voice of Auschwitz."

58. In the Jewish tradition there is a total of 613 commandments. See Fackenheim, *God's Presence in History*, p. 84 and passim; *Quest for Past and Future*, p. 20 and passim; cf. *Encounters between Judaism and Modern Philosophy*, pp. 166–67, and discussion of Jewish martyrdom, pp. 20–21, 73, 75–77; "Jewish Values in the Post-Holocaust Future," pp. 272, 273, 295; and see p. 78 in this volume for a longer presentation of the 614th commandment. See also Eckardt, *Your People, My People*, p. 228–31.

59. Eckardt, *Your People, My People*, p. 244. There is perhaps an analogue here to the Christian persuasion of love as the "fulfilling" of "the law." But the parallel assumes that the imperative "Thou shalt love" is transformed—through the power of love itself?—into a declarative "We do love." It seems clear that the way for human beings to live a fulfilled life is for them to love.

60. The renowned medieval philosopher Moses Maimonides ruled that any Jew "who is killed, though this may be for reasons other than conversion, but simply because he is a Jew, is called *Kaddosh*"—one who has sanctified God's name; cited in Pesach Schindler, "The Holocaust and Kiddush Hashem in Hassidic Thought," p. 88. From the standpoint of Maimonides, those Jews killed in the Holocaust were martyrs. But cf. Richard L. Rubenstein: "One of Hitler's greatest victories was that he deprived the Jews of *all* opportunity to be martyrs. There can be no martyrdom without free choice"; "Some Per-

spectives on Religious Faith after Auschwitz," in Littell and Locke, eds., *German Church Struggle and the Holocaust*, p. 263.

61. Manès Sperber, . . . *than a Tear in the Sea*, pp. xii–xiv.

62. Cf. Rubenstein, *After Auschwitz*, pp. 32–39; Terrence Des Pres, *The Survivor*, pp. 51–72.

63. Pesach Schindler, consultation, Jerusalem, 18 June 1976.

64. Fackenheim, *God's Presence in History*, pp. 75–76. Fackenheim points to the cunning with which "the Nazi empire" was designed "to murder Jewish martyrdom"; "Reflections on Aliyah," p. 26.

65. The affirmation of sovereignty for the Jewish people is further considered in this chapter under the heading "Political Power and the People of God." In *Encounters Between Judaism and Modern Philosophy*, Fackenheim deals with the question of whether "pre-Messianic suffering, risked for the sake of a Messianic future" counts "against the assertion that God is merciful." He contends that in contrast to the Christian eschatological expectation, the Jewish expectation is "at least in part falsifiable by future history. . . . After Auschwitz, it is a major question whether the Messianic faith is not *already* falsified—whether a Messiah who could come, and yet at Auschwitz did not come, has not become a religious impossibility" (pp. 20–21). Cf. Gregor in Wiesel's *Gates of the Forest*: "Whether or not the Messiah comes doesn't matter; we'll manage without him. It is because it is too late that we are required to hope" (p. 223).

66. Thomas A. Idinopulos and Roy Bowen Ward, "Is Christology Inherently Anti-Semitic? A Critical Review of Rosemary Ruether's *Faith and Fratricide*," p. 209. Ruether clearly shows that human behavior cannot be separated from human beliefs. The former follows the latter, rather than the reverse. In arguing that political factors, instead of theological ones, were the real root of tensions between Christians and Jews, Idinopulos and Ward fail to see that the original struggle was thoroughly religious. Social prejudices and political rivalries were ancillary to the church's main goal of establishing itself as the true —that is, God's—instrument of salvation. In their endeavor to undermine Ruether's understanding that "the anti-Judaic structure of Christian thought . . . has retarded Christian theological maturation," the two critics trivialize her challenge to a genuine Christian *metanoia*.

67. Alistair Kee, ed., *A Reader in Political Theology*, p. ix.

68. Here is the place where Jürgen Moltmann's emphasis upon the Godforsakenness of Jesus on the cross gains its force, in contrast to his erroneous effort to extract ultimate theological significance from Jesus' cry of abandonment.

69. Greenberg, "Cloud of Smoke," p. 54.

70. Rubenstein, "Some Perspectives on Religious Faith after Auschwitz," pp. 265, 266.

71. We are indebted to Irving Greenberg for this item concerning Eldridge Cleaver.

72. Irving Greenberg, "Some Thoughts on the Meaning of the Restoration of Israel and Jerusalem for Days of Commemoration," in Alice L. Eckardt, ed., *Jerusalem: City of the Ages* (Lanham, Md.: University Press of America, 1987), p. 282.

73. Abba Lessing, "Jewish Impotence and Power," *Midstream* 22, 8 (Oct. 1976): 56.

74. Pinchas Hacohen Peli, "The Future of Israel," p. 15.

75. Ibid., p. 13.

76. Manès Sperber, . . . *than a Tear in the Sea*, p. xv.

77. Mordecai Waxman, "The Dialogue: Touching New Basis?" in Helga Croner, ed., *More Stepping Stones to Jewish-Christian Relations*, p. 29; and Peli, "The Future of Israel," pp. 1–3.

78. Calvin Keene, "Prophecy and Modern Israel," pp. 1–3.

79. Peter R. Powell, Jr., letter in *The Christian Century* 101, 16 (19 May 1984): 500.

80. Uriel Tal, "Möglichkeiten einer jüdisch-christlichen Begegnung und Verständigung, Jüdische Sicht" (*Possibilities of a Jewish-Christian Encounter and Agreement: Jewish View*), p. 606. Cf. Reinhold Niebuhr: "patriotism transmutes individual unselfishness into national egoism" (*Moral Man and Immoral Society*, p. 91). Niebuhr understood sin as "the hidden pride that insinuates itself even into our most selfless endeavors. And this pride is particularly dangerous at the collective level"; June Bingham, "Carter, Castro, and Reinhold Niebuhr," p. 776.

81. See among others, these works by Reinhold Niebuhr: *The Children of Light and the Children of Darkness; Christianity and Power Politics; Moral Man and Immoral Society; The Structure of Nations and Empires.*

82. Fadiey Lovsky, written communication, 1 Dec. 1975.

83. Niebuhr, *Children of Light*, p. xiii.

84. Emil Fackenheim, "Foreword" to Yehuda Bauer, *The Jewish Emergence from Powerlessness*, p. xiv.

85. David Hartman, "The Moral Challenge of Israel," *Jerusalem Post*, 20 June 1982, p. 8.

86. On the link between politics and forgiveness, our debt to Reinhold Niebuhr is as great as it is obvious. See especially his essay "The Peace of God," in *Discerning the Signs of the Times*, pp. 174–94.

87. Greenberg, "Cloud of Smoke," p. 34.

7. TURN TO THE
KINGDOM OF DAY

1. Greenberg, from "To the Mount of Corpses in the Snow," in *Anthology of Modern Hebrew Poetry* 2: 260–61.

2. Peck, "From Cain to the Death Camps," p. 162; Arthur A. Cohen, "The Holocaust and Christian Theology," p. 430; Stefan Zeroniski, cited in David Rosenthal, "Thirty Years after the Liberation of Auschwitz and Bergen-Belsen," p. 9.

3. Metz, "Facing the Jews," p. 29.

4. Fackenheim, "The People Israel Lives," *The Christian Century* 87, 18 (6 May 1970): 565.

5. Donald McEvoy professes to be haunted by the gospel hymn "Were you There When They Crucified My Lord?" For him the words recall the failure of the churches in the years 1933–1945. He has made it his life calling to try to rectify that silence, that averted gaze, that turning away in any situation that has appeared to threaten the security of Jews, and others in danger. As vice president in charge of programming for the National Conference of Christians and Jews at the time when the American Nazi Party

was given court sanction to march, in full regalia including swastikas, in Skokie, Illinois (a community with an especially large number of Holocaust survivors in residence), Mc-Evoy rallied the NCCJ membership and other interested Christians to go to Skokie and be on the streets wearing a yellow star to show their solidarity with the Jews whom the party continues to threaten.

6. Manès Sperber, "Hurban or the Inconceivable Certainty," in . . . *than a Tear in the Sea*, pp. xi, xiii. Alexander Donat made a similar testimony: "We paid a terrible price for our hope, which turned out to be a delusion." The Nazi "stage managers" used many tactics, including "the torture of hope." On the other hand, a Polish journalist speaks of the "illusion of hope by which people without any alternatives try to save themselves"; Donat, "Armageddon," *Dissent* 2 (Spring 1963): 125, 128, 127.

7. Yet this question, often in the slightly veiled form of an accusation, continues to be one most persistently raised, as if the atrocities of the murderers are easier to comprehend than the helplessness of the trapped victims. The exact opposite question was asked by Elie Wiesel's mother, as she read about the Warsaw ghetto uprising in a Hungarian newspaper at Passover 1943: "Why did they revolt?" She did not know that the only alternative to dying while fighting was dying at Treblinka in a mass gas chamber; cited in Abrahamson, *Against Silence*, 1: 105.

8. Paul Celan, as cited in Langer, *Holocaust and the Literary Imagination*, p. 9.

9. "Todesfuge" was composed on a train en route to the East and a forced labor camp. Celan's parents were murdered; he took his own life in Paris in 1970. See Paul Celan, *Selected Poems*; Paul Celan, *Nineteen Poems*; see also George Steiner, *Language and Silence*; Samuel Hux, "The Holocaust and the Survival of Tragedy."

10. Manès Sperber, . . . *than a Tear in the Sea*, pp. xiii–xiv.

11. David Wolf Silverman, "The Holocaust: A Living Force," p. 25.

12. See Irving Greenberg, "Clouds of Smoke," p. 27, and Gregory Baum, "Christian Theology After Auschwitz," p. 16.

13. From Uri Zvi Greenberg, "A Jew Stands at the Gates of Tears," in Joseph Leftwich, ed. and trans. *The Golden Peacock*, p. 199.

14. Israeli school children are brought to Yad Vashem to learn of the dark night experienced by their people. Yet the ebullience of youth, in a free society, prevents them from being overwhelmed by the horror. On the lawns near the waiting buses they soon are engaged in the typical play activities of young people the world over. Nearby is a piece of sculpture: a large anonymous mother figure. Her outstretched arms clasp lifeless figures of children. Here is a strange convergence: the national memorial to the victims of the Holocaust, in the newly reborn State of Israel, the dark shadow that the Shoah casts, beneath the usually sun-lit sky, the memory of one and one-half million murdered children, and the laughter of living Israeli children.

15. Yizhak Orpaz, "A Literature of Siege and Survival," p. 14. Most man-centered societies or cultures presuppose a transcendent frame of reference by way of justifying, implicitly, their humanism. The only exception to this, in principle, is a humanistic world view that seeks for a self-contained or perhaps self-evident justification of itself through a positing of strictly human needs and purposes as its ultimate norms. An illustration of a transcendent frame of reference for humanistic, political goals is found in David Polish's position respecting the contemporary State of Israel. After observing with entire truth, that "a state is not a state if power is not its primary concern," Polish continues that the Jewish people must concern themselves with that, but also with more than that. The

"more" is "the messianic component out of which the idea of the state emerged." Polish concludes that the very existence and viability of the Galut, the Dispersion, "prevent Israel from being like all the nations"; *Israel—Nation and People*, pp. 166, 174.

16. Gyorgy Kemeny, as cited in *Der Widerstandskampfer* (The Resistance Fighter) [Vienna] 23 (Spring 1975): 6.

17. Contrary to many assertions that studying the Holocaust and keeping its memory alive will be a strong preventive against a repetition, David Biale believes the opposite. "Once an event has occurred, once it has been conceived of as possible, its recurrence is likely, regardless of memory, perhaps even as a result of it"; "Power, Passivity and the Legacy of the Holocaust," in "Rethinking the Holocaust," p. 72. But Arthur Waskow thinks that "the looming Planetary Auschwitz [a worldwide nuclear annihilation] is a "little less hard to avoid because we have already experienced the Nazis"; "Between the Fires," in ibid., p. 86.

18. Orpaz, "Literature of Siege and Survival," p. 15; Aharon Megged, "Letter from Israel," p. 13.

19. Elie Wiesel, "Ominous Signs and Unspeakable Thoughts." The artist's sketch placed next to Wiesel's lament portrays a man wearing an Arab headdress blowing out the candles of a menorah, whose seven flames are human skulls.

20. Rudolf Pfisterer, written communication, 14 Oct. 1975.

21. "Conversation with Elie Wiesel," p. 5.

22. From an address by Moshe Dayan at Lehigh University, 13 Feb. 1977.

23. Louis Halle sustains political realism in international politics, a position for which Reinhold Niebuhr and Hans J. Morgenthau also have been eloquent spokesmen. Halle shows how the high degree of instability that characterized relations between the United States and the Soviet Union at the end of the 1950s was subsequently overcome "not by disarmament, but by its opposite." Peace has been made possible by the increase and technical improvement of nuclear weaponry, together with effective espionage satellites, all of which foster mutual deterrence. Accordingly, those who automatically equate disarmament with morality are urged to think twice. "Applying Morality to Foreign Policy," in Kenneth W. Thompson, ed., *Foreign Policy and Morality*, pp. 30–32.

24. See, for example, Robert M. Lawrence and Joel Larus, eds., *Nuclear Proliferation*, esp. Avigdor Haselkorn, "Israel: From an Option to a Bomb in the Basement?," pp. 149–82.

25. See Mihail Agursky, "Russian Neo-Nazism: A Growing Threat."

26. David Roskies, *Against the Apocalypse*, pp. 305, 310; emphasis added.

27. Cf. Moltmann, *Crucified God*, pp. 251–52.

28. John Pawlikowski has repeatedly called attention to the fact that Hitler and his National Socialist creation were the culmination of a "new sense of freedom" within modern humankind—a freedom from any and all transcendent norms, a freedom to re-create Creation in a new mold. "The Nazi experiment is liberated man's first attempt to use his new [uninhibited] powers in a wholesale fashion. It is the ultimate achievement of man without God. "The Holocaust as Rational Event," *Reconstructionist* 40, 3 (April 1974): 8; see also "Christian Perspectives and Moral Implications," in Henry Friedlander and Sybil Milton, eds., *The Holocaust: Ideology, Bureaucracy, and Genocide*, pp. 295–308.

29. Bertrand Joseph, written communication, Strasbourg, 27 Oct. 1975. To be sure, Jews have not been nor are they, totally free of intolerance. The greatest venom has always been directed toward other Jews, e.g., Karaite-Rabbanite, Hasidim-Mitnaggedim.

221

30. Rubenstein, *Cunning of History*, p. 93.

31. Cf., for example, Rabbi Judah Löw, the Maharal, of sixteenth-century Prague: God created a plurality of nations, peoples, each with its essence and form, its own appropriate place, and its own spiritual distinctions. Division belongs to the very order of the world; Lionel Kochan, *The Jew and His History* (New York: Schocken, 1977), p. 36. See also Irving Greenberg, "Models of Pluralism," *Perspectives* 2, 5 (April 1987): 1–5 in which Rabbi Soloveitchik's views are cited.

32. Baum, "Christian Theology After Auschwitz," p. 13.

33. Finn Henning Lauridsen, consultation, Copenhagen, 31 July 1975.

34. We do not, alas, know his name. The statement was reported to us in a conversation with Avraham Soetendorp, The Hague, 22 January 1976.

35. Robert McAfee Brown, *Theology in a New Key: Responding to Liberation Themes*, p. 187.

36. See Appendix 2. In the United States, since 1979, National Days of Remembrance have been established by Congress and are being ever more widely observed in state houses and local communities as well as synagogues, some churches, and some interfaith services. In the Netherlands the memory of the destruction of Dutch Jews has been incorporated into commemoration of liberation from the suffering imposed on the Dutch people by the Nazi occupiers. In Israel, Yom HaShoah is an annual and national day of solemn remembrance.

37. Cf. David Roskies, *Against the Apocalypse*, p. 9.

38. Elie Wiesel, in Abrahamson, ed., *Against Silence*, I, pp. 240, 28.

39. Jesus' coming Resurrection will be distinctive for Christians because his is the history through which they were brought into the covenant with Israel—just as the future resurrection of Abraham and Moses will have peculiar significance for the eschatological community of Jews, as, secondarily, for Christians. For the Christian of the end-time, what joy will surpass that of meeting face-to-face the transfigured Jesus?

APPENDIX 1

1. *New York Times*, May 3, 1985.

2. Among Christian sources consult, e.g., Alan Davies, ed., *Antisemitism and the Foundations of Christianity* (New York: Paulist, 1979); A. Roy Eckardt, *Your People, My People* (Quadrangle/New York Times, 1974), chap. 2; A. Roy Eckardt and Alice L. Eckardt, "Christentum und Judentum, Die theologische und moralische Problematik der Vernichtung des europäischen Judentums," *Evangelische Theologie* 36 (1976): 406–26; idem, *Long Night's Journey into Day* (Detroit: Wayne State University Press, 1982); Friedrich Heer, *God's First Love*, trans. Geoffrey Shelton (New York: Weybright and Talley, 1970); Charlotte Klein, *Theologie und Anti-Judaismus* (Munich: Chr. Kaiser Verlag, 1975); Franklin H. Littell, *The Crucifixion of the Jews* (New York: Harper & Row, 1975); Rolf Rendtorff and Ekkehard Stegemann, eds., *Auschwitz—Krise der christlichen Theologie* (Munich: Chr. Kaiser Verlag, 1980); and Rosemary Radford Ruether, *Faith and Fratricide* (New York: Seabury, 1974).

3. David S. Wyman, *Paper Walls: America and the Refugee Crisis, 1938–1941* (Amherst: University of Massachusetts Press, 1969); idem, *The Abandonment of the Jews: America and the Holocaust, 1941–1945* (New York: Pantheon, 1984).

4. John Tagliabue, "SS Veterans Feel 'Rehabilitated' by Reagan Visit," *New York Times*, May 3, 1985. It was not until after 1943 that, because of a high attrition rate, SS members were conscripted; before then the units were wholly composed of volunteers.

5. On April 22, 1985, a *Washington Post*–ABC News poll found that 51 percent of respondents disapproved of the cemetery visit, 39 percent approved, and the remainder voiced no opinion. True, the poll showed an immediate drop in the president's approval rating to 54 percent (*Washington Post*, May 8, 1985). Yet the Bitburg "incident" was all too soon forgotten. President Reagan was probably right that his Bitburg visit was not "of that much concern" to most Americans. Of great relevance here is the peculiar social-psychological truth that national, majority attitudes to Mr. Reagan show over the long range little if any connection to his personal policies and behavior.

6. Consult, e.g., the exchange of correspondence reproduced in *European Judaism* (London), Spring 1985, pp. 5–17.

7. Consult, e.g., Edward H. Flannery, *The Anguish of the Jews*, rev. ed. (New York: Paulist, 1985); and Hyam Maccoby, *The Sacred Executioner* (New York: Thames and Hudson, 1982).

8. *The Times* (London), June 8, 1985.

9. Dietrich Bonhoeffer, *The Cost of Discipleship*, trans. R. H. Fuller and Irmgard Booth (London: SCM, 1959), p. 35.

10. On balance, the ongoing American record respecting its own Jewish citizens is among the best in the world. But the preeminent moral source for this achievement is a trans-Christian and constitutionally guaranteed cultural pluralism.

11. *New York Times*, April 30, 1985.

12. Such participation does not require fervent or active religiousness; the most nominal gentile lives under the power of Christian history.

13. By Ronald Reagan's good intentions at the conscious level, we mean both his self-image and his image as received by many other people. Objectively speaking, Mr. Reagan is of course not above the use of falsehood to advance his position. Thus, one young Jewish woman wrote to urge him not to go to Bitburg. In his speech at the U.S. air base there, the president said she had advised him to *go* to Bitburg (Anthony Lewis, "The One-Track Mind," *New York Times*, May 9, 1985: see "Press Commentaries.")

14. Erich Simenauer, "The Return of the Persecutor," in *Generations of the Holocaust*, ed. Martin S. Bergmann and Milton E. Jucovy (New York: Basic Books, 1982), pp. 172, 173.

15. Alexander and Margarete Mitscherlich, *Die Unfähigkeit zu trauern, Grundlagen kollektiven Verhaltens* (Munich: R. Piper Verlag, 1967).

16. One can readily interject that the vigorous protests against Mr. Reagan's visit on the part of the Congress of the United States and from many other quarters were closely affinal to, or were at least made possible by, a true Christian consciousness (contra Christian ideology). In the United States a secular ethic in behalf of justice for Jews has (good) Christian roots—which is another way of saying that it has Jewish prophetic and rabbinic roots. However, the present essay is delimited by self-identifiably Christian praxis respecting Jews.

17. Advertisement in the *New York Times*, April 28, 1985.

18. There is a limited but real sense in which entire nations may express repentance. At the fortieth anniversary of the United Nations, Prime Minister Yasuhiro Nakasone of Japan expressed profound regret, in the name of his country, for "the ultranation-

alism and militarism it unleashed, and the untold suffering the war inflicted upon peoples around the world and, indeed, upon its own people" (*New York Times*, Oct 24, 1985). Even Chancellor Kohl is reported to have spoken to a group of American Jewish leaders "as a German and as a Christian" in seeking forgiveness for the Holocaust (*New York Times*, October 26, 1985).

19. Consult Part III, "The Persecutors' Children," in Bergmann and Jucovy, eds., *Generations of the Holocaust*.

APPENDIX 2

1. The fact that a few Christians here and there acted lovingly and sacrificially does not expunge or redeem the dreadful record of most church members and officials.

2. A. Roy Eckardt, "Christian Responses to the *Endlösung*," *Religion in Life* 47, 1 (Spring 1978): 34–35. Gregory Baum is cited within this passage.

3. This type of service may be observed in conjunction with the Jewish date of Yom HaShoah, or the date of *Kristallacht*, or Anne Frank day, etc. See later comments regarding questions about Holy Week. A Roman Catholic priest in Memphis, Tennessee, suggested the addition of a "Feast of Atonement" to the Christian liturgical calendar.

4. Robert Willis, "Christian Theology After Auschwitz," *Journal of Ecumenical Studies* 12, 4 (Fall 1975): 494–95.

5. Cf. the Rev. Theodore Loder, "Your People, My People," sermon in Marcia Sachs, Littell, ed., *Liturgies on the Holocaust* (Lewiston, N.Y.: The Edwin Mellen Press, 1986), pp. 84–85, 86.

6. Goals may include: to educate; to share the suffering vicariously (as on Good Friday); to become sensitized to the consequences of hatred and idolatries; to remember the victims; to see the broader implications of moral issues; to help us understand our Jewish neighbors and the State of Israel; to become more aware of the past persecutions of Jews and of our own attitudes; to comprehend Christian failure to respond adequately to the needs of desperate people; to see where our teachings need changing, along with our rituals; to dedicate ourselves to Never Again; to raise theological questions.

7. McEvoy, "A Holocaust Memorial Service for Christians" (New York: National Conference of Christians and Jews, 1978), pp. 5–6.

8. Hochhuth, *The Deputy* (New York: Grove Press, 1964), p. 289.

9. Robert Gram, "Christ and the Auschwitz Experience," *The Church Herald*, 27, January 1978, pp. 4–5.

10. Emil Fackenheim, "The People Israel Lives," *The Christian Century* 87, 18 (6 May 1970): 568.

11. H. David Leuner, *Holocaust Memorial Service*, Jerusalem, 1975.

12. Joan Ringelheim related how working with the abstract numbers of women victims from one ghetto community after another made her *more* conscious of the persons they represented; "Women and the Holocaust: Taking Numbers into Account" (Lecture at Lehigh University, 19 March 1987).

13. Franklin H. Littell, *The Crucifixion of the Jews* (New York: Harper & Row, 1975), p. 131.

14. Hermann Adler, quoted in Elisabeth Orsten, "Light in Darkness," *The Bridge*, III, John M. Oesterreicher, ed. (New York: Pantheon Books, 1958), pp. 338–39.

15. In Albert Friedlander, ed., *Out of the Whirlwind* (New York: Schocken, 1976).

16. Elisabeth Orsten and *Stimmen der Zeit* in *The Bridge*, pp. 335–38.

17. McEvoy, "A Holocaust Memorial Service," p. 6.

18. *The Diary of Eva Heyman* (Jerusalem: Yad Vashem, 1964), p. 65.

19. See *Liturgies on the Holocaust*, pp. 103–4.

20. Barry Ulanov, "Abraham Rattner, Painter of Anguish," and Elisabeth Orsten, "Light in Darkness," in *The Bridge*, pp. 388–98, 377–79.

SELECTED
BIBLIOGRAPHY

Abella, Irving, and Harold Troper. *None is Too Many*. Toronto: Lester and Orpen Dennys, 1982.

Abrahamson, Irving, ed. and comp. *Against Silence: The Voice and Vision of Elie Wiesel*. 3 vols. New York: Holocaust Library, 1985.

Adam, Uwe Dietrich. *Judenpolitik im Dritten Reich*. Dusseldorf: Droste Verlag, 1972.

Adler, Hermann G. *Der Verwaltete Mensch: Studien zur Deportation der Juden aus Deutschland*. Tübingen: J. C. B. Mohr, 1975.

Agursky, Mikhail. "Russian Neo-Nazism: A Growing Threat." *Midstream* 22, no. 2 (Feb. 1976): 35–42.

Alexander, Edward. "Abba Kovner: Poet of Holocaust and Rebirth." *Midstream* 23, no. 8 (Oct. 1977): 50–59.

————. *The Resonance of Dust: Essays on Holocaust Literature and Jewish Fate*. Columbus: Ohio State University Press, 1980.

Améry, Jean. *At the Mind's Limits: Contemplation by a Survivor on Auschwitz and Its Realities*. Translated by Sidney and Stella Rosenfeld. Bloomington: Indiana University Press, 1980.

Annals of the American Academy of Political and Social Science 450 (July 1980). Special number on "Reflections on the Holocaust: Historical, Philosophical, and Educational Dimensions."

Anthology of Modern Hebrew Poetry. Vol. 2 Selected by S. Y. Penueli and A. Ukhmani. Jerusalem: Institute for the Translation of Hebrew Literature and Israel Universities Press, 1966.

Arad, Yitzhak. *Ghetto in Flames: The Struggle and Destruction of the Jews in Vilna in the Holocaust*. New York: Holocaust Library, 1982.

Arad, Yitzhak, Shmuel Krakowski and Shmuel Spector, eds. *The Einsatzgruppen Reports: Selections from the Official Dispatches of the Nazi Death Squads' Campaign Against the Jews*. Foreword by William Donat. New York: Holocaust Library, 1987.

Aron, Robert. *Lettre ouverte à l'église de France*. Paris: Albin Michel, 1975.

"Auschwitz," *Encyclopaedia Judaica* 3: 854–58.

Bar-on, Abraham Zvie. "The Holocaust: Who is to Blame?" Unpublished preparatory paper for International Scholars Conference on the Holocaust, New York, 3–6 March 1975.

SELECTED BIBLIOGRAPHY

Bartrop, Paul. "Indifference and Inconvenience: The Australian Government's Policy Toward Refugees from Nazi Persecution, 1933–1939." Ph.D. thesis, Monash University, Australia.

Bastiaans, Jan. "The KZ-Syndrome: A Thirty Year Study of the Effects on Victims of Nazi Concentration Camps." *Revistâ Medico-Chirurgicala* [Belgrade] 63, no. 3 (July-Sept. 1974): 573–78.

———. *Psychosomatische Gevolgen van Onderrdrukking en Verzet.* Amsterdam: N. V. Noord-Hollandische Uitgevers Maatschappij, 1957.

———. "Vom Menschen im KZ und vom KZ in Menschen: Ein Beitrag zur Behandlung des KZ-Syndroms und dessen Spätfolgen." In *Essays über Naziverbrechen: Simon Wiesenthal Gewidmet*, pp. 177–201. Amsterdam: Wiesenthal Fonds, 1973.

Bauer, Yehuda. *A History of the Holocaust.* New York: Franklin Watts, 1982.

———. *The Holocaust in Historical Perspective.* Seattle: University of Washington Press, 1978.

———. *The Jewish Emergence from Powerlessness.* Buffalo and Toronto: University of Toronto Press, 1979.

———. *My Brothers Keeper: The American Jewish Joint Distribution Committee 1939–1945.* Detroit: Wayne State University Press, 1981.

———. *They Chose Life: Jewish Resistance in the Holocaust.* New York: Institute of Human Relations, American Jewish Committee; Jerusalem: Institute of Contemporary Jewry, Hebrew University, 1973.

Baum, Gregory G. *Christian Theology after Auschwitz.* London: Council of Christians and Jews, 1976.

———. "The Holocaust and Political Theology." In Fiorenza and Tracy, eds., *The Holocaust as Interruption*, pp. 34–42.

———. *Man Becoming: God in Secular Experience.* New York: Herder and Herder, 1971.

———. "Theology after Auschwitz: A Conference Report." *The Ecumenist* 12, no. 5 (July-Aug. 1974): 65–80.

Baumgärtel, Friedrich. *Wider die Kirchenkampf-Legenden.* Neuendettelsau: Freimund-Verlag, 1976.

Bea, Augustin Cardinal. *The Church and the Jewish People.* London: Geoffrey Chapman, 1966.

Berenbaum, Michael J. "Elie Wiesel and Contemporary Jewish Theology." *Conservative Judaism* 30, no. 3 (Spring 1976): 19–39.

———. *The Vision of the Void: Theological Reflections on the Works of Elie Wiesel.* Middletown, Conn.: Wesleyan University Press, 1979.

Berger, Alan. *Crisis and Covenant: The Holocaust in American Jewish Fiction.* Albany: State University of New York Press, 1985.

Bergmann, Martin S., and Milton E. Jucovy, eds. *Generations of the Holocaust*. New York: Basic Books, 1982.

Berkovits, Eliezer. *Faith after the Holocaust*. New York: Ktav Publishing House, 1973.

————. "The Hiding God of History." In Israel Gutman and Livia Rothkirchen, eds., *The Catastrophe of European Jewry*, pp. 684–704.

————. *With God in Hell: Judaism in the Ghettos and Death Camps*. New York and London: Sanhedrin Press, 1979.

Bethge, Eberhard. *Bonhoeffer: Exile and Martyr*. Edited by John W. De Gruchy. New York: Seabury Press, 1975.

————. *Dietrich Bonhoeffer*. New York: Harper and Row, 1970.

Bingham, June. "Carter, Castro, and Reinhold Niebuhr." *The Christian Century* 94, no. 28 (14 Sept. 1977): 775–76.

Bishop, Claire Huchet. *How Catholics Look at Jews: Inquiries into Italian, Spanish, and French Teaching Materials*. New York: Paulist Press, 1974.

Blumenkranz, Bernhard. "L'Holocauste dans l'enseignement public en France." *Archives Juives* 11, no. 2 (1975): 127–34.

Bokser, Ben Zion. *Judaism and the Christian Predicament*. New York: Alfred A. Knopf, 1967.

Boon, Rudolf. *Outmoeting Met Israël: Het Volk van de Torah*. Kampen: Uitgevers-maats-chappij J. H. Kok, 1974.

Bor, Josef. *Theresienstädter Requiem*. Berlin: Buchverlag der Morgen, 1975.

Borkin, Joseph. *The Crime and Punishment of I. G. Farben*. New York: Free Press, 1978.

Borowitz, Eugene B. *Contemporary Christologies: A Jewish Response*. New York and Ramsey: Paulist Press, 1980.

————. *How Can a Jew Speak of Faith Today?* Philadelphia: Westminster Press, 1969.

Bracher, Karl Dietrich. *The German Dilemma: The Throes of Political Emancipation*. Translated by Richard Barry. London: Weidenfeld and Nicolson, 1974.

Brandon, S. G. F. *The Trial of Jesus of Nazareth*. London: B. T. Botsford, 1968.

Brenner, Reeve Robert. *The Faith and Doubt of Holocaust Survivors*. New York: Free Press, 1980.

Brown, Robert McAfee. *Elie Wiesel: Messenger To All Humanity*. Notre Dame and London: Notre Dame University Press, 1983.

————. "From the Death Camps to Israel." *Christianity and Crisis* 40, no. 2 (18 Feb. 1980): 18, 27–31.

————. "The Holocaust: The Crisis of Indifference." *Conservative Judaism* 31, no. 1–2 (Fall-Winter 1976–77): 16–20.

———. *Theology in a New Key: Responding to Liberation Themes*. Philadelphia: Westminster Press, 1978.

Browning, Christopher. *Fateful Months: Essays on the Emergence of the Final Solution, 1941–1942*. New York and London: Holmes and Meier, 1985.

Busi, Frederick. "The Impact of Fascism: The Jew in Twentieth Century French Thinking." *Patterns of Prejudice* 8, no. 1 (Jan.-Feb. 1974): 9–16.

Campion, Joan. *In the Lion's Mouth: Gisi Fleischmann and the Jewish Fight for Survival*. Lanham, Md.: University Press of America, 1987.

Cargas, Harry James. *Harry James Cargas in Conversation with Elie Wiesel*. New York: Paulist Press, 1976.

———. *A Christian Response to the Holocaust*. Denver: Stonehenge Books, 1981.

———. *The Holocaust: An Annotated Bibliography*. Chicago: American Library Association, 1985.

Celan, Paul. *Nineteen Poems*. Translated by Michael Hamburger. Oxford: Carcanet Press, 1972.

———. *Selected Poems*. Translated by Michael Hamburger and Christopher Middleton. Harmondsworth: Penguin Books, 1972.

Cernyak-Spatz, Susan E. *German Holocaust-era Literature*. New York and Munich: Peter Lang, 1985.

Charny, Israel, ed. *Toward the Understanding and Prevention of Genocide*. Boulder, Colo., and London: Westview Press, 1984.

Cholawski, Shalom. *Soldiers from the Ghetto*. New York: Herzl Press, 1981.

Chopp, Rebecca. "The Interruption of the Forgotten." In Fiorenza and Tracy, *The Holocaust as Interruption*, pp. 19–25.

Cohen, Arthur A. "The Holocaust and Christian Theology: An Interpretation of the Problem." In *Judaism and Christianity Under the Impact of National Socialism (1919–1945)*, pp. 415–34.

———. "In Our Terrible Age: The *Tremendum* of the Jews." In Fiorenza and Tracy, eds., *The Holocaust as Interruption*, pp. 11–16.

———. "Messianism and Sabbatai Zevi." *Midstream* 20, no. 8 (Oct. 1974): 30–49.

———. *The Tremendum: A Theological Interpretation of the Holocaust*. New York: Crossroad, 1981.

Cohen, Jeremy. *The Friars and the Jews: The Evolution of Medieval Anti-Judaism*. Ithaca: Cornell University Press, 1982.

Cohn, Haim. "Reflections on the Trial and Death of Jesus." *Israel Law Review* 2, no. 3 (July 1967): 279–332.

———. *The Trial and Death of Jesus*. New York: Harper and Row, 1971.

229

Cohn-Sherbok, Dan. *On Earth As It Is in Heaven: Jews, Christians, and Liberation Theology*. Maryknoll, N.Y.: Orbis Books, 1987.

Concilium [Mainz] 10, no. 10 (Oct. 1974). Special number on "Christians and Jews."

"Conversation with Elie Wiesel." *Women's American ORT Reporter* [New York], Mar.-Apr. 1970.

Costanza, Mary. *The Living Witness: Art in the Concentration Camps and Ghettos*. New York: The Free Press; London: Collier Macmillan Publishers, 1982.

Cox, Harvey. *Feast of Fools: A Theological Essay on Festivity and Fantasy*. Cambridge, Mass.: Harvard University Press, 1969.

A Crime of Silence: The Armenian Genocide. The Permanent People's Tribunal (Paris). London: Zed Books, 1985.

Croner, Helga, ed., *More Stepping Stones to Jewish-Christian Relations*. New York: Paulist Press/Stimulus Books, 1985.

―――. *Stepping Stones to Further Jewish-Christian Relations*. New Malden, Surrey: Stimulus Books, 1977.

Croner, Helga, and Leon Klenicki, eds. *Issues in the Jewish-Christian Dialogue: Jewish Perspectives on Covenant, Mission, and Witness*. New York and Ramsey: Paulist Press, 1979.

Dadrian, Vahakn N. "The Role of Turkish Physicians in the World War I Genocide of Ottoman Armenians." *Holocaust and Genocide Studies*. 1, no. 2 (1986): 169–92.

―――. "Some Determinants of Genocidal Violence in Intergroup Conflict—With Particular Reference to the Armenian and Jewish Cases." *Sociologies* 26, no. 2 (New Series 1976) [Berlin]: 129–49.

Davies, Alan T. *Anti-Semitism and the Christian Mind: The Crisis of Conscience after Auschwitz*. New York: Herder and Herder, 1969.

―――. "Anti-Zionism, Anti-Semitism, and the Christian Mind." *The Christian Century* 87, no. 33 (19 Aug. 1970): 987–89.

――――, ed. *Antisemitism and the Foundations of Christianity*. New York, Ramsey, and Toronto: Paulist Press, 1979.

―――. "The Contemporary Encounter of Christians and Jews," *The Ecumenist* 10, no. 4 (May-June 1972): 56–60.

Dawidowicz, Lucy S. *The War against the Jews, 1933-1945*. New York: Holt, Rinehart and Winston, 1975.

De Graaf, Theo. "Pathological Patterns of Identification in Families of Survivors of the Holocaust." *Israel Annals of Psychiatry and Related Disciplines* 13, no. 4 (Dec. 1975): 335–63.

Delbo, Charlotte. *None of Us Will Return*. Translated by John Githens. Boston: Beacon Press, 1978.

Des Pres, Terrence. *The Survivor: An Anatomy of Life in the Death Camps*. New York: Oxford University Press, 1976.

Dicks, Henry V. *Licensed Mass Murder: A Socio-Psychological Study of Some SS Killers*. Columbus Centre Series, Studies in the Dynamics of Persecution and Extermination. London: Sussex University Press, 1972.

Diem, Hermann. *Ja Oder Nein: 50 Jahre Theologie in Kirche und Staat*. Stuttgart: Kreuz Verlag, 1974.

Diner, Dan. "The Historians' Controversy—Limits to the Historization of National Socialism." In "Rethinking the Holocaust," pp. 74–78.

Donat, Alexander. "A Letter to My Grandson." *Midstream* 16, no. 6 (June-July 1970): 41–45.

———. *The Death Camp Treblinka*. New York: Holocaust Library, 1979.

———. "The Voice of the Ashes." Unpublished preparatory paper for International Scholars Conference on the Holocaust, New York, 3–6 Mar. 1975.

Downs, Donald Alexander. *Nazis in Skokie: Freedom, Community, and the First Amendment*. Notre Dame: Notre Dame University Press, 1985.

Driver, Tom. "Toward a Theocentric Christology." *Christianity and Crisis* 45, no. 18 (11 Nov. 1985): 449–52.

Dubois, Marcel-Jacques. "The Challenge of the Holocaust and the History of Salvation." In *Judaism and Christianity Under the Impact of National Socialism (1919-1945)*, pp. 441–53.

———. "Theological Implications of the State of Israel: The Catholic View." *Encyclopaedia Judaica Year Book 1974*, pp. 167–73. Jerusalem: Keter Publishing House, 1974.

Dupuy, Bernard. "Un théologien juif de 1 'Holocauste, Emil Fackenheim." *Foi et Vie* 73, no. 4 (Sept. 1974): 11–21.

"The Echo of *Mein Kampf* in Arab Antisemitism." *Patterns of Prejudice* [London] 9, no. 2 (Mar.-Apr. 1975): 15–16, 25.

Eckardt, Alice L. "Bystanders? Resisters? Killers? Which Category Is Ours? Biomedical Issues After the Holocaust." In Ryan, ed. *Human Responses to the Holocaust*, pp. 239–59.

———. "Christian Response to the Holocaust." In Robert S. Hirt, and Thomas Kessner, eds., *Issues in Teaching the Holocaust: A Guide*. New York: Yeshiva University, 1981, pp. 69–95.

———. "The Holocaust: Christian and Jewish Responses. "*Journal of the American Academy of Religion* 42, no. 3 (Sept. 1974): 453–69.

———. "The Holocaust, the Church Struggle, and Some Christian Reflections." In Richard Libowitz, ed., *Faith and Freedom*, pp. 31–44.

———. "'The Kingdom of Night' in the Classroom." *Shofar* 2, no. 2 (1984): 6–20.

————. "Post-Holocaust Theology: A Journey Out of the Kingdom of Night." *Holocaust and Genocide Studies* 1, no. 2 (1986): 229–40.

————. "Power and Powerlessness: The Jewish Experience." In Charny, ed., *Toward the Understanding and Prevention of Genocide*, pp. 183–96.

Eckardt, Alice L., and A. Roy Eckardt. "The Achievements and Trials of Interfaith." *Judaism* 27, no. 3 (Summer 1978): 318–23.

————. "After the Holocaust: Some Christian Considerations." In Norma H. Thompson, and Bruce K. Cole, eds., *The Future of Jewish-Christian Relations*. Schenectady: Character Research Press, 1982.

————. "Christentum and Judentum: Die theologische und moralische Problematik der Vernichtung des europäischen Judentums." *Evangelische Theologie* 36, no. 5 (Sept.-Oct. 1976): 406–26. English version, "The Theological and Moral Implications of the Holocaust." *Christian Attitudes on Jews and Judaism* [London] 52 (Feb. 1977): 1–7, 53 and (Apr. 1977): 7–12.

————. *Encounter with Israel: A Challenge to Conscience*. New York: Association Press, 1970.

————. "German Thinkers View the Holocaust." *The Christian Century* 93, no. 9 (17 Mar. 1976): 249–52.

————. "The Holocaust and the Enigma of Uniqueness: A Philosophical Effort at Practical Clarification." *Annals of the American Academy of Political and Social Science* 450 (July 1980): 165–78.

————. "Studying the Holocaust's Impact Today: Some Dilemmas of Language and Method." *Judaism* 27, no. 2 (Spring 1978): 222–32; reprinted in Alan Rosenberg and Gerald Myers, eds., *Echoes from the Holocaust*.

Eckardt, A. Roy. Anti-Semitism Is the Heart." *Theology Today* 41, no. 3 (October 1984): 301–8.

————. "Christian Responses to the Endlösung." *Religion in Life* 47, no. 1 (Spring 1978): 33–45.

————. *Christianity and the Children of Israel*. New York: King's Crown Press, 1948.

————. "Christians and Jews: Along a Theological Frontier." *Encounter* [Indianapolis] 40, no. 2 (Spring 1979): 89–127.

————. "Christians, Jews and the Women's Movement." *Christian Jewish Relations* [London] 19, no. 2 (June 1986): 13–22.

————. "Contemporary Christian Theology and a Protestant Witness for the Shoah." *Shoah* 2, no. 1 (Spring-Summer 1980): 10–13; also in *Union Seminary Quarterly Review* 38, no. 2 (1983): 139–45.

————. "Covenant-Resurrection-Holocuast." In Josephine Knopp, ed., *Proceedings of the Second Philadelphia Conference on the Holocaust*, pp. 39–47.

232

——. "Death in the Judaic and Christian Traditions." In Arien Mack, ed. *Death in American Experience*, pp. 123–48. New York: Schocken Books, 1973.

——. "The Devil and Yom Kippur." *Midstream* 20, no. 7 (Aug.-Sept. 1974): 67–75.

——. *Elder and Younger Brothers: The Encounter of Jews and Christians*. New York: Charles Scribner's Sons, 1967; Schocken Books, 1973.

——. *For Righteousness' Sake: Contemporary Moral Philosophies*. Bloomington: Indiana University Press, 1987.

——. "Ha'Shoah as Christian Revolution: Toward the Liberation of the Divine Righteousness." *Quarterly Review* [Nashville] 2, no. 4 (Winter 1982): 52–67.

——. "Is the Holocaust Unique?" *Worldview* 17, no. 9 (Sept. 1974): 31–36.

——. "Is There a Way Out of the Christian Crime? The Philosophic Question of the Holocaust." *Holocaust and Genocide Studies* [Oxford] 1, no. 1 (1986): 121–26.

——. *Jews and Christians: The Contemporary Meeting*. Bloomington: Indiana University Press, 1986.

——. "Jürgen Moltmann, the Jewish People, and the Holocaust." *Journal of the American Academy of Religion* 44, no. 4 (Dec. 1976): 675–91.

——. "One *Ruse de Guerre* on the Devil." In Richard Libowitz, ed., *Faith and Freedom*, pp. 17–23.

——. "The Recantation of the Covenant?" In Rosenfeld and Greenberg, eds., *Confronting the Holocaust*, pp. 159–68.

——. "Recent Literature on Christian-Jewish Relations." *Jewish Book Annual* 38 (1980–81): 47–61.

——. "The Shadow of the Death Camps." *Theology Today* 34, no. 3 (Oct. 1977): 285–90.

——. "Theological Implications of the State of Israel: The Protestant View." *Encyclopaedia Judaica Year Book 1974*, pp. 158–66. Jerusalem: Keter Publishing House, 1974.

——. "Toward a Critical Assessment of Christian Theology in the Aftermath of the Holocaust." Unpublished preparatory paper for "Thinking About the Holocaust: An International Scholars' Conference Devoted to Historiographical and Theological Questions," Bloomington, Ind., 3–5 Nov. 1980.

——. "Toward a Secular Theology of Israel." *Religion in Life* 48, no. 4 (Winter 1979): 462–73.

——. *Your People, My People: The Meeting of Jews and Christians*. New York: Quadrangle, New York Times Book Co., 1974.

——, ed. *The Theologian at Work A Common Search for Religious Understanding*. New York and London: Harper and Row; and London: SCM Press Ltd., 1968.

Eckert, W. P. "The Final Solution and the Response of the Catholic Church." Unpublished paper for International Conference on the Chruch struggle and the Holocaust, Hamburg, 8–11 June 1975.

———, ed. *Jüdisches Volk-gelobtes Land: Die Biblischen Landesverheissungen als Problem des jüdischen Selbstverständnisses und der christlichen Theologie.* Munich: Chr. Kaiser Verlag, 1970.

Eckert, W.P., N. P. Levinson, and M. Stöhr, eds. *Antijudaismus im Neuen Testament? Exegetische und systematische Beiträge.* Munich: Chr. Kaiser Verlag, 1967.

Eckman, Lester, and Chaim Lazar. *The Jewish Resistance: The History of the Jewish Partisans in Lithuania and White Russia During the Nazi Occupation 1940–1945.* New York: Shengold, 1977.

Eitinger, Leo. *Concentration Camp Survivors in Norway and Israel.* Translated by Peggy Houge. The Hague: Martinus Nijhoff, 1972.

Eitinger, Leo, Robert Krell, and Miriam Rieck. *The Psychological and Medical Effects of Concentration Camps and Related Persecutions on Survivors of the Holocaust: A Research Bibliography.* Vancouver: University of British Columbia Press, 1985.

Eitinger, Leo, and Axel Strom. *Mortality and Morbidity after Excessive Stress.* New York: Humanities Press, 1973.

Eliach, Yaffa. *Hasidic Tales of the Holocaust.* New York: Oxford University Press, 1985.

Elyashiv, Vera. "Germans, Jews, Israelis: The Indissoluble Complicity." *Jewish Quarterly* [London], 21, no. 1–2 (1973): 31–41.

Ellis, Marc H. *Toward a Jewish Theology of Liberation.* Maryknoll, N.Y.: Orbis Books, 1987.

Engelmann, Bernt. *Deutschland ohne Juden: Eine Bilanz.* Munich: Franz Schneekluth Verlag, 1970.

Epstein, Helen. "The Heirs of the Holocaust." *New York Times Magazine,* 19 June 1977, pp. 12–15, 74–77.

Ericksen, Robert P. *Theologians Under Hitler.* New Haven: Yale University Press, 1985.

Evangelische Theologie 34, no. 3 (May-June 1974). Special number on "Toward Christian-Jewish Dialogue."

Everett, Robert A. "Zionism, Israel, and the Hope of Christianity." *Reflection* [Yale Divinity School] 82, no. 2 (April 1985): 13–17.

Ezrahi, Sidra de Koven. "Holocaust Literature in European Languages." *Encyclopaedia Judaica Year Book 1973,* pp. 106–19. Jerusalem: Keter Publishing House, 1973.

———. *By Words Alone: The Holocaust in Literature.* Chicago: University of Chicago Press, 1979.

Fackenheim, Emil L. "Concerning Authentic and Unauthentic Responses to the Holocaust." Unpublished preparatory paper for International Scholars Conference on the Holocaust, New York, 3–6 Mar. 1975.

————. *Encounters between Judaism and Modern Philosophy: A Preface to Future Jewish Thought*. New York: Basic Books, 1973.

————. "Foreword." In Bauer, *The Jewish Emergence from Powerlessness*, pp. vii–xiv.

————. *From Bergen-Belsen to Jerusalem: Contemporary Implications of the Holocaust*. Jerusalem: Institute of Contemporary Jewry, Hebrew University, 1975.

————. *God's Presence in History: Jewish Affirmations and Philosophical Reflections*. New York: New York University Press, 1970.

————. "The Holocaust and the State of Israel: Their Relation." *Encyclopaedia Judaica Year Book 1974*, pp. 152–57. Jerusalem: Keter Publishing House, 1974.

————. "The Human Condition after Auschwitz: A Jewish Testimony a Generation After." *Congress Bi-Weekly* 39, no. 7 (28 Apr. 1972): 6–10; no. 8 (19 May 1972): 5–8.

————. *The Jewish Return into History: Reflections in the Age of Auschwitz and a New Jerusalem*. New York: Schocken Books, 1978.

————. "The Nazi Holocaust as a Persisting Trauma for the Non-Jewish Mind." *Journal of the History of Ideas* 36, no. 2 (Apr.-May 1975): 369–76.

————. "The People Israel Lives." *The Christian Century* 87, no. 18 (6 May 1970): 563–68.

————. *Quest for Past and Future*. Boston: Beacon Press, 1970.

————. "Reflections on Aliyah." *Midstream* 31, no. 7 (1985): 25–28.

————. "The Spectrum of Resistance During the Holocaust: An Essay in Description and Definition." *Modern Judaism* 2, no. 2 (1982): 113–30.

————. *To Mend the World*. New York: Schocken Books, 1982.

————. *What Is Judaism?* New York: Summit Books, 1987.

Falk, Harvey. *Jesus the Pharisee*. New York: Paulist Press, 1985.

Farber, Klaus, and Heinz Kremers, eds. *Juden: Ein Beitrag zur Behandlung der Vorurteilsproblematik im Unterricht*. Dortmund: W. Crüwell Verlag, 1974.

Feingold, Henry. *The Politics of Rescue*. New York: Holocaust Library, 1980.

Ferencz, Benjamin B. *Less than Slaves: Jewish Forced Labor and the Quest for Compensation*. Cambridge, Mass. and London: Harvard University Press, 1979.

Fine, Ellen. *Legacy of Night: The Literary Universe of Elie Wiesel*. Albany: State University of New York Press, 1982.

Fink, Heinrich, ed. *Stärker als die Angst: Den sechs Millionen, die keinen Retter fanden*. Berlin: Union Verlag, 1968.

Fiorenza, Elisabeth Schussler and Tracy, David; eds. *The Holocaust as Interruption* [*Concilium* 175]. Edinburgh: T. & T. Clark, 1984.

Fischel, Jack and Sanford Pinsker, eds. *The Churches' Response to the Holocaust*. Greenwood, Fla.: Penkville, 1986.

Fisher, Eugene. "Ani Maamin: Directions in Holocaust Theology." *Interface* 5, 1980.

———. *Faith without Prejudice*. New York, Ramsey, and Toronto: Paulist Press, 1977.

Flannery, Edward. *The Anguish of the Jews: Twenty-three Centuries of Anti-Semitism*. Rev. ed. New York: Paulist Press, 1985.

Fleischner, Eva, ed., *Auschwitz: Beginning of a New Era? Reflections on the Holocaust*. New York: Ktav Publishing House, 1977.

———. *Judaism in German Christian Theology since 1945: Christianity and Israel Considered in Terms of Mission*. Metuchen, N.J.: Scarecrow Press, 1975.

Fleming, Gerald. *Hitler and the Final Solution*. Berkeley: University of California Press, 1984.

Flinker, Moshe. *Young Moshe's Diary: The Spiritual Torment of a Jewish Boy in Nazi Europe*. Jerusalem: Yad Vashem; New York: Board of Jewish Education, 1971.

Flusser, David. "The Crucified One and the Jews." *Immanuel* [Jerusalem] no. 7 (Spring 1977), pp. 25–37.

———. *Jesus*. Translated by Ronald Walls. New York: Herder and Herder, 1969.

———. "Thèses sur l'émergence du christianisme à partir du judaïsme." *Vav* 7, no. 11 (Mar. 1975): 4–16.

Forster, Arnold, and Benjamin R. Epstein. *The New Anti-Semitism*. New York: McGraw-Hill, 1974.

Frank, Anne. *The Diary of a Young Girl*. New York: Doubleday, 1952.

———. *The Works of Anne Frank*. Introduction by Ann Birstein and Alfred Kazin. New York: Doubleday, 1959.

Franke, Manfred. *Morderläufe 9./10. XI 1938*. Darmstadt: Luchterhand Verlag, 1973.

Frankl, Viktor. *From Death Camp to Existentialism: A Psychiatrist's Path to a New Therapy*. Boston: Beacon Press, 1959.

Frey, Robert Seitz, and Nancy Thompson-Frey. *The Imperative of Response: The Holocaust in Human Context*. Lanham, Md.: University Press of America, 1985.

Friedlander, Albert H. "Kafka's Ape: A Meditation on Religious Dialogue." *European Judaism* 10, no. 1 (Winter 1975–76): 30–36.

———, ed. *Out of the Whirlwind: A Reader of Holocaust Literature*. New York: Schocken Books, 1976.

———. "Stations Along the Way: Christian and Jewish Post Holocaust Theology." *Common Ground* [London] 2 (1978): 6–15.

Friedlander, Henry. "Historians on the Holocaust: An Analysis." Unpublished preparatory paper for International Scholars Conference on the Holocaust, New York, 3–6 Mar. 1975.

Friedlander, Henry, and Sybil Milton, eds. *Ideology, Bureaucracy, and Genocide*. Millwood, N.Y.: Kraus International Publications, 1980.

Friedländer, Saul. *L'Antisémitisme Nazi: Histoire d'une psychose collective*. Paris: Seuil, 1971.

———. *Reflections on Nazism*. New York: Harper and Row, 1984.

———. "Some Aspects of the Historical Significance of the Holocaust." *Jerusalem Quarterly* 1 (Fall 1976): 36–59.

———. *When Memory Comes*. New York: Avon Books, 1980. From French original *Quand vient le sourvenir*. . . .

Friedman, Philip. *Martyrs and Fighters*. New York: Frederick A. Praeger, 1954.

Friedman, Saul S. "Arab Complicity in the Holocaust." *Jewish Frontier* 42, no. 4 (Apr. 1975): 9–17.

———. *No Haven for the Oppressed: United States Policy Toward Jewish Refugees, 1938–1945*. Detroit: Wayne State University Press, 1973.

———. *The Oberammergau Passion Play: A Lance Against Civilization*. Carbondale and Edwardsville: Southern Illinois University Press, 1984.

———. "Universal Anti-Semitism." *Jewish Frontier* 43, no. 7 (August-September 1976): 14–18.

Gallin, Alice. *Midwives to Nazism: University Professors in Weimer Germany, 1925–1933*. Macon, Ga.: Mercer University Press, 1986.

Gaon, Solomon and M. Mitchell Serels, eds. *Sephardim and the Holocaust*. New York: Yeshiva University Press, 1988.

Gerlach, Wolfgang. *Als die Zeugen schwiegen. Bekennende Kirche und die Juden (When the Witnesses Kept Silent. Confessing Church and the Jews)*. Mit einem Vorwort von Eberhard Bethge; herausgegeben von Peter von der Osten-Sachen. Berlin: Institut fur Kirche und Judentum, 1987.

Gerssen, Samuel. *Het Grote Schisma: Israël in de theologie van dr. K. H. Miskotte*. Kampen: Uitgeversmaatschappij, J. H. Kok, 1975.

Gibson, James L., and Richard D., Bingham. *Civil Liberties and Nazis: The Skokie Free-Speech Controversy*. New York: Praeger, 1985.

Gilbert, Martin. *Auschwitz and the Allies*. New York: Holt, Rinehart and Winston, 1981.

———. *The Holocaust: The History of the Jews of Europe During the Second World War*. New York: Holt, Rinehart and Winston, 1986.

———. *The Macmillan Atlas of the Holocaust*. New York: Macmillan, 1982.

Giniewski, Paul. *L'antisionisme*. Brussels: Éditions de la Librairie Encyclopedique, 1973.

Glatstein, Jacob. *Selected Poems of Jacob Glatstein*. Translated by Ruth Whitman. New York: October House, 1972.

Glatstein, Jacob, Israel Knox, and Samuel Margoshes, eds. *Anthology of Holocaust Literature*. Philadelphia: Jewish Publication Society of America, 1973.

Goes, Albrecht. *The Burnt Offering*. Translated by Michael Hamburger. New York: Pantheon, 1956.

Goldschmidt, Dietrich, and Hans-Joachim Kraus, eds. *Der Ungekündigte Bund: Neue Begegnung von Juden und christlicher Gemeinde. Im Auftrag der Arbeitsgemeinschaft Juden und Christen beim Deutschen Evangelischen Kirchentag*. Stuttgart: Kreuz-Verlag, 1962.

Gollwitzer, Helmut, and Eleonore Sterling, eds. *Das Gespaltene Gottesvolk: Im Auftrag der Arbeitsgemeinschaft Juden und Christen beim Deutschen Evangelischen Kirchentag*. Stuttgart: Kreuz-Verlag, 1966.

Gordon, Sarah. *Hitler, Germany, and the "Jewish Question."* Princeton: Princeton University Press, 1984.

Graham, Robert A. *Pius XII's Defense of Jews and Others: 1944-1945*. Milwaukee: Catholic League for Religious and Civil Rights, n.d.

Greenberg, Irving. "Are We Focusing on the Holocaust Too Much? *Martyrdom and Resistance* 10, no. 1 (September-October 1983): 6, 7.

——. "Cloud of Smoke, Pillar of Fire: Judaism, Christianity, and Modernity after the Holocaust." In Fleischner, ed., *Auschwitz*, 7-55.

——. "The Ethics of Jewish Power," I and II. *Perspectives* [New York] (January 1984): pp. 1-8.

——. *The Holocaust: The Need to Remember*. New York: National Jewish Resource Center, n.d.

——. "Lessons to Be Learned from the Holocaust." Unpublished paper at International Conference on the Church Struggle and the Holocaust, Hamburg, 8-11 June 1975.

——. "New Revelations and New Patterns in the Relationship of Judaism and Christianity." *Journal of Ecumenical Studies* 16, no, 2 (Spring 1979): 249-67.

——. "On the Third Era in Jewish History: Power and Politics." *Perspectives* [New York] (October 1980): 1-22.

——. "Some Lessons From Bitburg." *Perspectives* [New York] (May 1985): 3-4.

——. "Some Thoughts on the Meaning of the Restoration of Israel and Jerusalem for the Days of Commemoration." In Alice L. Eckardt, ed., *Jerusalem: The City of the Ages*. Lanham, Md. and London: University Press of America, 1987, pp. 281-85.

——. "The Third Great Cycle in Jewish History." *Perspectives* [New York] (September 1981): 1-32.

——. "Voluntary Covenant." *Perspectives* [New York], (October 1982): 2-36.

Greenberg, Uri Zvi. "A Jew Stands at the Gates of Tears." In Leftwich, ed., *The Golden Peacock*, pp. 193-99.

————. "To God in Europe," translated by Robert Friend; "To the Mound of Corpses in the Snow," translated by A. C. Jacobs. In *Anthology of Modern Hebrew Poetry*, vol. 2, pp. 264–78, 259–61.

Grobman, Alex, and Daniel Landes, eds. *Genocide: Critical Issues of the Holocaust*. Los Angeles: Simon Wiesenthal Center, and Chappaque, N.Y.: Rossel Books, 1983.

Grossman, Chaika. *The Underground Army: Fighters of the Bialystok Ghetto*. New York: Holocaust Library, 1984.

Grossmann, Wassilij. *Die Hölle von Treblinka*. Moskau: Verlag für Fremdsprachige Literatur, 1946.

Gruenagel, Friedrich. *Die Judenfrage, Die geschichtliche Verantwortung der Kirchen und Israels*. Stuttgart: Calwer Verlag, 1970.

Guroian, Vigen. "A Comparison of the Armenian and Jewish Genocides: Some Common Features." *Thought* 58, no. 229 (June 1983): 207–23.

Gutman, Israel/Yisrael. *The Jews of Warsaw, 1939–1943*. Bloomington: Indiana University Press, 1982.

————. "Remarks on the Literature of the Holocaust." *In the Dispersion* [Jerusalem], no. 7 (1967).

————. Gutman, Israel/Yisrael, and Shmuel Krakowski. *Unequal Victims: Poles and Jews During World War II*. New York: Holocaust Library, 1986.

Gutman, Israel/Yisrael, and Livia Rothkirchen, ed. *The Catastrophe of European Jewry: Antecedents—History—Reflections*. Jerusalem: Yad Vashem, 1976.

Gutteridge, Richard. *Open Thy Mouth for the Dumb!: The German Evangelical Church and the Jews 1879–1950*. Oxford: Basil Blackwell, 1976.

Haffner, Sebastian. *The Meaning of Hitler*. Translated by Ewald Osers. New York: Macmillan Publishing, 1979.

Haft, Cynthia. *The Theme of Nazi Concentration Camps in French Literature*. The Hague and Paris: Mouton, 1973.

Hallie, Philip P. *Lest Innocent Blood Be Shed: The Story of the Village of Le Chambon and How Goodness Happened There*. New York: Harper and Row, 1979.

Hancock, Ian. *The Pariah Syndrome: An Account of Gypsy Slavery and Persecution*. Ann Arbor, Mich.: Karoma Publishers, Inc., 1987.

Harkabi, Yehoshafat. *Arab Attitudes to Israel*. Jerusalem: Israel Universities Press, 1971.

Hartman, Geoffrey, ed. *Bitburg in Moral and Political Perspective*. Bloomington: Indiana University Press, 1986.

Hartmann, Dieter. "Compliance and Oblivion: Impaired Compassion in Germany for the Victims of the Holocaust." In Charny, ed., *Toward the Understanding and Prevention of Genocide*, pp. 197–201.

Hay, Malcolm. *Thy Brother's Blood: The Roots of Christian Anti-Semitism.* New York: Hart Publishing Co., 1975; also published as *The Roots of Christian Anti-Semitism,* New York: Freedom Library, 1981.

Heer, Friedrich. "The Catholic Church and the Jews Today." *Midstream* 17, no. 5 (May 1971): 20–31.

————. *God's First Love: Christians and Jews over Two Thousand Years.* Translated by Geoffrey Skelton. New York: Weybright and Talley, 1970.

Heering, H. J. *Franz Rosenzweig: Joods Denker in de 20e EEUW.* The Hague: Martinus Nijhoff, 1974.

Heimler, Eugene. *A Link in the Chain.* London: Bodley Head, 1962.

————. *Night of the Mist.* New York: Vanguard Press, 1960.

Helmreich, Ernst Christian. *The German Churches under Hitler: Background, Struggle, and Epilogue.* Detroit, Mich.: Wayne State University Press, 1976.

Herberg, Will. *Faith Enacted as History: Essays in Biblical Theology.* Edited by Bernhard W. Anderson. Philadelphia: Westminster Press, 1976.

Herman, Simon N. *Israelis and Jews: The Continuity of an Identity.* New York: Random House, 1970.

Hertzberg, Arthur. *Anti-Semitism and Jewish Uniqueness: Ancient and Contemporary.* Syracuse: Syracuse University, 1975.

————. "Response to Uriel Tal." *Union Seminary Quarterly Review* 26, no. 4 (Summer 1971).

Herzberg, Abel J. *Amor Fati: Zeven opstellen over Bergen-Belsen.* Amsterdam: Moussault's Uitgeverij, 1950.

————. *Brieven aan mijn kleinzoon: De geschiedenis van een joodse emigrantenfamilie.* Amsterdam: Em. Querido's Uitgeverij B. V., 1975.

Heyman, Eva. *The Diary of Eva Heyman.* Introduction and notes by Moshe M. Kohn. Jerusalem: Yad Vashem, 1974.

Hilberg, Raul. *The Destruction of the European Jews.* Rev. ed. Chicago: Quadrangle Books, 1967.

————. *The Destruction of the European Jews.* Rev. and Def. ed. 3 vols. New York: Holmes and Meier, Inc., 1985.

————. ed. *Documents of Destruction: Germany and Jewry, 1933–1945.* Chicago: Quadrangle Books, 1971.

Hirshfeld, Gerhard, ed. *The Policies of Genocide: Jews and Soviet Prisoners of War in Nazi Germany.* Boston: Allen & Unwin, 1986.

Hirszowicz, Lukasz. *The Third Reich and the Middle East.* London and Toronto: Routledge & Kegan Paul and the University of Toronto Press, 1966.

Hochhuth, Rolf. *The Deputy*. Translated by Richard and Clara Winston. New York: Grove Press, 1964.

Holland, Joseph. "Hunger: Global Holocaust or Global Exodus?" *The Ecumenist* 13, no. 2 (Jan.-Feb. 1975): 17–21.

Holocaust. Jerusalem: Keter Publishing House, 1974.

The Holocaust. Jerusalem: Yad Vashem, 1975.

Holocaust and Rebirth: A Symposium. Jerusalem: Yad Vashem, 1974.

"The Holocaust: Our Generation Looks Back." *Response* 25 (Spring 1975).

Hommel, Gisella. "Anti-Semitic Tendencies in Christian Feminist Theology in Germany." *European Judaism* 1 (1987): 43–48.

Hoppe, Klaus D. "The Aftermath of Nazi Persecution Reflected in Recent Psychiatric Literature." In Henry Krystal and William G. Niederland, eds., *Psychic Traumatization: Aftereffects in Individuals and Communities*. Boston: Little, Brown, 1971.

Housepian, Marjorie. "The Unremembered Genocide." *Commentary* 42, no. 3 (Sept. 1966): 55–61.

Houtart, Francois and Geneviève Lemercinier. *Les Juifs dans la catèchése: Étude sur la transmission des code religieux*. Louvain: Université Catholique de Louvain, 1972.

Hovannisian, Richard, ed. *The Armenian Genocide in Perspective*. Washington, D.C.: Armenian Assembly of America, 1987.

Huberband, Shimon. *Kiddush Hashem: Jewish Religious and Cultural Life in Poland During the Holocaust*. Jeffrey S. Gurock and Robert S. Hirt, eds. Translated from Yiddish by David E. Fishman. New York: Ktav/Yeshiva University Press, 1988.

Huneke, Douglas. *The Moses of Rovno*. New York: Dodd, Mead and Co., 1985.

Hux, Samuel. "The Holocaust and the Survival of Tragedy." *Worldview* 20, no. 10 (Oct. 1970): 4–10.

Idinopulos, Thomas A., and Roy Bowen Ward. "Is Christology Inherently Anti-Semitic? A Critical Review of Rosemary Ruether's *Faith and Fratricide*." *Journal of the American Academy of Religion* 45, no. 2 (June 1977): 193–214.

Interpreting the Holocaust for Future Generations: Proceedings of a Symposium. New York: Memorial Foundation for Jewish Culture, 1974.

Isaac, Jules. *Genèse de l'antisémitisme*. Paris: Calmann-Levy, 1956.

———. *Jesus and Israel*. Edited by Claire Huchet Bishop. Translated by Sally Gran. New York: Holt, Rinehart and Winston, 1971.

———. *The Teaching of Contempt: Christian Roots of Anti-Semitism*. Translated by Helen Weaver. New York: Holt, Rinehart and Winston, 1964.

Israel, Gérard. *Hereux Comme Dieu en France . . . 1940-1944*. Paris: Editions Robert Leffont, 1975.

241

Jaffe, Ruth. "The Sense of Guilt within Holocaust Survivors." *Jewish Social Studies* 32, no. 4 (Oct. 1970): 307–14.

Jansen, John Frederick. *The Resurrection of Jesus Christ in New Testament Theology.* Philadelphia: Westminster Press, 1980.

Jersild, Paul T., and Dale A. Johnson, eds. *Moral Issues and Christian Response.* 2d ed. New York: Holt, Rinehart and Winston, 1976.

"Jesu Verhältnis zum Judentum. Das Judentumsbild in christlichen Religionsunterricht." *Freiburger Rundbrief* 26, nos. 97/100 (1974): 21–30.

Jewish Resistance during the Holocaust: Proceedings of the Conference on Manifestation of Jewish Resistance. [Jerusalem, 7–11 Apr. 1968]. Supervised by Meir Grubsztein. Jerusalem: Yad Vashem, 1971.

"Jewish Values in the Post-Holocaust Future." (A Symposium). *Judaism* 16, no. 3 (Summer 1967): 266–99.

Jonas, Hans. "The Concept of God After Auschwitz." In Albert Friedlander, ed., *Out of the Whirlwind.* pp. 465–76.

Judaism and Christianity Under the Impact of National Socialism (1919–1945). International Symposium, June 1982. Jerusalem: The Historical Society of Israel, 1982.

Les Juifs dans la catéchèse: Étude des manuels de catéchèse. Louvain: Centre de Recherches socie-religieuses, 1969.

Kallenbach, Hans, and Willi Schemel, eds. *Judentum im christlichen Religionsunterricht.* Frankfurt: Verlag Evangelischer Pressverband fur Hessen und Nassau, 1972.

Kalow, Gert. *Hitler—des deutsche Trauma.* Munich: Piper, 1974.

Katznelson, Yitzhak. *The Song of the Murdered Jewish People.* Translated by Noah H. Rosenbloom. Asherat, Israel: Ghetto Fighters' House, 1980.

Kee, Alistair, ed. *A Reader in Political Theology.* Philadelphia: Westminster Press, 1974.

Keene, Calvin. "Prophecy and Modern Israel." *The Link* 10, no. 3 (Summer 1977): 1–3.

Kellen, Konrad. "*Seven Beauties:* Auschwitz—the Ultimate Joke?" *Midstream* 22, no. 8 (Oct. 1976): 59–66.

Kenrich, Donald, and Gratton Puxon. *The Destiny of Europe's Gypsies.* New York: Basic Books, 1972.

Kestenberg, Judith S. "Psychoanalytic Contributions to the Problem of Children of Survivors of the Nazi Persecution." *Israel Annals of Psychiatry and Related Disciplines* 10, no. 4 (Dec. 1972): 311–25.

Klausner, Joseph. *The Messianic Idea in Israel.* Translated by W. F. Stinespring. New York: Macmillan, 1955.

Klein, Charlotte. *Anti-Judaism in Christian Theology.* Translated by Edward Quimm. Philadelphia: Fortress Press, 1978. (Originally published as *Theologie und Anti-Judaismus: Eine Studie zur deutschen theologischen Literatur der Gegenwart.* Munich: Chrs. Kaiser Verlag, 1975.)

————. "Vatican View of Jewry, 1939–1962." *Christian Attitudes on Jews and Judaism* [London] 43 (1975): 12–16.

————. "The Vatican and Zionism, 1897–1967." *Christian Attitudes on Jews and Judaism* [London] 36–37 (1974): 11–16.

Klein, Hilel. "Families of Holocaust Survivors in the Kibbutz: Psychological Studies." In Henry Krystal and William G. Niderland, eds., *Psychic Traumatization: Aftereffects in Individuals and Communities*, pp. 67–92. Boston: Little, Brown, 1971.

————. "Holocaust Survivors in Kibbutzim; Readaptation and Reintegration." *Israel Annals of Psychiatry and Related Disciplines* 10, no. 1 (Mar. 1972): 78–91.

Klein, Hilel, and Uriel Last. "Cognitive and Emotional Aspects of the Attitudes of American and Israeli Jewish Youth towards the Victims of the Holocaust." *Israel Annals of Psychiatry and Related Disciplines* 12, no. 2 (June 1974): 111–31.

Klein, Hilel, and Shulamit Reinharz. "Adaptation in the Kibbutz of Holocaust Survivors and Their Families." In Louis Miller, ed. *Mental Health and Rapid Social Change*, pp. 302–19. Jerusalem: Jerusalem Academic Press, 1972.

Knitter, Paul. *No Other Name?: A Critical Survey of Christian Attitudes Toward the World Religions*. Maryknoll, N.Y.: Orbis Books, 1985.

Knopp, Josephine. *The Trial of Judaism in Contemporary Jewish Writing*. Urbana: University of Illinois Press, 1975.

————, ed. *International Theological Symposium on the Holocaust*. October 15–17, 1978. Philadelphia: National Institute on the Holocaust, 1979.

————, ed. *Proceedings of the Second Philadelphia Conference on the Holocaust* [16–18 Feb. 1977]. Philadelphia: Temple University, 1977.

Knutson, Mary. "The Holocaust in Theology and Philosophy: The Question of Truth." In Fiorenza and Tracy, eds., *The Holocaust as Interruption*, pp. 67–74.

Koch, H. W. *The Hitler Youth: Origins and Development 1922–1945*. Briar Cliff Manor, N.Y.: Stein and Day, 1976.

Kogon, Eugen. *The Theory and Practice of Hell: The German Concentration Camps and the System Behind Them*. Translated by Heinz Norden. New York: Octagon Books, 1979. (Originally published as *Der SS-Staat: Das System der deutschen Konzentrationslager*. Munich: Kindler Verlag, 1974.)

Kohn, Hans. *The Mind of Germany: The Education of a Nation*. New York: Harper Torchbooks, 1965.

Kohn, Murray J. *The Voice of My Blood Cries Out: The Holocaust as Reflected in Hebrew Poetry*. New York: Shengold Publishers, 1979.

Kolinsky, Martin, and Eva Kolinsky. "The Treatment of the Holocaust in West German Textbooks." In Livia Rothkirchen, ed., *Yad Vashem Studies on the European Jewish Catastrophe and Resistance*, vol. 10, pp. 149–216. Jerusalem: Yad Vashem, 1974.

243

Kolitz, Zvi. "Yossel Rakover's Appeal to God." In Friedlander, ed., *Out of the Whirlwind*, pp. 390–99.

Konigsberg, Leslie. "Remember." Unpublished poem written at Lehigh University, 1978.

Korey, William. *The Soviet Cage: Anti-Semitism in Russia*. New York: Viking Press, 1973.

Korman, Gerd, ed. *Hunter and Hunted: Human History of the Holocaust*. New York: Viking Press, 1973.

Kovner, Abba, "A First Attempt to Tell"; "The Miracle in the Midst of Destruction"; "Threnody for a Movement." Unpublished preparatory papers for International Scholars Conference on the Holocaust, New York, 3–6 Mar. 1975.

Kovner, Abba, and Nelly Sachs. *Selected Poems*. Harmondsworth: Penguin Books, 1971.

Kowalski, Isaac, ed. *Anthology on Armed Jewish Resistance 1939–1945*. 3 vols. Brooklyn, N.Y.: Jewish Combatants Publishers House, 1983, 1984, and forthcoming.

Krakowski, Shmuel. *The War of the Doomed: Jewish Armed Resistance in Poland 1942–1944*. New York: Holmes and Meier, 1984.

Krausnick, Helmut, Hans Buccheim, Martin Broszat, and Hans-Adolf Jacobsen. *Anatomy of the SS State*. Translated by Richard Barry, Marian Jackson, and Dorothy Long. London: Collins, 1968.

Kremers, Heinz, ed. *Juden und Christen Lesen Dieselbe Bibel*. Duisburg: Walter Braun Verlag, 1973.

——. *Judenmission heute? Von der Judenmission zur bruderlichen Solidarität und zum ökumenischen Dialog*. Neukirchen-Vluyn: Neukirchener Verlag, 1979.

——. *Das Verhältnis der Kirche zu Israel*. Düsseldorf: Presseverband der Evangelischen Kirche im Rheinland, 1965.

Kulka, Erich. *Die Massenvernichtung der Juden Wird Geleugnet: Eine Studie über die beunruhigenden Perspektiven der Vergangenheit*. Jerusalem: Yad Vashem, 1975.

Küng, Hans. *On Being a Christian*. Translated by Edward Quinn. New York: Pocket Books, 1978. (Originally published as *Christsein*. Munich: R. Piper Verlag, 1974).

Langbein, Hermann. *Hommes et Femmes à Auschwitz*. Translated by Denise Meumer. Paris: Fayard, 1975.

——. "Überblick über neonazistiche Literatur." *Zeit Geschichte* [Salzburg] 9–10 (1975): 236–42.

Langer, Lawrence. L. *The Age of Atrocity*. Boston: Beacon Press, 1978.

——. *The Holocaust and the Literary Imagination*. New Haven, Conn.: Yale University Press, 1975.

——. *Versions of Survival: The Holocaust and the Human Spirit*. Albany: State University of New York Press, 1982.

Lapide, Pinchas E. "Jesu Judesein: Christliches Unbehagen." *Tribüne* [Frankfurt-am-Main] 14, no. 55 (1975): 6356–66.

———. *Juden und Christen.* Cologne: Benziger Verlag, 1976.

———. "Vom 'Gottesmord' zum Volkermörd." *Tribüne* [Franfurt-am-Main] 14, no. 53 (1975): 6134–50.

Lapide, Pinchas E., and Luz Ulrich. *Jesus in Two Perspectives: A Jewish-Christian Dialog.* Minneapolis: Augsburg Press, 1987.

Lapide, Pinchas E., and Jürgen Moltmann. *Jewish Monotheism and Christian Trinitarian Doctrine. A Dialogue.* Translated by Leonard Swiddler. Philadelphia: Fortress Press, 1981. (Originally published as *Jüdischer Monotheismus, christliche Trinitätslehre: Ein Gesprach.* Munich: Chr. Kaiser Verlag, 1979.)

Laqueur, Walter. *The Terrible Secret: Suppression of the Truth About Hitler's "Final Solution."* Boston: Little, Brown and Co., 1981.

Latour, Amy. *The Jewish Resistance in France (1940-1944).* Translated by Irene Ilton. New York: Holocaust Library, 1982.

Lauran, Annie. *La casquette d'Hitler ou le temps de l'oubli.* Paris: Éditions Francais Réunis, 1974.

Lawrence, Robert M., and Joel Larus, eds. *Nuclear Proliferation: Phase II.* Lawrence, Kan.: University Press of Kansas, 1974.

Leftwich, Joseph, ed. and trans. *The Golden Peacock: A Worldwide Treasury of Yiddish Poetry.* New York and London: Thomas Yoseloff, 1961.

Lelyveld, Arthur J. *Atheism is Dead: A Jewish Response to Radical Theology.* Cleveland and New York: World Publishing Co., 1968.

Lendvai, Paul. *Anti-Semitism without Jews: Communist Eastern Europe.* New York: Doubleday, 1971.

Lessing, Abba. "Jewish Impotence and Power." *Midstream* 22, no. 8 (Oct. 1976): 52–58.

Leuner, H. David. "Das Rätsel des Antisemitismus in kommunistischen Ländern." *Dokumentation: Ein Informationsdienst.* Frankfurt-am-Main: Haus der Evangelischen Publizistik, 18 Sept. 1972.

———. "Versagen und Bewährung—Die Welt und das Brandopfer der Juden." *Israel-Forum* 17, no. 2 (1975): 2–9.

———. *Zwischen Israel und den Völkern: Vorträge eines Judenchristen.* Edited by Peter von der Osten-Sacken. Berlin: Institut Kirche und Judentum, 1978.

Levi, Primo. *The Drowned and the Saved.* Translated by Raymond Rosenthal. New York: Summit Books, 1988.

———. *Moments of Reprieve.* New York: Summit Books, 1988.

———. *The Periodic Tables.* New York: Schocken Books, 1984.

Levin, Dor. *Fighting Back: Lithuanian Jewry's Armed Resistance to the Nazis, 1941–1945.* New York: Holmes and Meier, 1985.

Levin, Nora. *The Holocaust: The Destruction of European Jewry 1933–1945.* New York: Schocken Books, 1973.

———. "Life over Death." *Congress Bi-Weekly* 40, no. 8 (18 May 1973): 22–23.

Levine, Herbert H. "Munich Thirty Years Later: Trying to Erase the Shadow." *Present Tense* 2, no. 3 (Spring 1975): 31–35.

Lewy, Guenter. *The Catholic Church and Nazi Germany.* New York: McGraw-Hill, 1964.

Libowitz, Richard, ed. *Faith and Freedom: A Tribute to Franklin H. Littell.* Oxford and New York: Pergamon Press, 1987.

Lind, Jakov. *Counting My Steps: An Autobiography.* London: Jonathan Cape, 1970.

———. *Soul of Wood and Other Stories.* Translated by Ralph Manheim. New York: Fawcett Crest Books, 1966.

Lindsey, Robert L. "A New Approach to the Synoptic Gospels." *Christian News from Israel* [Jerusalem] 22, no. 2 (1971): 56–63.

Littell, Marcia Sachs, ed. *Liturgies on the Holocaust: An Interfaith Anthology.* Lewiston and Queenston: Edwin Mellen Press, 1986.

Littell, Franklin H. "Christendom, Holocaust, and Israel: The Importance for Christians of Recent Major Events in Jewish History." *Journal of Ecumenical Studies* 10, no. 3 (Summer 1973): 483–97.

———. "Christians and Jews in the Historical Process," *Judaism* 22, 3 (Summer 1973): 264–77.

———. "The Credibility Crisis of the Modern University." In Friedlander and Milton, eds., *The Holocaust: Ideology, Bureacracy, and Genocide,* pp. 271–83.

———. *The Crucifixion of the Jews: The Failure of Christians to Understand the Jewish Experience.* New York: Harper and Row, 1975; Macon, Ga.: Mercer University Press, 1986.

———. "*Kirchenkampf* and Holocaust: The German Church Struggle and Nazi Anti-Semitism in Retrospect." In James E. Wood, Jr., ed., *Jewish-Christian Relations in Today's World.* Waco, Tex.: Baylor University Press, 1971.

———. "Particularism and Universalism in Religious Perspective." Unpublished lecture at Beth Tzedec Congregation, Toronto, 11 May 1972.

Littell, Franklin H., and Hubert G. Locke, eds. *The German Church Struggle and the Holocaust.* Detroit, Mich.: Wayne State University Press, 1974.

Locke, Hubert G., ed. *The Church Confronts the Nazis: Barmen Then and Now.* New York and Toronto: Edwin Mellen Press, 1984.

———. *Exile in the Fatherland: Martin Niemöller's Letters from Moabit Prison.* Translated by Ernst Kaemke, Kathy Elias, and Jacklyn Wilferd. Grand Rapids, Mich.: William B. Eerdmans Publishing Co., 1986.

Lookstein, Haskel. *Were We Our Brother's Keepers? The Public Response of American Jews to the Holocaust, 1938–1944.* New York and Bridgeport, Conn.: Hartmore House, 1985.

Lorenz, Friedebert, ed. *Juden und Deutsche: Ihr Weg zum Frieden. Vortrag gehalten anlässlich des 13. Evangelischen Kirchentags Hannover 1967.* Stuttgart: Kreuz-Verlag, 1967.

Lovsky, Fadiey. *La Déchirure de l'absence: Essai sur les rapports de l'église du Christ et du peuple d'Israël.* Paris: Calmann-Levy, 1971.

Lubetkin, Zivia. *In the Days of the Destruction and Revolt.* Asherat, Israel: Ghetto Fighters House, 1981.

Lukas, Richard C. *The Forgotten Holocaust: The Poles Under German Occupation, 1939–1944.* Lexington: University of Kentucky Press, 1986.

McEvoy, Donald W., ed. *Christians Confront the Holocaust: A Collection of Sermons.* New York: National Conference of Christians and Jews, 1980.

McGarry, Michael B. *Christology after Auschwitz.* New York: Paulist Press, 1977.

Maccoby, Haim. *The Sacred Executioner: Human Sacrifice and the Legacy of Guilt.* New York: Thames and Hudson, 1982.

Ma'oz, Moshe. *The Image of the Jew in Official Arab Literature and Communications Media.* Jerusalem: Shazar Library, Institute of Contemporary Jewry, 1976.

Mark, Ber. *Uprising in the Warsaw Ghetto.* New York: Schocken Books, 1975.

Marquardt, Friedrich-Wilhelm. *Die Bedeutung der biblischen Landesverheissungen für die Christen. Theologische Existenz heute, no. 116.* Munich: Chr. Kaiser Verlag, 1964.

———. *Die Juden und ihr Land.* Hamburg: Siebenstein Taschenbuch Verlag, 1975.

Marrus, Michael R. *The Unwanted: European Refugees in the Twentieth Century.* New York: Oxford University Press, 1985.

Matheson, Peter. *The Third Reich and the Christian Churches.* Grand Rapids, Mich.: William B. Eerdmans Publishing Co., 1981.

Matussek, Paul, et al. *Internment in Concentration Camps and Its Consequences.* Translated by Derek and Inge Jordan. Berlin: Springer-Verlag, 1975.

Maybaum, Ignaz. *Creation and Guilt.* London: Vallentine, Mitchell, 1970.

———. *The Face of God after Auschwitz.* Amsterdam: Polak and Van Gennep, 1965.

Mayer, Reinhold. *Judentum und Christentum.* Aschaffenburg: Paul Pattloch Verlag, 1973.

247

Megged, Aharon. "Letter from Israel." *Jewish Quarterly* [London] 22, no. 4 (Winter 1975).

Merk, Hans Gunther. "Rechtsradikalismus in der Bundesrepublik Deutschland." *Tribüne* [Frankfurt-am-Main] 14, no. 56 (1975): 6496–500.

Metz, Johann-Baptist. *The Emergent Church: The Future of Christianity in a Post-Bourgeois World*. New York: Crossroad, 1981.

———. "Facing the Jews. Christian Theology After Auschwitz." In Fiorenza and Tracy, eds., *The Holocaust as Interruption*, pp. 11–16.

———. *Faith in History and Society*. New York: Seabury Press, 1980.

Mitscherlich, Alexander, and Margarete Mistscherlich. *Die Unfähigkeit zu trauern: Grundlagen kollektiven Verhaltens*. Munich: R. Piper Verlag, 1967.

Modern Language Studies. 16, no. 1 (Winter 1986). Special issue on the Holocaust in literature.

Moltmann, Jürgen. *The Church in the Power of the Spirit*. Translated by Margaret Kohl. New York: Harper and Row, 1975. (Originally published as *Kirche in der Kraft des Geistes*. Munich: Chr. Kaiser Verlage, 1975).

———. *The Crucified God*. Translated by R. A. Wilson and John Bowen. New York: Harper and Row, 1974.

Morgenthau, Henry. *The Murder of a Nation*. 2d ed. Los Angeles: Ararat Press, 1982.

Morley, John F. *Vatican Diplomacy and the Jews during the Holocaust 1939–1943*. New York: Ktav Publishing House, 1980.

Morse, Arthur D. *While Six Million Died*. New York: Hart Publishing Co., 1975.

Neher, André. *The Exile of the Word: From the Silence of the Bible to the Silence of Auschwitz*. Translated by David Maisel. Philadelphia: The Jewish Publication Society of America, 1981. (Originally published as *L'Exil de la parole: Du silence biblique au silence d'Auschwitz*. Paris: Editions du Seuil, 1970.)

Neven-du Mont, Jürgen. *After Hitler: Report from a West German City*. Translated by Ralph Manheim. Harmondsworth: Penguin Books, 1970.

Niebuhr, Reinhold. *The Children of Light and the Children of Darkness: A Vindication of Democracy and a Critique of its Traditional Defense*. New York: Scribner Lyceum Editions, 1960.

———. *Christianity and Power Politics*. Hamden, Conn.: Archon Books, 1969.

———. *Discerning the Signs of the Times*. New York: Charles Scribner's Sons, 1946.

———. *Moral Man and Immoral Society: A Study in Ethics and Politics*. New York: Charles Scribner, 1941.

———. *The Structure of Nations and Empires: A Study of the Recurring Patterns and Problems of the Political Order in Relation to the Unique Problems of the Nuclear Age*. New York: Charles Scribner's Sons, 1959.

Niebuhr, Ursula M., ed. *Justice and Mercy.* New York: Harper and Row, 1974.

Novitch, Miriam. *Sobibor: Martyrdom and Revolt.* New York: Holocaust Library, 1980.

Nomberg-Przytyk, Sara. *Auschwitz: True Tales from a Grotesque Land.* Translated by Roslyn Hirsch. Chapel Hill and London: University of North Carolina Press, 1985.

Oberman, Heiko A. *The Roots of Anti-Semitism.* Translated by James I. Porter. Philadelphia: Fortress Press, 1984.

O'Collins, Gerald. *What Are They Saying about the Resurrection?* New York, Ramsey, and Toronto: Paulist Press, 1978.

Opsahl, Paul D., and Marc H. Tanenbaum, eds. *Speaking of God Today: Jews and Lutherans in Conversation.* Philadelphia: Fortress Press, 1974.

Orpaz, Yizhak. "A Literature of Siege and Survival." *Jewish Quarterly* [London] 22, no. 4 (Winter 1975).

Osten-Sacken, Peter von der. "Anti-Judaism in Christian Theology." *Christian Attitudes on Jews and Judaism* [London] 55 (Aug. 1977): 1–6.

————. *Christian-Jewish Dialogue: Theological Foundations.* Philadelphia: Fortress, 1986.

———— ed. *Treue zur Thora: Beiträge zur Mitte des christlich-jüdischen Gesprächs. Festschrift für Günther Harder zum 75. Geburtstag.* Berlin: Institut Kirche und Judentum, 1977.

————, ed. *Zionismus: Befreiungsbewegung des jüdischen Volkes.* Berlin: Institut Kirche und Judentum bei der Kirchlichen Hochschule Berlin, 1977.

Ozick, Cynthia. "The Uses of Legend: Elie Wiesel as Tsaddik." *Congress Bi-Weekly* 36, no. 9 (9 June 1969): 16–20.

Pannenberg, Wolfhart. *Jesus—God and Man.* Translated by Lewis L. Wilkins and Duane A. Friebe. Philadelphia: Westminster Press, 1968.

————. "Zukunft und Einheit der Menschheit." *Evangelische Theologie* [Munich] 32, no. 4 (July-Aug. 1972): 384–402.

Parkes, James. *Antisemitism.* London: Vallentine, Mitchell, 1963.

————. *The Conflict of the Church and the Synagogue: A Study in the Origins of Antisemitism.* Cleveland: World Publishing Co., 1961.

————. *A History of the Jewish People.* Harmondsworth: Penguin Books, 1964.

————. *The Jew in the Medieval Community: A Study of His Political and Economic Situation.* 2d ed. New York: Hermon Press, 1976.

————. *Judaism and Christianity.* Chicago: University of Chicago Press, 1948.

————. *Prelude to Dialogue: Jewish-Christian Relationships.* London: Vallentine, Mitchell, 1969.

————. *Whose Land? A History of the Peoples of Palestine.* New York: Taplinger Publishing Co., 1971.

SELECTED BIBLIOGRAPHY

Pauley, Bruce F. *Hitler and the Forgotten Nazis: A History of Austrian National Socialism*. Chapel Hill: University of North Carolina Press, 1986.

Pawlikowski, John T. *Catechetics and Prejudice: How Catholic Teaching Materials View Jews, Protestants, and Racial Minorities*. New York: Paulist Press, 1973.

——. *The Challenge of the Holocaust for Christian Theology*. New York: Anti-Defamation League of B'nai B'rith, 1978.

——. *Christ in the Light of the Christian-Jewish Dialogue*. New York: Paulist Press, 1982.

——. "The Contemporary Jewish-Christian Theological Dialogue Agenda." *Journal of Ecumenical Studies* 11, no. 4 (Fall 1974): 599–616.

——. "The Dialogue Agenda." *ADL Bulletin* 31, no. 9 (Nov. 1974).

——. "The Holocaust and Contemporary Christology." In Fiorenza and Tracy, eds., *The Holocaust as Interruption*, pp. 43–49.

——. *What Are They Saying about Christian-Jewish Relations?* New York: Paulist Press, 1980.

Peck, Abraham J., ed. *Jews and Christians After the Holocaust*. Philadelphia: Fortress Press, 1982.

Peck, William Jay. "From Cain to the Death Camps: An Essay on Bonhoeffer and Judaism." *Union Seminary Quarterly Review* [New York] 28, no. 2 (Winter 1973): 158–76.

Peli, Pinchas Hacohen. "The Future of Israel." *Proceedings of the Rabbinical Assembly 74th Annual Convention* [5–9 May 1974], pp. 8–19.

Penkower, Monty. *The Jews Were Expendable: Free World Diplomacy and the Holocaust*. Urbana: University of Illinois Press, 1983; Paperback edition, Detroit: Wayne State University Press, 1988.

Pennie, David A., ed. *A Bibliography of the Printed Works of James Parkes*. Compiled with bibliographical notes by Sidney Sugarman and Diana Bailey. Southampton: University of Southampton, 1977.

Pfisterer, Rudolf. "Alter Feind in neuem Kleid: Erwägungen über den Antisemitismus." *Tribüne* [Frankfurt-am-Main] 12, no. 48 (1973): 5462–88.

——. "Antizionismus und Antisemitismus." *Tribüne* [Frankfurt-am-Main] 8, no. 32 (1969): 3407–18.

——. *Im Schatten des Kreuzes*. Hamburg-Bergstedt: Herbert Reich Evang. Verlag, 1966.

——. "Judaism in the Preaching and Teaching of the Church." *Lutheran World* [Geneva] 11, no. 3 (July 1964): 311–25.

——. *Von-A-Bis Z: Quellen zu Fragen um Juden und Christen*. Schriftenmissions-Verlag Gladbeck, 1971.

————. "Wiederum Schweigen?" *Tribüne* [Frankfurt-am-Main] 14, no. 53 (1975): 6116–33.

"Philosophy and the Holocaust." *The Philosophical Forum* 45, 1–2 (Fall-Winter 1984–85).

Poliakov, Léon. *The Aryan Myth: A History of Racist and Nationalist Ideas in Europe.* London: Heinemann Educational Books and Sussex University Press, 1974.

————. *Auschwitz.* Paris: Rene Julliard, 1964.

————. "The Catholic Church and the Jews: The Vatican's New Guidelines." *Midstream* 22, no. 8 (Oct. 1976): 29–35.

————. *The Harvest of Hate: The Nazi Program for the Destruction of the Jews of Europe.* Westport, Conn.: Greenwood Press, 1971; New York: Holocaust Library, 1975.

————. *The History of Anti-Semitism.* 4 vols. New York: Vanguard Press, 1964, 1974, 1975, and 1986.

————. *De l'antisionisme à l'antisémitisme.* Paris: Calmann-Levy, 1969.

Polish, David. *Israel—Nation and People.* New York: Ktav Publishing House, 1975.

————. "The Tasks of Israel and Galut." *Judaism* 28, no. 1 (Winter 1969): 3–16.

Postal, Bernard, and Samuel H. Abramson. *The Traveler's Guide to Jewish Landmarks of Europe.* New York: Fleet Press, 1971.

Presser, Jacob. *The Destruction of the Dutch Jews.* Translated by Arnold Pomerans. New York: E. P. Dutton, 1969. Paperback edition published as *Ashes in the Wind: The Destruction of Dutch Jewry.* Detroit: Wayne State University Press, 1988.

Rabi, Wladimir. "La théologie juive aprés Auschwitz." *Dispersion et Unité* [Jerusalem] 12 (1972): 186–204.

Rabinowitz, Dorothy. *New Lives: Survivors of the Holocaust Living in America.* New York: Alfred A. Knopf, 1976.

Ramras-Rauch, Gila and Joseph Michman-Meekman, eds. *Facing the Holocaust: Selected Israeli Fiction.* Philadelphia: The Jewish Publication Society of America, 1985.

Rash, Yohoshua. "French, Foreigners, and Jews." *Patterns of Prejudice* [London] 10, no. 1 (Jan.-Feb. 1976): 6–13.

Rat der Evangelischen Kirche in Deutschland. *Christen und Juden: Eine Studie des Rates der Evangelischen Kirche in Deutschland.* Gütersloh: Gütersloher Verlagshaus Gerd Möhn, 1975.

Rautkallio, Hannu. *Finland and the Holocaust: The Rescue of Finland's Jews.* Translated by Paul Sjöblom. New York: Holocaust Library, 1987.

Reid, James J. "The Armenian Massacres in Ottoman and Turkish Historiography." *Armenian Review* 37, no. 1 (Spring 1984): 22–40.

Reitlinger, Gerald. *The Final Solution: The Attempt to Exterminate the Jews of Europe, 1939–1945.* New York: A. S. Barnes, 1961.

Rencontre: Chrétiens et Juifs [Paris] 10, no. 46 (1976). Special issue on "Après l'Holocaust."

Rendtorff, Rolf, ed. *Arbeitsbuch Christen und Juden.* Gütersloh: Gütersloher Verlagshaus Gerd Möhn, 1979.

―――. "Ende oder Erfüllung der Geschichte? Das Problem des jüdischen Nationalstaats." *Evangelische Kommentare* [Stuttgart] 6, no. 5 (May 1973): 273–75.

―――. *Israel und sein Land: Theologische Überlegungen zu einem politischen Problem.* Munich: Chr. Kaiser Verlag, 1975.

―――. "Juden sind keine potentiellen Christen." *Evangelische Kommentare* [Stuttgart] 5, no. 6 (June 1972): 358–60.

―――. "Die neutestamentliche Wissenschaft und die Juden: Zur Diskussion zwischen David Flusser und Ulrich Wilckens." *Evangelische Theologie* [Munich] 36, no. 2 (Mar.-Apr. 1976): 191–200.

―――. "Der Staat Israel und die Christen." *Zeitwende* [Gütersloh] 45, no. 3 (May 1974): 183–96.

"Rethinking the Holocaust." In *Tikkun* 2, no. 1, 54–91, 139–43.

Reznikoff, Charles. *Holocaust.* Los Angeles: Black Sparrow Press, 1975.

Robinson, Jacob. *Psychoanalysis in a Vacuum: Bruno Bettelheim and the Holocaust.* New York: Yad Vashem-Yivo Documentary Projects, 1970.

Robinson, Jacob, assisted by Mrs. Philip Friedman. *The Holocaust and After: Sources and Literature in English.* Yad Vashem Martyrs' and Heroes' Memorial Authority, Jerusalem, and Yivo Institute for Jewish Research, New York, Joint Documentary Projects; Bibliographical Series, no. 12. Jerusalem: Israel Universities Press, 1973.

Rosenbaum, Irving J. *The Holocaust and Halakhah.* New York: Ktav Publishing House, 1976.

Rosenberg, Alan, and Gerald Myers, eds. *Echoes from the Holocaust.* Philadelphia: Temple University Press, 1988.

Rosenfeld, Alvin H. *A Double Dying: Reflections on Holocaust Literature.* Bloomington, Ind., and London: Indiana University Press, 1980.

―――. *Imagining Hitler.* Bloomington: Indiana University Press, 1985.

Rosenfeld, Alvin H., and Irving Greenberg, eds. *Confronting the Holocaust: The Impact of Elie Wiesel.* Bloomington, Ind., and London: Indiana University Press, 1978.

Rosenthal, David. "Thirty Years after the Liberation of Auschwitz and Bergen-Belsen." *Jewish Frontier* 41, no. 3 (Mar. 1975): 4–10.

Rosenzweig, Franz. *The Star of Redemption.* Translated by William W. Hallo. New York: Holt, Rinehart and Winston, 1970.

Roskies, David H. *Against the Apocalypse: Responses to Catastrophe in Modern Jewish Culture.* Cambridge, Mass., and London: Harvard University Press, 1984.

Roskies, Diane K. *Teaching the Holocaust to Children: A Review and Bibliography.* New York: Ktav Publishing House, 1975.

Rotenstreich, Nathan. *Reflections on the Contemporary Jewish Condition.* Jerusalem: Institute of Contemporary Jewry, Hebrew University, 1975.

Roth, John K. *A Consuming Fire: Encounters with Elie Wiesel and the Holocaust.* Atlanta, Ga.: John Knox Press, 1979.

Rothkirchen, Livia. "The Stand of the Churches vis-à-vis the Persecution of the Jews of Slovakia." In *Judaism and Christianity Under the Impact of National Socialism (1919-1945)*, pp. 273–86.

Rottenberg, Isaac C. "Fulfillment Theology and the Future of Christian-Jewish Relations." *Christian Century* 97, no. 3 (23 Jan. 1980): 66–69.

———. "Should There Be a Christian Witness to the Jews?" *The Christian Century* 94, no. 13 (13 Apr. 1977): 352–56.

Rubenstein, Richard L. *After Auschwitz: Radical Theology and Contemporary Judaism.* Indianapolis: Bobbs-Merrill Co., 1966.

———. "Auschwitz and Covenant Theology." *The Christian Century* 86, no. 21 (21 May 1969): 716–18.

———. *The Cunning of History: Mass Death and the American Future.* New York: Harper and Row, 1975.

———. "Jewish Theology and the Current World Situation." *Conservative Judaism* 28, no. 4 (Summer 1974): 3–15.

———. "Job and Auschwitz." *Union Seminary Quarterly Review* 25, no. 4 (Summer 1970): 421–37.

Rubenstein, Richard L., and John K. Roth. *Approaches to Auschwitz: History and Its Legacy.* Atlanta: John Knox Press, 1987.

Ruether, Rosemary Radford. "Christian-Jewish Dialogue: New Interpretations." *ADL Bulletin* 30, no. 5 (May 1973): 3–4.

———. *Faith and Fratricide: The Theological Roots of Anti-Semitism.* New York: Seabury Press, 1974.

———. "The Future of Christian Theology about Judaism." *Christian Attitudes on Jews and Judaism* [London] 49 (Aug. 1976): 1–5.

———. "An Invitation to Jewish-Christian Dialogue: In What Sense Can We Say that Jesus Was "'The Christ'?" *The Ecumenist* 10, no. 2 (Jan.-Feb. 1972): 17–24.

———. *Liberation Theology: Human Hope Confronts Christian History and American Power.* New York: Paulist Press, 1972.

Ryan, Allan A. *Quiet Neighbors: Prosecuting Nazi War Criminals in America.* New York: Harcourt Brace Jovanovich, 1984.

Ryan, Judith. *The Uncompleted Past: Postwar German Novels and the Third Reich.* Detroit: Wayne State University Press, 1983.

Ryan, Michael. *The Contemporary Explosion of Theology.* Metuchen, N.J.: Scarecrow Press, 1975.

———. *Human Responses to the Holocaust: Perpetrators and Victims and Bystanders and Resisters.* New York and Toronto: Edwin Mellen Press, 1981.

———. "Some Protestant Theological Reflections on Jews and Judaism since 1945: Towards a Definition of Theological Anti-Semitism." Unpublished paper at Annual Scholars' Conference on the Church Struggle and the Holocaust, New York, 17–20 Mar. 1974.

Rylaarsdam, J. Coert. "Jewish-Christian Relationship: The Two Covenants and the Dilemmas of Christology." *Journal of Ecumenical Studies* 9, no. 2 (Spring 1972): 249–70.

Sachar, Howard. *The Emergence of the Middle East 1914–1924.* New York: Alfred A. Knopf, 1971.

Sachs, Nelly. *O the Chimneys: Selected Poems.* New York: Farrar, Straus and Giroux, 1967.

Sanders, E. P. *Jesus and Judaism.* Philadelphia: Fortress Press, 1985.

———. *Paul and Palestinian Judaism: A Comparison of Patterns of Religion.* Philadelphia: Fortress Press, 1977.

Sanders, Wilm. *Antisemitismus bei den Christen? Gedanken zur christlichen Judenfeindschaft am Beispiel der Oberammergau Passionsspiele.* Leutesdorf-am-Rhein: Johannes-Verlag, 1970.

Sandmel, Samuel. *Anti-Semitism in the New Testament?* Philadelphia: Fortress Press, 1978.

———. "The New Movement." *Common Ground* [London] 23, no. 2 (Summer 1969).

———. *We Jews and Jesus.* New York: Oxford University Press, 1965, 1973.

Schenk, Rosemarie; Otto Schenk; Eva Nessler; and Udo Nessler . . . *Und gruben Brunnen in der Wuste: Junge Deutsche ziehen Bilanz ihrer 8 Aufbaujahre zwischen Jerusalem und Beer Shava.* Darmstadt: Eduard Roetther Verlag, 1975.

Schindler, Pesach. "Faith after Auschwitz in Light of the Paradox of Tikkun in Hassidic Documents." *Sidic* [Rome] 7, no. 3 (1974): 24–30.

———. "The Holocaust and Kiddush Hashem in Hasidic Thought." *Tradition* 13, no. 4 and 14, no. 1 (Spring-Summer 1973): 88–104.

Schmid, Herbert. "Holokaust, Theologie, und Religionsunterricht." *Judaica* [Zurich] 35 (1979): 5–11.

Schneider, Gertrude. "Survival and Guilt Feelings of Jewish Concentration Camp Victims." *Jewish Social Studies* 37, no. 1 (Jan. 1975): 74–83.

Schorsch, Ismar. "German Anti-Semitism in the Light of Post-War Historiography." Unpublished preparatory paper for International Scholars Conference on the Holocaust, New York, 3–6 Mar. 1975.

———. "Historical Reflections on the Holocaust." *Conservative Judaism* 31, nos. 1–2 (Fall-Winter 1976–77): 26–33.

Schulz, Gerhard. *Faschismus-Nationalsozialismus: Versionen und theoretische Kontroversen*. Frankfurt-am-Main: Verlag Ullstein, 1974.

Schwarz-Bart, André. *The Last of the Just*. Translated by Stephen Becker. New York: Atheneum, 1961.

Schweitzer, Frederick M. *A History of the Jews since the First Century A.D.* New York: Macmillan, 1971.

Seiden, Morton Irving. *The Paradox of Hate: A Study in Ritual Murder*. New York and London: Thomas Yoseloff, 1967.

Senesh, Hannah. *Hannah Senesh: Her Life and Diary*. Translated by Martha Cohn. New York: Schocken Books, 1973.

Sereny, Gitta. *Into That Darkness: From Mercy Killing to Mass Murder*. New York: McGraw Hill, 1975.

Shabbetai, K. *As Sheep to the Slaughter: The Myth of Cowardice*. New York and Tel Aviv: World Association of the Bergen-Belsen Survivors Associations, 1963.

Shapiro, Susan. "Hearing the Testimony of Radical Negation." In Fiorenza and Tracy, eds. *The Holocaust as Interruption*, pp. 3–10.

Sherman, Franklin. "Speaking of God after Auschwitz." *Worldview* 17, no. 9 (Sept. 1974): 26–30.

Sherwin, Byron L., and Susan G. Ament. *Encountering the Holocaust: An Interdisciplinary Survey*. Chicago: Impact Press, 1979.

Sichrovsky, Peter. *Born Guilty: Children of Nazi Families*. Translated by Jean Steinberg. New York: Basic Books, 1988.

———. *Strangers in Their Own Land: Young Jews in Germany and Austria Today*. Translated by Jean Steinberg. New York: Basic Books, 1987.

Sidic [Rome] 7, no. 2 (1974), special number on the Holocaust; 8, no. 3 (1975), special number on Jewish-Christian relations, 1965–75.

Siegele-Wenschkewitz, Leonore. "The Contribution of Church History to a Post-Holocaust Theology: Christian Anti-Judaism as the Root of Anti-Semitism." In Fiorenza and Tracy, eds. *The Holocaust as Interruption*, pp. 60–64.

———. "Mitverantwortung und Schuld der Christen am Holocaust." *Evangelische Theologie* 42 (1982): 171–90.

255

Silbermann, Alphons. "Antisemitismus in der Bundersrepublik." Offprint from *Bild der Wissenschaft* (June 1976), pp. 68–74.

Silverman, David Wolf. "The Holocaust: A Living Force." *Conservative Judaism* 31, no. 1–2 (Fall-Winter 1976–77): 21–25.

Simon, Ulrich E. *A Theology of Auschwitz.* London: Victor Gollancz, 1967; SPCK, 1978.

Sloyan, Gerard S. *Is Christ the End of the Law?* Philadelphia: Westminster Press, 1978.

Snoek, Johan M. *The Grey Book. A Collection of Protests Against Anti-Semitism and the Persecution of Jews Issued by Non-Roman Catholic Churches and Church Leaders During Hitler's Rule.* Assen, Neth.: Van Gorcum & Co. N.V., 1969.

Sontag, Frederick. *The God of Evil: An Argument from the Existence of the Devil.* New York: Harper and Row, 1970.

Sosnowski, Kiryl. *The Tragedy of Children under Nazi Rule.* Warsaw: Western Agency Press, 1962.

Sperber, Manès. . . . *Than a Tear in the Sea.* Translated by Constantine Fitzgibbon. New York and Tel Aviv: Bergen-Belsen Memorial Press, 1967.

———. *Die Wasserträger Gottes.* Vienna: Europaverlag, 1974.

Stein, André L. "A Chronicle: The Necessity and Impossibility of 'Making Sense' at and of Auschwitz." *Jewish Social Studies* 45, no. 3–4 (Summer-Fall 1983), 323–36.

Steiner, George, *In Bluebeard's Castle: Some Notes Towards the Re-definition of Culture.* New Haven: Yale University Press, 1979.

———. *Language and Silence: Essays on Language, Literature, and the Inhuman.* London: Penguin Books, 1969.

Steiner, Jean-Francois. *Treblinka.* Translated by Helen Weaver. London: Weidenfeld and Nicholson, 1967.

Steinitz, Lucy Y., and David M. Szonyi, eds. *Living after the Holocaust: Reflections by the Post-War Generation in America.* New York: Bloch Publishing Co., 1976.

Stern, Ellen. *Elie Wiesel: Witness for Life.* New York: Ktav, 1982.

Stiegnitz, Peter. "Angst und Antisemitismus: Sozialpsychologie der Judenfeindschaft in Deutschland und Österreich." *Tribüne* [Frankfurt-am-Main] 14, no. 55 (1975): 6368–74.

Stierlin, Helm, *Adolf Hitler: Familienperspektiven.* Frankfurt-am-Main: Suhrkamp, 1975.

Stimmt unser Bild vom Judentum? Fazit aus 20 Jahren christlich-jüdischen Dialogs. Papers given before a conference at the Evangelical Academy, Bad Boll, 7–9 Nov. 1975.

Stöhr, Martin, Johann Maier, Heinz Kremers, J. F. Konrad, and Pinchas E. Lapide. *Judentum im christlichen Religionsunterricht.* Frankfurt: Verlag Evangelischer Presseverband fur Hessen und Nassau, 1972.

Stow, Kenneth R. *Catholic Thought and Papal Policy 1555–1593*. New York: Ktav and Jewish Theological Seminary, 1977.

Strober, Gerald S. *Portrait of the Elder Brother: Jews and Christians in Protestant Teaching Materials*. New York: American Jewish Committee-National Conference of Christians and Jews, 1972.

Stroh, Hans. "Die gegenseitige Befragung: Zum Stand des jüdisch-christlichen Gesprächs." *Zeitwende* [Gütersloh] 45, no. 3 (May 1974): 196–99.

―――. "Gibt es Verständigung zwischen Juden und Christen? *Zeitschrift für Theologie und Kirche* [Tübingen] 71, no. 2 (June 1974): 227–38.

Suhl, Uri, ed. and trans. *They Fought Back: The Story of the Jewish Resistance in Nazi Europe*. London: MacGibbon and Kee, 1968.

Syrkin, Marie. *Blessed Is the Match: The Story of Jewish Resistance*. Philadelphia: The Jewish Publication Society of America, 1976.

Szonyi, David M., ed. *The Holocaust: An Annotated Bibliography and Resource Guide*. Hoboken, N.J.: Ktav, 1985.

Tal, Uriel. *Christians and Jews in Germany: Religion, Politics, and Ideology in the Second Reich, 1870–1914*. Translated by Noah J. Jacobs. Ithaca, N.Y.: Cornell University Press, 1975.

―――. "Möglichkeiten einer jüdisch-christlichen Begegnung und Verständigung, Jüdische Sicht." *Concilium* [Mainz] 10, no. 10 (Oct. 1974): 605–9.

―――. "On the Study of the Holocaust and Genocide." In *Yad Vashem Studies*, edited by Livia Rothkirchen, vol. 13, pp. 7–52. Jerusalem: Yad Vashem Martyrs' and Heroes' Remembrance Authority, 1979.

―――. "Zur neuen Einstellung der Kirche zum Judentum." *Freiburger Rundbrief* 24, nos. 89–92 (Dec. 1972): 150–60.

Talmage, Frank Ephraim, ed. *Disputation and Dialogue: Readings in the Jewish-Christian Encounter*. New York: Ktav Publishing House, 1975.

Tec, Nechama. *When Light Pierced the Darkness: Christian Rescue of Jews in Nazi-Occupied Poland*. New York: Oxford University Press, 1986.

Thoma, Clemens. *A Christian Theology of Judaism*. Translated and edited by Helga Croner. New York and Ramsey: Paulist Press, 1980.

―――. *Kirche aus Juden und Heiden: Biblische Informationen über das Verhältnis der Kirche zum Judentum*. Vienna: Herder and Co., 1970.

Thompson, Kenneth W., ed. *Foreign Policy and Morality: Framework for a Moral Audit*. New York: Council on Religion and International Affairs, 1979.

Toland, John. *Adolf Hitler*. Garden City, N.Y.: Doubleday and Co., 1976.

Trachtenberg, Joshua. *The Devil and the Jews: The Medieval Conception of the Jews and Its Relation to Modern Antisemitism*. Cleveland, Ohio: Meridian Books, 1961; Philadelphia: The Jewish Publication Society, 1983.

Trunk, Isaiah. *Jewish Responses to Nazi Persecution*. New York: Stein and Day, 1982.

———. *Judenrat: The Jewish Councils in Eastern Europe Under Nazi Occupation*. New York: Macmillan, 1972.

"Tuchin." *Encyclopaedia Judaica*, vol. 15, pp. 1420–21.

Tyson, Joseph B. *A Study of Early Christianity*. New York: Macmillan, 1973.

Vago, Bela, and George Mosse, eds. *Jews and Non-Jews in Eastern Europe, 1918–1945*. New York: John Wiley and Sons; and Jerusalem: Israel Universities Press, 1974.

Van Buren, Paul M. "Affirmation of the Jewish People: A Condition of Theological Coherence." *Journal of the American Academy of Religion* 45, no. 3, Supplement (Sept. 1977): 1075–100.

———. *The Burden of Freedom: Americans and the God of Israel*. New York: Seabury Press, 1976.

———. *Christ in Context: A Theology of the Jewish-Christian Reality*. New York: Harper and Row, 1988.

———. *Discerning the Way: A Theology of the Jewish-Christian Reality*. New York: Seabury Press, 1980.

———. "The Status and Prospects for Theology." *CCI Notebook* 24 (Nov. 1975).

Vermes, Geza. *The Gospel of Jesus the Jew*. Newcastle upon Tyne: University of Newcastle, 1981.

———. *Jesus the Jew: A Historian's Reading of the Gospels*. London: Collins, 1973.

———. *Jesus and the World of Judaism*. Philadelphia: Fortress Press, 1984.

Vogt, Judith. "Old Images in Soviet Anti-Zionist Cartoons." *Soviet Jewish Affairs* [London] 5, no. 1 (1975): 20–38.

Volavkora, Hana, ed. *Children's Drawings and Poems—Terezin 1942–1944*. Prague: State Jewish Museum, 1959.

Wallimann, Isidor, and Michael N. Dobkowski, eds. *Genocide and the Modern Age: Etiology and Case Studies of Mass Death*. New York: and Westport, Conn.: Greenwood Press, 1987.

Wardi, Charlotte, *Le juif dans le roman francais*. Paris: Nizet, 1973.

Wasserstein, Bernard. *Britain and the Jews of Europe, 1939–1945*. Oxford: Oxford University Press, 1979.

Weller, Georges. *L'Étoile jaune à l'heure de Vichy: De Drancy à Auschwitz*. Paris: Fayard, 1973.

Wiesel, Elie. *Against Silence: The Voice and Vision of Elie Wiesel*. 3 vols. Edited and compiled by Irving Abrahamson. New York: Holocaust Library, 1985.

———. *"Ani Maamim": A Song Lost and Found Again*. Translated by Marion Wiesel. New York: Random House, 1973.

————. *A Beggar in Jerusalem*. Translated by Lily Edelman and the author. New York: Random House, 1970.

————. *The Fifth Son*. Translated by Marion Wiesel. New York: Summit Books, 1985.

————. *Five Biblical Portraits*. Notre Dame, Ind. and London: Notre Dame University Press, 1981.

————. *The Gates of the Forest*. Translated by Frances Frenaye. New York: Holt, Rinehart and Winston, 1966.

————. *A Jew Today*. Translated by Marion Wiesel. New York: Random House, 1978.

————. *Jewish Legends: A Teachers' Guide*. New York: Archdiocese of New York and Anti-Defamation League of B'nai B'rith, n.d.

————. "Jewish Values in the Post-Holocaust Future." *Judaism* 16, no. 3 (Summer 1967): 281–84.

————. *Legends of Our Time*. Translated by Stephen Donadio. New York: Avon Books, 1968.

————. *Messengers of God: Biblical Portraits and Legends*. Translated by Marion Wiesel. New York: Random House, 1976.

————. *Night*. Translated by Stella Rodway. New York: Hill and Wang, 1960.

————. *The Oath*. Translated by Marion Wiesel. New York: Random House, 1973.

————. "Ominous Signs and Unspeakable Thoughts." *New York Times*, 28 Dec. 1974.

————. *The Testament*. Translated by Marion Wiesel. New York: Summit Books, 1981.

————. *The Town beyond the Wall*. Translated by Stephen Becker. New York: Avon Books, 1964.

————. *The Trial of God*. Translated by Marion Wiesel. New York: Random House, 1979.

————. *Zalmen or, The Madness of God*. Translated by Marion Wiesel. New York: Random House, 1974.

Wiesenthal, Simon. *The Sunflower*. New York: Schocken Books, 1976.

Wilken, Robert L. *Judaism and the Early Christian Mind: A Study of Alexandria's Exegesis and Theology*. New Haven: Yale University Press, 1971.

Williamson, Clark. *Has God Rejected His People?* Nashville: Abingdon Press, 1982.

Willis, Robert E. "Auschwitz and the Nurturing of Conscience." *Religion in Life* 44, no. 4 (Winter 1975): 432–37.

————. "Christian Theology after Auschwitz." *Journal of Ecumenical Studies* 12, no. 4 (Fall 1975): 493–519.

Wistrich, Robert. *Hitler's Apocalypse: Jews and the Nazi Legacy*. New York: St. Martin's Press, 1985.

World Council of Churches. *The Church and the Jewish People.* Newsletter no. 4 (1975). Newsletter no. 2 (1977). Geneva: World Council of Churches, Consultation on the Church and the Jewish People.

Wormser-Migot, Olga. *L'Ère des camps.* Paris: Union Générale d'Éditions, 1973.

Wundheiler, Luitgard N. "Paul Celan, Poet of the Holocaust." *Worldview* 19, no. 12 (Dec. 1976): 24–26.

Wyman, David. *The Abandonment of the Jews: America and the Holocaust, 1941–1945.* New York: Pantheon, 1984.

————. *Paper Walls: America and the Refugee Crisis, 1938–1941.* New York: Pantheon, 1985.

Wyschogrod, Michael. "Faith and the Holocaust." *Judaism* 20, no. 3 (Summer 1971): 268–94.

Yahil, Leni. "The Holocaust in Jewish Historiography." *Yad Vashem Studies,* edited by Livia Rothkirchen, vol. 7, pp. 57–73. Jerusalem: Yad Vashem, 1968.

Zeitwende [Gütersloh] 46, no. 6 (Nov. 1975). Special number on Paul Celan.

Zerner, Ruth. "Dietrich Bonhoeffer and the Jews: Thoughts and Actions, 1933–1945." *Jewish Social Studies* 37, nos. 3–4 (Summer-Fall 1975): 235–50.

Zimmels, H. J. *The Echo of the Nazi Holocaust in Rabbinic Literature.* New York: Ktav Publishing House, 1977.

Zucker, Wolfgang. "Thirty Years after the Holocaust: A Midrash for the Church." *Lutheran Forum* 9, no. 3 (Sept. 1975).

INDEX

Abraham, 70, 90, 100, 110, 125, 131, 147, 222 n.39. *See also under* Jesus
Absolutism, Christian, 109–14, 118, 121, 127, of "the law", 99; political, 152, 154; religious, 152
Accountability: divine, 55; human, 55
Adler, Hermann G., 58
Adorno, T. W., 53
Adversus Judaeos, 16
Aichinger, Ilse, 162
Aktion Sühnezeichen/Friedens- dienste, 17, 45–46, 196 n.26
Americans: and Jews and Judaism, 172, 174, 223 n.10; and State of Is- rael, 172
Amichai, Yehuda, 161
Amnestia, 32, 36–38, 49, 195 n.20; concept of, 32
Anarchism/anarchy, 154, 155
Ani Ma-amin, 87, 170
Anthropotheism, 167
Anti-Israelism, 59, 208 n.6, 211 n.30
Anti-Judaism, 15, 16, 71, 107, 118, 120, 121, 140, 142, 211 n.30
Antisemitism, 15, 27, 34, 35, 42, 50–62, 64–70, 71, 98, 101, 131, 140, 144, 145, 165, 175, 176, 194 n.15, 196 n.32, 199 n.21; blame on Jews for, 72, 73, 99, 202 n.48; Christian, 15, 26, 27, 53, 58, 70–75, 98, 101, 119, 125, 126, 138, 140, 172, 202 n.48; and Christian liturgy, 199 n.22; Christian opposition to, 70; condemnation of, 98; converted from, 131; freedom from, 122–23; and Germans today, 34, 40–42; gov- ernmental, 193 n.29; and Holocaust, 57–67, 119; Nazi, 15, 73, 74; and Passion story, 128–29, 214 n.11; pro-

fessionalized, 67; religion of, 62; and Resurrection, 140; roots of, 98; and secularization, 166; singularity of, 50–62, 64–70, 109. *See also un- der* Devil; Germans; Guilt; New Testament; Passion story
Anti-Sinai, 67
Anti-Zionism, 67, 101, 172
Apocalyptic, Christian, 120; struggle of Hitler, 23
Apostasy, 77, 180
Arabs, 49, 153, 163, 164, 165; and State of Israel, 208 n.6
Arendt, Hannah, 51
Armenians, 53, 197 n.8
Aronsfeld, Caesar C., 35
Aryans, 53, 66
Aschkenasy, Yehuda, 95
Auschwitz, 25, 31, 50, 76, 114, 150–51, 152, 153, 158, 159, 161, 170, 182, 186; Christianization of, 114; Christians in, 183; Christ in, 183; God and 159; resistance in, 25, 161; as symbol for Final Solution, 62. *See also* Command; Voice
"Auschwitz Planet," 62

Baal Shem Tov, 49
Babi Yar, 186
Baeck, Leo, 88, 205 n.19
Bak, Samuel, 166
Bastiaans, Jan, 23
Baum, Gregory, 71–72, 83–84, 86, 87, 124, 105 n.19; on ideology 213 n.1; on Moltmann, 213 n.61
Bea, Cardinal Augustin, 98
Belzec, 80, 91, 115, 152, 158, 186
Bergen-Belsen, 79
Berkovits, Eliezer, 89–90, 94, 206 n.36

261

Bethge, Eberhard, 41
B.F.S., usage of, 54, 68, 70, 146, 147, 148, 158
Biale, David, 221 n.17
Biblical perspectives, 138, 147
Biblical scholarship, 104, 106, 107–108; German, 107
Birkenau, 158, 195 n.10
Bitburg, 34, 41, 171–79, 223 nn.5, 13, 16; as Christian issue, 171, 173; Christian opposition to visit, 173, 177–78; morality/immorality of, 177
Black power, 151
Blacks, 126
"Blasphemer," Jesus as, 103, 105
Blasphemy, 84, 86, 92, 100, 105, 114, 117, 129, 139, 144, 147, 150; meaning of, 210 n.20; and theology, 144
Blumhardt, Christoph, 111
Body-soul dualism, 142
Borowitz, Eugene, 136
Borowski, Tadeusz, 160
Brown, Robert McAfee, 15, 72, 168
Buchenwald, 115, 186

Cain, and God, 193 n.30
Cambodians, 63–64
Cammerer, Joseph S., 162
Campbell, Will D., 126
Camus, Albert, 82
Canetti, Elias, 29–30, 192 n.25, 194 n.5
Celan, Paul, 160, 220 n.9
Chagall, Marc, 184
Children, 40, 52, 146, 151, 159–60, 162, 220 n.14; burning of, 134–35, 156, 178, 215 n.27; as genocide victims, 63; in Holocaust, 29, 52, 85, 128, 134–35, 146, 156, 159, 162, 170, 178, 220 n.14; of survivors; 37. See also under Kingdom of day; Kingdom of night; Victims
Chmielnicki, 17
Chopp, Rebecca, 122
Chosen. See Election
Christ, 110, 114, 115, 209 n.12; in Auschwitz, 183, 184; and covenant, 132; faith in, 103; and freedom,

108; as God, 146; as "hidden," 116; and Jews, 99, 120, 201 n.48; Messiah of God, 109; Messiah of Israel, 120; rejection of, 20, 129; as sacrifice, 108; second advent of, 120; suffering of 108, 115; among victims of Holocaust, 184. See also Jesus; Messiah

Christian faith, 77, 101, 107, 115, 125, 131; as ally of Jews, 167; and crucifixion of Jesus, 115–16, 134; foundation of, 135; and Jewishness, 136–37; need for regeneration of, 117; rethinking of, 143, 158; and new revelations, 137; and salvation, 137. See also Christ; Christianity; Church; Jesus; and see under Relativization; Revolution; Triumphalism
Christianity, 16, 77, 107, 108, 138; claims of, 166, 181, 209 n.10, 215 n.32; contribution to Holocaust of, 100, 114–15, 122–23, 125, 126–27, 132, 171; credibility of, 71, 100; crisis of, 123; cynic's definition of, 142; God of, 86; and history, 137; and idolatry, 136; impact of Holocaust on, 85, 100, 101, 115–17, 132–33, 209 n.7; and Jewishness, 167; and Jews and Judaism, 12, 13, 16, 21–22, 26, 71, 98, 99, 101, 107–21, 124, 127, 131, 132, 136–37, 141, 143, 152, 158, 175, 178, 180, 187, 201 n.48, 209 nn.10, 12, 213 n.3, 215 n.32; and New Testament, 122, 129; as nonconversionist, 131, 132, 136; and other faiths, 136–37; plight of, 121; transformation of, 124, 127, 143, 166–68, 213 n.3; values and virtues of, 15, 175. See also Christian faith; Christians; Church; Culpability; and see under Holocaust; Ideology; Israel; Jewishness; Justice; Nazism; Revolution; Supersessionism; Theology; Triumphalism
Christianizing Holocaust testimony, 184–85

Idinopulos, Thomas A., 150, 218n.66
Idolatry, idols, 15, 97, 100, 116, 136, 150, 167; and self, 167. *See also under* Jesus
Imperialism, Christian. *See* Supersessionism
"Inability to mourn," 37–38, 176; and inability to repent, 38
Incarnation, 140; of Jewish people, 148, 176
Indifference, 24, 186, 202n.48
Inquisition, the, 67, 115
Interdependence of God and humans, 85–86
Intolerance, 137, 167; Jews and, 221n.29
Isaac, 70, 90, 100, 131
Isaac, Jules, 21, 210n.24
Israel, 81, 109, 110, 131, 137, 141; calling of, 118; Christian solidarity with, 117, 118, 140, 158; covenant with, 76, 129; demands upon, 74, 82, 90–91, 92–94, 119, 144–47; election of, 10, 81, 92–94, 99, 110, 111, 131, 132, 145, 147–48, election to life, 147–48; and God, 145, 161, 162, 170; as hope of church, 118; integrity of, 131; Paul and, 120; People, 10, 140–47; purifying of, 77; sins of, 91. *See also under* Church; Jews; Messianic hope; People of God; Suffering
Israel, State of, 12, 13, 16, 101, 145, 151–53, 155–58, 160–63 passim; as answer to spiritual power, 152; and children, 220n.14; and Christians, 118, 145, 153; demands upon, 153; double-standard toward, 153; as faith-orienting event, 181; and Holocaust, 161; hostility toward, 208n.6; and Jewish survival 141, 161; meaning of, 152; and news media, 155, 208n.6; and redemption, 151; as response to evil and Holocaust, 151, 152; as sign of hope, 16; and the German Federal Republic, 46–47, 101, 196n.27; as will to live, 151. *See also* Political do-

main; Political power; Hope and the People Israel

Jacob, 70, 100, 131
Jesus, 21, 107, 144, 169–70, 186; as Christ, 129, 144; claims of, 105; and covenant, 131; condemnation of, 105, 129; crucifixion of, 11, 41, 54, 98, 107, 109, 114–17, 129–30, 133, 135, 137, 138, 144, 147, 156, 210n.20; death of, 108, 114, 115, 120–30, 133–34, 137; as fulfillment of divine promise, 209n.10; as false messiah, 71, 105; and forgiveness, 103, 104; and Godforsakenness, 85, 106, 133–34, 147, 156, 218n.68; and Holocaust, 21, 183; and idolatry, 136; Jewishness of, 64, 104–5, 109, 131, 133, 158, 210n.17; and Judaism, 106, 107, 210n.17; and kingdom of God, 140; and "the law," 103–106, 110–111, 139; nonresurrection of, 141; and Pharisees, 103–104; rejection of, 129; as second Abraham, 136; suffering of, 108, 133, 137, 159; and Torah, 104, 141; trial of, 103–5, 129–31, 210n.20; words on cross, 80, 85, 107, 109, 147, 150, 161, 210n.20, 218n.66. *See also under* Cross; Crucifixion; Gentiles; Jews; Messiah; Resurrection
Jewish Christianity, 133, 136; and Holocaust, 115
Jewish historicalness, 136–38, 161; and Christians, 136
Jewish theology, 112; and Holocaust, 16, 82, 93, 144
Jews, Jewish people, 35, 43, 55–62 passim, 80, 100–101, 109, 115; abandoned, 80, 150, 172, 174, 186; accusations against, 25, 58, 72, 99, 128–30, 160, 201n.48; and blame for antisemitism, 72–73, 99, 202n.48; calling of, 71, 118–20, 144; and the Christ, 73, 99, 120;

Pauck, Wilhelm, 107
Paul (apostle), 99, 107, 120, 122,
  136–37, 138, 142, 168; on Judaism,
  120, 168, 212 n.59; and Resurrec-
  tion, 142
Pawlikowski, John, 72; on Eckardt
  and devil, 199 n.22
Peck, William Jay, 77, 157, 193 n.30
Peli, Pinchas, 152
Penitence, 38. *See also under* God
People of God, 68, 69, 76–77, 81, 101,
  147, 158; and Christians, 158; and
  hope, 158, 159–66; Israel as, 141;
  and political power, 159–66; and
  suffering, 77, 81. *See also under*
  Suffering; Suffering servant
Perfection: of God, 119; and Judaism,
  73, 74, 119; of world, 86, 159
Perfectionism, 143, 153, 203 n.57; of
  God, rejected, 143
Pfisterer, Rudolf, 99
Pharisees: and Jesus, 103–5
Phillips, A. C. J., 173–74
Philosophy: contribution to Holocaust,
  14, 67; of history, 54–55; task of, 68
Poland, 48
Polish, David, 60, 92, 220 n.15
Political domain: 125, 152, 155,
  219 n.80. *See also under* Kingdom
  of day; Theology
Political power, 125, 128, 150–56,
  161. *See also* Democracy; Israel,
  State of; Kingdom of day; People of
  God; Niebuhr, Reinhold; Theology
Post-Christian era, 166
Post-concentration-camp syndrome,
  37
Post-Holocaust theology, 35, 92, 93,
  96, 106, 116, 117, 124–33, 141,
  144–70, 207 n.46, 212 n.60, 214 n.13,
  215 n.32; and "blasphemy," 147
Powell, Peter R., Jr., 153
Power, 150–51, 160, 161, 162. *See
  also* Political domain; Political
  power
Powerlessness, 119, 144, 151, 160, 162;
  of God, 119. *See also* Theology of

suffering; Suffering
Prayer, 22; of Donat, 80; Jewish daily,
  108; of Rakover, 88–89; of Schwarz-
  Bart, 79–80
Pre-Holocaust theology, 86–90, 92–94,
  96–97, 99–100, 107, 116–17, 121,
  135, 147, 193 n.4, 213 nn.61, 66,
  215 n.27
Prejudice, 58, 130
Propositions: moral-historical, 39–49
Protest, 112, 147, 196 n.32, 217 n.56
Protestant Church in Germany, 89,
  132; Council of, 100–2, 132,
  209 nn.10, 12
Protestantism, 107, 202 n.48, 210 n.24
Providence, 83, 87, 90
Psychological plight: of Germans, 34,
  35–36, 37–38, 175–76; of victims,
  23, 24, 36–37, 63

"Race of the dead," 23
Racial doctrines, racism, 15, 55, 66,
  99; American, 126
Rakover, Yossel, 88–89, 184–85
Reagan, Ronald, 34, 42, 171–74,
  223 nn.5, 13, 16
"Realized eschatology": repudiation
  of, 122–23
Rebirth, 82
Reconciliation, 43, 126, 136–37,
  176–79 passim; of Christians and
  Jews, 99, 101, 109, 116, 126,
  212 n.60; of German Federal Re-
  public and the U.S., 176–78
Redemption, 11, 73, 109, 116, 142,
  151, 169; future, 109–110; lack of,
  110, 116; of world, 76, 77, 86, 110,
  151. *See also under* God; Man
Red Sea, 148
Reductionism, 136
Reformed Church of Holland, Gen-
  eral Synod of, 131
Refugees, Jewish, policies toward,
  194 n.15
Relativization, of Christian faith, 109,
  194 n.15, 167; need for, 111, 122
Religion: pluralism in, 166; rescue

INDEX

Yom haShoah, 36, 180, 222 n.36;
  Christian observance of, 180–88
Yom Kippur War, 163, 199 n.21

Zeffirelli, Franco, 128

Zeroniski, Stefan, 157
Zimmels, H. J., 55–56
Zionism, 163
Zucker, Wolfgang, 50, 73, 74, 100

277

Alice L. and A. Roy Eckardt are Professors Emeriti of Religion Studies at Lehigh University and have been Visiting Scholars at the Centre for Post Graduate Hebrew Studies, University of Oxford. Alice L. Eckardt has taught Holocaust studies and Christian-Jewish relations and history, and has served as chairperson of the Christian Study Group on Judaism and the Jewish People. She is on the editorial review board of the journal *Holocaust and Genocide Studies* and the board of directors of the Anne Frank Institute of Philadelphia. A. Roy Eckardt has been a Ford fellow at Harvard University, a Lilly fellow at the University of Cambridge, a Rockefeller Foundation humanities fellow at the University of Tubingen and the Hebrew University, and editor of the *Journal of the American Academy of Religion*. The first edition of this book, *Long Night's Journey into Day: Life and Faith after the Holocaust*, was published by Wayne State University Press in 1982. Among Alice L. Eckardt's other publications is *Jerusalem: City of the Ages* (1987). A. Roy Eckardt's earlier books include *For Righteousness' Sake: Contemporary Moral Philosophies* (1987); *Jews and Christians: The Contemporary Meeting* (1986); *Your People, My People* (1974); and *Elder and Younger Brothers* (1967). The Eckardts also collaborated on *Encounter with Israel* (1970). Their articles have appeared in *The Christian Century*, *Judaism*, and *Christian Jewish Relations*.

The manuscript for this revised and enlarged edition was prepared for publication by Lisa Nowak Jerry. The book was designed by Mary Primeau. The typeface for the text and the display is Caledonia. The text is printed on 60-lb. Glatfelter text paper. The cloth edition is bound in Holliston Mills' Roxite Linen. The stock for the paper cover is Hammermill Antique.

Manufactured in the United States of America.